Networking Device Drivers

VNR COMMUNICATIONS BOOKS

Networking Device Drivers

Sanjay Dhawan

VAN NOSTRAND REINHOLD
I(T)P™ A Division of International Thomson Publishing Inc.

New York • Albany • Bonn • Boston • Detroit • London • Madrid • Melbourne
Mexico City • Paris • San Francisco • Singapore • Tokyo • Toronto

Copyright © 1995 by Van Nostrand Reinhold.

I(T)P ™ Published by Van Nostrand Reinhold, a division of
International Thomson Publishing Inc.
The ITP logo is a trademark under license.

Printed in the United States of America.
For more information, contact:

Van Nostrand Reinhold
115 Fifth Avenue
New York, NY 10003

International Thomson Publishing GmbH
Königswinterer Strasse 418
53227 Bonn
Germany

International Thomson Publishing Europe
Berkshire House 168-173
High Holborn
London WCIV 7AA
England

International Thomson Publishing Asia
221 Henderson Road #05-10
Henderson Building
Singapore 0315

Thomas Nelson Australia
102 Dodds Street
South Melbourne, 3205
Victoria, Australia

International Thomson Publishing Japan
Hirakawacho Kyowa Building, 3F
2-2-1 Hirakawacho
Chiyoda-ku, 102 Tokyo
Japan

Nelson Canada
1120 Birchmount Road
Scarborough, Ontario
Canada M1K 5G4

International Thomson Editores
Campos Eliseos 385, Piso 7
Col. Polanco
11560 Mexico D.F. Mexico

1 2 3 4 5 6 7 8 9 10 QEBFF 01 00 99 98 97 96 95

Library of Congress Cataloging-in-Publication Data
Dhawan, Sanjay
      Networking device drivers / Sanjay
   Dhawan.
            p.   cm.
      Includes bibliographical references and index.
      ISBN 0-442-01943-2
      1. Computer networks—Computer programs. 2. Device drivers
      (Computer programs) I. Title.
   TK5105.9D 49   1995
   005.7 13—dc20   95-46462
                                                CIP

Project Management: Raymond T. Campbell • Art Director: Jo-Ann Campbell • Production: mle design, 562 Milford Point Rd., Milford, CT 06460 • Proofreading: Joan P. Radin

To Anjali
and Samay

Trademarks

8086, 80286, 80386, and 80486 are trademarks of Intel Corporation.

AppleTalk is a trademark of Apple Computer.

ARCNET is a trademark of DATAPOINT Corporation.

Ethernet is a trademark of Digital, Intel and Xerox.

IBM PS/2, IBM PC LAN, SNA, and AIX are trademarks of International Business Machines Corporation.

MS-DOS, Microsoft, Microsoft Windows, and Microsoft Windows NT are trademarks of Microsoft Corporation.

NetWare, NetWare 386, NLM, Novell, SPX, IPX, and VAP are trademarks of Novell, Inc.

Network File System (NFS), Sun, and SunOS are trademarks of Sun Microsystems, Inc.

Network General and Sniffer are trademarks of Network General Corporation.

SCO is a trademark of Santa Cruz Operation, Inc.

UNIX and STREAMS are trademarks of AT&T.

VAX and VMS are trademarks of Digital.

Word is a trademark of Microsoft Corporation.

Contents

CHAPTER 4   **NDIS 2.0.1 DRIVERS** **167**

Preface

This book is written for networking professionals who would like to understand the complexities and interactions in the various networking components like network interface cards, device drivers, protocol stacks and the operating system. This book focuses on the practical real life aspects of implementing the networking environment in today's systems. There are a number of very well written books on the subject of networking. A number of these books cover the various networking architectures such as TCP-IP, NetBIOS, 7 Layer OSI reference model. A number of these books also cover the various LAN and WAN technologies like Ethernet, Token Ring, X.25. This book covers the networking technology from a different aspect. The main focus here is to define the architecture of the major networking device drivers. The networking device drivers act as the glue between the networking hardware (Network Interface Card) and the software protocol layers and the operating system. By understanding the architecture of the networking device drivers, the reader should be able to learn the networking architecture of the various networking products used today by millions of users.

This book describes the various networking device driver architecture's used in the industry. The device drivers are the lowest software component in the networking 7 layer protocol stacks. They are also the most important component in the complete networking stack implementation because they tie the networking hardware to the protocol stacks. The networking device drivers are responsible for sending frames, receiving frames, multiplexing frames between multiple protocol stacks, maintain statistics.

Various networking device driver standards exist in the industry which specify the device driver architecture's for a particular network operating environment. The most common device driver architectures like NDIS (Network Driver Interface Standard) from 3COM and Microsoft, ODI (Open Data-Link Interface) from Novell, Packet Driver from FTP Software, DLPI (Data Link

Provider Interface) from USL, Inc., are all covered in great detail in this book. The book starts with giving complete background on networking, various networking media like CSMA/CD, Token Ring, etc. The various popular network operating systems like Novell NetWare, Microsoft LAN Manager, Windows, and Windows NT, are also covered from the networking and device driver standpoint. The introduction to basic concepts is followed by the details of various networking device drivers.

The first chapter is titled Networking Basics. This chapter introduces various basic networking concepts to the reader. This chapter defines the 7 layer OSI networking model. It defines the functions performed by each layer. It provides some real examples of the networking protocols like TCP-IP, NetBIOS, Novell IPX/SPX and shows how they fit in the 7 layer OSI model.

The second chapter provides introduction to various Media Access Control layers. The MAC layer of the 7 layer OSI model is the key layer to understand from the networking device driver standpoint. This chapter explains the architecture of the various IEEE 802 MAC layers like CSMA/CD, Token Ring, FDDI. The details of the frame formats and the description of various fields is also provided in this chapter. This chapter lays the framework for further discussion on the networking device drivers.

The third chapter is titled *Networking Operating Systems and the Device Drivers*. This chapter provides very essential background information about various network operating systems and there internal architecture. The network operating systems which are covered in this chapter are Novell NetWare, Microsoft LAN Manager, UNIX operating system, and various peer-to-peer network operating systems like Artisoft Lantastic, NetWare Lite, Windows for Workgroups. This chapter also defines the term "device driver." It explains the device driver architecture's for MS-DOS, Windows, NetWare, OS/2, and UNIX operating systems. It also links the basic device driver architecture of an operating system to the networking device driver for the corresponding network operating system.

Chapters four through eight provide detailed information on various networking device drivers.

Chapter 4 covers the NDIS 2.0.1 Drivers. The NDIS 2.0.1 (Network Driver Interface Specification) originated from Microsoft and 3COM. This driver specification is the most popular networking device driver specification. This chapter defines the architecture of the NDIS 2.0.1 device drivers. It defines various internals of the NDIS 2.0.1 architecture like multiple ways to implementing reception of a packet from the network.

Chapter 5 is on NDIS 3.0 Drivers for Microsoft's Windows for Workgroups 3.11 and Windows NT. The NDIS 3.0 specification is developed by Microsoft for implementing networking device drivers under WFW 3.11 and Windows NT. This chapter provides the internals of this new and very portable architecture called NDIS 3.0. Various data transmission and reception techniques are discussed.

Chapter 6 covers the Packet Driver architecture. The packet driver specification originated from FTP Software Inc. The packet drivers are used in the TCP-IP implementations for DOS operating systems. This chapter provides a complete understanding of the TCP-IP protocol stacks and how they interact with packet drivers. It also gives the complete internal implementation of the packet drivers.

Chapter 7 covers the Novell NetWare ODI Drivers. The Novell Open Data-Link Architecture (ODI) was released by Novell to provide an interface between the protocol stacks and the network device drivers. The ODI architecture exists for various operating systems like Novell NetWare, DOS, OS/2, and Windows NT. This chapter defines ODI architecture and various layers that exist in the ODI architecture. It also defines the ODI protocol and device driver implementation as applicable to the above mentioned operating systems.

Chapter 8 covers the UNIX DLPI Driver architecture. The UNIX Data Link Provider Interface (DLPI) is the networking device driver interface for UNIX. This chapter describes the DLPI specification. It also provides a complete tutorial on the STREAMS communication mechanism which is used for implementing networking layers under UNIX.

There are three appendices in this book. Appendix A covers a typical hardware/software implementation of networking solution. This appendix explains a network interface controller chip (PCNet-ISA from AMD) and its hardware and software interfaces. It also explains the implementation of pseudo device driver routines for this device. This appendix provides a quick start for the reader who wants to understand writing networking device drivers. Appendix B covers the Remote Program Load (RPL) protocol. The RPL protocol is designed by IBM and is based on Find/Found frames. The RPL protocol provides the capability of a diskless workstation to boot from a network server over a network. Appendix C is a reference appendix which provides the main header file for the UNIX DLPI drivers. The header file DLPI.H lists the main data structures used in the DLPI drivers. This appendix provides the user some reference material for understanding the DLPI drivers.

I would like to thank a number of people for providing me with the inspiration for writing this book. The person on the top of the list is my wife, Anjali Dhawan. Anjali read every single page of this book and provided me with comments to make this book more readable. I would also like to thank my parents, Mr. S.R. Dhawan and Mrs. Sunita Dhawan and Anjali's parents, Dr. M.R.Tehri and Mrs. Sudhi Tehri, for their moral support. Neil Levine, the editor of this book from *Van Nostrand Reinhold* provided me with very valuable guidance during the whole project. I would also like to thank Mike Sherry from *Van Nostrand Reinhold* for his prompt actions to the many, many questions that needed resolution during this complete project. Finally, I would like to thank Jo-Ann Campbell, *mle design* and Chris Grisonich, *Van Nostrand Reinhold* for copyediting and preparing the layout of this book.

Sanjay Dhawan

1

Networking Basics

INTRODUCTION TO NETWORKING

The computer industry has been going through a period of very rapid growth during the last several years. In the 1970s, various organizations and universities had one or two main frame computers which were shared by users. The users brought their computing jobs to the main frame computer operators and took the final results back with them.

With the explosion of the microprocessor industry in the 1980s, the above model of the user coming to a computer was transformed. Today, most individuals in any organization have computers at their desks. The main computer room in a university or an organization has been replaced by small but very powerful computers distributed in different offices and various other locations. With the distribution of the computing power came the need for smoother information flow between computers. Users expressed the need to send electronic messages to one another. They also wanted to share resources such as files, and printers. This need gave birth to the concept of computer networks.

A computer network is an infrastructure that connects a number of computers to achieve the automatic information flow between different computers. A computer network, consists of electrical cables or phone lines or RF medium and connects various computers to carry information between them. In addition, each computer has dedicated networking hardware and software. The dedicated networking hardware is responsible for providing access to the underlying transport (cable, phone lines, etc.). The software running in each computer implements a basic protocol that works as the language for computers and is implemented and understood by the computers that are exchanging information. For a computer to exchange information with other computers on a network, it has to use the language (protocol) which is understood by the other computers. It is also possible for a computer to run multiple protocols simultaneously. This enables this computer to successfully talk to multiple groups of computers running different protocols.

The physical medium which connects various computers on a network can have broadcast channels or point-to-point channels. A broadcast channel has a single communication medium which is shared by all the computers on the network. This means that when a computer sends a packet of information in a broadcast, channel-based computer network, it is screened by all the other computers on the broadcast network. The information packet usually has a destination computer address in the packet. This address is used by all the computers screening the packet to decide whether or not they want to receive the packet. A point-to-point channel computer network is a store-and-forward network. This means that when an information packet is sent by a computer, one or more intermediate computers receive this packet. These intermediate computers may store this packet until their output medium is ready to send this packet to the next computer. In some networks, these intermediate computers may also take the decision on whether or not to forward the packet. The point-to-point computer networks can be designed to follow a certain addressing hierarchy and the intermediate computers can take the decision of forwarding or not forwarding the packets based upon the destination address of the incoming packet. Figure 1-1 illustrates a broadcast channel and point-to-point, channel-based computer network systems.

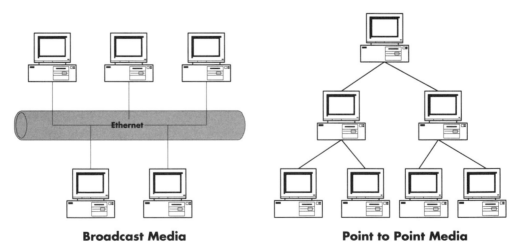

Broadcast Media   **Point to Point Media**

Figure 1-1. Different Physical Media

Computer networks can be broadly categorized into three different categories. They are:

- Local Area Networks (LANs)

- Metropolitan Area Networks (MANs)

- Wide Area Networks (WANs)

The three categories are based on the geographical distance that a network is designed to cover. The network characteristics (time-out values, capacity, network technology used etc.) depend upon the type of network. The LAN technology offers the highest speed connectivity but sacrifices the network distance. A LAN spans small areas like a computer room, a building, or a small campus. The LAN technologies available today operate between 4 Mbps to 100 Mbps or even more. The distance spanned by them may be from a few meters to couple of kilometers.

The WAN technology is intended for use over very large distances. The distance spanned by WAN technologies can be several thousand kilometers. The WANs operate at a slower speed. The speed for WANs range from few kbps to few tens of kbps.

The MANs fall between the LANs and WANs in speed and distance spanned. Typical MANs cover a large metropolitan area ranging from a few kilometers to tens of kilometers. The speed of MANs is in the range of 56kbps to 10Mbps. LANs, MANs, and WANs together provide the complete infrastructure for connecting computers, both locally and remotely, based on the need. The speed of the network operation is inversely proportional to the distance covered by that network. A well written network protocol design hides the differences between various LAN/MAN/WAN technologies from network users. This means that the user is unable to tell the difference between working over a LAN or a WAN network.

At this time, it is also important to understand all the major standards groups involved in standardization of the various network technologies. A list of these standardization groups is given below. This is not an exhaustive list; its intent is to introduce major network standardization organizations which are involved in standardization of computer networking components. The organizations discussed here are:

- International Standards Organization (ISO)

- American National Standards Institute (ANSI)

- National Bureau of Standards (NBS)

- Institute of Electrical and Electronics Engineers (IEEE)

- International Telecommunication Union (ITU)

- Comité Consultatif International de Télégraphique et Téléphonique (CCITT)

- Network Information Center (NIC)

ISO is the organization that is responsible for producing worldwide standards. Over ninety national standards organizations are ISO members. For example, the U.S. National Standards Organization, ANSI, is a member of ISO, and so is the British National Standards Organization, BSI (British Standards Institute). ISO develops standards on a number of subjects including computer networks. ISO is divided into several technical committees, which are then divided into working groups. ISO working group meetings are attended by individuals from organizations interested in developing and contributing to the standard on which the group is working. This is where all the technical work in developing the standard is done.

ANSI is a private organization within the U.S. that is responsible for producing American national standards in the required areas. ANSI standards are generally routed to the ISO to be made international standards. ANSI has technical groups responsible for doing the standards work. One such group is X3T9. The Fiber Distributed Data Interface (FDDI) computer networking standard was produced by X3T9.5 working group. ANSI members are various companies interested in participating in American standards development.

The National Bureau of Standards (NBS) is an agency of the U.S. Department of Commerce. The NBS is responsible for developing and issuing standards which the suppliers must meet to sell to the various government organizations. One example of the standards issued by NBS is GOSIP (Government OSI Profile). This standards document defines various computer networking requirements.

IEEE is a major player in networking standards. IEEE is the organization with engineer members located all over the world. IEEE has a standards group that develops standards in the area of electrical engineering and computer networks. The IEEE 802 is the standards group responsible for producing the 802 LAN standards (Ethernet, Token Bus, Token Ring, etc.). The 802 LAN standards define the most popular LAN infrastructure in the world. IEEE's 802 LAN standards are the basis for the ISO LAN standards ISO 8802.

ITU is a United Nations agency responsible for coordinating the telecommunication issues between various countries. Phone lines connecting people and computers are managed in different ways in different countries. ITU is responsible for coordinating the inter-country phone connections so that the people and computer equipment between different countries can communicate. ITU has three main groups—two of these three groups deal with radio broadcasting. The third group deals with telephone and data communication standards. This group is called CCITT. CCITT is based in Geneva, Switzerland and its main function is to make technical recommendations on telephone, telegraph and data communication interfaces. One example of the interface dealt with by CCITT is X.25 computer networking (packet switched) interface.

The various standards groups mentioned above produce networking standards responsible for connecting computers with each other. The protocol level standardization is also done in some of these standards groups. However, when it comes to protocol standardization it is important to mention a group called Network Information Center (NIC). The NIC is funded by Defense Communication Agency (DCA) for maintaining and distributing the information about TCP-IP technology. The TCP-IP protocol suite is the most used networking protocol suite. Most of the other networking protocol standards are maintained by the vendors who originated them (Novell's IPX/SPX, IBM's NetBEUI, etc.).

SEVEN LAYER OSI MODEL

The Open Systems Interconnection (OSI) is a computer networking reference model defined in ISO 7498 : 1984, Information Processing Systems, Open Systems Interconnection, Basic reference model standard.

In the mid 1970s, the development and use of computer networks began to achieve considerable attention. The early success of the ARPANET and CYCLADES made computer networking an important field.

In 1978, the International Organization for Standardization (ISO) Technical Committee 97 on Information processing, recognizing that standards for networks of heterogeneous systems were urgently required, created a new subcommittee (SC 16) for "Open Systems Interconnection." The term "Open" was chosen to emphasize that by conforming to OSI (Open Systems Interconnection) standards, a system would be open to communication with any other system obeying the same standards anywhere in the world.

Initial discussions revealed that a consensus could be reached rapidly on a basic, layered architecture that would satisfy most requirements of OSI and that could be extended later to meet new requirements. It was decided to develop this standard model of architecture that would constitute the framework for the development of standard protocols.

The reference model of OSI was developed, and this model was taken as the basis for development of standards for OSI within the ISO. This Basic Reference Model went in as a Draft Proposal (DP) for an International standard in 1980. It progressed to a Draft international Standard (DIS) in Spring of 1982 and became an International Standard (ISO 7498) in Spring of 1983.

In most cases, the job of a standards committee is to take sets of commercial practices and the current research results, if applicable, and convert these procedures into standards that can be utilized by commercial products. SC 16 had to develop a set of standards that new and emerging products could adopt before commercial practices were in place and while many of the more fundamental research problems remained unsolved.

The approach adopted by SC 16 was to use a layer architecture to break up the problem into manageable pieces. The OSI Reference Model is a framework for coordinating the development of OSI standards. In OSI, the problem is approached in a top-down fashion, starting with a description at a high level of abstraction which imposes few constraints, and proceeding to more and more refined description with tighter and tighter constraints. In OSI, three levels of abstractions are explicitly recognized: the architecture, the service specifications, and the protocol specifications (see Figure 1-2).

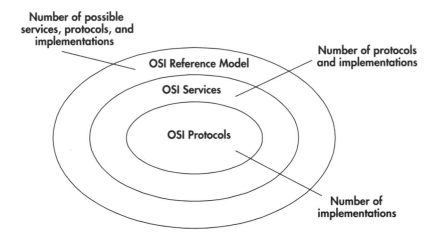

Figure 1-2. Three levels of Abstraction in OSI

(a)   The document that describes the OSI Architecture, ISO 7498, defines the types of objects that are used to describe an open system, the general relations among these types of objects, and the general constraints on these types of objects and their relations. It also defines a seven layer model for interprocess communication constructed from these objects, relations, and constraints. These are used as a framework for coordinating the development of layer standards by OSI committees, as well as the development of standards built on top of OSI.

(b) The OSI Service Specification represents a lower level of abstraction that defines in greater detail the service provided by each layer. The service specification lays tighter constraints than the Reference Model on the protocols and implementations that will satisfy the requirements of the layer. A service specification defines the facilities provided to the user of the service, and that specification is independent of the mechanisms used to accomplish the service. It also defines an abstract interface for the layer by defining the primitives that a user of the layer may request with no implication of how or whether that interface is implemented.

(c) The OSI Protocol Specification represents the lowest level of abstraction in the OSI standards scheme. Each protocol specification defines precisely what control information is to be sent and what procedures are to be used to interpret this control information. The protocol specifications represents the tightest constraints placed on implementations built to conform to OSI standards.

The OSI Reference Model does not describe the implementation approach for various protocol stacks. It is a model for describing the concepts for coordinating the parallel development of interprocess communication standards. The purpose of OSI is to allow any computer anywhere in the world to communicate with any other, as long as they obey the OSI standards.

The elements of the OSI architecture are divided into two major sections. The first section describes the elements of the OSI architecture. These constitute the building blocks that are used to construct the seven layer model. The second section describes the services and functions of the layers.

Systems, Layers, and Entities

The OSI Reference Model is an abstract description of interprocess communication. In the OSI Reference Model, communication takes place between application processes running in distinct systems. A system is considered to be one or more autonomous computers and their associated software, peripherals, and users that are capable of information processing and/or transfer.

Layering is used as a structuring technique to allow the network of open systems to be logically decomposed in independent smaller subsystems (see Figure 1-3). A layer is viewed as being locally composed of subsystems of the same rank in all inter-connected systems. Entities in the same layer are termed as peer entities. For simplicity, any layer is referred to as the (N)-layer, while its next lower layer and next higher layer are referred to as the (N-1)-layer and the (N+1)-layer, respectively. The same notation is used to designate all concepts relating to layers, for example, an entity in the (N) layer is termed as (N)-entity, and is illustrated in Figure 1-4.

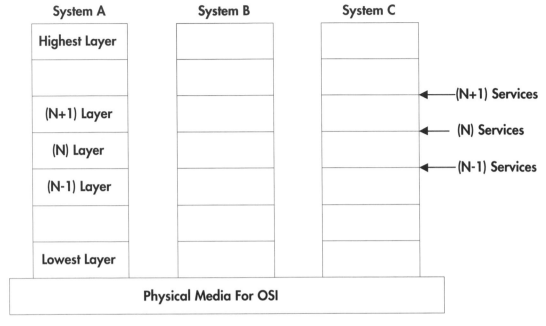

Figure 1-3. Open System Layering

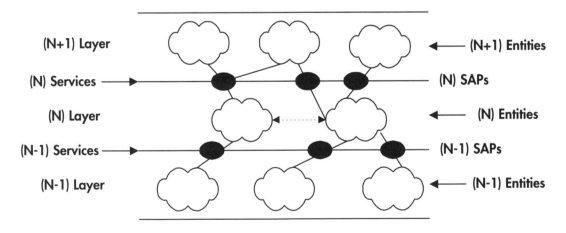

Figure 1-4. N Layer Entities and SAPs

The basic idea of layering is that each layer adds value to services provided by the set of lower layers in such a way that the highest layer is offered the full set of services needed to run distributed applications. Layering thus divides the total problem into smaller pieces.

SERVICES AND SERVICE ACCESS POINTS.

Each layer provides services to the layer above it. A service is a capability of the (N)-layer which is provided to the (N+1)-entities. But it is important to note that not all functions performed within the (N)-layer are services. Only those capabilities that can be seen from the layer above are services.

The (N)-entities add value to the (N-1) service they get from the (N-1)-layer and offer this value added service i.e., the (N)-service to the (N+1)-entities.

The (N)-services are offered to the (N+1)-entities at the (N)-service access points, or (N)-SAPs. A (N+1)-entity communicates with a (N)-entity in the same system through a (N)-SAP. A (N)-SAP can be served by only one (N)-entity and used by only one (N+1)-entity, but one (N+1)-entity can serve several (N)-SAPs and one (N+1)-entity can use several (N)-SAPs. A (N)-SAP is located by its (N)-address.

FUNCTIONS AND PROTOCOLS

A (N)-function is part of the activity of a (N)-entity. Flow control, data transformation, sequencing are all examples of (N)-functions. A (N)-protocol is a set of rules and formats which govern the communication between (N)-entities performing the (N)-functions in different open systems, e.g., for sharing resources.

NAMING

Objects within a layer or at the boundary between adjacent layers need to be uniquely identifiable, in order to establish a connection between two SAP's, one must be able to identify them uniquely. The OSI architecture defines identifiers for entities, SAPs, and connections as well as relations between these identifiers.

Each (N)-entity is identified with a global title that is unique and identifies the same (N)-entity anywhere in the network of open systems. Each (N)-SAP is identified by an (N)-address which uniquely locates the (N)-SAP at the boundary between the (N)-layer and (N+1)-layer. The concepts of titles and addresses are illustrated in Figure 1-5.

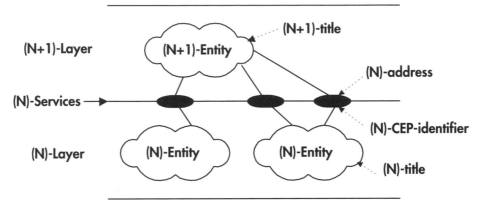

Figure 1-5. OSI Naming Concepts

CONNECTIONS

A common service offered by all layers consists of providing associations between peer SAPs which can be used in particular to transfer data. More precisely (see Figure 1.6), the (N)-layer offers (N)-connections between (N)-SAPs as part of the (N)-services. The most usual type of connection is the point-to-point connection, but there are also multiend point connections which correspond to multiple association between entities (e.g., broadcast or multidrop communications). The end of an (N)-connection at an (N)-SAP is called an (N)-connection end point or (N)-CEP for short. Several connections may coexist between the same pair (or N-tuple) of SAPs.

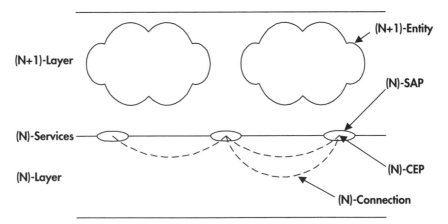

Figure 1-6. (N)-Connections between (N)-SAPs

Information is transferred in various types of data units between peer entities and between entities attached to a specific service access point. The logical relationships between data units in adjacent layers is shown in Figure 1-7.

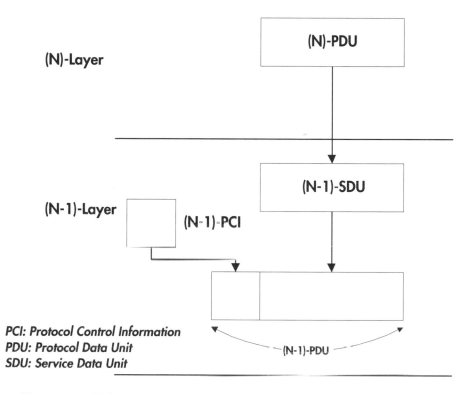

Figure 1-7. Relationship between Data Units

The Seven Layer Model

In OSI, interprocess communication is subdivided into seven independent layers. Each (N)-layer uses the services of the lower (N-1)-layer and adds the functionality peculiar to the (N)-layer to provide service to the (N+1)-layer. Layers have been chosen to break the problem into reasonably sized smaller problems that can be considered relatively independently. The seven layers are described in the following section and are illustrated in Figure 1-8.

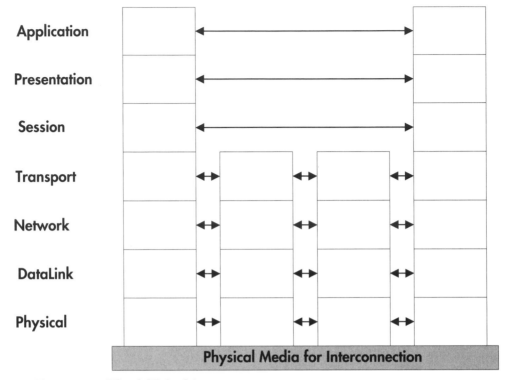

Figure 1-8. The OSI Architecture

APPLICATION LAYER

The Application layer, the highest layer of OSI, does not provide services to any other layer. The primary concern of the Application layer is the semantics of the application. All application processes reside in the Application layer. However, only part of the Application layer is in the real OSI system. Those aspects of the Application process concerned with interprocess communication (called the application entity) are within the OSI environment.

PRESENTATION LAYER

The primary purpose of the Presentation layer is to provide independence to application processes from differences in data representations, i.e., syntax. The presentation layer protocol allows the user to select a "Presentation Context." The Presentation context may be specific to an application such as a library protocol or virtual terminal, to a type of hardware such as a particular machine representation, or to some standard or canonical representation.

SESSION LAYER

The primary purpose of the Session layer is to provide the mechanism for organizing and structuring the interactions between application processes. The mechanisms provided in the session layer allow for two-way simultaneous and two-way alternate operation, the establishment of major and minor synchronization points, and the definition of special tokens for structuring exchanges. In essence, the Session layer provides the structure for controlling the communication.

TRANSPORT LAYER

The purpose of the Transport layer is to provide transparent transfer of data between end systems, thus relieving the upper layers from any concern with providing reliable and cost effective data transfer. The Transport layer optimizes use of network services and provides additional reliability over that supplied by the Network service.

NETWORK LAYER

The Network layer provides independence from the data transfer technology and independence from relaying and routing considerations. The Network layer masks from the Transport layer all the peculiarities of the actual transfer medium. The Network layer also handles relaying and routing data through as many concatenated networks as necessary while maintaining the quality of service parameters requested by the Transport layer.

DATA LINK LAYER

The purpose of the Data Link layer is to provide the functional and procedural means to transfer data between network entities and to detect, and possibly correct, errors which may occur in the Physical layer. Data link layer protocols and services are very sensitive to the physical layer technology. While in the upper layers there is one protocol specified per layer, in the lower layers this is not the case. In order to ensure efficient and effective use of the variety of cabling technologies, protocols designed to their specific characteristics are required.

PHYSICAL LAYER

The Physical layer provides the mechanical, electrical, functional, and procedural standards to access the physical medium. The physical layer is concerned with transmitting bits over a communication channel. This layer defines the electrical characteristics of the transmission medium. This layer also ensures that multiple stations can communicate electrically on the same medium.

BRIDGES AND ROUTERS

Various computer networks rarely run the same protocols or access methods. These different networks have to coexist so that the users on these networks can exchange, among other features, files, mail, and data. If all users used the same protocol stack and the same physical layer access methods, internetworking would be very easy. However, it would be naive even to consider that the protocols or the network technology used by different users can be controlled to make homogeneous networks. In actual practice, a number of heterogeneous networks exist in the computer networking environment. These different networks have to be interconnected so that the users can exchange data. In the past, some researchers believed that the introduction of OSI would solve the problem of heterogeneous networks. They believed that everyone would eventually migrate to OSI-based protocols, and hence interoperation would be easy. However, it is now believed that heterogeneous networks are here to stay. The main reason for this is that the installed base of non-OSI-based networks is very large and still growing. IBM is still selling SNA based new systems. The TCP-IP architecture, which was initially installed in UNIX environment has grown tremendously in non-UNIX environments also. Even different departments within the same organization are installing LANs following different technologies (Ethernet or Token Ring). The problem to be solved is that of interconnecting the various computer networks. Computer networks can be interconnected using four different types of devices/architectures. They are:

- Repeaters
- Bridges
- Routers
- Gateways

Repeaters are physical layer devices that are used to extend the cable lengths of a computer network. For example, in a 802.3-based network running thick coaxial cable, the cable length cannot exceed 500 meters. This restriction is made because of the electrical signal degradation. If the user wants to extend the length of the cable, he or she has to use repeaters. Repeaters regenerate the electrical signal going between the two coaxial cables and hence the signal strength does not become an issue. A repeater is a very dumb device, and it only regenerates electrical signals. It does not do any protocol level interpretation. Figure 1-9 illustrates the concept of a repeater.

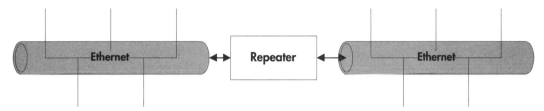

Figure 1-9. Repeater in an Ethernet Network

Bridges operate at data link layer and are responsible for interconnecting LANs following different media access technology (see Chapter 2). Bridges are used for several different reasons in a LAN environment. The first and the most important reason is to interconnect LANs based on different technologies. For example, one LAN may be based on Ethernet, and the second LAN may be based on token bus technology. These two LANs can be interconnected using a bridge. The second reason for installing bridges is for data traffic flow. LANs with a large number of users can be separated into logical and physical segments using a bridge. A bridge can also be programmed to filter certain traffic between the LAN segments. This would ensure that not all LAN traffic from one LAN is transmitted on the other LAN and vice versa.

Figure 1-10 illustrates a bridge interconnecting an Ethernet (802.3) network with a Token Ring (802.5) network.

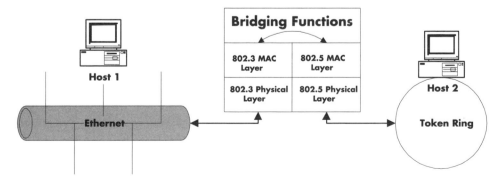

Figure 1-10. Bridge between 802.3 and 802.5

As illustrated in Figure 1-10, a token ring based network and an Ethernet-based network are interconnected using a bridge. The bridge is responsible for translating the frame formats between the two networks and also the electrical signal characteristics and the media access mechanisms. If a piece of information needs to go from host 1 to host 2 (see Figure 1-10), host 1 bundles this information into a 802.3 packet and transmits it on the Ethernet network. The bridge receives this 802.3 packet via its 802.3 interface and passes it to the bridging functions running on top of its 802.3 interface. The bridging functions take this packet and pass it to the 802.5 interface to transmit it on the 802.5 network. The 802.5 MAC and physical layers construct the packet in the 802.5 formats (described in Chapter 2) and transmit it on the token ring network. This packet is received by host 2 and is passed onto the application within host 2 which is waiting for this piece of information.

The use of a bridged network raises several issues. The first is with regard to the speed of dissimilar networks. In the above example, the Ethernet (802.3) networks run at 10Mbps and the Token Ring (802.5) networks run at 4 Mbps or 16 Mbps. This means that packets come and go at different speeds between the two networks. This also means that the some kind of buffering mechanism has to used within a bridge so that the packets are not lost. The second issue which is raised because of the bridge architecture is that of maximum frame size. On an Ethernet network, the maximum frame size is 1518 bytes. On a token ring network there is no maximum frame size specified. The only restriction on the token ring network is that a station cannot transmit longer than the token hold time which results into a frame size of around 5000 bytes (default value of token hold time). This means that it is possible to receive a packet on the token ring network which is larger than 1518 bytes and needs transmission on the Ethernet side. There is no solution to this problem because the bridges do not understand how to split frames as they are MAC layer devices. This means that the maximum size of the frame on a bridged network is the lowest common denominator of the maximum size. This means that in the example given in Figure 1-10, the maximum size of the frame which may pass through the bridge (in either direction) cannot be more than 1518 bytes.

A router is a device that connects dissimilar networks together. The main difference between a router and a bridge is the OSI layer at which the two operate. The bridge is a layer 2 device, however the router operates above layer 3, the network layer. This makes the router a slower device than a bridge because it has to go through more overhead than a bridge. However, the router provides more flexibility when it comes to interconnecting dissimilar networks. When a router is present between two or more dissimilar networks, the packet size problem explained above is handled by the router by packet segmentation and reassembly of packets larger than a certain size. This means that the restriction on packet size, which exists in a bridged network, is not a restriction in networks connected by a router.

The segmentation and the transmission of various segments is a simple process, but the reassembly of the segments is a complicated process. This reassembly process is further complicated by the fact that one of the segmented packets is lost in the transmission and an error recovery algorithm is necessary to recover the packet. The router segmentation and reassembly issues are discussed in detail in the following reference [Tanenbaum 1988]. Figure 1-11 illustrates networks connected using a router.

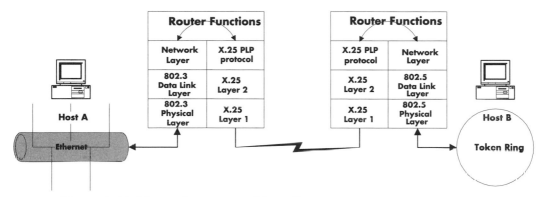

Figure 1-11. Networks connected by a Router

Gateways are devices which have all seven layers of the OSI model implemented and they make the interconnection between the two or more dissimilar networks at the seventh layer. Gateways are not used very often and are considered beyond the scope of this chapter.

PROTOCOL STACK EXAMPLES

This section focuses on three main protocol stacks that are used in the real world. They are:

- TCP-IP Protocol Stack

- NetBIOS Protocol Stack

- Novell IPX/SPX Protocol Stack

The relationship of these protocol stacks with the 7 layer OSI model is also explained here. In the real world, the 7 layer OSI model is followed where applicable. However, in certain cases it is more important to interoperate with the existing protocol stacks and network operating systems than to follow the 7 layer architecture. The next three sections are based on real world examples of networking protocol stacks.

TCP/IP Protocol Stack

The TCP-IP protocol stack is named after the two main standards included in the TCP-IP protocol suite. They are Transport Control Protocol (TCP) and Internet Protocol (IP). The communication protocols that run over IP, alongside TCP protocol, are grouped together and are often referred to as TCP-IP protocol suite. The TCP-IP protocol suite evolved from the research funded by Defense Advanced Research Projects Agency (DARPA). Today, TCP-IP is by far the most used protocol stack/suite and several applications use this protocol suite under the UNIX, DOS, OS/2, Windows, and NetWare operating systems.

The generic term "TCP-IP" usually means anything and everything related to the specific protocols of TCP (Transmission Control Protocol) and IP (internet Protocol). It also is used to refer to some other protocols like UDP, ARP, and ICMP. Some applications that are also part of TCP-IP suite are TELNET, FTP, and RCP. Figure 1-12 shows the TCP-IP architecture, including applications, transport protocols, and the Internet protocol.

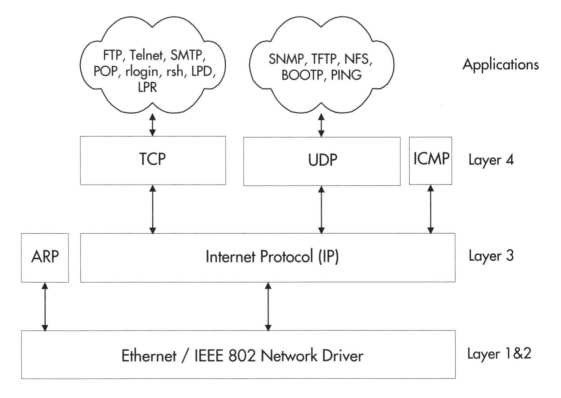

Figure 1-12. TCP-IP Protocol Suite

The TCP-IP applications use the TCP protocol or UDP protocol to transport data across a network. The applications include file transfer, terminal emulation, mail, network management, and printing. The Transport Control Protocol (TCP) offers a connection oriented byte stream. The TCP service is reliable, and it transfers data sequentially between local or remote hosts. TCP guarantees that the data will reach its destination, and it retransmits any data that did not go through. User Datagram Protocol (UDP) is a connectionless datagram delivery service that does not guarantee delivery. UDP does not maintain an end-to-end connection with the remote UDP modules. UDP pushes the datagram out on the network and accepts incoming datagrams off the network.

Internet Control Message Protocol (ICMP) sends error and control messages from routers or hosts to the message originator. ICMP is considered to be a network management protocol which uses the services provided by the IP layer.

Internet Protocol (IP) receives data bytes from data link layer, assembles them into an IP datagram, and routes this datagram to the appropriate protocol address on a subnet. If the IP datagram is assembled for a certain host, then IP layer of that host will pass it to TCP or UDP protocol. If the IP datagram is intended for a host residing on another subnetwork, then IP will send the datagram to a router to be forwarded to that subnetwork.

Address Resolution Protocol (ARP) is used to translate IP addresses to Ethernet addresses. The translation is done for outgoing IP packets because this is when the IP header and the Ethernet header are created. Each TCP-IP protocol suite implementation maintains an ARP table. If the ARP table cannot be used to translate an address, an ARP request packet is transmitted with a broadcast ethernet address. All ethernet nodes receive this packet. If the receiving ethernet node's IP address matches the IP address of the ARP request, the receiving node has to respond with an ARP response which contains its IP address. This is how the ARP table is built in the host machine.

Figure 1-13 shows the relationship between the 7 layer OSI model and the TCP-IP protocol stack implementation.

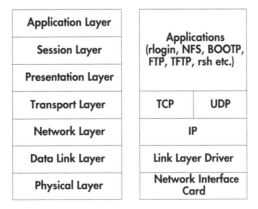

Figure 1-13. TCP-IP and 7 Layer OSI Model Relationship

As illustrated in Figure 1-13, the TCP-IP protocol layers are the applications running on top of the protocol stack that do not fit very well in the 7 layer OSI model and the layered functions defined in the OSI model. The key differences between the 7 layer OSI model and the TCP-IP protocol suite are the layers 5-7 and the way the application programs, like rlogin and FTP, are implemented in TCP-IP protocol suite. However, the fact is that TCP-IP protocol suite is the protocol suite which is used by a large number of users.

NetBIOS Protocol Stack

NetBIOS is a defacto standard which defines a protocol and services at the session layer. The NetBIOS standard is defined by IBM. The NetBIOS interface specification was first introduced in 1984 along with IBM's PC LAN software. This specification was designed by Sytek. A number of other products which were introduced around that time were also based on the NetBIOS specification. Microsoft designed and introduced Microsoft Networks ("MS-Net") software which was based on NetBIOS interface and protocols. DOS 3.1 also uses NetBIOS functions to access files located on remote networks. Since then, all IBM LAN software (PC LAN Program, LAN Server, OS/2, etc.) and Microsoft LAN software (MS-Net, LAN Manager, Windows, etc.) provides NetBIOS interfaces. This early acceptance of the NetBIOS interfaces and a huge application support forced a number of other LAN software vendors like Novell to provide NetBIOS support in their operating systems.

The NetBIOS interface operates at session layer (layer 5) and provides functions associated with the session, transport, and network layers. The NetBIOS implementations run on top of the standard network device driver interfaces discussed in the next few chapters. The NetBIOS Extended User Interface is called NetBEUI. The NetBEUI is a protocol that manages the packaging of data and application messages. Figure 1-14 illustrates the NetBIOS interface and its relation to the 7 layer OSI model.

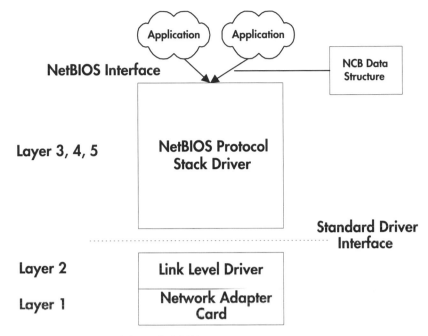

Figure 1-14. NetBIOS and OSI layers

The NetBIOS defines a programming interface that applications can use to request services. NetBIOS drivers can be implemented as, for example, an application, a Terminate and Stay Resident (TSR), a DOS device driver, or a UNIX program. A 64-byte data structure called a Network Control Block (NCB) is the means by which the applications send commands to the NetBIOS driver. The NCB data structure is shown in Figure 1-15. The method by which the NCB is sent to the driver depends upon the operating system. In the MS-DOS operating system, the address of the NCB is put in the ES and BX registers and then the Interrupt 5Ch is called.

```
typedef struct NCB {
      BYTE     ncb_command;
      BYTE     ncb_retcode;
      BYTE     ncb_lsn;
      BYTE     ncb_num;
      DWORD    ncb_buffer;
      WORD     ncb_length;
      BYTE     ncb_callName[16];
      BYTE     ncb_name[16];
      BYTE     ncb_rto;
      BYTE     ncb_sto;
      DWORD    ncb_post;
      BYTE     ncb_lana_num;
      BYTE     ncb_cmd_cplt;
      BYTE     ncb_reserved[14];
} NCB;
```

Figure 1-15. Network Control Block (NCB) Data Structure

The ncb_command field specifies the action to be performed. The ncb_ret-code field contains the command complete status (success or failure). The ncb_lsn field specifies the logical session number (LSN). A logical session number is established between remote applications and is then used in future communications. The next few fields are used to communicate the length and the address of the NCB buffer and the logical names of the local and remote processes. A complete description of the NCB fields is provided in the reference [Sinha 1992].

The NetBIOS services which are available to the applications running above the NetBIOS interface are divided into four services:

- Name Management

- Status and Control

- Connectionless Data Transfer Services

- Session Services

The Name Management service allows the NetBIOS based station to have logical names. Each network adapter card residing in a computer contains a unique physical address assigned by the manufacturer of the adapter card. The NetBIOS allows each computer to have 254 logical names for each LAN adapter. This allows for multiple users/applications to run on top of a single adapter card. The logical name, also known as the NetBIOS name, is the name that the application creates to refer to a physical address. The names create a level of abstraction. Applications can communicate with each other by using these logical names without being concerned with the physical address of the adapter. A NetBIOS name can have a maximum of 16 characters. The name management services provided by the NetBIOS interface provide functions for name management. Applications can use these functions to add a name to the NetBIOS name table. The NetBIOS driver checks the table for duplicate name entries. If a name is unique the NetBIOS driver assigns it a name number between 1–254 (0 and 255 are reserved) and returns the name number to the application.

The Status and Control functions provide general purpose services to the application programs running above NetBIOS. Commands that provide status reporting and control related to NetBIOS interface are available. For example, the application program can use the adapter status query to check the status of the underlying adapter card.

The NetBIOS session services are also known as Connection-Oriented Data Transfer services. The NetBIOS session services provide reliable data transfer based on the establishment of a session, or virtual circuit, between names. A session is created between two or more applications. Once a session is created, the data is transferred directly between the session participants. The applications can submit data between 0–64KB. The NetBIOS breaks the data into smaller chunks if needed and sends it as a sequence of one or more frames. The size of each data frame is dependent on the underlying network media access layer. For example, an IEEE 802.3 (Ethernet) based network can send frame with data size between 0–1500 bytes.

The Connectionless data transfer services allows data transmission to take place without first establishing a session. The connectionless mode of operation does not guarantee the delivery of the data, and there is no acknowledgment of data packets. The connectionless data transfer service is not considered reliable.

Novell's IPX/SPX Protocol Stack

This section examines Novell's IPX and SPX protocols. These protocols are responsible for transmitting, receiving, sequencing, and error checking packets between the server and the client machines. They use the services provided by the network interface card and its drivers to send and receive packets to and from the network. Novell core protocol stacks are IPX and SPX. IPX stands for Internetwork Packet Exchange. The IPX protocol is used to provide connectionless data exchange between the client and the server. SPX stands for Sequenced Packet Exchange protocol. The SPX services are used for providing connection oriented data exchange between the client and the server. The IPX protocol does not guarantee the delivery of the packet. An IPX packet can arrive in any sequence at its destination. SPX packets are sequenced, so they arrive in proper order. SPX protocol provides guaranteed delivery service. However, SPX is slower than IPX because of the packet overhead and the acknowledgment required for each packet.

When a station transmits data, it places a header around the data. The header information is used to indicate, for example, the destination address of the data, source of the data, and length. IPX and SPX protocols require additional headers to be placed in front of the data. These headers include routing data, sequencing information, and upper layer protocol identification.

Novell's networking protocols are derived from Xerox Network Systems (XNS). The Novell protocol stack is based on the XNS layer 3 and 4 protocols. XNS includes a protocol at layer 3 called IDP (Internetwork Datagram Protocol) which is the basis of Novell's IPX protocol. XNS also includes two transport layer protocols: PEP (Packet Exchange Protocol) and SPP (Sequenced Packet Protocol). XNS's PEP and SPP form the basis for Novell's Sequenced Packet Exchange (SPX) protocol.

IPX protocol stack performs the functions of a network layer of the 7 layer OSI model. The basic service which is provided by this protocol is forwarding the packet, segmenting and reassembly of packet, and routing the packet.

SPX is a connection-oriented protocol. This protocol first establishes a connection with another SPX protocol on a remote computer and then starts sending sequenced packets to the destination node. The SPX packets arrive in proper order. This overhead communication in the SPX environment makes SPX based communications a little slower. The SPX protocol is used by the Novell NetWare server for its print server services, and remote console services.

IPX and SPX protocol stacks are used in the Novell environment to transmit and receive packets. However, a standardized language is used to define networking services (request and replies). The standardized language in the Novell NetWare environment is called NCP (NetWare Core Protocols). The Novell NetWare environment defines a set of NCP standards which define the format and conventions for various messages. The NCP language is spoken by all NetWare clients and servers. The NetWare client requests file reads, writes, print services, drive letter mapping among other functions. These client requests are NCP requests which are interpreted by the server and acted upon by the server. Once the request is completed by the server, it must attach to a server and request a NCP connection. Once the server grants a NCP connection, the client can make NCP requests to the server and the server replies with a NCP reply. The NCP protocol provides some basic services. These services are:

- Basic Operating System Services
- Basic Communications Services
- File Access
- Locking and Synchronization
- Queue Management
- Printer Access

Figure 1-16 illustrates the relationship between IPX/SPX and NCP protocols and the 7 layer OSI model.

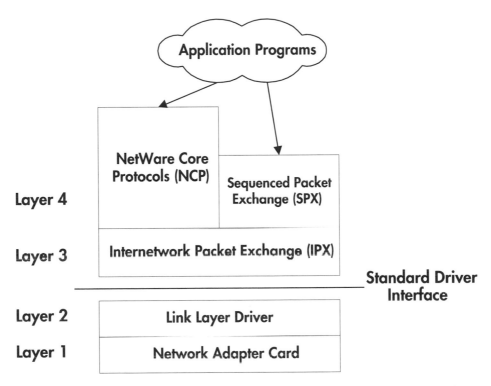

Figure 1-16. Novell Protocols and 7 Layer OSI Model

The IPX, SPX, and the NCP services of the NetWare client and server environments use the network interface card and driver to transmit and receive packets. The protocol stack is connected to the network interface card via the network device drivers. The network interface card device drivers follow an architecture called ODI (Open Data-Link Interface), described in Chapter 7.

SUMMARY

This chapter provides the basic concepts on networking. The 7 layer OSI model is always mentioned during computer networking discussions. This chapter provides the concepts of layering as defined in the OSI reference model. It also defines the various primitives which flow between various layers. The concept of Protocol Data Unit (PDU) and Service Data Unit (SDU) are also explained in this chapter. The real world of networking is little different from the OSI reference model. This is also discussed in this chapter. These three stacks and their relationship with the 7 layer OSI model is also explained in this chapter.

REFERENCES

Chappell, Laura 1993. *Novell's Guide to NetWare LAN Analysis*. Novell Press. San Jose, CA.

Comer Douglas E. 1991. *Internetworking with TCP-IP. Volume I. Principles, Protocols, and Architectures*. Prentice-Hall, Englewood Cliffs, NJ.

Martin, James and Chapman, Kathleen K. 1989. *Local Area Networks Architectures and Implementations*. Prentice-Hall, Englewood Cliffs, NJ.

Malamud, Carl 1990. *Analyzing Novell Networks*. Van Nostrand Reinhold, 115 Fifth Avenue, New York, NY.

Rose, Marshall T. 1990. *A Practical Perspective on OSI*. Prentice-Hall, Inc., Englewood Cliffs, NJ.

Rose, Marshall T. 1991. *The Simple Book. An Introduction to Management of TCP-IP based internets*. Prentice-Hall, Inc., Englewood Cliffs, NJ.

Sinha, Alok and Patch, Raymond 1992. *An Introduction to Network Programming Using the NetBIOS Interface*. Microsoft Systems Journal. March/April 1992.

Tanenbaum, Andrew S. 1988. *Computer Networks*. Prentice-Hall, Englewood Cliffs, NJ.

2

Introduction to Various MAC Layers

This chapter focuses on the Media Access Control (MAC) layer technologies. As explained in Chapter 1, the MAC layer is part of the Data Link Layer (layer 2) of the 7 layer OSI reference model. The real life network interface cards implement the media access control functions in a controller chip that resides on the adapter card. The software that drives the adapter card (device driver) must understand how the MAC controller chip operates. It must also understand how the media access control functions implemented in the controller chip operate. This chapter is focused on discussing the various MAC layer architectures.

MEDIA ACCESS CONTROL LAYER AND OSI MODEL

The Media Access Control (MAC) sub-layer resides within layer 2 of the OSI reference model. The other half of the layer 2 residing above the MAC layer is the Logical Link Control (LLC) sub-layer. The segmenting of the layer 2 of the OSI reference model into MAC and LLC layers is done in the IEEE 802 project. Figure 2-1 illustrates the organization of MAC and LLC layers with respect to the 7 layer OSI reference model.

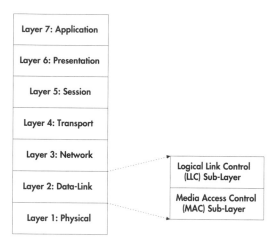

Figure 2-1. OSI Reference Model and MAC / LLC Layers

The data-link layer is the second layer of the OSI reference model. This layer resides on top of the physical layer. The physical layer is typically implemented in the hardware and is responsible for the actual electrical transmission and reception of data bits from the cable. The data-link layer is responsible for transmission of data from one network node to another. The data-link layer is responsible for taking the raw transmission from the physical layer, formatting it into a structure (which is called a frame), and presenting this structure to the network layer. The data-link layer is also responsible for managing the physical access of the medium. In general, there will be a number of nodes connected to the same media and hence some sort of protocol has to be implemented which defines the media access rules. This protocol is implemented in the data-link layer.

The data-link layer is further broken into the LLC and the MAC layers. This sub-partitioning of the data-link layer is done by the IEEE 802 project committee and the reasoning behind this is discussed in the next section.

IEEE 802 LAN Model

IEEE 802 has played a major role in the standards definition for Local Area Networks (LANs) by defining a flexible network architecture for local area networks. The IEEE 802 approach of layering the LAN architecture follows the 7 layer OSI reference model. IEEE 802 specifies only the bottom 2 layers of the networking architecture. The definition and implementation of layers above layer 2 is beyond the scope of the IEEE 802 project. Figure 2-2 lists all the standards published by the IEEE 802 standards committee for LANs. Figure 2-3 illustrates the relationships of these standards with one another.

Standard Ref#	Description
IEEE 802.1	The 802.1 produces the higher layer interface standards and is best known for its standards on MAC Layer bridges and LAN Management.
IEEE 802.2	Logical Link Control layer Standard. This standard defines the LLC sub-layer and the three classes of LLC—Type 1, 2 and 3.
IEEE 802.3	CSMA/CD (Ethernet) Standard. This standard specifies the CSMA/CD MAC protocol and the various types of media (Coaxial, Twisted Pair, Fiber Optics, etc.)
IEEE 802.4	Token Bus Standard. This standard specifies the Token Bus MAC protocol and various types of physical media (Coaxial, Fiber Optics, etc.)
IEEE 802.5	Token Ring Standard. This standard specifies Token Ring MAC protocol and various types of physical layer media (Twisted Pair, Fiber Optics, etc.)
IEEE 802.6	This standard specifies the Distributed Queue Dual Bus (DQDB) Subnetwork of a Metropolitan Area Network.
IEEE 802.7	IEEE 802.7 is not a standard. It is a recommendation specifying the physical, electrical and mechanical characteristics of a properly designed broadband cable medium.
IEEE 802.8	IEEE 802.8 is not a standard. It is a recommendation specifying the physical, electrical and mechanical characteristics of a properly designed fiber optics cable medium.
IEEE 802.9	IEEE 802.9 specifies the MAC and physical layers of Integrated Services LAN (ISLAN). The ISLAN allows integrated voice and data to be carried on the same medium.
IEEE 802.10	IEEE 802.10 is the standard for Interoperable LAN Security (SILS).
IEEE 802.11	IEEE 802.11 is the Wireless LAN standards group. This group is coming up with the MAC and Physical layer specifications for a wireless LAN.
IEEE 802.12	IEEE 802.12 specifies the MAC and Physical layers for a demand priority LAN (DPLAN).

Figure 2-2. List of IEEE 802 Standards

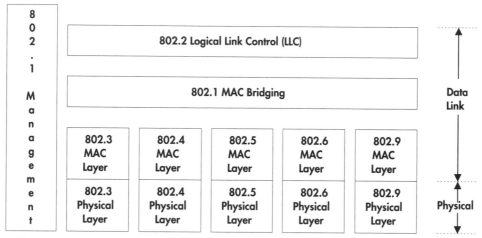

Figure 2-3. Relationships between IEEE 802 Standards

Figure 2-4 illustrates the relationship of the IEEE 802 standards with the 7 layer OSI reference model.

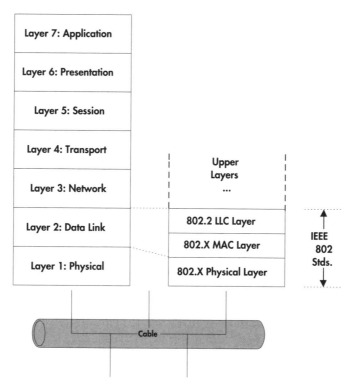

Figure 2-4. IEEE 802 and 7 Layer OSI Model

IEEE 802 publishes standards for Local Area Networks (LANs) and Metropolitan Area Networks (MANs). These standards try to cover a very wide variety of applications and hence IEEE 802 has to specify different types of media access control (MAC) technologies. There are five major MAC architectures covered by the 802 standards. This chapter discusses the three most popular 802 MAC architectures. They are 802.3, 802.4, and 802.5. Each of these MAC architectures may use different types of physical layers. The different physical layers are for different combinations of speed, cost, and distance. The MAC sub-layer performs access control functions for the shared medium. The shared medium on a LAN has a number of nodes connected to it, a protocol must be followed by all the nodes to access the shared medium. This protocol allows fair sharing of the medium by all the nodes on the LAN. The MAC sub-layer also performs address recognition and CRC generation and checks the outgoing and incoming MAC frames.

The logical link control (LLC) standard is used above the MAC standards. The LLC sub-layer standard describes three types of operations for data exchange. These three types of operations are:

- **Type 1**: Unacknowledged Connectionless
- **Type 2**: Connection-Oriented
- **Type 3**: Acknowledged Connectionless

The three types of LLC operations differ from each other on the basis of the reliability of the connection. In the Type 1 operation, there is no guarantee that the frame transmitted would arrive at its destination. There is no error recovery built in the Type 1 operation.

The Type 2 operation is used for applications that require guaranteed arrival of frames. Two or more LLC layers operating at Type 2 level first establish a connection and then exchange data. Error recovery mechanisms are provided in the Type 2 operation. The Type 3 operation is very similar to the Type 1 operation, that is, there is no need for connection establishment before information is transferred. However, the difference between Type 1 and Type 3 operation is that in Type 3 operation, critical frames can be sent with a request of acknowledgment from the receiving station. This ensures that the receiving station acknowledges the receipt of critical data.

The secure data exchange and the media access control bridging standards are used in conjunction with the MAC standards. The LAN Management standard (802.1) provides a set of tools that allow specific management applications to perform management tasks within LAN stations. Some of the performance management tasks are:

- Configuration Management

- Security Management
- Accounting Management

Logical Link Control (LLC) Layer

The Logical Link Control (LLC) sub-layer of the IEEE 802 architecture is the upper half layer of the data-link layer of OSI reference model layer 2. This is illustrated in Figure 2-1. The LLC layer provides services to the network layer (layer 3). It uses the services provided by the layers below it (MAC Layer) to accomplish some of the tasks assigned to it by the layers above it. The LLC service specification to the network layer provides a description of the various services that the LLC sub-layer and the underlying layers and sub-layers offer to the network layer. The LLC service specification to the MAC layer provides a description of the services that the LLC sub-layer requires of the MAC sub-layer. The LLC/MAC layer interface defined in IEEE 802.2 is implementation independent. This interface is also independent of the MAC layer protocol and the underlying physical layer.

IEEE 802.2 defines three types of data link operations. They are:

- **Type 1**: Connection-Less Mode
- **Type 2**: Connection-Oriented Mode
- **Type 3**: Acknowledged Connectionless Mode

In the Type 1: Connection-Less Mode of operation, the transmitting and the receiving stations do not have to form a connection. Data transfer is done transparently between these stations. Each data unit (frame) is transmitted and received independently. There is no acknowledgment in the connectionless mode. This means that the receiving station will not acknowledge the receipt of the incoming packet. The connectionless mode of operation is the simplest mode from implementation standpoint. Also, Type 1 operation is the most efficient because it does not have any major protocol overhead. This type of operation is most useful when the higher layers provide error recovery and sequencing of packets. This means that the LLC sub-layer can be operated without any error recovery and sequencing services.

The Type 2: Connection-Oriented Mode requires that the transmitting station establish a connection with the receiving station before it transmits any data to the receiving station. The transmitting station establishes and maintains the logical connection with the receiving station during the data transfer. Once the data transfer is completed, the connection is terminated. Type 2 mode of operation provides error recovery and sequencing services. The receiving station, in the Type 2 mode of operation, checks for the correct sequence of the receiving packets. It also acknowledges the receipt of the packet to the transmitting station. If a certain packet number is not received, the error recovery will take effect, and the same packet will be retransmitted. The connection oriented mode provides a reliable service for data transfer between two LLC stations. However, due to the overhead associated with this service, the data transfer is slower than in the Type 1 mode.

The Type 3: Acknowledged Connectionless Mode of operation was added to the LLC standard to provide the advantages of both the Type 1 and the Type 2 modes to the user. In this mode the general operation is same as in the Type 1: Connection-Less Mode. However, the Type 3 mode has another option available for critical data. In this mode, the transmitting station can ask for an acknowledgment of the received data from the receiving station. This means that for non-critical data, the stations can turn off the acknowledgment by operating in Type 1 mode and for critical data transfer, the transmitting station can ask for an acknowledgment.

Depending upon the type of services supported by an LLC implementation, there can be four classes of LLC implementations. These are listed in Figure 2-5.

	Type 1	Type 2	Type 3
Class I	X		
Class II	X	X	
Class III	X		X
Class IV	X	X	X

Figure 2-5. LLC Sub-layer Classes

As shown in Figure 2-5, Class I of the LLC sub-layer implements the Type 1 service only. The Class II implements the Type 1 and Type 2 services, Class III implements Type 1 and Type 3, and Class IV implements Type 1, 2, and 3 modes of operation.

The LLC sub-layer adds three bytes of header information to the packet passed to it by the network layer. Figure 2-6 illustrates the LLC header location, within an Ethernet packet.

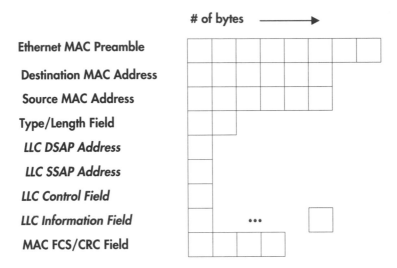

Figure 2-6. LLC Header Fields

The LLC DSAP address is the Destination Service Access Point Address, and the LLC SSAP address is the Service Access Point Address. The LLC sub-layer can have multiple data exchange sessions going on at any given time. The SAPs, or Service Access Points, are used to identify a particular access point located on the upper boundary of the LLC sub-layer which is involved in data transfer. SAPs can be considered as the addresses of the network layer access points onto the LLC sub-layer. The DSAP and the SSAP are 1 byte addresses. The control field byte is used to identify various types of operations and also the various commands used within the LLC sub-layer specification. The control byte is defined in the IEEE 802.2 Logical Link Control standard.

CSMA/CD ETHERNET (IEEE 802.3) MAC LAYER

The IEEE 802.3 standard specifies the CSMA/CD (Carrier Sense Multiple Access with Collision Detection) media access control protocol and the electrical and mechanical specifications for the various physical layers. The MAC sub-layer operates below the LLC layer and provides services to the LLC sub-layer. The CSMA/CD MAC access method defines the method for controlling the access to the physical transmission. The 802.3-based stations can use a number of different physical media for physical transmission. Figure 2-7 lists the various physical layer media available to the CSMA/CD-based stations.

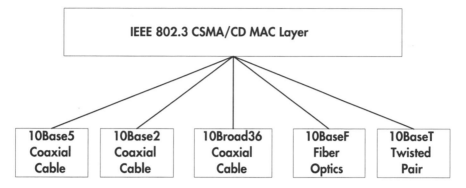

Figure 2-7. CSMA/CD Physical Layers

CSMA/CD MAC Architecture

The CSMA/CD MAC is the most used media access method. The CSMA/CD access method is derived from the Ethernet standard developed jointly by DEC/Intel/Xerox. The CSMA/CD-based networks are physically connected in either a bus or a tree topology. The main point to remember here is that in a CSMA/CD network, when a station transmits, all stations receive that transmission. The transmit and receive algorithm used by the stations are designed with fairness in mind.

When a station wants to transmit on the cable, it "listens" first to determine if it can sense some carrier on the cable. Carrier is a voltage level on the cable that indicates that the cable is being used by another station. If the transmitting station does not sense a carrier, it assumes that the cable is not in use and starts transmitting. It is very much possible that two stations looking for the carrier simultaneously, and not finding it, decide that no other station is transmitting and start transmitting at the same time. This results in what is known as collision on the CSMA/CD network. A collision results in increased voltage levels on the network and causes the data to get garbled. The transmitting and receiving stations monitor for collisions on the network. As stated earlier, a collision is indicated when the voltage levels on the cable are twice the strength of the voltage levels of a single station. If a collision is detected, the receiving station aborts the receive process and the transmitting station aborts the transmission. The transmitting station backs off for a random amount of time to allow multiple stations to be able to implement backoff algorithms that allow for transmission based on random time, to wait and then retry the transmission. The CSMA/CD stations retry their transmission for a maximum of 16 times (retry limit), and if the transmission is not done after 16 retrys, they give up.

If the cable is busy and the transmitting station senses a carrier, the transmitting station must defer its transmission for a set period of time and repeat the process of carrier sense. Figure 2-8 lists all the steps involved in a frame transmission under a CSMA/CD LAN.

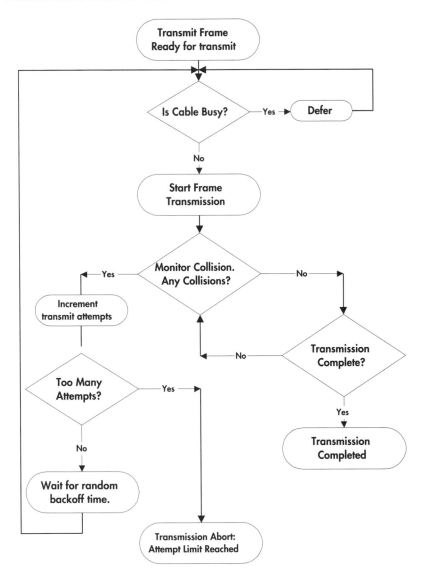

Figure 2-8. CSMA/CD Transmit Flow Diagram

The CSMA/CD receive process works in a very simple manner. All the stations on a CSMA/CD-based network are in the receive mode, if they are not transmitting. All of these stations are receiving bits from the network as CSMA/CD is a broadcast network. All the stations are examining the destination address and matching the destination address to their own MAC-level address. If the two addresses match, then the station continues to receive the rest of the packet. If the two addresses do not match, the reception of this packet is aborted and the station starts waiting for the next packet.

The receiving station also monitors for errors in the incoming packets. The very first error check performed is the frame fragment check. The receiving station checks to see if the received frame is less than 64 bytes. If the frame is less than 64 bytes, then the frame is assumed to be a collision fragment and hence the reception is aborted. The receiving station also checks the frame check sequence field. It is looking for a valid CRC (Cyclic Redundancy Check) in the 4 bytes of CRC field. If the receiving frame has a bad CRC, the station marks it as a frame with CRC error and optionally reports it to the user. If the received packet has a CRC error, the receiving station also checks for alignment error. A frame with an alignment error is defined as a frame which has a non multiple of 8 bits. This means that the number of bits in the frame is not a multiple of 8. Hence, frames that do not end on a byte boundary are considered as frames with bad alignment. The length field of the incoming frame is also checked. The length field of the frame should match the actual length of the data field of the frame. The length field should also be less than or equal to 1500 bytes (total frame size of 1518 bytes). The length field is checked for integrity. If the length field is not good, then the frame is marked as a frame with length field error. If there are no errors in the received frame, the receiving station completes the reception of the frame by marking it as a good frame and then passing it to the layer above it.

Figure 2-9 illustrates the complete frame receiving process for a CSMA/CD-based MAC layer.

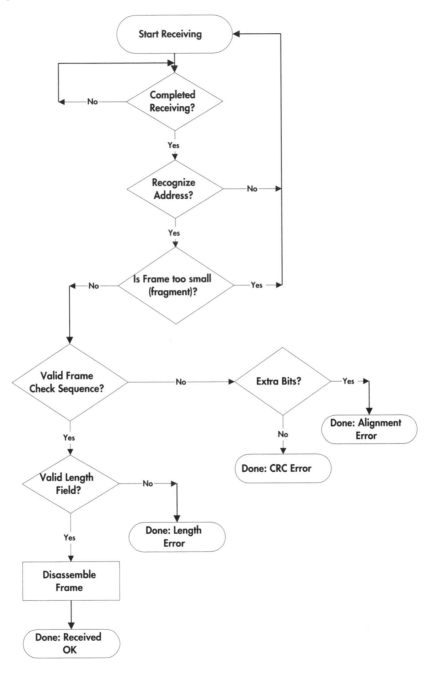

Figure 2-9. CSMA / CD MAC Frame Reception Process

CSMA/CD MAC Frame Format

The CSMA/CD MAC layer defines a MAC layer frame format which is used by all the CSMA/CD-based MACs. This frame format is used to encapsulate the data received from the LLC layer and then transmitted over the CSMA/CD network. The CSMA/CD MAC frame format contains the MAC-level destination and source addresses. These address fields provide information to the other MACs present on the broadcast medium about who should receive this frame. The preamble field provides electrical synchronization to the receiving station. The CSMA/CD frame format is described in Figure 2-10:

Preamble	Start Frame Delimiter	Destination Address	Source Address	Length	Data	PAD	Frame Check Sequence
7 Bytes	1 Byte	2 or 6 Bytes	2 or 6 Bytes	2 Bytes	0-n Bytes	0-x Bytes	4 Bytes

Figure 2-10. CSMA/CD MAC Frame Format

The various fields of the CSMA/CD MAC frame are described below.

Preamble:
The preamble field consists of 7 bytes of 0 bit followed by a 1-bit. These 56 bits of 0 followed by a 1 give a 5 MHz signal to the receiving station for clock synchronization. The preamble field is the key to clock synchronization between the transmitting and the receiving stations and hence very important to the frame reception.

SFD:
The Start of Frame Delimiter is a one byte field which always contains the value 10101011b. This fixed pattern indicates to the receiving station that the frame is starting after the SFD pattern.

Destination Address:
The destination address is a 2 byte or a 6 byte address which identifies the receiving station or stations. The address field length which is used most is the 6 byte address length. The complete CSMA/CD network has to have a 2 byte or a 6 byte address so that all the stations are looking for the same number of bytes as the source or destination address. The address can be individual, multicast, or broadcast. An individual address is the address of a single station. The multicast address is used to identify a group of stations. A broadcast address is used to identify all the stations on the network. The broadcast address is all 1s in the address field.

Source Address: The source address is a 2 byte or a 6 byte field which contains the address of the transmitting station. The source address format used most often is the 6 byte format. Also, all the stations on a CSMA/CD network have to use the same address format: 2 or 6 bytes.

Length: The length field is a 2 byte field which is used to indicate the length of the LLC data bytes (length of the data field).

Data: The data field contains the actual data bytes received by the CSMA/CD MAC from its upper layer. The size of the data field can be anywhere from 0 to 1500 bytes. The maximum frame size on a CSMA/CD LAN is 1518 bytes. The minimum frame size is 64 bytes. If the data bytes are less than 46 bytes, then Pad bytes are added to bring the size of the frame up to 64 bytes. The minimum frame size is required for correct CSMA/CD protocol operation.

Pad: The PAD field is an optional field. The length of the PAD field can be between 0–46 bytes. The actual length of the PAD field depends upon the length of the data supplied by the upper layer, and hence how many more PAD bytes are needed to bring the MAC frame length to its minimum size of 64 bytes.

FCS (Frame Check Sequence):   A cyclic redundancy check (CRC) is used by the transmit and receive algorithms to generate a CRC value for the FCS field. The transmit station performs a CRC generation on all the data bytes of the frame and generates a 4 byte CRC which is appended to the frame. The polynomial which is used to generate the CRC is described in the IEEE 802.3 standards documentation. The receiving station receives the MAC frame, computes the same CRC, and compares the received CRC with the computed CRC. For the frame to be transmitted and received without errors, the two values should match.

CSMA/CD Physical Layers

Figure 2-7 shows five different physical layers which can be used by a CSMA/CD-based node to transmit and receive data from the network cable. These five physical layers are:

- 10Base5 Coaxial Cable

- 10Base2 Coaxial Cable

- 10Broad36 Coaxial Cable

- 10BaseF Fiber Optics Cable

- 10BaseT Twisted Pair Cable

The 10Base5 coaxial cable physical media was the very first media type used in the CSMA/CD based networks. The 10Base5 physical layer attaches itself on a coaxial cable using Bee-Sting connectors. The data rate supported by this physical layer is 10 Mbps. The total distance covered by a 10Base5 cable is 500 meters or 1640 feet. The transmission on the coaxial cable is of the baseband type and the coaxial cable is of 50 ohms resistance. Repeaters are used in a 10Base5 network to regenerate the electrical signal beyond 500 m. In 802.3 networks, the maximum number of repeaters that can be used are 4 and hence the maximum network length is 2500 m (each segment of 500 m with 4 repeaters connecting 5 segments). Another restriction is placed on the number of stations that can exist in a single 500 m segments and the minimum distance between them. This restriction is placed because the signal reflection from stations placed too close on a cable can cause reflections and hence give false collision indications. The stations on a 10Base5 networks must be spaced by 2.5 meters, and any 500 meter segment may not have more than 100 stations connected to it. The 802.3 standard specifies the electrical and mechanical specifications of a 10Base5 physical layer.

The 10Base2 coaxial cable-based physical layer operates at 10 Mbps. The maximum distance covered by a single cable segment of 10Base2 based physical layer is 200 meters. The 10Base2 physical layer supports baseband transmission over a coaxial cable. The coaxial cable used in the 10Base2 implementation is a thinner coaxial cable than the 10Base5 based coaxial cable. The connectors used in the 10Base2 physical layer are called BNC. Hence, the 10Base2 based physical layer is also known as BNC cable or Thinnet.

The third physical layer listed above is called 10Broad36. This physical layer uses broadband transmission over CATV-type coaxial cable with taps, connectors and amplifiers. The coaxial cable used has a resistance of 75 ohms. The data rate supported on this physical layer is 10 Mbps and the maximum distance covered by s single 10Broad36 cable is 3600 meters. A coaxial broadband system permits the assignment of different frequency bands to multiple applications. For example, a band in the frequency spectrum can be utilized by local area networks while other bands are used by television, or audio signals.

The 10BaseF physical layer is the CSMA/CD based physical layer operating at 10 Mbps over a fiber link.

The 10BaseT physical layer operates at 10 Mbps over a twisted pair. The 10BaseT is the most popular physical layer today. The twisted pair based physical layer uses a star type network topology. In the 10BaseT network topology, the end stations are connected to a central hub using a twisted pair cable. The twisted pair length between the end station, and the hub may be between 0 to 100 meters. The 10BaseT physical uses 4 wires (2 pairs) of the twisted pair cable. One pair is used for differential transmit signals, and the other pair is used for differential receive signals.

TOKEN BUS (IEEE 802.4) MAC LAYER

The Token Bus MAC and Physical layer specifications were developed in response to the fact that baseband network standards, like CSMA/CD, are not suitable for factory floors. The Token Bus (IEEE 802.4) standard development was driven by General Motors. GM wanted a MAC layer protocol which provides deterministic time for frame transmission. In a CSMA/CD based network, if a station is hit by collisions, that particular station can sit in a collision path, and the frames from that station may be delayed due to excessive collisions on the network. Furthermore, this delay could be caused due to some unimportant data transmission. The Token Bus based architecture eliminates this problem. In IEEE 802.4 standard, each station has to wait for a token before it can transmit. Also, each station can hold the token for a defined maximum amount of time. This provides a means of calculating the worst-case frame latencies.

The physical layer of Token Bus standard is broadband versus baseband for CSMA/CD. Broadband electrical signaling is more immune to noise on a factory floor. The Token Bus group adopted a logical ring architecture on a broadcast bus over a physical ring architecture. This is done to provide a greater degree of flexibility from the cabling standpoint in a factory floor. Also, physical rings are more prone to single points of failure as compared to a physical bus architecture.

The next few sections provide more details with regards to the Token Bus MAC layer operation and the physical layer signaling.

Token Bus MAC Architecture

The Token Bus MAC architecture is based on a token passing mechanism. Each station has to wait for a token before it can transmit on the network. When a station receives a token, it looks into its transmit queue. If any frames are present, it will transmit those frames. The station then passes the token to the next station. The next station then goes through the same exercise. In the

IEEE 802.4 Token Bus architecture, all the stations are connected on a broadcast medium. Each station can see the transmission from every other station. Another very important point to remember for token bus architecture is that the physical location of the station has absolutely nothing to do with the logical location of a station on a ring. This means that the logical token passing ring is constructed on the token bus network without giving any consideration to the physical location of the station. The concept of a logical ring on a physical bus is illustrated in Figure 2-11.

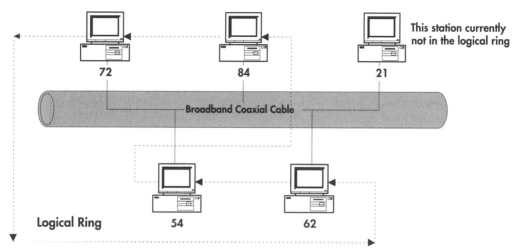

Figure 2-11. Logical Ring on a Physical Bus

As shown in Figure 2-11, the token bus is a linear cable with a number of stations connected to it. Logically, these stations are connected as a ring and each station has a MAC level address assigned to it. When the ring is initialized, the station with the highest address gets the right to create a token and pass the token to the next station in the ring. As shown in Figure 2-11, the stations are formed into a logical ring according to their station addresses. The token is passed in the logical ring from the highest station address to the next lower station address. The station with the lowest address in the ring finally passes the token back to the highest address station. The token holder is the only station that has the permission to transmit a frame on the network. The token holding station has this permission to transmit for only a limited amount of time. Once the allowed time is up, the station must pass the token onto the next station. The IEEE 802.4 is a broadcast medium, and hence every station receives the transmission from all other stations. The stations connected on the broadcast medium are responsible for filtering out the information not needed by them. Hence, regardless of the physical location of the station, the station can send a frame or token to any other station on the network. Another very important point of the token bus protocol is the fact that the token bus protocol has the provision to add or delete a station from the ring. A user of a station may decide to power on the station but not include the station in to the logical ring. Later on, when the user is ready, he or she can instruct the station to connect itself onto the logical ring.

The use of the token guarantees that only one station transmits at any one time. This eliminates the chances of collisions on token bus networks. Data frames are transmitted by a station only when the station receives a token. The token bus MAC receives the data units from the LLC sub-layer, packages the data units with the MAC header information (destination address, source address, etc.), and then waits for the token. Once the token arrives, the MAC layer holds the token and then transmits the MAC frame on the network. All the stations receive the data frame and monitor the destination address of the data frame. If the destination address matches the source address, the data frame is received by the MAC layer. Once the complete data frame is received by the MAC layer, it strips all the MAC-related headers and passes the data frame to the LLC layer above it.

The token passing MAC protocol is much more complicated than any other 802 MAC-level protocol. A number of steps are defined for token bus ring maintenance. Without going into too much detail, the major token bus ring maintenance steps are discussed briefly below.

(i) **Adding a Station**: From time to time, stations are powered on and want to join the ring. Each station gives an opportunity to other stations to join in between itself and its successor. The station that is already in the logical ring initiates the reconstruction of the ring if the data traffic on the ring is low. This ensures that data traffic is given priority over ring maintenance functions. The station maintains a timer called the ring maintenance timer. If the current token rotation time is less than what is specified by the ring maintenance timer, the data traffic is low, and the station can start the process of adding another station. However, if the current token rotation time is higher than what is specified by the ring maintenance timer, the station does not initiate the station addition process. When the token holding station determines that data traffic is low and other stations can be added in to the ring, it sends a special control frame called SOLICIT_SUCCESSOR frame. This frame contains the MAC address of the sender station and also the address of the sender's current next station. The station(s) with MAC address(es) inside the range of the SOLICIT_SUCCESSOR MAC addresses are invited to join the ring. The sending station waits for a predefined period, and if no response is obtained, the token passing continues without any changes in the logical ring. If one and only one station responds, that station is inserted in the logical ring. If more than one stations respond to the SOLICIT_SUCCESSOR frame, the transmission is garbled and the station that started the ring maintenance starts a resolve contention process. The resolve contention process is designed to limit the number of stations which can be inserted in to the ring to avoid contention between these stations. This process is defined in the IEEE 802.4 standard.

(ii) **Deleting a Station**: The process of deleting a station from the logical ring is much more simple than the process of adding a station to the ring. The station that wishes to be deleted from the ring waits for a token. When it receives a token, it sends a SET_SUCCESSOR control frame to its predecessor station requesting the predecessor to change its next station address. For example, if the station with MAC address 62 wants to leave the ring (see Figure 2-11), it waits for the token. When it receives the token, it sends a SET_SUCCESSOR frame to the MAC station with address 72 requesting it to change its successor address from 62 to 54. This means that the station with address 72 would now pass the token to the station with address 54, and hence the station with address 62 is deleted from the logical ring. When the station with address 54 receives a transmission from the station with address 72, it changes its predecessor address from 62 to 72. This completes the deletion of a station from the logical ring.

(iii) **Ring Initialization**: The process of ring initialization is very similar to the process of adding stations to the ring. The only major difference between the ring initialization and adding the stations to the ring is claim tokens. When a station first powers on and does not detect any activity on the network, it starts the process of ring initialization by sending a control frame called CLAIM_TOKEN. The stations receiving the claim token frame are required to participate in the process of deciding which station has the highest address to initiate a token. If none of the stations participate in the claim token process, then the station that initiated this process makes a one node ring and starts passing the token to itself. Other stations can join this one station ring later.

(iv) **Fault Recovery**: It is possible that a station participating in the logical ring fails for one or the other reason. A very clear process is defined to recover from such a situation. In a logical ring of four station: A, B, C, and D in which station A is passing token to station B, B is passing token to C, C is passing token to D, and D is passing token back to A, if station C fails, a process by which this failure will be detected is initiated. When station B passes the token to station C, station B monitors the cable for a defined period of time to see if station C has made a valid transmission (a token or a data unit). If station B does not see any transmission from station C, it passes the token one more time. If this also fails, station B sends a WHO_FOLLOWS frame specifying station C's address. The station located after station C is required to monitor its predecessor's address and then to respond to the WHO_FOLLOWS frame.

In this case, station D sees its predecessor's address (i.e., C) in the WHO_FOL-LOWS frame, and hence station D responds to the WHO_FOLLOWS frame by sending a SET_SUCCESSOR frame to station B. The SET_SUCCESSOR frame is received by station B, and station B changes its successor from C to D. Hence station C is deleted from the logical ring. It may also be possible that there was a dual fault, and stations C and D went down at the same time. This means that the WHO_FOLLOWS frame from station B will go unnoticed by other stations as the WHO_FOLLOWS frame has station C's address, and the only station qualified to respond is station D. When station B does not get a response for a pre-defined period of time, station B sends a control frame called SET_SUCCESSOR_2 frame to see if any other station is alive. It is also possible that the station that becomes faulty takes the token with it. This is known as lost token case, and the problem is solved in a manner similar to ring initialization via claim tokens. It is also possible that for some reason, multiple tokens are generated on a ring. If a station holding a token sees a transmission on the network, it assumes that there is duplicate token and drops its own token. This process reduces the number of tokens on the network until only one token is left.

The IEEE 802.4 Token Passing MAC is very complicated, and only the very basic concepts have been covered in this section. Readers who would like more details on this subject should read the IEEE 802.4 standard.

Token Bus MAC Frame Format

This section defines the IEEE 802.4 Medium Access Control (MAC) frame formats. It also gives some examples of the MAC control frames such as token frames. The MAC data frames contain the data passed to the MAC sub-layer by the LLC sub-layer. Figure 2-12 illustrates the general frame format for IEEE 802 MAC sub-layer.

Preamble	Start Delimiter	Frame Control	Destination Address	Source Address	Data Unit	Frame Check Sequence	End Delimiter
1 or more Bytes	1 Byte	1 Byte	2 or 6 Bytes	2 or 6 Bytes	0-8182 Bytes	4 Bytes	1 Byte

Figure 2-12. IEEE 802.4 MAC General Frame Format

The various fields of the IEEE 802.4 MAC frame are described below.

Preamble: The preamble is a bit pattern that precedes every transmitted frame. The receiving station uses the preamble bits for synchronization. In the case of IEEE 802.4 physical layers, the preamble is used to acquire signal level and phase lock by using a known pattern. The preamble pattern and length is different for each physical layer modulation scheme discussed in the next section. Another purpose of the preamble is to guarantee a minimum time between End Delimiter of the previous frame and Start Delimiter of the next frame. This minimum time allows the stations to process the previous frame before the next one starts. The minimum time (or length) of the preamble should be 2 μs, regardless of the data rates. This means that for the data rates of 1 Mb/s, the station has to transmit a minimum of 1 byte of preamble, and for data rates of 10 Mb/s, the station has to transmit a minimum of 3 bytes of preamble.

Start Delimiter: The Start Delimiter (SD) is used to indicate to the receiving station that the frame is starting. The SD consists of signaling patterns that are always distinguishable from the data. The SD field is 1 byte long.

Frame Control: The Frame Control (FC) field is 1 byte long. The FC field identifies the type of frames being sent. The IEEE 802.4 MAC has two types of frames: MAC data frames and MAC control frames. The MAC control frames contain a number of frames like claim_token, solicit_successor_1, solicit_successor_2, and who_follows. The MAC data frames contain the LLC data bytes. The frame control byte in the MAC data frame also represents the priority of the frame. Figure 2-13 shows a token frame and its frame control field.

Preamble	SD	FC 00001000	DA	SA	FCS	ED

Figure 2-13. MAC Token Frame

Destination Address: The destination address field length can be either 2 or 6 bytes. The 6 byte address field format is the one that is used most commonly in the IEEE 802.4-based networks.

The address field length has to be consistent throughout the network. The destination address field contains the MAC address of the station which should receive the frame. The destination address can be a broadcast (All 1s), group (bit 48 = 1), or individual (bit 48 =0), followed by a unique 47-bit address. The frame with a broadcast destination address is received by all stations. The group address frame is received by a group of frames and the individual address frame is received by a single station.

Source Address: The source address field length can be either 2 or 6 bytes. The 6 byte address field format is the one that is used most commonly in the IEEE 802.4-based networks. The address field length has to be consistent throughout the network. The source address field contains the MAC address of the frame transmitting station.

Data Unit: The Data Unit field contents depend upon the value in the frame control field. If the FC field specifies a frame as a MAC control frame, then the data unit field contains a value (or values) specific to that MAC control frame. If the FC field specifies a frame as a MAC data frame, the MAC data unit field contains the LLC data bytes.

Frame Check Sequence: The Frame Check Sequence (FCS) is a 4 byte field. A cyclic redundancy check (CRC) is used by the transmit and receive algorithms to generate a CRC value for the FCS field. The transmit station performs a CRC generation on all the data bytes of the frame and generates a 4 byte CRC which is appended to the frame. The polynomial which is used to generate the CRC is described in the IEEE 802.4 standards documentation. The receiving station receives the MAC frame, computes the same CRC, and compares the received CRC with the computed CRC. For the frame to be transmitted and received without errors, the two values should match.

End Delimiter: The IEEE 802.4 MAC frame format requires an End Delimiter (ED), which ends the frame and determines the position of the FCS. The ED field contains a signaling value that is always distinguishable from data. The bytes between the SD and the ED fields are covered by FCS.

Token Bus Physical Layers

The IEEE 802.4 physical layer uses coaxial cable supporting data rates of 1, 5 and 10 Mbps. The 10 Mbps data rates based physical layers are used most in the IEEE 802.4-based networks. The token bus standard specifies three different types of physical layers. Figure 2-14 shows the different types of physical layers used in IEEE 802.4-based networks.

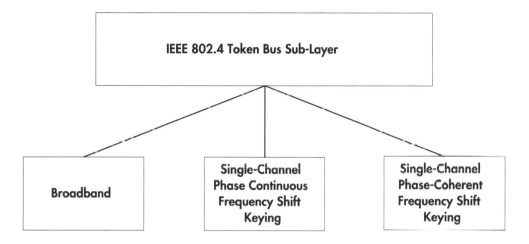

Figure 2-14. IEEE 802.4 Physical Layers

The broadband physical layer uses the 75 ohm broadband coaxial cable used for cable television. The broadband system can use a single cable with transmit and receive channels running at different frequency bands or a dual-cable configuration. In the broadband-based system, the information is encoded, modulated onto a carrier, and band-pass filtered to occupy a limited frequency spectrum on the coaxial transmission medium. In such a transmission scheme, many information signals can be present on the medium at the same time without disruption, provided that they all occupy nonoverlapping frequency regions within the cable system's range of frequency. The modulation technique used is called three-level duo binary AM/PSK. In the AM/PSK modulation an RF carrier is both amplitude modulated (AM) and phase shifted (PSK). The three-level duo binary signaling has three different signaling levels. The duo binary signaling uses different pulse shapes to reduce the frequency spectrum required to transmit the information.

The single-channel Phase-Coherent FSK uses baseband transmission and frequency modulation. In this physical layer, the frequency changes between two distinct values, rather than varying continuously. The phase-coherent frequency shifted keying mechanism is a particular type of FSK where two signaling frequencies are integrally related to the data rate, and transitions between the two signaling frequencies are made at the zero crossings of the carrier waveform. This physical layer uses 75 ohm CATV type cable. The data rates supported are 5 Mbps and 10 Mbps. The 5 Mbps data rate uses frequencies between 5 MHz and 10 MHz. The 10 Mbps data rate uses frequencies between 10 MHz and 20 MHz.

The single-channel phase-continuous FSK physical layer is based on baseband transmission. The modulation in this physical layer is provided by frequency-shift keying. In phase-continuous FSK modulation, the frequency changes continuously. The cable used in this physical layer is the 75 ohm CATV type cable. The data rates supported are 1 Mbps. The carrier frequency is around 5 MHz. The frequency shift keying modulation varies from 3.75 MHz to 6.25 MHz.

TOKEN RING (IEEE 802.5) MAC LAYER

The Token Ring (IEEE 802.5) standard is another very important MAC and physical layer standard. This standard is used in almost all IBM local area networking architectures. A number of different types of token ring architectures have existed in the LAN marketplace. However, the most popular token ring architecture is the one documented in the IEEE 802.5 specifications. As specified in the other 802 standards, the 802.5 token ring standard specifies the token ring MAC protocol and the various physical layers which can be used under the MAC layer. The MAC layer of the token ring specification interfaces with the LLC layer. The interface between the MAC and the LLC layer is also documented in the IEEE 802.5 standard.

The token ring network uses a physical ring architecture where the stations are connected on a physical ring using shielded or unshielded twisted pair cables. Data bits are transmitted from one station to another in a given direction. Each station observes the data bits and decides if it should use those data bits or not. Each station also acts as a repeater, repeating the data bits so that the next station in the physical station can receive the data bits. The data bits transmitted on the station eventually reach the originator and the originator is responsible for removing the data bits from the network. More details of the token ring MAC, physical layer architecture, and the MAC frame format are discussed in the following sections.

Token Ring MAC Architecture

The token ring MAC layer is a logical ring architecture where stations are connected in physical rings. The access to a station is controlled by a device called MAU (Media Access Unit). MAU is a collection of relays that come into play to either allow access to a station or to prohibit access to a station. The token ring network and the station bypass functions are shown in Figure 2-15.

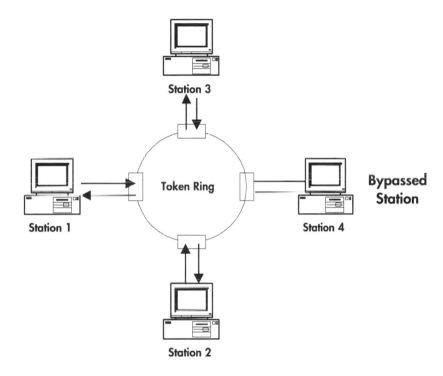

Figure 2-15. Token Ring Architecture

As indicated earlier, a token ring consists of a set of stations connected serially by a transmission medium. Information is transferred sequentially from one station to another. The information flows in the form of bits in one single direction. Each station regenerates and repeats each bit. Only one station at any time has the right to transmit on the ring. The right to transmit on the ring is controlled by a token. A station can only transmit information on the ring if it captures a token first. The token is a control signal comprised of a unique signaling sequence that circulates on the medium following each information transfer. The token is also passed from one station to another. When a station receives a token, it has the right to transmit data on the medium for a limited and predefined amount of time. Each station maintains a token holding timer that controls the maximum period of time a station can hold the token and make data transmission. When the defined amount of time expires, the station has to complete the transmission and then release the token. The token then travels to the next station and the same process is repeated. The station that transmits data bits on the network is also responsible for removing the data bits from the ring. When the station is transmitting data bits, it ignores all the data bits coming to it. If the station is in "listen" mode, it monitors all the incoming data bits and looks for frames addressed to it. It also watches for token frames which it can capture and be able to start a transmission.

Each token ring network has a set of server stations that are the main stations through which the systems manager manages the other stations in a token ring system. Servers are data collection and distribution points on each ring. Each station on the ring reports various error conditions to the server stations. All the stations also report the change in ring status such as addition and removal of stations to the server stations. The IEEE 802.5 specification lists a protocol and message format for exchanging data information between regular stations and server stations.

The token ring network can have error conditions which can prohibit data transmission on the network. One of the error conditions that can happen on the token ring network is a lost token. The token ring architecture has a way of recovering from this condition. In a token ring network, one of the active stations is assigned the function of an active monitor. The active monitor station is selected during ring initialization. During ring initialization, a station transmits a CLAIM_TOKEN frame. Each station on a token ring network has the capability of becoming an active monitor. Each station monitors the CLAIM_FRAME it receives and if the source address in the claim frame is higher then the source address of this station, then the station repeats the CLAIM_TOKEN frame.

When a station receives its CLAIM_TOKEN frame, it assumes that it is the active monitor. The main responsibility of the active monitor is to monitor the token ring network for errors. The active monitors have the worst case token rotation timer. If the active monitor does not see the token during the time specified by the timer, then the active monitor station assumes that the token is lost and it generates another token. The active monitor station takes action when a ring is broken. It also performs ring purging functions. The token ring network can have garbled frames which appear as a result of aborted transmission. These frames should be removed from the token ring. The active monitor station detects these frames by looking for frames with, for example, invalid formats or bad checksums. The active monitor opens the ring, drains all the bad frames and then restarts the ring by issuing a new token.

The token ring MAC architecture is not as complicated as the token bus MAC architecture. The main difference between the token ring and the token bus architectures is the active monitor station. One of the disadvantages of the token ring is that if the active monitor station goes down, the token ring will have major problems. This means that the token ring architecture has a single point of failure, whereas in the token bus architecture, all stations share the responsibility of ring maintenance and error recovery, which makes the architecture more complicated.

Token Ring MAC Frame Format

The token ring general frame format is very similar to the frame format of other 802 MAC layer frames. Figure 2-16 lists all the fields in the IEEE 802.5 Token Ring MAC layer frame.

Starting Delimiter	Access Control	Frame Control	Destination Address	Source Address	Data Unit	Frame Check Sequence	End Delimiter	Frame Status
1 Byte	1 Byte	1 Byte	2 or 6 Bytes	2 or 6 Bytes	0 - N Bytes	4 Bytes	1 Byte	1 Byte

Figure 2-16. IEEE 802.5 MAC General Frame Format

The various fields of the IEEE 802.5 MAC frame are described below.

Start Delimiter: The Start Delimiter (SD) is used to indicate to the receiving station that the frame is starting. The SD consists of signaling patterns that are always distinguishable from the data. The SD field is 1 byte long. The data sequence included in the SD field is such that it is not mistaken with the actual data (0s and 1s).

Access Control: The access control field is 1 byte long. This field specifies if the following frame is a token frame or a data frame. This field also identifies the priority of the data frames.

Frame Control: The Frame Control (FC) field is 1 byte long. The FC field identifies the type of frame being sent. This field contains bits that distinguish between a MAC data frame and an LLC data frame. If the frame is LLC data frame, this byte reserves 3-bits to indicate the LLC data frame priority level.

Destination Address: The destination address field length can be either 2 or 6 bytes. The 6 byte address field format is the one that is used most commonly in the IEEE 802.5 based networks.

The address field length has to be consistent throughout the network. The destination address field contains the MAC address of the station which should receive the frame. The destination address can be a broadcast (all 1s), group (bit 48 = 1), or individual (bit 48 =0), followed by a unique 47-bit address. The frame with a broadcast destination address is received by all stations. The group address frame is received by a group of frames and the individual address frame is received by a single station.

Source Address: The source address field length can be either 2 or 6 bytes. The 6 byte address field format is the one that is used most commonly in the IEEE 802.5 based networks. The address field length has to be consistent throughout the network. The source address field contains the MAC address of the frame transmitting station.

Data Unit: The Data Unit field contents depend upon the value in the frame control field. If the FC field specifies a frame as a MAC control frame, then the data unit field contains value specific to the MAC control frames. If the FC field specifies a frame as a MAC data frame, the MAC data unit field contains the LLC data bytes.

Frame Check Sequence: The Frame Check Sequence (FCS) is a 4 byte field. A cyclic redundancy check (CRC) is used by the transmit and receive algorithms to generate a CRC value for the FCS field. The transmit station performs a CRC generation on all the data bytes of the frame and generates a 4 byte CRC which is appended to the frame. The polynomial which is used to generate the CRC is described in the IEEE 802.5 standards documentation. The receiving station receives the MAC frame, computes the CRC and compares the received CRC with the computed CRC. For the frame to be transmitted and received without errors, the two values should match.

End Delimiter: The IEEE 802.4 MAC frame format requires an End Delimiter (ED), which is used to indicate the end of the frame. The ED field contains a unique pattern which indicates the end of the frame. The ED field also contains an error-detected bit which is set by a station if it detects any errors in the frame. The ED also contains another bit that is labeled as intermediate frame bit. The intermediate frame bit is used to indicate whether or not this frame is the last frame of a multiframe transmission.

Frame Status: The frame status field is a one byte field. This field has two main bits defined. They are address recognized bit (A bit) and frame copied bit (C bit). The station transmitting the frame sends the A and C bits = 0. If a station's address matches the destination address of the frame, it sets the A bit. If this station successfully copies the frame into its buffer, then the station sets the C bit. These two bits indicate whether or not the frame was successfully received by the destination station.

Token Ring Physical Layers

The IEEE 802.5 standard specifies two types of physical layers. Figure 2-17 lists the two types of physical layers specified for the token ring standard.

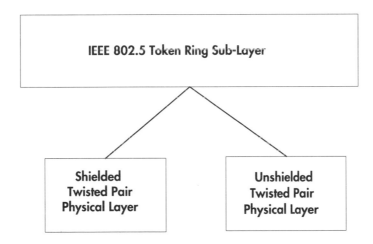

Figure 2-17. IEEE 802.5 Physical Layers

The two physical layers listed in Figure 2-17 use the same form of encoding called differential manchester encoding. In the manchester encoding scheme, the bits 1 and 0 are represented by transitions in the middle of a bit. This allows the encoded data to be self clocking, that is, the receiving station can regenerate the clock from the data bits. In the differential manchester encoding, a 1 is represented by a lack of transition on a bit boundary. A transition on a bit boundary represents an 0 in a differential manchester encoding. In the differential manchester encoding, a 1 is represented by keeping the polarity as previous polarity until the middle of the bit and then a transition is made to change the polarity. An 0 is represented in differential encoding by changing the polarity at the beginning of the bit and also at the middle of the bit. A transition always occurs during each bit time in manchester and differential manchester encoding. Figure 2-18 illustrates the manchester encoding and differential manchester encoding.

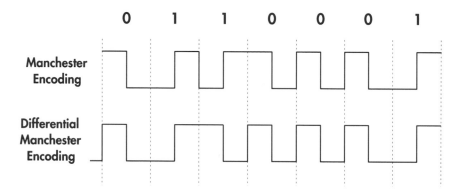

Figure 2-18. Manchester Encoding and Differential Manchester Encoding

The shielded twisted pair and the unshielded twisted pair physical layer run at 4 Mbps data rates. The shielded twisted pair used is of 150 ohm type. The unshielded twisted pair used has the resistance of 100 ohm.

FDDI MAC LAYER

Fiber Distributed Data Interface (FDDI) is a new multivendor local area network standard which was developed by ANSI X3T9.5 standards committee. The FDDI LANs operate at 100 Mbps speed and can support a maximum of 500 stations covering 100 km of geographical area.

The need for FDDI came from the ever-increasing use of the existing LANs. Before FDDI, the two most popular LANs were Ethernet (10 Mbps) and Token ring (4 or 16 Mbps). The number of stations supported by either of these LAN technologies was small. For example, an ethernet LAN can support a maximum distance of 500 meters with a maximum of 200 stations on it (without repeaters). This imposed a limitation on the total distance covered by the LAN and on the number of users on the LAN. The increasing computing power and the need to support increasing data traffic on the LAN backbones drove the need for a high speed LAN-like FDDI.

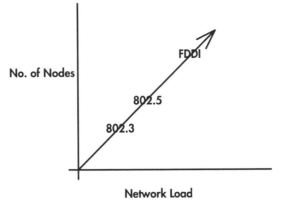

Figure 2-19. Relationship of FDDI to 802

The FDDI standard defines the physical layer and the data link layer functions of the 7 layer OSI model. The data link layer functions are not completely defined in the FDDI standard because the partial data link layer functions are defined in the logical link control (IEEE 802.2) standard. The FDDI standard sub-layers are defined in Figure 2-20.

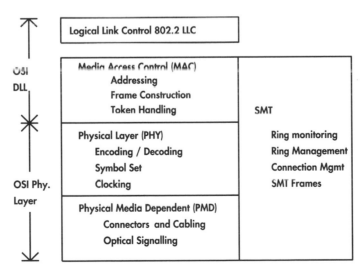

Figure 2-20. FDDI and OSI Layers

The PMD standard of FDDI defines the transmitter and the receiver characteristics. It defines the cable types, the connectors to be used, and the fiber cable plant characteristics like the total optical loss. The PHY standard specifies the 4B/5B encoding and decoding rules, the clocking and data and clock recovery requirements. It also introduces the concept of line state which is a certain number and sequence of bits. The MAC standard defines the timed—token protocol, addressing, and token handling, frame transmission and reception function, ring initialization and steady state operation of the ring. The SMT defines how to manage the PMD, PHY, and MAC portions of FDDI. It also introduces the concept of local and remote management for various FDDI stations on the ring.

FDDI System Architecture

An FDDI end station can have three possible internal configurations.

- Single Attach Station (Figure 2-21)
- Single MAC Dual Attach Station (Figure 2-22)
- Dual MAC Dual Attach Station (Figure 2-23)

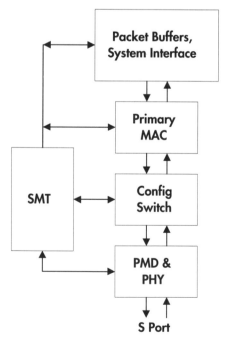

Figure 2-21. Single Attach Station

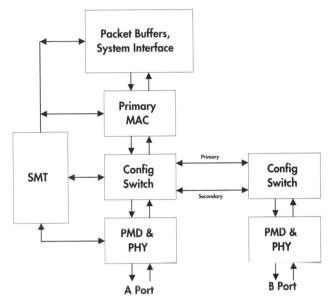

Figure 2-22. Single MAC Dual Attach Station

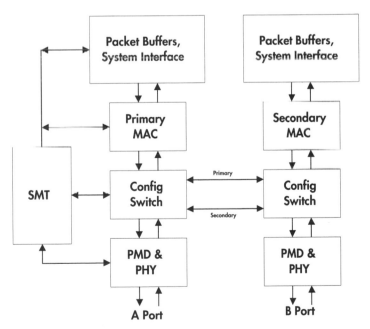

Figure 2-23. Dual MAC Dual Attach Station

These station configurations differ on the basis of the number of ports attaching to the FDDI network and also on the number of MACs available for data transfer.

Each of these architectures has its own advantages and disadvantages. For example, the SAS station architecture is the simplest and the lowest cost architecture. However, it does not offer the flexibility and redundancy built into a dual attach station. Similarly, the single MAC station is less complex and less expensive than a dual MAC station. The dual MAC station has the capability of transmitting data on both rings (primary and secondary) at the same time.

Another FDDI system type is the FDDI concentrator. A concentrator connects a single or dual attach station to the FDDI ring. The single attach station or the slave ports may be inserted on a primary or a secondary ring by a FDDI concentrator.

The various components described in the section above can participate in the FDDI protocol in various ways. Figure 2-24 below illustrates the FDDI topology.

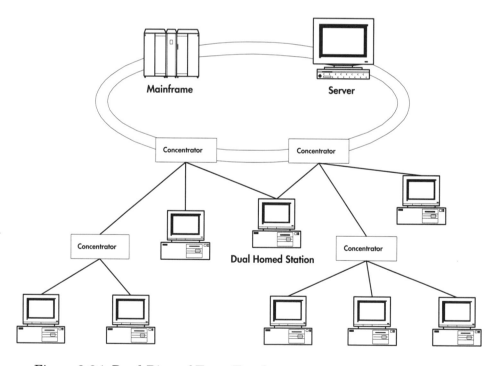

Figure 2-24. Dual Ring of Trees Topology

A station has to be a dual attach station to connect to the dual ring. However, a concentrator can be a single attach or a dual attach concentrator. A single attach concentrator has to connect like a slave station. A dual attach concentrator can be connected to the dual ring or like a slave on another FDDI concentrator. These flexible connectivity rules make FDDI very desirable for the complex networks that are being built today.

FDDI MAC Architecture

The very first event that takes place on a FDDI network is between the adjacent links of the two stations. Each link between two stations tries to initialize by exchanging information such as port type, connection rules, and link confidence information. Once the link is "up," the configuration switch will configure the station's MAC layer into the internal path so that the token can be generated on the ring. In the FDDI ring architecture, every station has equal rights. This means that it needs to be decided which station will initiate a token. This is done by a process called claim process which is very similar to auctioning. Each station bids for the token, and its bid is placed in a frame called claim frame. If a station receives a bid larger than its own bid, it keeps sending its own bid. However, if a station receives a bid smaller than its own bid, it repeats the smaller bid. This means that the station with the smallest bid will see its claim frame coming back to itself. The station which receives its own claim frame back has the right to initiate a token.

Once a token is initiated on the ring, each station has to wait for the token, capture it, and then perform data transmission. Once the station has completed data transmission, it releases the token. On the receive side, each station repeats all the frames. If the destination address of the incoming frame matches the receiving station's address, the station copies the frame into its local buffers and processes it. If the source address of the incoming frame matches the receiving station's address, the station strips the frame from the network. Also each station maintains a number of timers, like valid transmission timer (TVX), to keep a watch on the network. If a fault is detected by any station, then a number of predefined recovery procedures are executed by the station.

FDDI MAC Frame Format

The FDDI MAC frame format is very similar to the Token Bus and Token Ring MAC frame formats. The FDDI frame format and various fields of frames are illustrated in Figure 2-25.

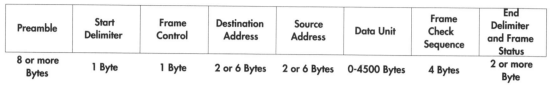

Preamble	Start Delimiter	Frame Control	Destination Address	Source Address	Data Unit	Frame Check Sequence	End Delimiter and Frame Status
8 or more Bytes	1 Byte	1 Byte	2 or 6 Bytes	2 or 6 Bytes	0-4500 Bytes	4 Bytes	2 or more Byte

Figure 2-25. FDDI MAC General Frame Format

The various fields of the FDDI MAC frame are described below.

Preamble: The preamble is a bit pattern that precedes every transmitted frame. The receiving station uses the preamble bits for synchronizing the incoming frame with the receiver logic in the physical layer. The FDDI MAC has to append 8 bytes of preamble to every frame transmitted.

Starting Delimiter: The Starting Delimiter (SD) is used to indicate to the receiving station that the frame is starting. The SD consists of the unique symbol pair (JK) and is recognizable across any symbol boundary. The SD field is 1 byte long.

Frame Control: The Frame Control (FC) field is 1 byte long. The FC field identifies the types of frames being sent. The FC field distinguishes between LLC data frames, SMT frames, and MAC control frames. The frame control field also contains the priority of the data frame. The MAC maintains the queue for various priority levels and hence the data frame with higher priority gets serviced before the data frame with lower priority. Figure 2-26 shows a token frame and its frame control field.

Preamble	SD	FC 1000 0000	ED

Figure 2-26. MAC Token Frame

Destination Address: The destination address field length can be either 2 or 6 bytes. The 6 byte address field format is the one that is used most commonly in the FDDI-based networks. The address field length has to be consistent throughout the network. The destination address field contains the MAC address of the station that should receive the frame. The destination address can be a broadcast (all 1s), group (bit

48 = 1), or individual (bit 48 =0), followed by a unique 47 bit address. The frame with a broadcast destination address is received by all stations. The group address frame is received by a group of frames, and the individual address frame is received by a single station.

Source Address: The source address field length can be either 2 or 6 bytes. The 6 byte address field format is the one that is used most commonly in the FDDI based networks. The address field length has to be consistent throughout the network. The source address field contains the MAC address of the frame transmitting station.

Data Unit: The Data Unit field contents depend upon the value in the frame control field. If the FC field specifies a frame as a MAC control frame, then the data unit field contains values specific to the MAC control frames. For example, the MAC claim frames information field contains the bid value. If the FC field specifies a frame as a LLC data frame, the data unit field contains the LLC data bytes. The data unit field may also contain the station management related information for SMT frames.

Frame Check Sequence: The Frame Check Sequence (FCS) is a 4 byte field. A cyclic redundancy check (CRC) is used by the transmit and receive algorithms to generate a CRC value for the FCS field. The transmit station performs a CRC generation on all the data bytes of the frame and generates a 4 byte CRC which is appended to the frame. The polynomial which is used to generate the CRC is described in the FDDI standards documentation. The receiving station receives the MAC frame, computes the CRC, and then compares the received CRC with the computed CRC. For the frame to be transmitted and received without errors, the two values should match.

End Delimiter and Frame Status: The ending delimiter contains symbols that indicate the end of the frame. The symbol used as an ending delimiter is terminate symbol (T). The frame status field contains 3 (or optionally more) indicators. These three indicators are EAC. The indicator E is for error detection. If a station detects any error in the frame, it sets (S) the E indicator, otherwise the E indicator stays reset (R). The A indicator is for address match. If a station's address matches the address in the destination address of the frame, it sets the A indicator, otherwise it stays clear. The C indicator is for indicating frame copy status. If a station successfully copies a frame into its buffer, it sets the C indicator, otherwise the C indicator stays reset.

FDDI and Station Management

The Station Management (SMT) standard provides the necessary services at the station level to monitor and control a FDDI station. Each FDDI station can have multiple instances of the PMD, PHY, and MAC components, but has only one SMT entity. The SMT provides a mechanism for station insertion into and removal from the ring. It has some other functions for the connection and configuration management. Fault localization is another very important function provided by the SMT. There are a number of counters and timers which gather various statistics for the local station and for the complete FDDI network.

The FDDI SMT has three major components (see Figure 2-27):

- Connection Management (CMT)

- Ring Management (RMT)

- SMT Frame Services

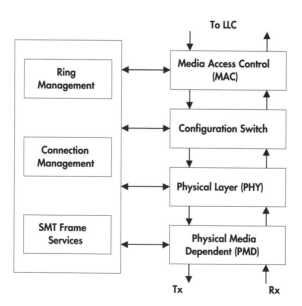

Figure 2-27. SMT and the FDDI Architecture

Connection Management

The Connection Management (CMT) entity of the SMT is responsible for the station insertion and removal. When a FDDI link is coming up, an initial bit signaling takes place. This bit signaling (exchange of 10 bits each) is performed by the connection management entity. The configuration switch which is responsible for managing the internal paths of the FDDI station is also controlled by the CMT.

Ring Management

The Ring Management (RMT) entity performs the duplicate address detection for each station on the ring. It is also responsible for taking corrective action if a duplicate address is detected on the ring. The RMT process also handles the MAC availability for transmitting LLC frames. If a duplicate is detected on the network, then RMT will make MAC not available for LLC transmission until the duplicate condition is fixed on the network. The RMT also implements a number of fault detection and correction protocols.

SMT Frame Services

The SMT frame services provide means to control and observe the FDDI network. These services are implemented by different SMT frame classes and frame types. The frame class identifies the function that the frame performs, such as neighborhood information frame (NIF) and station information frame (SIF). The frame type designates whether the frame is an announcement, a request, or a response to a request frame.

Alternative Media Types for FDDI

The installation of FDDI requires putting fiber optic cable, adapters and other similar connection components. The fiber installation, including putting a connector on the fiber, is a very labor intensive job, hence it is very expensive. The fiber optic transmitter and receiver which are built into an FDDI station are also very expensive components of the FDDI system.

Most of the existing buildings currently have a twisted pair cabling system in place to either run token ring- or Ethernet-type networks. The cost of implementing FDDI networks can be reduced considerably if the FDDI uses twisted pair as a transmission medium. This would eliminate the fiber optics transceivers from the FDDI stations and the existing copper wires could be used for connectivity. With these goals in mind, a new working group was formed in

ANSI, the X3T9.5 committee. The charter of this working group is to evaluate the possibility of running FDDI at 100 Mbps over Shielded Twisted Pair (STP) and Unshielded Twisted Pair (UTP) wires covering a distance of 100 meters or more. The most common twisted pair is unshielded, and has two types:

- Voice Grade

- Data Grade

The voice grade twisted pair is ordinary telephone wire. The difference between voice and data grades is the higher number of twists in a given length of the data grade cable. The biggest challenge against this working group is to propose a signaling scheme which would enable FDDI data rates transmission over twisted pair and also the products based on the signaling specification should be able to meet the FCC requirements for electromagnetic interference. It is easier to meet FCC requirements for electromagnetic interference with STP. It is also possible that to achieve the goal of running 100 Mbps over UTP, the PHY encoding scheme (currently NRZI) may be replaced by another scheme. The twisted pair PMD (TP-PMD) working group is currently considering various new encoding/decoding schemes to transmit 100 Mbps. The main philosophy behind the new encoding schemes is to lower the frequency of the transmitted signal without lowering the data rates.

SUMMARY

The main focus of this chapter is to provide information about layer 1 and layer 2 of the OSI reference model. The networking device drivers are software programs that operate at layer 2. Thus, before discussing various networking device driver architectures, it is important that the user understands the lower layer architectures of the 7 layer OSI model. This chapter covers the IEEE 802 local area network standards including LLC, CSMA/CD, Token Bus, and Token Ring. The networking device drivers are responsible for driving the network controller chips which implement the MAC layer standards. Hence, it is very important to understand the networking protocols and standards operating at the LLC and MAC layers. The FDDI standard provides high speed local area networking capabilities. The FDDI MAC and physical layers are also covered in this chapter. The decision to implement a FDDI network depends upon a number of factors. Network size, load on the network, and predicted future usage, play an important role in this decision. This chapter covers various FDDI topologies. FDDI can support various topologies, like dual attach stations, concentrator and single attach stations, or a mix of these two topologies. This chapter covers the management features included in the SMT part of the FDDI standard which is very complete. This makes FDDI very desirable as the next generation LAN.

REFERENCES

Chappel, Laura 1993. *Novell's Guide to NetWare LAN Analysis*. Novell Press.

Martin, James and Chapman, Kathleen K. 1989. *Local Area Networks Architectures and Implementations*. Prentice-Hall, Inc. Englewood Cliffs, NJ.

Mirchandani, Sonu and Khanna, Raman 1993. *FDDI Technology and Applications*. John Wiley & Sons, Inc., New York, NY.

Tanenbaum, Andrew S. 1988. *Computer Networks*. Prentice-Hall, Inc. Englewood Cliffs, NJ.

_____1990. ISO/IEC 8802-2. ANSI/IEEE Std 802.2. *Information Processing Systems–Local Area Networks—Part 2: Logical Link Control.*

_____1990. ISO/IEC 8802-3. ANSI/IEEE Std 802.3. *Information Processing Systems–Local Area Networks—Part 3: Carrier Sense Multiple Access with Collision Detection (CSMA/CD) Access Method and Physical Layer Specifications.*

_____1990. ISO/IEC 8802-4. ANSI/IEEE Std 802.4. *Information Processing Systems–Local Area Networks—Part 4: Token-passing Bus Access Method and Physical Layer Specifications.*

_____1990. ISO/IEC 8802-5. ANSI/IEEE Std 802.5. *Information Processing Systems–Local Area Networks—Part 5: Token Ring Access Method and Physical Layer Specifications.*

_____1990. ANSI/IEEE Std 802.6 *Local and Metropolitan Area Networks. Distributes Queue Dual Bus (DQDB) Subnetwork of a Metropolitan Area Network (MAN).*

3

Networking Operating Systems and the Device Drivers

INTRODUCTION

This chapter focuses on providing the architecture of the main operating systems and their networking sub-systems. It also details the device driver architecture of these operating systems. The information presented in this chapter should help the reader understand the specifics of the various networking device driver architectures that are discussed in the next few chapters. This chapter is essential in understanding the concepts of networking device drivers.

The operating systems that are covered in this chapter are DOS, Windows 3.1, Windows NT 3.1, OS/2 2.x, Novell NetWare, and UNIX. These operating systems are very different from each other, and hence their device driver architectures are also very different. Some of these operating systems allow loading the device drivers from command line. However, the other operating systems make the device driver part of the main operating system kernel. Some of these operating systems have the networking sub-system designed as an integral part of the operating system. The other operating systems have networking added to them as an enhancement later, and hence the design is not very clean.

This chapter will provide background information on all operating systems and their corresponding device driver architectures. Readers may skip sections of this chapter if they are already familiar with the information in them.

Device drivers are very complex pieces of software that are responsible for manipulating the hardware devices present in a system. Every hardware device in a computer system requires a device driver. For example, in IBM PCs or compatibles, the hardware devices that require a device driver to be loaded are the keyboard, the mouse, the video, the disks, serial and parallel ports, the network card, and the sound card, to name a few. The device driver understands the hardware architecture of the device very well, and is responsible for performing all the I/O to that device. Device drivers make the hardware device initialize and operational. In addition, device drivers hide the complexities of the hardware device from rest of the operating environment. This means that the device driver provides a simple, generic interface for that device to the rest of the operating environment. For example, a hard disk device driver will contain all the hardware details of initializing, sending read command, and sending write command, to the hard disk controller. The disk driver presents a very simple interface to various applications running in the system to access the disk and to perform read and write operations on the disk. All the complicated translations of handling the simple application interface calls are done within the device driver.

Device drivers are very complex, low-level programs that are responsible for manipulating the I/O devices/hardware attached to them. Their main function is to operate the hardware for which they are responsible. They also insulate the rest of the operating system from the complexities of the hardware components. The kernel and the applications involved with the hardware device do not need to understand the operational details of the hardware device. The device driver understands the device registers and I/O ports, device commands, and error recovery, and the device driver provides the rest of the system with an interface for manipulating the hardware device. The role of the device driver is very transparent at the application level. In earlier operating systems (the 1970s), the operating systems and the applications were hardware-dependent. The applications were written for a certain hardware, and they expected that hardware while they were running. The complete operating system evolution has focused mainly on interfaces, and hence the device drivers today offer a very simple interface to their applications. This makes the applications completely hardware-independent. The drivers make the kernel and the applications hardware-independent, and hence they can be used across a wide variety of hardware platforms by just rewriting the device driver portion.

This chapter provides the basic architecture and the device driver architecture of various operating systems. The operating systems which are covered in this chapter are DOS, Windows 3.1, Windows NT 3.1, OS/2 2.x, NetWare, and UNIX. The networking device driver aspect of these operating systems is also covered in this chapter. This chapter provides the background information needed for the reader to proceed into the detailed description of the various networking device drivers provided in the next few chapters.

DOS OPERATING SYSTEM

DOS is the acronym for Disk Operating System. DOS was first introduced in 1981 by Microsoft Corporation. This operating system was the one used on the first IBM PCs. Since then DOS has undergone various major enhancements and is used in millions of PCs around the world. Today there are three main versions of DOS available. They are:

- MS-DOS (Microsoft)

- PC-DOS (IBM)

- Novell-DOS (Novell)

MS-DOS is by far the main DOS operating system used by users all over the world. The base operating system is very similar among the three versions of DOS, and hence various DOS applications are very compatible. The three DOS versions do offer some different advanced functions, like disk compression, which are not compatible across the three types of DOS. In this section, we focus on the MS-DOS operating system. The concepts presented in this section also apply to the other DOS types.

MS-DOS provides generic, device-independent access to the resources of the computer. A typical MS-DOS computer is a 8086 microprocessor compatible computer with various devices like disks, keyboard, screen, mouse, serial, and parallel interfaces. The main component of the MS-DOS operating system is a set of system-level functions provided by MS-DOS. This provides access to various hardware devices and some other general housekeeping services, such as memory management, and national language support. The programs and applications that use these system level functions provided by MS-DOS are device-independent. These programs have no knowledge of the operation of the device. They rely on the MS-DOS operating system and the device drivers resident along with the operating system to interact with the hardware devices. The systems functions provided by various MS-DOS versions have grown steadily from version 1.0 to the current version 6.22. The systems interface provided by MS-DOS is forward- and backward-compatible, and hence the programs written for one version run on the other versions, and so on. The MS-DOS application programs use the MS-DOS system functions to allocate memory, load programs, read and write files and devices, connect to a network, and so on. The main features of MS-DOS operating system are listed on the following pages.

1. **File System**: The MS-DOS file system consists of files, directories, and data structure holding the complete file system information. MS-DOS has the master control of the complete file system. The various application programs can create, read, write, and delete files from the computer storage media. The data structure that holds the complete MS-DOS file system is called File Allocation Table (FAT). Programs do not access the FAT data structure directly. The programs use the system functions to create, read, write, and delete a file. When MS-DOS receives such a request, it updates the FAT table and also uses the disk device driver to pass the actual disk I/O commands to the disk controller hardware.

2. **Memory Management**: The complete system memory (RAM) is managed by MS-DOS operating system. When the user wants to load a program, MS-DOS allocates memory for the program code and data. It then copies the program from the disk to the memory and executes it. The program can allocate or deallocate memory as it is running. The MS-DOS operating system provides several system functions to allocate and free memory from the main system pool of memory.

3. **Program Execution**: MS-DOS is a single tasking operating system. It runs one program at a time. The program that is being executed can load and run another program. The MS-DOS operating system provides resources to the new program also. The original program is in a suspend state until the second program is completed.

4. **Character Device Management**: MS-DOS provides a very simple interface to use the various character devices present in the computer system. The character devices are the devices which handle data, one byte at a time. The example of such devices are keyboard, screen, and serial port. MS-DOS assigns logical name to various devices in the system. For example PRN is the printer device, CON is the console device which contains screen as output and keyboard as input, and AUX is the serial port. MS-DOS programs can communicate to these character devices in the same way as they manipulate files. This means that a program can open a device by the name PRN and then write to it, and the net effect would be to print on an attached printer.

5. **Interrupt Handling**: MS-DOS programs provide system functions to install interrupt handlers for various programs. This means that a program can install its custom handler that would be called by the operating system when the corresponding interrupt occurs in the computer system.

6. **Networks**: The MS-DOS operating system provides support programs that communicate over a network. A network enables programs running on one computer to use the resources and communicate to another com-

puter. MS-DOS programs connect to network drives, and access files and character devices by opening, reading, and writing to the files located on network drives.

Major Components of MS-DOS

It is important to understand the DOS internal structure and the MS-DOS booting process to understand the role of the device drivers and their structure which is discussed later in this section. MS-DOS has three main components that are loaded and executed during the MS-DOS boot process. These three components reside in three separate files. They are:

IO.SYS   This is a hidden file. This file contains the DOS basic I/O device drivers. The device drivers contained in this file include drivers for the following devices: CON (Keyboard and Screen), PRN (Printer), AUX (Serial Interface), CLOCK (Clock), Hard disks, and Floppy disks. These drivers are always loaded and cannot be installed or changed by the user. These drivers interact with the ROM BIOS present in the system.

MSDOS.SYS   This is a hidden read only systems file. This file is also called as the MS-DOS kernel. This file contains all the file access routines and the character input/output routines. This file contains the MS-DOS systems functions which are called using the interrupt 21h. These MS-DOS system functions provide routines for accessing the keyboard, screen, and disk. The MS-DOS int 21h interface is completely independent of the hardware. Internally, these routines use the hardware-dependent device drivers located in IO.SYS file. Any MS-DOS application program can call these functions by using the software interrupts (int 21h) and passing the function number and parameters in the processor registers.

COMMAND.COM   This file is a regular file placed in the root directory when MS-DOS is installed. This is the MS-DOS command interpreter. This command processor is responsible for displaying the "A:>" or "C:>" prompts on the screen and processing any user inputs. The COMMAND.COM is a MS-DOS user level program running under MS-DOS control. The COMMAND.COM program has three portions: an initialization routine, a resident portion, and a transient portion. The initialization routine loads during the booting process and initializes MS-DOS. The resident portion of COMMAND.COM contains the most used MS-DOS commands such as COPY, RENAME, and DIR. When a user types any of the resident commands, the COMMAND.COM can process these commands quickly because the code for these commands is already resident in the memory. The resident portion also contains various routines for error handling. The transient portion contains the code for displaying the MS-DOS prompt, reading user input, and executing the input. The memory location of the transient portion is unprotected and can be overwritten by a new program load. After a program has completed its execution, the resident portion of COMMAND.COM performs a checksum calculation on the memory area where the transient portion was located. If the checksum fails, the resident portion of COMMAND.COM reloads the transient portion of COMMAND.COM.

The PC startup process starts with the execution of the ROM based BIOS code followed by the power on self test for various hardware components of the PC. After the hardware is initialized and labeled functional, the MS-DOS boot process starts. The first sector on the bootable floppy disk or the hard disk is called boot sector. The MS-DOS format command places a loader on this boot sector. This program is first loaded into PC memory and is executed. This program checks for the presence of IO.SYS and MSDOS.SYS files. These two files are loaded and executed in the memory. The DOS kernel (MSDOS.SYS) builds several important tables and data areas and initializes the device drivers loaded via IO.SYS. Next, the MS-DOS kernel searches for a file by the name CONFIG.SYS. This file contains various user installable device drivers for system peripherals like network card, and sound card. These device drivers contained in the CONFIG.SYS files are loaded and initialized. The command processor (COMMAND.COM) is loaded after CONFIG.SYS file. The COMMAND.COM initializes and looks for a file called AUTOEXEC.BAT. If this file is present, the command processor executes all the MS-DOS command contained in this file. The MS-DOS user prompt is displayed at the end of this process.

MS-DOS File Formats (EXE vs. COM vs. SYS)

MS-DOS supports EXE, COM, and SYS file formats. It also has another file extension to support batch files called BAT. In this discussion, we ignore the BAT file extension because the MS-DOS batch files are nothing but text files containing MS-DOS commands. The COM, EXE, and SYS file extensions indicate that these files have different properties. All three file formats are for executable files which can be executed by MS-DOS. The COM and EXE files can be executed from the MS-DOS prompt. However, the SYS files are mainly used for the MS-DOS device drivers and can only be loaded from CONFIG.SYS processing using a <device=driver.sys> line.

A *.COM program contains an absolute binary image of a program. This absolute binary image contains all the information needed in the memory in the exact order to run this program. In MS-DOS the *.COM program must fit in a single segment (64K bytes). This means that program code, data, and stack are all stored in a 64K segment for the *.COM program under MS-DOS. The 8086 microprocessor's segment registers all point to the start of the program and remain fixed during the execution of the *.COM program. The code of the *.COM program can be addressed via the CS segment register, the data can be referenced via the DS segment register and the stack via the SS segment register. Figure 3-1 illustrates the structure of a *.COM MS-DOS program.

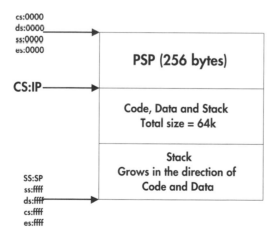

Figure 3-1. COM Program in Memory

The Program Segment Prefix (PSP) is a 256 byte data structure that contains information about programs environment such as the amount of memory that the system allocates for the program, the location of the program's environment block, and the command-line arguments supplied to the program. The PSP is located in the first 256 bytes of the program memory followed by the code and data associated with the program. In the *.COM program the PSP is not present in the binary image. The MS-DOS allocates and fills the first 256 bytes which contain the PSP data structure. The *.COM file size should be less than 64k bytes minus 256 bytes for PSP and at least 256 bytes for the initial stack. The MS-DOS allocates the required memory for the program, builds the PSP in the first 256 bytes, loads the *.COM file, starting immediately after the PSP (100h), allocates the initial stack and then transfers control to the instruction at offset 100h.

The *.SYS files represent the MS-DOS device drivers. A MS-DOS device driver is also a memory image file. However, unlike the *.COM programs, the DOS device drivers do not start at location 100h. The *.SYS MS-DOS device drivers start at location 0. There is no PSP data structure present in the *.SYS device drivers. The MS-DOS device drivers are considered as extensions to the MS-DOS kernel, and MS-DOS allocates memory and specific internal data structures to manage the location and operation of each device driver in the system. The MS-DOS device drivers start at location 0 with a device driver header. This device driver header has a very specific format which is discussed in the *MS-DOS Device Drivers* section. The main thing to note is that the *.SYS files represent the MS-DOS device drivers which contain the memory image of the program and code starting with the device driver header at location 0.

The *.EXE program format is not restricted by the single segment restriction. In EXE files, the code, the data, and the stack are distributed over various different segments in the memory. The CS, DS, and SS segment registers of the 8086 compatible microprocessor point to different segments when an EXE program is loaded in the memory. A *.EXE program contains a file header and a relocatable program image. The file header contains information that MS-DOS uses when loading the program, such as the size of the program and the initial values of the registers. The file header also points to a relocation table containing a list of pointers to a relocatable segment addresses in the program image. The *.EXE file header is described in Figure 3-2.

Offset	Length	Contents	Description	Comments
0	Word	4D5Ah	EXE file signature	
2	Word		Bytes in last partial page	Modulo 512
4	Word		Size of file	In 512-byte pages
6	Word		No.of pointers in relocation table	
8	Word		Size of header	In 16-byte paragraphs
A	Word		Minimum space needed above program	In 16-byte paragraphs
C	Word		Maximum space desired above program	In 16-byte paragraphs
E	Word		Initial SS register value	
10	Word		Initial SP register value	
12	Word		Checksum	Two's complement
14	Word		Initial IP register value	
16	Word		Initial CS value	
18	Word		Byte offset to relocation table	Relative to start of file
1A	Word		Overlay number	

Figure 3-2. EXE File Header Format

The program image, which contains the processor code and the initialized data for a program, starts immediately after the file header. Its size in bytes is equal to the size of the *.EXE file minus the size of the file header. The MS-DOS loads the *.EXE program by copying the program image directly from the file into memory and then adjusts the relocatable segment addresses specified in the relocation table pointed by the file header. The format of the EXE program in the memory is illustrated in Figure 3-3.

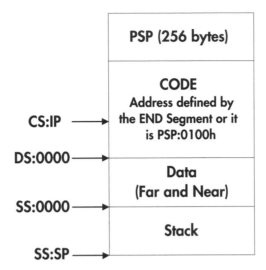

Figure 3-3. EXE Program in Memory

The EXE file loader is present in the COMMAND.COM program of MS-DOS operating system. This loader is available only after the MS-DOS kernel (MSDOS.SYS) is loaded and the CONFIG.SYS file is loaded including all the device drivers. This means that the EXE file loader is not present when the MS-DOS device drivers are being loaded, and therefore a device driver must be the binary image of a single segment program.

Networking Under MS-DOS

The MS-DOS operating system is mainly used as a client operating system in client/server environment. A client/server architecture consists of a server connected to a network consisting of several clients (also known as workstations). The server executes the network operating system and contains a wide variety of peripheral devices like disk drivers, modems, and printers. The clients contain operating system such as DOS and/or Windows 3.x. The clients also run some networking software that manages each client and allows the clients to access the resources of the server (files and printers, etc.). The client networking software runs in conjunction with the client operating system (DOS, Windows 3.1x, or OS/2). This software extends the services of the client operating system over the network. The client operating system services stay intact while the user can also use the resources available at the server. The most common use of networks is for file sharing between various clients. This is achieved by installing a server accessible to all the clients and placing the shareable file on the server which is providing the file sharing services.

The MS-DOS operating system is used as a client operating system. The server is used simultaneously by many users, and hence running the server capabilities on a multitasking system is useful. The server rarely operates under MS-DOS because MS-DOS can be too slow to process numerous simultaneous access requests. In the most common client/server environments, the server runs on a high-end multitasking operating system like OS/2, Windows NT, or NetWare. These server operating systems are discussed later in this chapter.

The MS-DOS operating system is used as a client (also known as a workstation) by installing a network redirector or network shell. The network shell was the first network redirection mechanism used by Novell. The architecture of a network shell like NETX.COM from Novell is based upon intercepting the MS-DOS INT 21h file I/O requests and watching every function call. In the Novell NetWare environment an MS-DOS client is connected to a Novell NetWare server via a network cable. The MS DOS client has the following software components loaded:

- **LSL.COM**: Link Support Layer "Glue between driver and protocol"

- **NE2100.COM**: NE2100 network interface card driver

- **IPXODI.COM**: IPX/SPX protocol stack

- **NETX.COM**: Network Shell for MS-DOS (all versions)

LSL, NE2100, and IPXODI are standard device drivers and protocol stacks needed by the Novell architecture (for more on the Novell architecture, see Chapter 7). The NETX.COM hooks on to the MS-DOS INT 21h and monitors every file I/O requests. If the user enters a command "dir c:", the COMMAND.COM MS-DOS command interpreter interprets this command and generates a INT 21h file I/O request to get the directory contents of c: drive. The NETX.COM intercepts this request and analyzes the drive letter information. As the c:1 drive is a local drive, the NETX.COM passes this request to the MS-DOS kernel to complete the command. Let us now consider that the user enters a command "dir f:." Assume here in this example that the f: drive is a network drive located on the NetWare file server. The COMMAND.COM MS-DOS command interpreter generates a file I/O request (INT 21h) to get the directory contents of the f: drive. The NETX.COM intercepts this file I/O request and analyzes the drive information letter. Since the f: drive is a network drive, the NETX.COM takes this request and generates a network packet to be transmitted via IPXODI protocol stack and the interface card driver (NE2100.COM) to the NetWare file server. The file server generates the f: directory information and sends the information via another network packet to the NETX.COM shell. This information is displayed on the screen to the user. The MS-DOS kernel never sees this file I/O request for a network drive. The concept of network shell is illustrated in Figure 3-4.

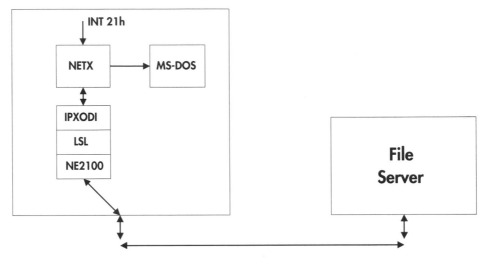

Figure 3-4. Network Shell

The network shell sees the INT 21h calls before MS-DOS sees it. In the case of network drives, the MS-DOS may never see the INT 21h calls. The term shell is used for the NETX type of redirectors because they put a shell around the MS-DOS API (Application Programming Interface).

The second type of redirector which is used in the MS-DOS environment is based on the largely undocumented network redirector interface which was introduced in MS-DOS, Version 3. This interface provides transparent support of network devices. The concept of network redirector interface present in MS-DOS operating system is similar to the network shell interface. In case of network redirector interface, the MS-DOS handles the local devices, however MS-DOS invokes various functions of network redirector interface to perform various operations on non-local (network) devices. This means that the MS-DOS is proactively generating the redirector interface function calls in the case of MS-DOS redirector interface versus the network shell where the burden was on the network shell to intercept the calls. The most recent implementation of MS-DOS client software is based on the network redirector interface of MS-DOS. The Novell NetWare VLM (Virtual Loadable Module) interface is based on the Network Redirector interface of MS-DOS. The previous implementation of Novell NetWare client software (NETX) was based upon the network shell approach.

The network redirector interface is implemented via software interrupts INT 2Fh. Microsoft uses this interface for implementing the Microsoft LAN Manager clients on MS-DOS. The redirector interface can be used for networking or for any other file system alien to MS-DOS. Microsoft also uses this interface to provide CD-ROM access under MS-DOS through the Microsoft CD-ROM Extensions (MSCDEX). Owing to the fact that the MS-DOS does some preprocessing, the redirector interface is simpler to implement because a smaller number of generally simple functions need to be implemented as compared to the shell approach. The negative associated with the redirector approach is that Microsoft has not documented this interface and does not support it. The INT 2Fh network redirector interface is documented in the following reference [Brown & Kyle 1994]. The concept of network redirector is illustrated in Figure 3-5.

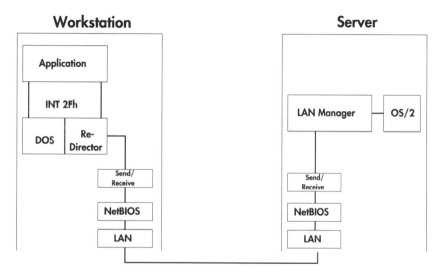

Figure 3-5. Network Redirector for MS-DOS

MS-DOS Device Drivers

The MS-DOS networking device drivers are written in two main file formats. The first format is a Terminate and Stay Resident (TSR) file format. This driver is usually in a COM file format which continues to reside in the memory after the user invokes it from the command line. The second format of a driver is the native MS-DOS device driver format which follows the SYS file format and is loaded via a "device=" line in the CONFIG.SYS file. In the networking MS-DOS device drivers discussed in the following chapters, the following formats are followed (the following example assumes the network adapter name is NETCARD).

NETCARD.COM: A TSR for Novell DOS-ODI driver (see Chapter 7)

NETCARD.COM: A TSR for Packet Driver (see Chapter 6)

NETCARD.SYS: An MS-DOS device driver for NDIS 2.0.1 (see Chapter 4)

The following discussion applies to the MS-DOS device driver format and to the terminate and stay resident drivers for MS-DOS.

Terminate and Stay Resident Programs

The Terminate and Stay Resident (TSR) programs are very popular under to MS-DOS operating system. A TSR is a program that moves to the "background" once it has started. A typical TSR program executes some initialization code in the beginning and then executes a MS-DOS function call (INT 21h, Function Call 31h–Terminate and Stay Resident) instructing MS-DOS to terminate the current executing program and return the control to the calling program. It also instructs MS-DOS to keep the current program in the memory for later recall. TSRs are used for several functions under MS-DOS. The TSR programs under MS-DOS service other programs. PRINT.EXE is a TSR that maintains the print queue and provides functions to manage the print queue under MS-DOS. Another very popular application of the TSR programs is as hardware support programs. These hardware support programs stay resident under MS-DOS and provide support functions for the hardware. This is the application of the TSR program which is used for networking device drivers under MS-DOS. Typically the entry into the TSR program is via hardware or software interrupts or callback addresses which are established during the initialization time of the TSR.

A networking TSR program consists of at least two parts: an initialization routine and an interrupt handler. The initialization routine initializes the hardware, initializes the interrupt vector table (IVT), and initializes other similar components. The interrupt handler contains the software for handling various possible interrupt conditions. For example, a networking interface card would generate a hardware interrupt when it receives a packet. This hardware interrupt is handled by the interrupt handler of the TSR which serves this particular networking hardware.

A TSR is a very complex program. The programmer of the TSR program has to be very cautious with his or her programming practice because a TSR, by its definition, ignores the single tasking nature of MS-DOS. A TSR program can be called asynchronously by the hardware device by generating a hardware interrupt at any time. It is possible that a MS-DOS function call may be in the process of being executed when the hardware device generates an interrupt, and the TSR programs interrupt handler is called. If the TSR completes its task and returns to the MS-DOS executing function properly, nothing happens.

However, the problem may arise when the TSR tries to call the MS-DOS function itself. This means that an MS-DOS function is being executed from within another MS-DOS function. This demonstrates a problem of re-entry, which MS-DOS is not designed to handle. Calling an MS-DOS function from within a TSR program while another function is executing leads to problems because the processor register SS:SP register is loaded with the address of the MS-DOS stack when an MS-DOS function is called. The MS-DOS stack is used to store the temporary data as well as to return the address to the calling program. If the MS-DOS function is called again, the processor register SS:SP is reloaded with the stack address and the contents of old stack are overwritten with new values. This means that the current function call is executed properly, but the problem will occur when the TSR program ends and the control is returned to the interrupted DOS function. Since the contents of the stack have been changed, the DOS function will probably crash the system. There are two methods that can be used to avoid this re-entry problem. The first method is not to use the MS-DOS function calls within the TSR. This is a difficult approach because the programs will have to implement a lot of code to perform very simple tasks which the MS-DOS implements. The other method is for the TSR interrupt handler to check the InDOS flag before calling an MS-DOS function. The InDOS flag is a counter located at a specified address after MS-DOS has booted. This flag keeps a count of the number of times the MS-DOS functions have been called. The MS-DOS function call INT 21h, function 34h returns the address of the InDOS flag. The TSR interrupt handler which uses a MS-DOS function call should check the contents of the InDOS flag before calling MS-DOS functions. If the InDOS flag is zero, then it is safe to call another MS-DOS function. If the InDOS flag is non-zero, the MS-DOS is currently processing a system function, and hence the TSR should not call any other MS-DOS functions.

MS-DOS Device Drivers

The MS-DOS device drivers are programs that are loaded from the CONFIG.SYS file and mostly have file extension of *.SYS. The device driver under MS-DOS becomes part of the operating system and is responsible for controlling and communication with the hardware device. The MS-DOS device driver is the lowest part of the operating system. It is typically written in assembly language. The MS-DOS device driver knows the hardware that it services very well. It hides hardware dependencies from the rest of the applications. The MS-DOS applications can communicate directly with the device driver and accomplish hardware tasks without ever knowing the details of the hardware implementation of the hardware device.

MS-DOS device drivers are similar to TSRs. They do not run on their own. They stay in the memory and wait for either MS-DOS or the hardware device to call them and ask for a service to be performed. For example, an MS-DOS application program like a TCP-IP protocol stack may call the networking device driver to transmit a packet on the network. The network device driver will take this request and manipulate the network interface card registers to instruct the network interface card to transmit the packet. Hence, MS-DOS calls the device driver's routine whenever the system needs the access to the device. The device driver then carries out the device specific operation and pass the operation information back to the MS-DOS.

The MS-DOS operating system is shipped with device driver support for a number of resident devices in the IBM PC architecture. These devices are keyboard, screen, serial port, parallel port, real time clock, and disk drive. Some of these drivers are resident as part of the system BIOS (Basic Input Output System) provided by the computer manufacturer. The MS-DOS device drivers implement installable device driver architecture which is used to support installable devices such as a networking card, printers, and pointing devices.

An MS-DOS device driver is a memory image file (like *.COM) that contains all the code to handle various device functions. The main difference between a *.COM file and a MS-DOS device driver is the start location. As discussed earlier, all *.COM files are required to start at location 100h. This allows the MS-DOS to load a 256 byte Program Segment Prefix (PSP) in the memory prior to loading the *.COM file. The MS-DOS device drivers start at location 0h. This is because the MS-DOS device drivers are an extension to the MS-DOS kernel. Hence, MS-DOS has allocated the memory and specific, internal data structures to manage the location and operation of each device driver in the system. Therefore, the MS-DOS does not need a PSP to manage a device driver. The MS-DOS manages the device driver with the help of a standard device driver header structure located at location 0 of the device driver. This structure is discussed later in this section.

An MS-DOS device driver always has a unique name. The application program accesses a hardware device by opening a device driver for that device by its unique name. The MS-DOS kernel contains a number of device drivers for standard hardware devices which are automatically installed during the MS-DOS boot process. Figure 3-6 lists the MS-DOS device driver names and functions.

Driver Name	Description of the Device
NUL	NUL Device (Imaginary Device)
CLOCK$	Real Time Clock Device
CON	Console Device (Keyboard and Screen)
AUX	Serial Port
PRN	Parallel Port

Figure 3-6. MS-DOS Device Driver Names

The MS-DOS device drivers are arranged sequentially in memory and are linked to each other. When the user wants to install another device driver in the linked chain of the device drivers, he or she places the device driver in the CONFIG.SYS file as a "device=" line. MS-DOS reads all the "device=" lines from the CONFIG.SYS file and installs the device drivers by linking them to the standard drivers. The installable device drivers have a device driver header data structure located at location 0. The device driver header is analogous to the PSP at location zero for the *.COM files. MS-DOS uses the device driver header to link all device drivers in a single linked list of device drivers. The structure defining the MS-DOS device driver header is listed below.

```
DEVICEHEADER STRUC
dhlink           dd        ?              ; link to next driver
dhAttributes     dw        ?              ; device attributes
dhStrategy       dw        ?              ; strategy routine offset
dhInterrupt      dw        ?              ; Interrupt routine offset
dhNameOrUnits    db        '????????'     ; logical device name or units
DEVICEHEADER ENDS
```

The device header identifies the device driver, and specifies the driver's strategy and interrupt routines. It also specifies the link to the next device driver header and the name of the device driver. The link field is used by the MS-DOS device driver writer to indicate to MS-DOS if there are more than one device drivers in the file that MS-DOS is loading under the "device=" line. In most cases, there is one device driver per file, and hence the contents of the dhLink field is 0FFFFh. MS-DOS sets this field to point to the driver in the chain at the load time. The second field contains the attribute word. The attribute word specifies additional information and capabilities of the device driver. The capabilities of the device driver that are specified by the attribute word are input versus output device, support for logical drive mapping, and replacement for standard clock device. The most important bit in the attribute word is bit 15, which indicates whether the device driver is a character device driver or a block device driver. More information on character or block device driver will be provided later. The detailed list and the description of the attribute word is provided in Microsoft, 1991.

The dhStrategy and dhInterrupt fields contain the offsets to the entry points of the strategy and interrupt routines. Since these fields are 16-bit values, the entry points must be in the same segment as the device driver file header. The dhNameOrUnits field is a 8 byte field containing either a device name for the character device drivers or a 1 byte value specifying the number of units supported for block device driver. MS-DOS supports two types of device drivers: *character* and *block*. The character device driver handles data one character or byte at a time. The examples of character device drivers are network device drivers, modem device drivers, and keyboard device driver. The block device driver handles a block of data (512 bytes for hard drives) at a time. The example of block device driver is the hard disk driver which handles a block of characters at a time. The discussion here is limited to the character device drivers because the networking device drivers are character device drivers.

Figure 3-7 illustrates the addition of NETCARD driver in the standard chain of MS-DOS device drivers.

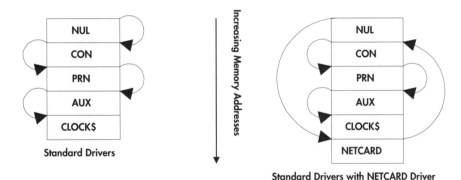

Figure 3-7. MS-DOS Device Drivers

A typical MS-DOS device driver contains five parts as shown in Figure 3-8.

Figure 3-8. MS-DOS Device Driver Format

The strategy and the interrupt routine are the two entry points for MS-DOS. Both these routines are called by MS-DOS, however, the interrupt routine does the actual work. Let us analyze from an application down to a device driver as to how the communication takes place. An application opens a device by using its name through the MS-DOS Open service (INT 21h, Function 3Dh). MS-DOS sets up a file handle and returns the file handle to the applications. The application uses this file handle to communicate to the device driver using the MS-DOS service calls. When MS-DOS receives a service request, it checks if the service request requires a device driver to get involved. If an MS-DOS device driver has to be involved, the MS-DOS constructs a request packet and passes the request packet to the device driver. The request packet contains command and data for the device driver. The command tells the device driver what action to perform (e.g., write) and the data is the actual data associated with the command. The request packet, also known as the request header, is passed to the device driver via the ES:BX registers containing the segment:offset address of the request packet. MS-DOS constructs the request packet, puts the address in the ES:BX register, and makes a call to the device driver's strategy routine. The strategy routine is the setup routine for the call. It saves the address of the request packet and returns immediately. MS-DOS then makes a call to the device driver's interrupt routine. At this point the device driver analyzes the request packet and performs the actual work. Figure 3-9 lists the format of the request packet.

Field Name	Length (bytes)	Description
Length Field	1	Length in bytes of the request packet
Device #	1	This field contains the device number
Command	1	Command code for the request packet
Status	2	Status information valid upon completion
Reserved	8	Reserved for future use
Data	Variable	Data associated with the command

Figure 3-9. Request Packet Format

The length field of the request packet contains the length of the request packet. The Device Number field contains the actual number of the device. This field makes sense for multiple devices attached to a single controller. For example a floppy disk controller often controls two devices: drive a: and drive b:. The request packet being passed to the floppy device drive has to indicate which device the command is for. This information is passed via the Device # field. The command field contains the actual command that needs to be executed by the device driver. MS-DOS requires the device drivers to support 19 commands. These 19 commands are listed in Figure 3-10. The fourth field is the status field and is used by the device driver to pass the command completion status back to MS-DOS. The next field is reserved. The last field is the data field, and the contents and the length of the data field depend upon the command field.

Command Name	Command Code	Description
Initialize	00h	Initialize the device driver and the associated hardware
Media Check	01h	Used with a block device driver only
Build BPB	02h	Build BIOS Parameter Block (BPB). Used with Block device driver only.
IOCTL Input	03h	This is the custom I/O control interface between the device driver and the application.
Read	04h	This command reads the data from the device to a buffer specified in the calling request packet.
Nondestructive Read	05h	This is used by character device driver to test for unread characters in the input buffer.
Input Status	06h	Command to obtain the input status
Input Flush	07h	This command clears the input buffers of a character device driver.
Write	08h	This command transfers the characters from the buffer to the device.
Write and Verify	09h	This command is same as Write command however, it verifies the data written.
Output Status	0Ah	This command obtains the status of the last write operation.
Output Flush	0Bh	This command clears the output buffer.
IOCTL Write	0Ch	This command passes the control information from the application to the device driver.
Open Device	0Dh	Opens the device.
Close Devices	0Eh	Closes the device.
Removable Media	0Fh	This command applies only to a block device driver. It is used to check if the media available is a removable media.
Output Until Busy	10h	This command sends data to the device until it can take no more data (i.e. until its busy).
Get Logical Device	17h	This command is for block device driver only. This command gets the logical device number.
Set Logical Device	18h	This command is for block device driver only. This command sets the logical device number

Figure 3-10. Commands supported by MS-DOS device drivers

The MS-DOS device drivers support the above commands. They also implement the IOCTL interface for custom commands not listed in Figure 3-10.

WINDOWS 3.X OPERATING SYSTEM

This section is focused on presenting the concepts behind the most popular operating system—Windows. This section provides the background information about Microsoft's Windows operating system, the architecture of Windows networking sub-system and the device driver architecture.

Introduction to Microsoft Windows

Microsoft Windows operating system was introduced by Microsoft in 1985 after enjoying the success of its MS-DOS operating system. The Microsoft Windows operating system is considered a very popular graphical user interface for MS-DOS. Today over 40 million users worldwide use the Microsoft Windows environment. The application base for Microsoft Windows is huge. Thousands of vendors worldwide support the Windows environment. From a user's perspective, the Windows environment brings a very simple to use user interface and the capability of performing multiple tasks from within Windows.

The Microsoft Windows provides multitasking, graphically-based windowing environment that runs Windows and MS-DOS programs. MS-DOS programs can be run from within Windows via the MS-DOS shell support. Windows has built in program manager, file manager, and print manager for managing various tasks. Most Windows programs have a common look and feel for a user and hence they are easier to learn. Windows programs can exchange data between themselves. The user can have multiple programs running at the same time and can switch between programs. Figure 3-11 illustrates the history of Windows Operating System. The discussion in this section is centered around Windows Versions 3.0 and above.

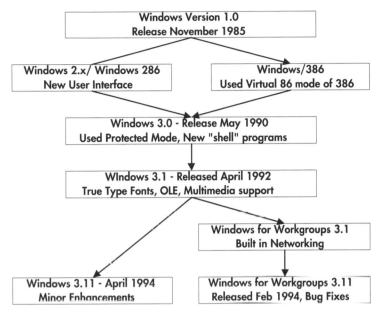

Figure 3-11. History of Microsoft Windows

The main feature of Windows is its Graphical User Interface (GUI). Personal computer users today are demanding easy to use interfaces. The Microsoft Windows operating system has been improving the user interface consistently since its 1.0 release. The Windows user interface make use of graphics on a bitmapped video display. As the video display hardware is getting better in performance and cheaper in price, the Microsoft Windows operating systems user interface capabilities are providing users with easier interfaces to personal computers. The concept of WYSIWYG (What You See Is What You Get) is becoming very popular. The multitasking environment of Windows is also very much liked by the users. The operating system keeps the active programs in the RAM and provides them a slice of the CPU time. The net results to the user is the effect that multiple programs are running at the same time.

The memory management under Windows is the core behind the multitasking feature of Windows and is very complex. The Windows 3.0 operating system supports three modes:

(1)   Real Mode

(2)   Standard Mode

(3)   Enhanced Mode

The real mode of Windows 3.0 is for machines based on 8086 microprocessor with a minimum of 640k of memory. The standard mode of Windows 3.0 uses the protected mode of 286 and higher microprocessors. In this mode, Windows programs can use up to 16 MB of conventional and extended memory. The Windows 3.0 enhanced mode is based around the 80386 and higher microprocessors. In this mode, Windows uses the paging register of the 386 processor to implement virtual memory, and it also uses the Virtual-86 mode of the 386 processor to support multiple virtual MS-DOS sessions. Microsoft decided to abandon real mode in Windows versions starting Version 3.1. In the current version of Windows 3.11, only two modes are available: standard and enhanced. The enhanced mode is available on 386 or higher processor. The operating mode of Windows 3.1 is determined by the processor type (286-standard, 386-enhanced), and any startup switches defined by the user (win /s-standard mode on any processor). The enhanced mode supports 32-bit performance on 386-based and higher computers. Standard mode helps to preserve an organization's investment in 286 computers and machines with limited memory. The enhanced mode is the most popular mode of Windows. The Windows virtual device drivers (VxDs) run in Windows enhanced mode only.

Networking Architecture for Windows

The discussion for the networking architecture for Windows is broken into two major sections: the networking architecture for Windows 3.1/3.11 and the architecture for Windows for Workgroups 3.1/3.11. The Microsoft Windows operating system is primarily used as the desktop operating system which acts as a client to a file/printer server. As discussed in the last section on MS-DOS networking, the client/workstation functionality of the Microsoft Windows operating system is obtained by using the network redirectors or shells. The Windows for Workgroups 3.1 introduced the peer-to-peer network operating system functions to Microsoft Windows. A peer-to-peer service is slightly different from a client server architecture. In a client/server architecture, the server offers the services such as file sharing, and all the clients can share the files present on the file server. The same concept applies to print server and so on. In a peer-to-peer network architecture, all the clients also offer some server services to all other clients. This means that each station can access every other station's files and other resources. This architecture distributes the server capabilities across each station. This architecture is called peer-to-peer networking and was introduced in Microsoft Windows for Workgroups 3.1 (WFW 3.1).

The Microsoft Windows 3.1 and 3.11 have no networking capabilities built in. They depend upon add on products to offer the networking capabilities to the user. The most popular mechanism of offering networking under Microsoft Windows 3.1x is to load the network interface card drivers, protocol stack, and the network redirector or shell under MS-DOS before starting Windows. This means that the network drives are available as MS-DOS drives before starting Windows. When the Microsoft Windows 3.1x is started, it realizes that the network drives are present, and it passes the networks drivers on to its file manager so that the file manager can provide access to the network drives. This means that the user can access the network drives from within Windows like any other local drives. The flow of I/O request to the network drive follows the path which is very similar to the MS-DOS path, as discussed in the last section. The network shell is responsible for trapping the INT 21 calls and if the request is for network drive, it constructs a network packet and passes the packet to the protocol stack for delivery to the server (see *Networking Under MS-DOS*). The network redirectors also work in the same way as discussed in *Networking Under MS-DOS*.

The Windows for Workgroups 3.1x operating system contains the integrated networking components. The Windows for Workgroups 3.1x (WFW 3.1x) has built in messaging and file and printer sharing to bring network workgroup features to every desktop. The WFW 3.1x is built with networking in mind. The WFW supports various networks such as LAN Manager, IBM LAN Server, Novell NetWare, and Banyan Vines. It supports Network Dynamic Data Exchange (NDDE). The Microsoft Windows 3.1 supports three methods of inter-process communication: DDE (Dynamic Data Exchange), Windows Clipboard, and Dynamic Link Libraries (DLL). The DDE is based on the messaging system built into Windows. Two windows programs carry on a DDE conversation by posting messages to each other. The WFW extends the DDE concepts of Windows 3.1 to the network. With NDDE (Network Dynamic Data Exchange), users can exchange data between applications running on different computers. A user can copy some data in its clipboard and another user on the network can paste the same data from the clipboard located on a different computer. This permits better use of network resources and brings workgroup computing to the desktop.

A workstation running WFW in 386 enhanced mode can act as both client and a server in a workgroup. This WFW workstation can access other resources on the network (client) and share its own resources with others on the network (server). The network capabilities of WFW 3.1 are based upon the following components of the operating system.

- NDIS compatible network adapter driver

- Protocol Manager

- NETBEUI protocol stack

- Network Redirector

- WinNet driver

- Virtual Devices (VxDs)

The NDIS (Network Driver Interface Specification) was developed by 3COM and Microsoft. This interface specification defines an interface between the protocol stacks and network adapter card drivers. The network hardware and its associated NDIS driver are independent of the protocol stack and can communicate with each other and transmit and receive packets if the NDIS specification is used. The NDIS specifications allows multiple protocols to run on the same interface card. The NDIS specification has two versions: 2.0.1 and 3.0. The NDIS 2.0.1 interface is the real mode definition of the interface between the network card drivers and protocols. The NDIS 3.0 is the 32-bit device driver specification which is implemented as a virtual device driver. The Windows for Workgroups 3.1 supports NDIS 2.0.1 interface, and the WFW 3.11 supports the NDIS 2.0.1 interface and the NDIS 3.0 interface specification. The NDIS 2.0.1 and the NDIS 3.0 specifications and their architectures are discussed in Chapters 4 and 5, respectively. The Protocol Manager is used to associate the network protocols (NETBEUI) to an NDIS 2.0.1 network card driver (see Chapter 4 for more details). The NETBEUI is the default protocol stack for WFW. All WFW computers use the NETBEUI protocol stack to communicate with each other. The network redirector handles all calls to the remote file system. The WinNet driver provides a workstation with access to the network. This driver is responsible for maintaining the user interface and for accessing and sharing resources. The WFW virtual device driver (VxD) is a 32-bit, protected mode driver that manages system resources, such as a hardware, or an installed software so that more than one application can use the resource at the same time. The VxD drivers are used to offer various networking functions in a WFW system. This means that networking functions run in protected mode and hence deliver 32-bit performance. Figure 3-12 summarizes the networking VxD drivers for WFW systems.

Virtual Device Driver	Description
VNB.386	VxD driver version of the NetBEUI protocol stack
VNETBIOS.386	Protected mode NetBIOS Interface
VREDIR.386	VxD driver version of the network redirector
VSERVER.386	File and Print server
VBROWSE.386	Provides browsing services to the network
VNETSUP.386	Provides network support functions to VNB.386, VREDIR.386 etc.
VSHARE.386	VxD driver version of the share.exe for MS-DOS
VWC.386	Virtual workgroup client device driver—provides support to the real mode redirector

Figure 3-12. Virtual Device Drivers (VxDs) for Networking

Figure 3-13 illustrates the networking components and how they interact in a WFW 3.1 enhanced mode system. Figure 3-14 illustrates the networking components and their interaction in a WFW 3.1 standard mode system.

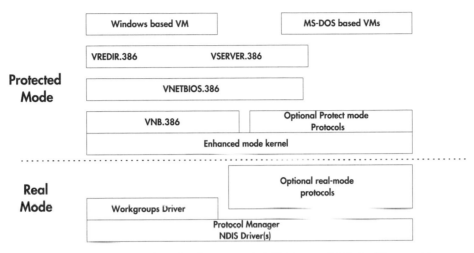

Figure 3-13. Windows for Workgroups 3.1 Enhanced Mode Networking

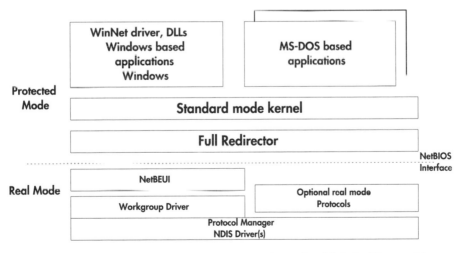

Figure 3-14. Windows for Workgroup 3.1 Standard Mode Networking

The WFW 3.11 operating system was improved further by Microsoft from a networking standpoint. The WFW 3.11 extends the 32-bit architecture to the networking device drivers by including NDIS 3.0 specification in its networking sub-system implementation. The 32-bit network adapter card drivers provide a full 32-bit code path from the network adapter card, through the network protocol and network client and server software, to the hard disk in the local computer. This provides improved performance for the network I/O. Windows for Workgroups 3.11 has the capability of running on top of Open Datalink Interface (ODI) network adapter card drivers. The ODI interface is like NDIS interface and provides the network adapter card driver to be implemented independent of the protocol stack. The ODI interface is discussed in Chapter 7.

The WFW 3.11 supports NDIS 2.0.1, NDIS3.0, and Novell ODI network card driver interface specifications. The next few figures provide the complete block diagrams of the networking architecture of WFW 3.11. The WFW 3.11 supports NDIS 2.0.1 network adapter card drivers. The NDIS 2.0.1 are real mode drivers. These real mode drivers have to be integrated with the WFW 3.11 networking components. Figure 3-15 shows the WFW 3.11 configuration using the NDIS 2.0.1 drivers. This configuration is similar to WFW 3.1 using NDIS 2.0.1 drivers.

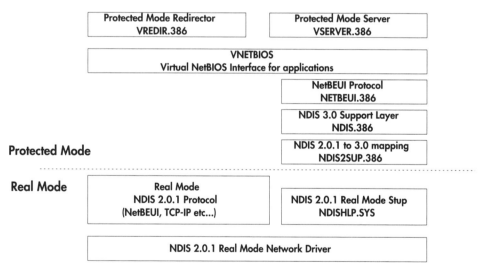

Figure 3-15. Windows for Workgroups 3.11 using NDIS 2.0.1 drivers

The difference between the WFW 3.1 and WFW 3.11 configuration using NDIS 2.0.1 drivers is the NDIS 2.0.1 to NDIS 3.0 mapping layer (NDIS2SUP.386) and the NDIS 2.0.1 real mode layer stub (NDISHLP.SYS). In WFW 3.1, the complete architecture was built around NDIS 2.0.1 drivers, and hence no mapping was required. In the case of WFW 3.11, the complete internal architecture (NETBEUI.386) is built around NDIS 3.0 drivers, and hence the mapping layers are needed. The NDIS2SUP.386 maps the real mode addresses into protected mode addresses and vice-versa. The NDIS2SUP.386 appears as a NDIS 3.0 network card driver to a NDIS 3.0 protocol driver and NDIS 2.0.1 protocol driver to an NDIS 2.0.1 network card driver. Hence, because of the presence of NDIS2SUP.386, the NDIS 2.0.1 network card driver thinks that it is running in a NDIS 2.0.1 environment and the NETBEUI.386 thinks that it running on top of a NDIS 3.0 network adapter card driver. The NDISHLP.SYS is a real mode stub for NDIS2SUP.386 VxD and assists in the real mode binding process.

The WFW 3.11 supports the 32-bit protected mode network adapter card drivers based on the NDIS 3.0. The NDIS 3.0 architecture is described in detail in Chapter 5. The WFW 3.11 network architecture using the NDIS 3.0 system contains three layers: NDIS 3.0 compliant network adapter card driver, NDIS 3.0 support layer, and the NDIS 3.0 protocol. The NDIS 3.0 network adapter card driver (protected mode) cannot bind to a NDIS 2.0.1 protocol (real mode). However, a NDIS 2.0.1 network adapter card driver (real mode) can bind to a NDIS 3.0 compliant (protected mode) stack. Figure 3-16 shows the NDIS 3.0-based networking components of the WFW 3.11 system.

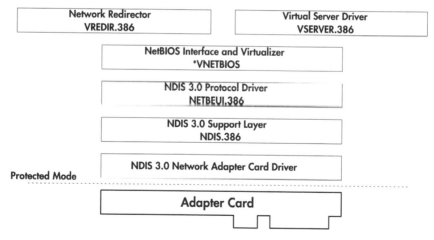

Figure 3-16. Windows for Workgroup 3.11 using NDIS 3.0

The NDIS 3.0 network adapter card driver is the Virtual Device Driver (VxD) that provides access to the networking hardware. The NDIS.386 is the NDIS 3.0 support layer also known as NDIS 3.0 wrapper. Any operating system request for hardware services are passed from NDIS.386 to the network adapter card driver. Also, any hardware requests for operating system services are passed from the NDIS 3.0 driver to the wrapper without any specific knowledge of the operating system. The NETBEUI.386 is a NDIS 3.0 protocol virtual device driver. This driver replaces the VNB.386 of the WFW 3.1. This is the NetBIOS interface provider. The *VNETBIOS, VREDIR.386 and VSERV-ER.386 provide the same functions as discussed in the previous section.

The WFW 3.11 also features the ability to run on top of Open Datalink Interface (ODI) drivers. The Novell NetWare integration is provided by Windows for Workgroups 3.11. This information consists of several components. All these components are available in the WFW 3.11 product package. Figure 3-17 shows the Novell NetWare components integrated with the WFW 3.11 components to enable connectivity to both Windows for Workgroups servers and the NetWare servers form a WFW 3.11 workstation.

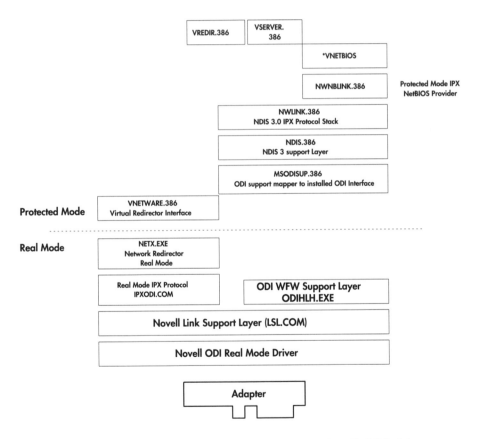

Figure 3-17. Windows for Workgroup 3.11 with Novell ODI drivers

The Windows for Workgroups 3.11 components for the Novell ODI drivers are very similar to the NDIS 2.0.1 real mode driver mapping. The concepts used by Microsoft are very similar to the ones that Microsoft used for the NDIS 2.0.1 mapping in the WFW 3.11. The ODIHLP.EXE program acts a ODI protocol stack to the Novell's LSL (Link Support Layer). Similarly, the NWLINK.386 is a protected mode implementation of the IPX protocol stack which is used in the Novell environment and binds to the NDIS 3.0 look alike network adapter layer (MSODISUP.386). The MSODISUP.386 VxD acts as a NDIS 3.0 compatible network card driver to the NWLINK.386 NDIS 3.0 compatible IPX protocol stack. All frames from the real mode environment (ODIHLP.EXE) are passed to the MSODISUP.386 VxD which does the address translation and passes them to the NWLINK.386 via the NDIS.386 wrapper. The net result is that the user can run the Windows for Workgroup 3.11 networking components on top of the Novell ODI network card device driver architecture.

This section's main focus was on the various architecture components of Windows operating system from networking standpoint. The next section describes the Windows Virtual Device Driver Model (VxDs). The VxD architecture which is presented in the next section applies to NDIS 3.0 device drivers only. The NDIS 2.0.1 drivers follow the MS-DOS real mode device driver architecture from an implementation standpoint. The Novell DOS ODI network adapter card drivers follow the MS-DOS TSR format.

Windows Device Driver Architecture

The Windows Device Driver Architecture is very complicated. We have to understand various Windows modes, especially the enhanced mode, to understand this complicated device driver.

As is discussed in the previous section, Windows Versions 3.1 and higher have two modes of operation: standard and enhanced. The standard mode requires a 286 processor or higher. This mode does not provide the ability to multitask with MS-DOS based applications. The MS-DOS applications runs on a full screen. When Windows starts, it keeps some of its components in the first 640K of memory. When the MS-DOS application is started in Windows standard mode, Windows transfers its components residing in memory below 640K to the disk in order to allow the MS-DOS-based application to run, and suspends any Windows based running applications. When the MS-DOS-based application is completed, Windows retrieves its components from the disk back into the memory and starts the suspended Windows application.

The second mode of Windows operation is the enhanced mode. In enhanced mode the user can run multiple MS-DOS based applications at the same time. The enhanced mode of Windows run on a 386 or higher processor. The

Windows enhanced mode runs under the virtual 8086 mode of 386 or higher processor. In the virtual 8086 mode, the MS-DOS applications run as if they are running in separate computers. In reality, these applications may be multi-tasking with other applications. The 386 processor separates each virtual 8086 mode task into its own virtual machine (VM). Each virtual machine running under the 386 processor is an executable task consisting of the application, supporting software such as MS-DOS, memory, and CPU registers. In Windows enhanced mode, there is a system VM in which Windows runs the Windows kernel, Windows core components and all Windows-based applications. Every MS-DOS based application is run in a separate machine called DOS Virtual Machine or DOS-VM. Also, Windows contains a Virtual Machine Manager (VMM) to manage the different VMs running in the Windows environment. The VMM manages the applications by creating and maintaining virtual machines. The VMM partitions the resources: CPU time, memory, keyboard, and other peripherals among the VMs. Each VM has its own address space, I/O port space and interrupt vector tables and operates under the illusion that it has complete control of the computer. Before we get into more details on the VMM, we will describe the Windows booting process. The Windows boot process for the enhanced mode is shown in Figure 3-18.

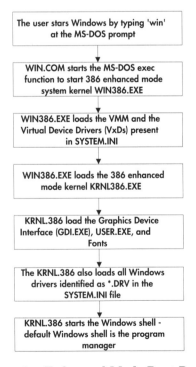

Figure 3-18. Windows 3.x Enhanced Mode Boot Process

VMM is used to manage the different VMs running in the Windows environment. It services the various VMs where various Windows and MS-DOS applications run. The VMM allocates the memory, manages the address pointers, and handles any communication from application to application, or an application to the hardware (see Figure 3-19). The VMM is a 32-bit operating system kernel that replaces the MS-DOS. Windows uses virtual device drivers (VxDs) to communicate between the system MS-DOS VMs and hardware devices. The term VxD is the acronym for Virtual Device Driver where x represents the type of device driver. For example, the virtual device driver for a display device is known as VDD. VxDs provide the virtual image of the hardware to each of the Windows and MS-DOS programs running in various VMs. A VxD is a 32-bit code and data that runs at 386 processor ring 0, and lets more than one application use the resource (including hardware) at the same time. The VxDs are running at 386 processor ring 0 and hence have access to all the system resources. The VxDs under windows enhanced mode are loaded from system.ini file. The typical VxD load line under SYSTEM.INI is "device=<VxD_Name>.386."

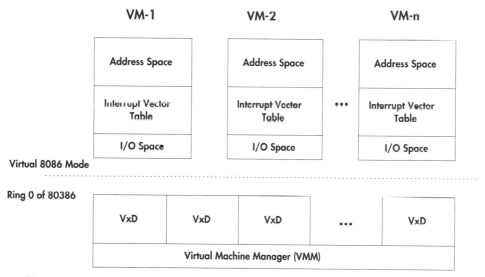

Figure 3-19. VMM, VxD, and VMs

The Windows enhanced mode virtualizes the various hardware components present in a typical computer including the keyboard, display adapter, serial and parallel ports, programmable interrupt controller (PIC), timer, DMA device, and disk controller. Any add-on hardware device, like a network adapter card, would need to have a VxD containing the device specific code to carry out the device specific operations. The VxD for the hardware device keeps track of the state of the device for each application and ensures that the device is in the correct state whenever the context of the application switches. The Windows operating system includes the VxDs for all the commonly used hardware and software devices. Any add-on hardware devices, like network adapter card, VxD are typically written by the hardware manufacturer and provided to the user. The VxD for the network adapter card hardware has to follow the NDIS 3.0 architecture interface. This ensures that it can interface with the other network-related VxDs present in the Windows system.

The applications interact with the VMM to communicate with each other and the VMM. These applications would also need to talk to the hardware. If the VxDs are not available for a certain device, the VMM can queue the VM requests (coming from applications) and pass the hardware access request via the MS-DOS device drivers (see Figure 3-20). The VxDs act as a device manager for the hardware device. They handle all the queue requests and perform the actual operation on the device that they manage. The VxDs can also communicate with other VxDs in the system, providing them with data that they need to be able to function. With the VxDs installed between VMM and the hardware (see Figure 3-21), various virtual computers are created in the Windows enhanced mode environment. The VxD should be able to handle the VM's request and provide a response similar to what the actual device would provide.

To summarize, the VxD provides managed access to the hardware device for any VM in the system. Figure 3-21 illustrates the configuration similar to that in Figure 3-20 with VxDs virtualizing the hardware.

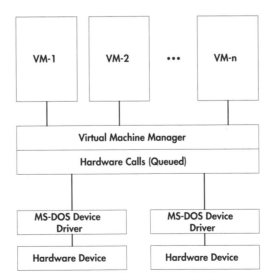

Figure 3-20. Windows Enhanced Mode—No VxD

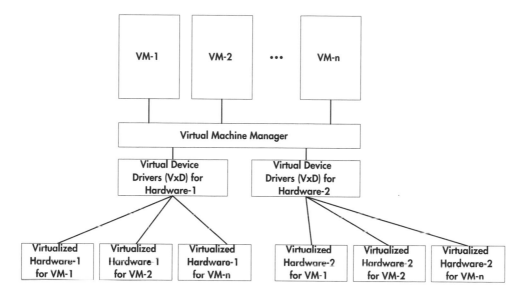

Figure 3-21. Windows Enhanced Mode with VxDs

The VxDs are very different from MS-DOS device drivers. The MS-DOS drivers (MS-DOS device drivers or the TSRs) use the segment:offset addressing architecture whereas the VxDs use the 32-bit flat addressing. The performance of the hardware sub-system is better with VxDs because the VxDs operate in linear memory, and hence there are no translation or performance penalties. Also, the MS-DOS device drivers are duplicated in each VM. The VxDs are loaded only once, and they service all the different VMs. This causes memory overhead with MS-DOS device drivers in the system.

The VMM is the base for the VxDs. The VMM is responsible for functions such as loading the VxDs, providing services to trap interrupts and I/O, and handling the memory management. The VMM provides to the VxD, the timing services, manages event processing, and services ring 3 transition calls. These transition calls are required when MS-DOS BIOS or MS-DOS device drivers need to be accessed by the VxD (MS-DOS is available in a VM which runs at 386 processor ring 3). VxDs access software interrupts and I/O via VMM.

The VMs communicate with the VMM by using the interrupts that are intended for specific hardware devices. The VMs function as if they are communicating directly with the hardware. If the VM expects an immediate response the VMM can suspend the VM until the VxD has serviced the request. The VMM and VxDs communicate via shared routines called services. VxDs use these services to handle interrupts, to initiate callback procedures and to process exception faults. Figure 3-22 illustrates the communication between VMs, VMM, and VxDs.

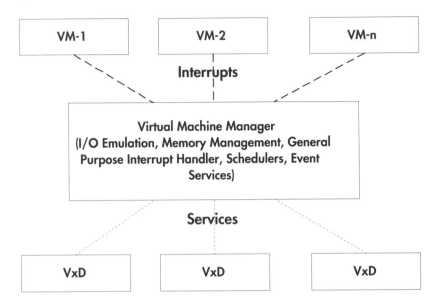

Figure 3-22. VMM Communication with VMs and VxDs

The most critical feature of the VxD model is its ability to hook interrupt and I/O services to each VM. Hooking the I/O ports to the VM is done by using a VMM service (Install_IO_Handler) which takes the I/O port address and the address of the procedure to be called and maps these in an I/O permission table (IOPM). MS-DOS applications can access the I/O ports directly. The VMM traps every VM call to the I/O port and allows a VxD to manage access to the port. Interrupt hooks are handled by a VxD called VPICD (Virtual Programmable Interrupt Controller Device). The PIC (Programmable Interrupt Controller) is a chip that is part of every PC. The PIC handles interrupts at the hardware level, and the VPICD virtualizes communication from the PIC to the VMM. The VPICD routes hardware interrupts to other VxDs, provides services that enable VxDs to request interrupts, and simulates hardware interrupts into VMs. Any VxD which supports a hardware interrupt interface will hook that interrupt service to the VPICD.

VxDs are loaded in two different ways:

(a) From the SYSTEM.INI file. The SYSTEM.INI file can contain a line which has the following format "`device=<VxD_Name>.386`"

(b) VxDs can be attached to any MS-DOS device driver or a TSR. A programmer may write a MS-DOS device driver or TSR to handle the hardware device and then write a VxD that supports the MS-DOS device driver in Windows.

VxDs can perform any 386 processor instruction without producing a protection violation. VxDs run at 386 processor ring 0. VxDs are written in 32-bit code. For all these reasons, VxDs are very powerful device drivers under Windows operating system. Usually, they provide performance gain and the ability to run multiple MS-DOS applications within a single computer.

MICROSOFT WINDOWS NT OPERATING SYSTEM

This section describes the general architecture of Windows NT operating system. This chapter also elaborates on the networking components of Windows NT operating system and the device driver architecture of Windows NT operating system. The version of Windows NT operating system discussed here is 3.1. Microsoft is coming out with a newer version of the operating system. The newer version is called Microsoft Windows NT 3.5. From a device driver architecture standpoint the two versions of the Windows NT operating system (3.1 and 3.5) are very similar, and hence the discussion in this section on Windows NT device driver applies to both 3.1 and 3.5 versions.

Windows NT Operating System Overview

The Windows NT (New Technology) Operating System was introduced in 1993 by Microsoft to provide a smooth growth for Windows 3.x customers to new software and hardware. The Windows NT operating system is not a replacement of Windows 3.x operating system. The Windows NT is complementary to the Windows 3.x operating system. Microsoft's strategy for Windows NT operating system included some very well defined goals for the design teams to meet. Some of these goals for Windows NT operating system are:

- **Portability**: The Windows NT operating system is portable. It can be ported to run on different processors. Some of the processors on which Windows NT is available are 386 and higher, DEC Alpha, Power PC, MIPS R4000 processors etc.

- **Compatibility**: The Windows NT operating system supports user interface which is very similar to Windows 3.x. The applications written for MS-DOS, Windows 3.x , OS/2 1.x and POSIX operating environments can run on Windows NT. The networking subsystem of Windows NT operating system supports connectivity to several different networks (Novell, Banyan, LAN Manager, LAN Server, etc.)

- **Scalability**: Windows NT can run on single and multiple processor machines (symmetric). This operating system scales along with the processors. This means that Windows NT operating system fully uses the capabilities of a symmetric multiprocessor machine.

- **Security**: The Windows NT has a very uniform security architecture which meets the U.S. government security guidelines. The operating system provides a secure environment to run corporate wide applications.

- **Reliability**: The reliability and robustness of the Windows NT operating system is very high as compared to some other operating system. This operating system guards itself and other applications running in the system from a misbehaved application. Each application runs in its own domain and cannot access other applications or the operating system. This structured exception handling is built in the complete operating system.

- **Distributed Computing**: Distributed computing means that a computer can distribute its tasks not only to multiple processors within a single machine but also across to other computers connected via some kind of networks. Windows NT implements networking into its core architecture, and hence enables the Windows NT applications to distribute their work across multiple computer systems connected by computer networks.

Windows NT is a preemptive, multitasking operating system which is based on a 32-bit design. It provides a 32-bit programming interface for writing 32-bit applications. This 32-bit interface is called Win32 API (Windows 32-bit Application Programming Interface). The API exported by the Win32 subsystem of Windows NT is a 32-bit version of the Windows 3.x 16-bit APIs. The 32-bit Win32 API is also available in a subset form on Windows 3.x via Win32s libraries. The Windows 95 ("Chicago") operating system from Microsoft will have Win32 API for applications and hence applications can run with the same binaries between Windows NT and Windows 95 operating system.

The Windows NT operating system is very modular. The complete operating system is built with various different modules communicating with each other like clients and servers. Interestingly, the inter-modular communication within various modules of Windows NT is based on the networking client/server architecture. Figure 3-23 illustrates the Windows NT architecture.

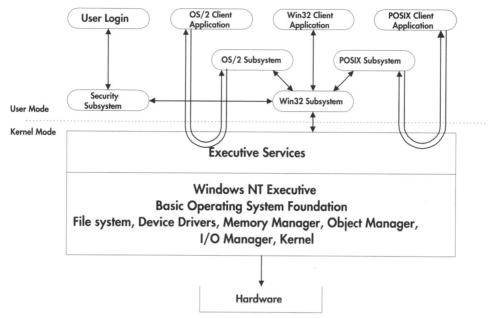

Figure 3-23. Windows NT Architecture (Client / Server Model)

Figure 3-23 shows the Windows NT architecture. The Windows NT executive performs the low level operating system functions like thread scheduling, interrupt dispatching, exception dispatching, and multiprocessor synchronization. The core of the Windows NT executive is the kernel. The kernel provides a set of routines that the rest of the operating system uses to implement other operating system services. Windows NT uses the client/server model to provide the operating system API services like Win32.

As shown in Figure 3-23, various operating system functions run as servers and the applications requiring services from the servers use the message passing services provided by the Windows NT executive. The OS/2 Subsystem runs as a server under Windows NT operating system. The OS/2 applications are clients to the OS/2 subsystem server and the applications communicate with the client using the NT executive's message passing services. This client/server model simplifies the base operating system and adds reliability. Each server runs as a separate process, partitioned into its own memory, and is protected from other processes.

Figure 3-24 shows the Windows NT executive details.

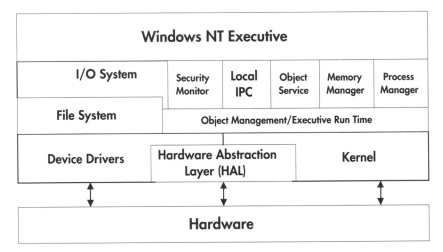

Figure 3-24. Windows NT Executive

The Hardware Abstraction Layer (HAL) is the thin layer of software under Windows NT which is provided by the hardware manufacturer and abstracts the hardware details from the rest of the operating system. The HAL makes sure that different types of hardware look alike to the operating system. A single processor machine and a multiprocessor machine will have different HAL implementations. The HAL layer hides the details of single versus multiprocessor information and complexity from the rest of the operating system.

The kernel is the main component of the Windows NT operating system. It schedules activities for the processor. The kernel also manages activities between a single or a multiple processors. Its key goal is to schedule task so that the processor is used to its maximum. If a higher priority tasks comes, the kernel makes sure that this task is scheduled first before any other lower priority tasks. The kernel also synchronizes various activities for I/O manager and the Process Manager. The Windows NT kernel runs in the kernel mode and is nonpageable (cannot be swapped to the hard drive). The software running inside the kernel (kernel code) is non-preemptible; however, the rest of the software running outside the kernel is preemptible and can be context switched.

The next major component of the Windows NT architecture is the Executive Services. The Windows NT executive manages the interface between the various different subsystems running in user mode and the kernel. As shown in Figure 3-24, the major groups of executive services are:

- I/O Manager
- Object Manager

- Process Manager

- Security Manager

- Local IPC (Inter Procedure Call)

- Memory Manager

The executive services perform the routing function. They basically pass messages from one Windows NT component to another. The I/O manager manages all the input and output for the operating system as well as all the device drivers (File system drivers, Network drivers, Hardware device drivers, and so on). The I/O manager also manages the communication between various different drivers in the Windows NT system. The I/O architecture in Windows NT has the typical driver functionality broken into two components: the first component is the piece of device driver that handles the hardware and the second piece is the device driver that interfaces with the O.S. The Windows NT file system drivers are managed by the I/O manager. Windows NT supports a new file system called NTFS (New Technology File System). Windows NT also support FAT (File Allocation Table) and the HPFS (High Performance File System).

The security manager within the Windows NT executive services is responsible for validating access to the objects, and checking user privilege level, among other functions. The Process Manager is responsible for process and thread objects. A process is defined as an address space, a set of resources visible to the process and a set of threads that run in the context of the process. A thread only contains some registers, a kernel and a user stack, and a thread environment block. Process manager manages the process of creating and deleting tasks. The memory manager under Windows NT is also known as virtual memory manager. The memory space that NT can address is a linear address space controlled by 32-bit addresses. The memory architecture is demand paged virtual memory. The reason the memory management architecture under Windows NT is called virtual is because the operating system can access memory up to 4 Gigabyte even though the physical memory present in the system is much less than that. The operating system uses the demand paging mechanism to do this. The demand paging refers to a method by which data is moved in pages from physical memory to a temporary paging file on the disk. When the operating system needs the data that it has paged to the disk, it reads the data back from the disk and makes it available to the application that needs it.

The Local IPC (Inter Procedure Call) is the module which is responsible for the client/server model of the Windows NT operating system. Client applications, like Win32 applications under Windows NT, need to talk to their server, which in the case of the Win32 application is Win32 Subsystem. The Local IPC also known as LPC (Local Procedure Calls) provides a message passing facility between the client and server modules of Windows NT operating system. The LPC messaging calls are very similar to the RPC (Remote Procedure Calls) which are used between applications running on different computers to communicate with each other.

The Windows NT kernel and the rest of the executive and its components are very modular and follow a very strict messaging and coding procedure to make the operating system portable between various operating systems.

Networking Under Windows NT Operating System

The Microsoft Windows NT goal was to build networking in the operating system as a core component and not as an add-on. The security component of the Windows NT operating system is integrated with the networking component. The networking component present within Microsoft Windows NT can be put into three categories:

- Windows NT as a network client to a server

- Windows NT as a peer-to-peer workstation

- Windows NT as a server

The Windows NT has the capability to act as a client to Novell NetWare Server, Microsoft LAN Manager Server, IBM LAN Server, Banyan Vines, and SUN NFS. It can also act as a peer-to-peer workstation with other Windows NT stations and Windows for Workgroups stations. In this mode the system can support limited networking capabilities like file sharing, electronic mail, and remote printing. The Windows NT system is also shipped with LAN Manager server packaged along with the base Windows NT operating system. This product is called Windows NT Advanced Server by Microsoft. The Windows NT Advanced Server system can act as a full functionality server to a number of clients on the network, providing the file sharing, printing, and other services.

The Windows NT operating system also has various transport layer stacks shipped with the base operating system. The three most popular transport stacks which are supported in the Windows NT operating system are TCP-IP, NetBEUI, and IPX/SPX (Novell). The network cards within the Windows NT environment are supported by a defined interface called NDIS (Network Driver Interface Specification) 3.0 (see Chapter 5 for detailed architecture). The NDIS 3.0 network driver architecture allows the transport layer stacks to be completely independent of the networking hardware. The NDIS 3.0 network adapter card drivers provide a interface as specified in the NDIS 3.0 specification for Microsoft Windows NT which all the transport stacks use. All the network interface card hardware functionality and manipulation resides within the NDIS 3.0 Windows NT driver. The networking components of Windows NT are illustrated in Figure 3-25.

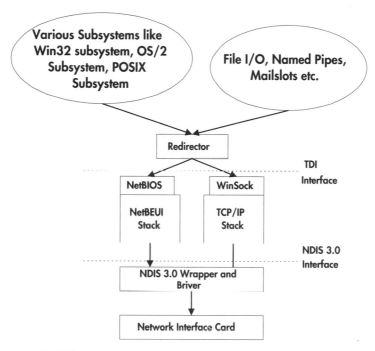

Figure 3-25. Windows NT Networking

As shown in Figure 3-25, the Windows NT networking subsystem contains three main interfaces: NDIS 3.0, TDI (Transport Driver Interface), and the Redirector Interface which mainly depends on the file system which the redirector is supporting.

Let us analyze the flow of an I/O within the networking subsystem of the Windows NT operating system. Let us say that the Win32 subsystem gets a I/O request from a application or a Win32 client. Let us assume that this I/O request is intended for a remote file system (file system located on a file server which is connected to the network). The I/O manager of the Windows NT executive services constructs a I/O request packet (IRP) and passes the request to one of the registered file system driver, in this case the file system redirector. The file system redirector passes the request to the appropriate transport layer via the TDI interface. The transport layer interacts with the network interface card driver (NDIS 3.0) to transmit the packet on the network cable. The server receives this packet and starts the processing of the packet. The server responds back to the Windows NT station with its response (depending upon what the request was). The response packet goes through the exact reverse of the request packet and the request is completed.

The Windows NT operating system provides a number of application programming interfaces (APIs) for various applications. Figure 3-26 describes the various network APIs supported by the Windows NT operating system.

Network API Name	Description
Win32 I/O API	The Win32 I/O API provides standard functions for open, close, read, write etc. on file. The Win32 functions access the network subsystem via the file system redirectors only when the file name contains a driver letter which is a network drive.
NetBIOS API	There are some applications (mainly MS-DOS) which access the NetBIOS API directly. This interface is provided in Windows NT for backwards compatibility with such applications.
Winsock API	The Windows Socket API provides 16-bits and 32-bits UNIX socket style networking interface.
RPC Interface	The Remote Procedure Call (RPC) interface allows the applications to call functions located in applications running on remote computers. This is the interface used to write distributed applications running on separate computers.
WNet API	The WNet (Win32 network) API provides functions for browsing remote file systems. This API is used by the file manager application of Windows NT to connect to remote file systems and to browse through it.
Win32 Named Pipes and Mailslots	The Win32 named pipes provide mechanism for two local or remote processes to exchange data. The mail slots provide mechanism for data exchange between many to one and one to many processes. The mail slots also operate between local and remote processes and hence the network component of the operating system is used.

Figure 3-26. Windows NT Network APIs

All the various network APIs that exist within the Windows NT network subsystem access the network transport layers via various interfaces. The APIs use the redirector interface, NetBIOS driver, Windows Socket driver and so on. However, only one interface is used to communicate to and from the network card. This interface is the NDIS 3.0 network interface. The Network interface card vendors have to provide a NDIS 3.0 compatible driver for their network interface card to function under Windows NT operating system. The rest of the network components are provided by the Windows NT operating system. The NDIS 3.0 interface is implemented as a network device driver under Windows NT. In the next section we will discuss the generic device driver architecture of the Windows NT. The NDIS 3.0 architecture is discussed in detail in Chapter 5.

Windows NT Device Driver Architecture

Microsoft Windows NT has two basic kinds of device drivers

- User Mode Drivers
- Kernel Mode Drivers

The user mode device drivers are the drivers which run in user mode and are specific to the subsystem they are running under. Examples of user mode drivers are the Win32 graphics display drivers, Win32 printers drivers, and Virtual Device Drivers (VDD) for MS-DOS applications.

The kernel mode device drivers run under the kernel mode and are present for logical, virtual, and physical devices. These drivers are part of the Windows NT executive, and hence are known as NT drivers.

The Windows NT NDIS 3.0 is a kernel mode device driver. From a networking standpoint, it is important to understand how the 16-bit MS-DOS drivers and TSRs integrate under Windows NT. The next few paragraphs talk about the user mode drivers and how MS-DOS applications and TSR that access the hardware devices exist on a Windows NT system. The rest of this section is focused on kernel mode device drivers.

In Windows NT, a key component called VDM (Virtual DOS Machine) provides a VDM within the Win32 subsystem to support the real and protected mode MS-DOS applications. Windows NT launches the VDM to support MS-DOS-based applications. There may be several copies of VDM running at any one time within Windows NT. This is based on what the user is trying to run at a given time. Also, only one copy of VDM is launched for multiple Windows 3.x applications running under Windows NT. Multiple copies of VDM set up self contained virtual DOS machines without resource conflicts among the various copies. The MS-DOS applications run in the VDM as if they were running in the native MS-DOS environment. The VDM provides an equivalent functionality that MS-DOS would supply to the applications. Most of the MS-DOS applications can run properly under the VDM. However, some applications and TSR that manipulate hardware by using the x86 I/O port IN and OUT instructions, or writing directly to the hardware memory, do not work as-are under the Windows NT VDM. The VDM does not permit the MS-DOS applications and TSRs to write directly to the hardware I/O ports and memory mapped ports as these applications run in a very protected environment. To support the MS-DOS applications and TSRs which write directly to the hardware, the application/TSR developer must write a 32-bit kernel mode device driver to access the board hardware. The developer must also provide a VDD (Virtual Device Driver) to intercept the hardware operations from the MS-DOS application/TSR and translate them into the corresponding kernel mode device driver calls for the particular hardware. The kernel mode device driver along with the VDD for the hardware device will enable it to run a MS-DOS application/TSR which manipulates a hardware run under Microsoft Windows NT.

There are three basic types of the kernel mode device drivers. They are:

- **Device Drivers (DD)**: The lowest level of device drivers that control physical devices such as disk driver, keyboard driver, network card driver, and so on. The NDIS 3.0-based network card driver is a NT device driver.

- **Intermediate Drivers (ID)**: The intermediate drivers are the drivers which run in kernel mode and reside between the FSD and the DD drivers. The transport interface driver, such as NetBIOS driver, is an intermediate driver.

- **File System Driver (FSD)**: These are the Windows NT supplied drivers for various file systems such as FAT, HPFS, and NTFS. The FSD drivers are very dependent upon the device drivers (DD) to access the hardware. The NT redirector is a specialized file system driver.

The NT device drivers are written in C. They are portable across different platforms along with the Windows NT operating system. The drivers are multiprocessor safe. This means that drivers have to make sure that when they are accessing hardware, nobody else is doing the same on another processor. This is achieved by obtaining a spin-lock from the system which puts the other processors in a spin state until the original spin-lock is returned. The NT device drivers are fully preemptible. The I/O requests under Windows NT device drivers is managed by the I/O manager. The I/O manager accepts requests from the user level applications, translates them to IRPs (I/O request packets), and routes them to the correct NT device driver. The I/O manager also returns the status of the original request to the original generator of the request. All this operation and interaction between the user mode applications, I/O manager, and the NT device drivers is asynchronous. Hence, no component of the Windows NT operating system waits for another component to finish, in order to proceed. This asynchronous operation is the key to the better performance of applications under Windows NT operating system.

The NT device drivers drive radically different hardware devices like network card, graphics controller, disk drive controller, and so on. The internal architecture of these device drivers is very different. However, from Windows NT's I/O manager standpoint, all these device drivers are very similar. The NT device driver architecture follows a layered approach. The I/O manager sends all its request to the NT device drivers as I/O Request Packets. The I/O manager defines a set of standard routines, which all NT drivers have to implement. The layering of the NT device drivers may be different between the network subsystem, disk subsystem, keyboard, and so on. However, conceptually they are all the same. Figure 3-27 shows the layering concept for NT device driver for IDE disk controller.

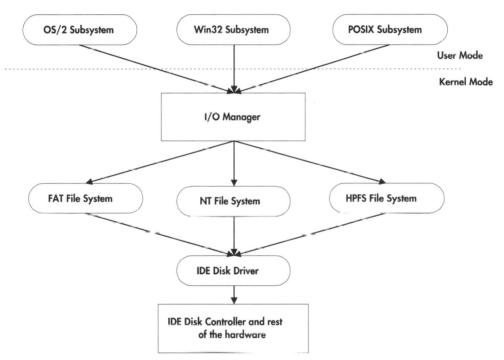

Figure 3-27. IDE Disk Driver Layers

In this example, the IDE disk driver controls the IDE disk controller present in a PC-AT system with up to two IDE disks attached to the IDE controller. Another example of layering is the SCSI subsystem architecture under Windows NT. The SCSI subsystem layers are illustrated in Figure 3-28.

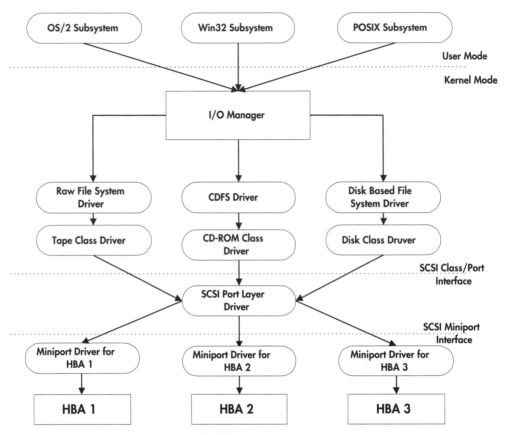

Figure 3-28. Windows NT SCSI Subsystem Layers

Figure 3-28 shows the various layers that exist in the Windows NT SCSI subsystem. The SCSI bus has a unique architecture. The SCSI bus allows various classes of devices to be connected on the bus. The various classes which are supported on the SCSI bus are disk drives, CD-ROM drives, tape backup units, scanners, and SCSI printers. The SCSI architecture in Windows NT is broken into various layers to support the concept of different classes of devices on the same bus. The heart of this architecture is the SCSI port layer driver. The SCSI port layer driver services the class drivers and the miniport drivers. The miniport drivers are written to a very tight specification provided by Microsoft. The specification covers the SCSI miniport interface and how the port layer communicates with the miniport layer. The miniport drivers are SCSI hardware (HBA–Host Bus Adapter)-dependent. A different type of SCSI hardware would require a different miniport driver (see Figure 3-28). The class drivers and their respective file system drivers are responsible for implementing the class device specific commands. For example, a disk device supports SCSI read and write commands; however, a SCSI CD-ROM supports the read command and not the write command. The various class device specific commands are implemented in the class driver. This architecture keeps the SCSI class drivers totally independent of the host bus adapters. Similarly, the miniport drivers are independent of the class driver specific commands.

The layering of the Windows NT networking subsystem is illustrated in Figure 3-29.

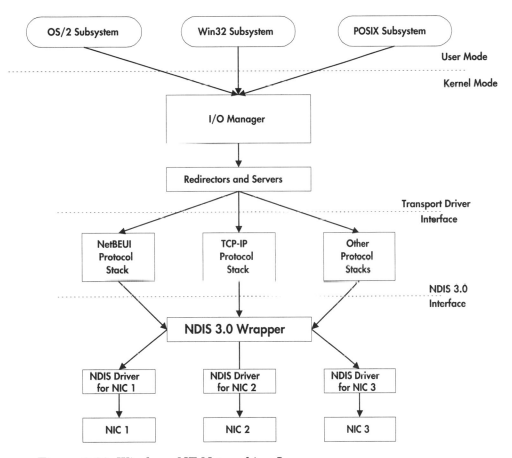

Figure 3-29. Windows NT Networking Layers

The various different components of the architecture and layering for Windows NT are discussed in the previous section. The key concept that the previous three examples convey is that the Windows device driver architecture is very modular. The Windows NT device drivers are always layered into components which are hardware dependent (SCSI miniport driver, NDIS Driver for NIC, and so on). The rest of the device drivers (intermediate and file system drivers) are responsible for providing the non hardware specific functions to the rest of the operating system and the hardware device driver.

All the various different types of device drivers are very different when it comes to implementing hardware specific routines. However, the basic structure of every NT driver consists of a standard set of routines. These routines are:

- Initialization routine
- Dispatch routines
- Start I/O routine
- Interrupt service routine
- DPC routine
- Unload routine
- Completion routine (optional)
- Error log routine (optional)
- Cancel I/O routine (optional)

Every Windows NT driver has an initialization routine which is named DriverEntry. The DriverEntry routine is called by the I/O manager when the operating system loads the driver. The DriverEntry routine is responsible for exporting the driver's other entry points, for initializing the NT objects the driver uses, and for setting up any other system resources that the driver uses. The DriverEntry routine exports the entry address of routines like StartIO, and Unload routine. It also exports routines which are driver-specific.

The Windows NT driver contains a set of dispatch routines. The dispatch routines offer the main function of the driver to other drivers. For example, a networking NDIS 3.0 driver has a dispatch routine for packet transmission. This packet transmit routine is called asynchronously by the NDIS wrapper to transmit a frame. The entry point (calling address) of the dispatch routine is exported by the DriverEntry routine. For SCSI miniport drivers the main dispatch routine is StartIO. The I/O manager generates a IRP (I/O Request Packet) which is then translated to a SRB (SCSI Request Block). The SRB is given to the SCSI miniport driver's StartIO routine. The SCSI SRB contains all the information about the SCSI command that should be sent on the SCSI bus and the return address which should be called when the SCSI command is completed.

A driver implements StartIO routine if it can support more than one concurrent I/O operation. Most of the NT drivers have StartIO routines because most PC peripheral devices are capable of handling only one device I/O operation at a time. The NT device driver has to set up internal request queues and manage its own queuing of the IRPs. The StartIO routine in a device driver is responsible for starting an I/O operation on the physical device.

The ISR (Interrupt Service Routine) is responsible for handling the interrupts from the physical device which is being serviced by this device driver. When a physical device generates a hardware interrupt, the Windows NT's kernel interrupt dispatcher transfers control to the device drivers ISR. In Windows NT architecture, which is multitasking, many interrupts are being generated all the time. Hence, it is recommended that no major processing is performed be the ISR context. An ISR queues a DPC (Deferred Processing Routine) to perform the real processing of the interrupt. This makes sure that low-level interrupts are not blocking each other.

A DPC (Deferred Processing Routine) is present in all drivers which have an ISR routine. A DPC routine performs all the work associated with the physical device interrupt. It runs at the IRQL (Interrupt Request Level) which is lower than the ISR, and hence other interrupts are not blocked while DPC is running.

The unload routine is called by the I/O manager requesting the device driver to release any system resources like memory. The I/O manager calls this routine before removing the device driver from the memory. The completion routine is implemented by device drivers that need to know when an I/O has finished. An intermediate device driver will have a completion routine, so that the I/O manager can call the intermediate device driver's completion routine when the device driver below it completes an I/O. A cancel I/O routine is implemented by the device driver to allow the layers above it cancel an I/O operation. The error logging routines log all the error conditions associated with the device operation and report them to the I/O manager.

The Windows NT device driver also contains a number of internal routines which are visible only to the device driver internally and are responsible for performing the low level functions such as device reset, initialize, etc. The implementation of the device driver internal routines is up to the device driver writer.

IBM OS/2 2.X OPERATING SYSTEM

The OS/2 (Operating System /2) operating system evolved from Microsoft planning a protected mode multitasking operating system based on the 286 or higher microprocessors. OS/2 operating system was developed by Microsoft under a joint marketing agreement between IBM and Microsoft. In parallel, Microsoft was also working on its earlier versions of Windows operating system. In 1990, Microsoft introduced version 1.3 of the OS/2 operating system. This was the last version of the OS/2 which was released by Microsoft. Microsoft wanted to focus on their very popular Windows operating system and hence they decided against OS/2. IBM picked up the development of the OS/2 operating system and released version 2.0 in 1992, followed by version 2.1 in 1993. Currently, the OS/2 operating system is one of the key components of the IBM personal computer strategy.

Introduction to OS/2

The OS/2 operating system has a number of key features over its predecessor MS-DOS. Some of these features are: new graphical user interface, Preemptive Multitasking, Application Programming Interface (API), Memory protection, virtual memory, IPC (Inter Process Communication), MS-DOS application support, Dynamic Linking, and so on.

The OS/2 graphical user interface is called the Presentation Manager. The Presentation Manager provides the capabilities to run and view multiple programs simultaneously. The application programs written to run under presentation manager provide a common look and feel for the user of the programs. The user can manipulate font sizes and shapes under the presentation manager GUI, use pull down menus, scroll bars to walk through documents, and so on. The Presentation Manager provides ease of use and flexibility and customization of the desktop to the user.

The API (Application Programming Interface) is a set of function calls provided by the OS/2 to the application programs. The services included in the API are functions to manage memory, inter-process communication, manipulate graphical user interfaces, create and manage Windows, and support multitasking, as well as timer and interrupt support functions. The multitasking capability of OS/2 is its ability to run multiple programs at the same time without the program or the user of one program being aware of the other program running simultaneously. The OS/2 achieves this by time slicing the processor time between multiple active tasks. The scheduler of the OS/2 is called every so often (fixed time slices), and the scheduler keeps track of the list of active tasks and their state and priority. Based on the state and the priority of the task, the scheduler decides which task gets the control of the processor time. The OS/2 operating system uses the capabilities of the protected mode of the 286 or another higher processor to protect the memory from one application to another and the operating system itself. This means that a misbehaving application cannot destroy another application or the operating system. The 286 protected mode adds a level of indirection in the memory addressing. The segment registers in the protected mode do not point to the physical segment;

instead they contain values called selectors. A selector is an index to an entry in a table called Local Descriptor Table (LDT) or Global Descriptor Table (GDT). The table entry contains the base address of the memory, the length of the memory segment and the protection information. The OS/2 operating system can only manipulate the descriptor tables which define the memory address space of the programs. Hence, a protected mode operating system like OS/2 can isolate one program from another program. The protected mode operating system can use the concept of virtual memory to gain access to memory much larger than the actual physical memory present in the system. The operating system along with the processor hardware swaps memory in and out of a swap file which is maintained on a disk. The operating system keeps part of its virtual memory in the physical memory, the rest in a swap file on the disk. When another portion of the virtual memory is needed, the operating system swaps some other portion of the memory from the physical to the swap file (to make space) and then swap in from the swap file to the physical memory the portion of virtual memory that it needs.

OS/2 provides various different mechanisms to inter-process communication. The inter-process communication is key for the operation of a multitasking operating system like OS/2 where multiple programs run at the same time and have to exchange data between themselves. The various methods of IPC which are supported by the OS/2 are:

- Signals
- Semaphores
- Named Pipes
- Shared Memory
- Queues
- Mail Boxes

The IPC methods listed above are similar in concept with the IPC mechanisms discussed in other operating system, and hence they are not discussed here in detail.

The OS/2 operating system introduced the concept of dynamic linking. This concept is very powerful. Traditionally, the programs are statically linked to resolve all function calls when the EXE of the program is being built. In OS/2, certain common functions are kept in files which are called Dynamic Link Libraries. A program that wants to use the functions out of a Dynamic Link Library informs the linker that a certain function is a dynamic link library function. It also informs the name of the dynamic link library file in which the function is resident. When the program is loaded for execution, the OS/2 loader tries to resolve the dynamic link library functions by loading the dynamic link library functions in the memory and passing their address to the calling program.

The OS/2 operating system has the following main components:

- OS/2 Kernel
- Device Drivers
- Command Processor
- Dynamic Link Libraries (DLL)
- Presentation Manager

The basic architecture of the OS/2 components is illustrated in Figure 3-30.

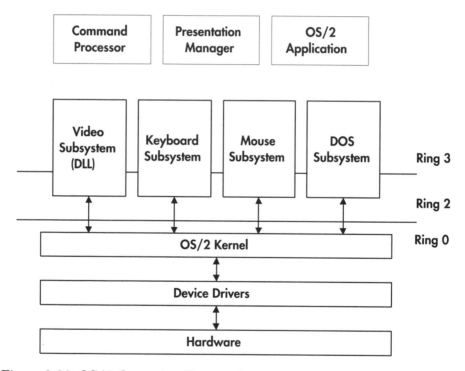

Figure 3-30. OS/2 Operating System Components

As in all the other operating systems, the purpose of the device drivers is the same in the OS/2 operating system: to provide hardware abstraction to the rest of the operating system. In a layered operating system architecture, like OS/2, the device drivers are the only component which are hardware implementation-dependent. The rest of the operating system uses the device drivers to access the hardware. The I/O request is passed to the device drivers in the form of a I/O request packet. The device drivers interpret this I/O request and translate it into its hardware-specific commands. The OS/2 kernel implements the standard set of kernel functions like memory management, file management, loading and managing the programs, supporting multitasking by scheduling programs execution, IPC, and MS-DOS emulation. The kernel provides its services via a rich set of API function calls. The major subsystems of OS/2 are listed in the Figure 3-30. The video, keyboard, and mouse subsystems are all implemented as DLLs. The OS/2 command processor is the protected mode command line interpreter for OS/2. It processes all the user commands and executes them.

The OS/2 operating system boot sequence is explained in Figure 3-31.

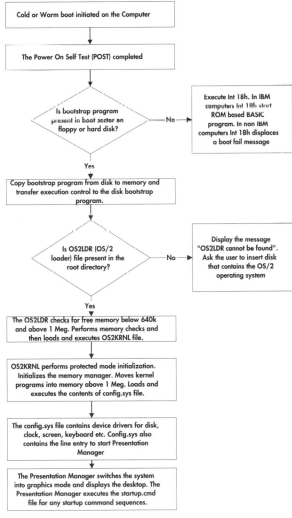

Figure 3-31. OS/2 Generic Boot Sequence

Networking Under OS/2

The OS/2 operating system can be used as a client (workstation) and/or as a server operating system. The multitasking capabilities of the OS/2 operating system provide the basis for the server capabilities of the operating system. Because of the history of the OS/2 (Microsoft and IBM involvement), a number of client and server products exist for OS/2 environment. The discussion of networking under OS/2 can be partitioned into three main sections:

- General discussion of networking under OS/2

- OS/2 and Microsoft LAN Manager and IBM LAN Server

- OS/2 and Novell NetWare

A number of other networking environments exist under OS/2. For example, Digital has a product called DEC Pathworks which has a client and server component. The server component of DEC Pathworks was derived from LAN Manager and hence runs on top of OS/2 (as described later in this section). Similarly, other derivative products and architectures exist for OS/2. A discussion of such architectures are beyond the scope of this book.

General Discussion of Networking Under OS/2

The IBM OS/2 operating system is a 32-bit multitasking operating system. The OS/2 operating system can be used as the base operating system for client services and/or server services. When the OS/2 operating system is acting as a client, it has the following components: network card, device driver for the network card, protocol stack, and network redirectors. Together, these software components running on OS/2 allow the OS/2 workstation to act as a client to a network server. These client software components allow the OS/2 workstation to access files, and printers. which are being managed by the network server. The OS/2 operating system can act as a client of almost any server which makes its protocol stack and other components of its client software working on the OS/2. The following environments have client software available for OS/2 operating system:

- Microsoft LAN Manager

- IBM LAN Server

- DEC Pathworks

- Novell NetWare

- UNIX

The IBM OS/2 can also act as a network server. The server services are very task intensive and hence need a multitasking operating system like OS/2. The OS/2 operating system supports various inter process communication mechanisms like Shared memory, semaphores, and named pipes. These inter process communication (IPC) are used by the server applications running under OS/2. The following server applications are available for OS/2 operating system:

- Microsoft LAN Manager

- IBM LAN Server

- Novell NetWare

The OS/2 networking environment uses the NDIS 2.0.1 device driver interface for LAN Manager and LAN Server environments. The NDIS 2.0.1 device driver interface provides a protocol-independent way of accessing the network hardware. The NDIS 2.0.1 device driver architecture is explained in detail in Chapter 4. The OS/2 networking environment uses the ODI network device driver architecture for Novell NetWare running under OS/2. The ODI network device driver architecture is discussed in detail in Chapter 7.

The OS/2 operating system is a single user operating system. This means that it assumes that all the processes are owned by one user. The server components which run on top of OS/2 operating system (LAN Manager, LAN Server or NetWare) add the concept of multiple users to the various processes which are running under OS/2. Any multitasking operating system has to provide mechanisms for various concurrently running processes to exchange data, start, and stop each other's execution, and synchronize execution by exchanging data. The OS/2 operating system supports five basic types of inter-process communication mechanisms. They are: Shared memory, Semaphores, Signals, Queues, and Pipes.

The shared memory IPC mechanism is used by processes when they need a simple mechanism for inter-process communication. The shared memory is allocated by the kernel when the process makes a function call to the OS/2 kernel. The second process which needs the access to this shared memory also makes a function call into the OS/2 kernel. After this initial setup is completed by the two or more processes, the shared memory can be used by these processes to exchange data, synchronization flags, and so on. The usage of shared memory IPC is limited to processes running on a single computer because the shared memory resides in a machine.

Semaphores have been used for IPC for a long time. Semaphores are special, protected variables with a defined set of operations that allow multiple processes to synchronize their execution. Various different processes may keep certain shared data in the shared memory. It is important that only one process modify any critical section of the shared data at any one time. This serialization of the data accesses by multiple processes can be achieved by a semaphore. Any process may use a single semaphore to indicate to others that it has the control of the shared data at any given time. A process uses the semaphore to tell to the other process when it is using the critical data. During that time, no other process can access the data. When the first process is done, it again uses the semaphore mechanism to indicate to other processes that it is finished handling the data.

Signals are another type of IPC mechanism that remain from the way DOS applications perform IPC. Signal is an asynchronous event from another process or the user informing the receiving process to perform certain functions.

The queues are another type of IPC mechanism that are used extensively within OS/2. Queues allow multiple client processes to communicate with a single server process. The server process creates a queue by making a call into the OS/2 kernel. The client processes open this queue and write elements into it. The server process reads elements from the queue. Figure 3-32 illustrates the use of a queue under OS/2.

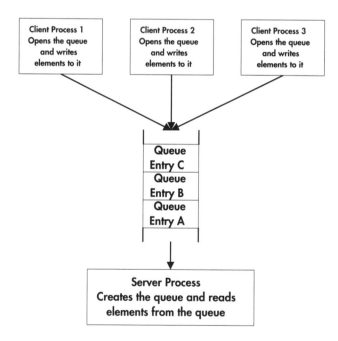

Figure 3-32. Queue-based Inter-Process Communication

The pipe IPC provides a data connection between two processes. Pipes can be of two types: Anonymous and Named. The anonymous pipes are like FIFO files. The process can open a pipe similar to the way in which it would open a file and then perform read/write function on a first-in-first-out basis. The named pipes are needed in the OS/2 networking environments to provide local and remote network transparency. A named pipe is like an anonymous pipe with a kernel specific value (name) that separates it from other pipes in a networking environment.

The IPC mechanisms described above provide the basic infrastructure within the OS/2 operating system to provide the rest of the networking components which are discussed in the following section.

OS/2 and Novell NetWare

OS/2 has support for NetWare Client and Server services. Traditionally, OS/2 has been used as the client operating system for NetWare servers connected on the network. Novell has provided the ODI (Open Data-Link Interface) driver interface based protocol stacks and network requester for the OS/2 operating system (see Chapter 7 for details on ODI based drivers). In 1991, IBM and Novell signed a relationship agreement. Under this agreement, IBM would distribute Novell NetWare products. Also, it was announced that Novell would port the NetWare operating system to OS/2, making OS/2 a NetWare server providing file sharing, printer sharing, and other server-based services to clients. The NetWare for OS/2 server products was announced in 1993. The purpose of this section is to explain the OS/2 environment as a client to the NetWare server.

The OS/2 client for NetWare includes the following components:

- Network Interface Card Driver

- Protocol Stack

- Network Requester

The network interface card driver for the OS/2 clients can follow two different types of architecture: ODI (Chapter 7) or NDIS 2.0.1 (Network Driver Interface Specification: Chapter 4). The ODI architecture is the native architecture for Novell NetWare client environment, and hence it is used in most of the OS/2 client stations for NetWare. The ODI architecture also contains a module called ODINSUP (ODI NDIS Support Layer). This module allows the IBM OS/2 native protocol stacks (which are based on the NDIS network driver architecture) to run on top of the ODI architecture. Figure 3-33 illustrates the relationship between the 7 layer OSI reference model and the NDIS and ODI specifications.

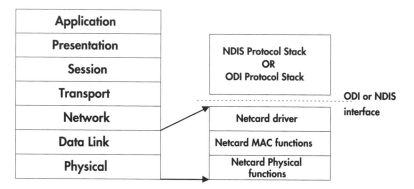

Figure 3-33. 7 Layer OSI Model and NDIS/ODI Architecture

Figure 3-34 illustrates the Novell ODI architecture layers. This architecture is discussed in detail in Chapter 7. The MLID stands for MAC Layer Interface Drivers. This module is responsible for managing the network interface card. It also constructs the MAC layer frames and is responsible for transmitting and receiving these frames to and from the network. The LSL (Link Support Layer) performs the LLC layer functions of multiplexing and de-multiplexing the protocols and MLIDs. The protocol stacks (IPX–Internet Packet Exchange) implement the layer 3 and 4 functions.

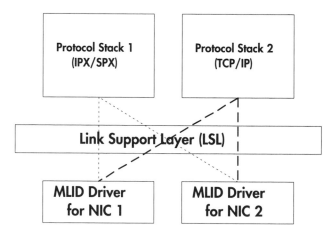

Figure 3-34. ODI Environment

Figure 3-35 illustrates the ODI layers embedded in the OS/2 environment providing the NetWare client services.

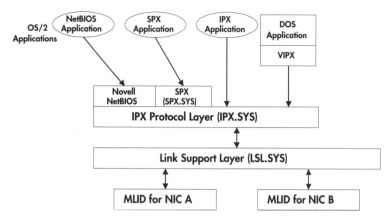

Figure 3-35. NetWare Client for OS/2

Figure 3-36 contains the ODINSUP the ODI NDIS support layer. The ODINSUP emulates the NDIS 2.0.1 interface for the NDIS interface based protocol manager and protocol stacks. With the support of ODINSUP, the NDIS protocol stacks can be used in the ODI architecture to transmit and receive frames and hence perform the client services. The NetWare client protocol stacks and requester can also run on top of network drivers based on NDIS 2.0.1 interfaces. This is illustrated in Figure 3-37. Figure 3-37 contains various NetWare client components with the exception of LSL and the MLID. The LSL and MLID are replaced by the NDIS 2.0.1 MAC driver and the ODI2NDI module.

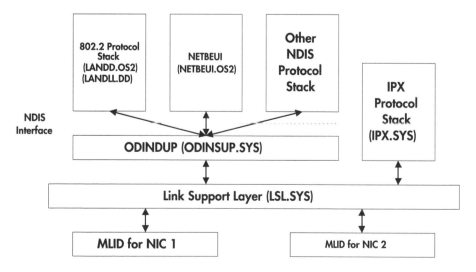

Figure 3-36. NDIS Protocol Stacks Over ODI Drivers

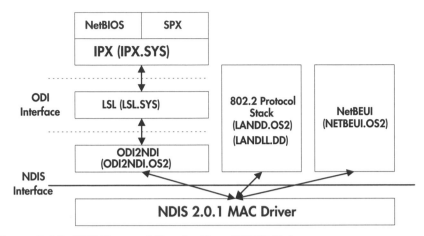

Figure 3-37. ODI Protocol Stacks Over NDIS Drivers

Figures 3-36 and 3-37 show the flexibility that is available to the OS/2 user to install, mix, and match various different components of client software from IBM and Novell. The OS/2 user has to decide whether he or she wants to keep the NDIS 2.0.1-based network card drivers or the ODI-based network card drivers, and then install the rest of the protocol stacks and network requestor components allowing the OS/2 workstation to access NetWare servers.

OS/2 and Microsoft LAN Manager and IBM LAN Server

This section is dedicated to the architecture (client and server) for Microsoft LAN Manager and IBM LAN Server environments running under OS/2. Microsoft LAN Manager is a OS/2 application running on top of OS/2 operating system providing network client and/or server services to local and remote applications. Similarly, IBM LAN Server is also a OS/2 application providing network client and/or server services. The Microsoft LAN Manager networking environment was supported on OS/2 version 1.3 and below. Since the shift in Microsoft product focus, the LAN Manager networking environment is now available on top of SCO UNIX and Windows NT. The OS/2 version 2.x does not have LAN Manager environment available on it. The IBM LAN server environment is available on all versions of OS/2. However, the IBM LAN Server is typically run on top of OS/2 2.x. For the rest of this chapter, LAN Server and LAN Manager server component are mentioned as the server components and the LAN Manager and LAN Server client components are referred to as the client component. This is done because the base versions of LAN Manager and LAN Server are very close in functionality, and hence the basic concepts are the same between the two networking environments.

The client environment of LAN Manager and LAN Server runs on OS/2 and DOS operating environments. The server environment of LAN Manager and LAN Server runs on OS/2 operating system only. The client and server environments under OS/2 use various components of the base operating system. Before we explore the server environment, let us explore the client environment. The client environment is based on the concept of network redirector. A network redirector is a software module which sits between the applications and the base operating system. When a user application needs to access a network drive, the network redirector intercepts the I/O call to the base operating system and gives it to the protocol stack to get information from the file server. When the information comes back from the protocol stack, the network redirector presents this information to the application. Hence, it appears to the application that the information came back from a local drive. In case of a DOS-based client, the network redirector monitors the INT 21h I/O requests and INT 2Ah or 2Fh network control functions. If the request is for a network driver it passes the request to the protocol stack or else it gives it to the local O.S., which in this case is DOS. This is illustrated in Figure 3-38.

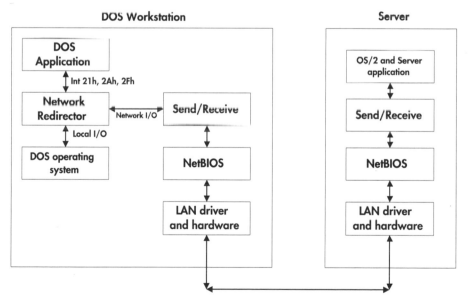

Figure 3-38. DOS Client Architecture for LAN Manager and LAN Server

The interface between the protocol stacks and the network interface card is based on the NDIS 2.0.1 (Network Driver Interface Specification) specification. The NDIS environment is very much like ODI architecture discussed in previous section. The main reason for having the NDIS based environment is to make protocol stacks independent of network interface card hardware. Also, the NDIS based environment contains protocol stacks and network card MAC layer drivers, both based on the NDIS stacks. In the NDIS environment multiple protocol stacks can coexist on top of one or more NDIS based MAC drivers. The NDIS environment is illustrated in Figure 3-39.

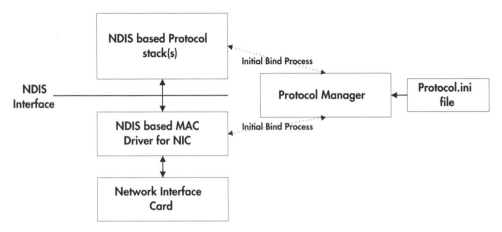

Figure 3-39. NDIS Environment Used in LAN Manager and LAN Server

The Protocol Manager is the component of the NDIS environment which reads the protocol.ini configuration file and helps the protocol and the NIC MAC driver bind to each other (exchange entry points) for future direct communication. The NDIS environment is used for DOS and OS/2 components of LAN Manager and LAN Server for communication between the protocol and network card hardware via NDIS MAC drivers. This means that the client and server environments both use the NDIS architecture. The NDIS environment is discussed in more detail in Chapter 4.

The IBM LAN Server and Microsoft LAN Manager server environments run on top of the base OS/2 operating system. The server environment is responsible for providing server type functions such as file sharing, printer sharing, and multiple users. The server components of LAN Manager and LAN Server use the basic services provided by the OS/2 operating system to offer the advanced server services to the users. The OS/2 file system HPFS (High Performance File System) is designed for file sharing. The file system is a multi-user file system. It can track a file's ownership, security, and access privileges. These functions are not present in some other file systems like the DOS FAT16 (File Allocation Table) file system. Every time a file is created, modified, or deleted, the file parameters are checked for proper operation. This means if the file was created by one user, another user cannot delete it, unless the owner provides permission for such an operation. The OS/2 operating system also allows installing other file systems along with or replacing HPFS.

The LAN Manager and LAN Server applications use the inter-process communications discussed in previous sections for communication within various services provided by these applications. The IPC mechanisms that are used most are pipes, shared memory, and queues. The server networking environment also uses Mail Slots for IPC between various different processes. The mail slots are store and forward message systems used by LAN Manager and LAN Server. Mail slots are an extension to the OS/2's queue mechanism for IPC. The main difference between mailslots and pipes is that mailslots are asynchronous in nature while pipes are synchronous.

Another very important module of the server environment is the SMBs (Server Message Blocks). The SMBs represent the core protocols used by the server. The NetBIOS protocol stack is the core network layer/transport layer protocol. The NetBIOS upper interface (application interface—also known as NetBEUI) is accessed by the applications via software interrupts with their associated function calls and a set of data structures called SMB's. The NetBIOS provides the network/transport layer functionality. The server environment supports other transport stacks like TCP-IP, etc. The server environment for OS/2 is illustrated in Figure 3-40.

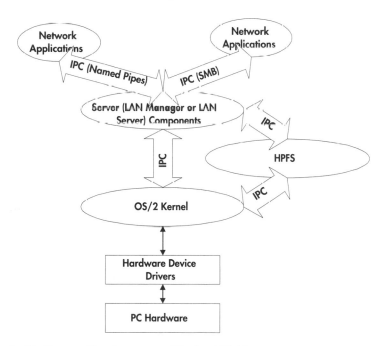

Figure 3-40. Server Environment Under OS/2

The OS/2 networking device driver falls into two categories:

- NDIS 2.0.1-based OS/2 driver

- Novell ODI-based OS/2 driver

The NDIS 2.0.1 generic architecture which covers DOS and OS/2 operating system implementation is covered in Chapter 4. The generic ODI architecture which covers the DOS, OS/2 and NetWare operating system is covered in Chapter 7. The next section covers the generic OS/2 device driver architecture.

OS/2 Device Driver Architecture

The OS/2 device drivers were introduced in the 1.x version of the operating system. The 1.x-based drivers were 16-bit device drivers. The 16-bit device driver model of OS/2 1.x is enhanced in the OS/2 version 2.x. The most important change in the device driver architecture for OS/2 2.x is the support for 32 bit driver model. The OS/2 2.x operating system uses the 80836 processor's virtual 8086 mode to run multiple DOS machines simultaneously. The device support in the virtual 8086 mode does not need to be a 16 bit real mode only driver. The driver in the virtual 8086 mode is running while the processor is still in the 32-bit protected mode. This results in two main types of device driver architectures under OS/2 2.x:

- Physical Device Drivers (PDD)

- Virtual Device Drivers (VDD)

The physical device drivers are the same as the OS/2 1.x device drivers. The PDD operate in real mode and support 16-bit data structures. The VDD support the new 32-bit device driver model and provide virtual DOS device I/O emulation. The VDD device drivers are similar in concept to the Windows VxDs. The VDD drivers can communicate with the device hardware directly, or can optionally call the VDD handler of the PDD. The physical device drivers that exist in a OS/2 system are the serial port driver, parallel port driver, and mouse driver keyboard driver. The virtual device drivers in a system include VPIC (Virtual Programmable Interrupt Controller), VTIMER (Virtual Timer), and VDMA (Virtual DMA).

The networking device drivers discussed in this book have two implementations under OS/2: NDIS 2.0.1-based OS/2 driver and ODI based OS/2 driver. The NDIS- and ODI-based networking device drivers are expected to run under OS/2 1.x and 2.x. Hence, typically, the device driver architecture used for the networking device drivers is the 16-bit OS/2 1.x compatible physical device driver architecture. The rest of this section is limited to the architecture of 16-bit physical device drivers. The OS/2 2.x VDD device driver architecture [Deitel 1992] is beyond the scope of this book.

The device drivers are the OS/2 operating system components which interact with the hardware devices in the system. The device drivers are the hardware-dependent portion of the operating system. They abstract the hardware and its low level functionality from the rest of the operating system and the OS/2 applications. The device drivers provide a common software interface to the device or adapter which the operating system or applications can use. The OS/2 operating system kernel and application can decouple themselves from the constraints of a hardware device and can depend on the device drivers to take care of hardware related constraints. The device drivers serialize the access to the device. This means that operating systems and applications can send multiple requests to the device and the device drivers, which know the capability of the device, and serialize the request according to the device capability. The OS/2 operating system loads some basic device drivers every time it boots. Some of these drivers are for keyboard device, display device, disk device, and so on. The other optional device drivers (for example network device drivers) are loaded by the DEVICE = <driver_path_and_name> line in the CONFIG.SYS file. These drivers are also called installable device drivers.

The OS/2 device drivers are similar to the DOS device drivers. One major DOS device driver drawback is carried in the OS/2 device driver: the calling convention is register based and not stack based. This makes the device driver architecture processor dependent. The calling convention for the OS/2 device driver is discussed later in this section. As in the case of DOS drivers, the OS/2 device drivers fall into two categories: block device drivers and character device drivers. The block device drivers transfer blocks of data between device and system memory. Usually the disk drivers are the block device drivers under OS/2. The character device drivers transfer one character at a time. The networking device drivers fall in the character device driver category. The OS/2 operating system assigns single letters A, B, C, etc. to block devices. The letter which is assigned to the block device depends on the order in which the block device drivers are loaded. The character device driver has a logical name (up to 8 characters). The application or the OS/2 kernel use this logical name to interface with the file system and to communicate with the device driver. This means an application can open a device by using the open file system command and perform a read or a write function with the file handle as if it were talking to a file, but in reality the I/O is going to a character device driver. Some examples of character device driver are SCREEN$, LPT1, COM1, and KBD$.

An OS/2 device driver operates in three different modes. These three modes are:

- Init Mode
- Kernel Mode
- Interrupt Mode

The driver runs in the init mode when the kernel calls the driver to initialize itself. The driver is in this mode when the driver is first loaded at the boot time. The driver runs at processor ring three mode in the init mode. In this mode, it is executing as an application. Very limited number of kernel level APIs (DevHlp functions discussed later in this section) are available to the driver in the init mode. The OS/2 driver is in kernel mode when the kernel calls the strategy routine of the driver. The driver strategy routine is explained later in this section. The kernel calls the driver's strategy routine to obtain some information or to perform some I/O. The driver runs at processor ring 0 in kernel mode. The driver has almost all the kernel level API functions (DevHelp) available to it during kernel mode. The driver interrupt mode is entered as a result of a hardware interrupt by the device. The interrupt produced by the hardware device goes to the PIC (Programmable Interrupt Controller) and then to the CPU and the OS/2 kernel. The kernel saves the context of the processor (saves all the register), and then transfers the execution to the device driver's interrupt handler. The driver, in interrupt mode, executes at processor ring 0 but has access to a subset of the DevHlp functions.

The communication between the OS/2 kernel and device driver is via a data structure called request packet. The request packet contains the I/O command and the pointers to buffers containing data (if applicable). The request packet is also used by the device driver to return status back to the kernel. Figure 3-41 shows the various fields of the request packet.

```
typedef struct _REQPACKET
{
     UCHAR   RPlength;        /* Request packet length */
     UCHAR   RPunit;          /* Unit code for block drivers */
     UCHAR   RPcommand;       /* Command code */
     USHORT  RPstatus;        /* Status word */
     UCHAR   RPreserved[4];   /* Reserved Bytes */
     ULONG   RPqlink;         /* Queue link */
     UCHAR   avail[19];       /* Command specific data */
} REQPACKET;
```

Figure 3-41. OS/2 device driver request packet

The OS/2 device driver file structure is shown in Figure 3-42.

EXE file header
Device Driver Header
Data Segment
Code Segment
Initialization Code
Other Segments

Figure 3-42. Device Drivers File Structure

The device driver has at least one code segment and one data segment. It may have other segments as well. The initialization code is discarded after the driver is loaded and the initialization code has been executed. This results in memory space saving. The device driver header is the first item in the data segment. The device driver header contains information about the device driver which the kernel can inspect when needed. The device driver header structure is shown in Figure 3-43.

```
typedef struct DeviceHdr
        {
                struct DEVICEHDR far *DHnext;    /* Pointer to the next header */
                USHORT DHattribute;              /* Device attribute word */
                USHORT DHstrategy;               /* Offset to strategy routine */
                USHORT DHidc;                    /* Offset to IDC routine */
                UCHAR  DHname[8];                /* Device Name or # of units */
                CHAR   reserved[8];              /* Reserved Bytes */
        } DEVICEHDR;
```

Figure 3-43. Device Driver Header Structure

The first element of the device driver header is a pointer to the next driver in the chain. If this driver is the last driver in the chain then this field is -1. This pointer is initialized to -1, and the kernel fills the correct value when the driver is loaded. The next field is the device driver attribute word. The attribute word defines the various attributes of the driver like block driver versus character driver. The next field is the offset to the strategy routine. The strategy routine is the main entry point for the requests from the kernel. The OS/2 kernel initiates an I/O operation by calling the driver's strategy routine with the address of the data structure called the request packet (see Figure 3-41). The driver looks at the command field of the request packet and executes the appropriate command. When the request is completed, the strategy routine returns the request packet with the status of the request back to the kernel.

The next field is the offset to the IDC routine (Inter Device Communication). The driver name for the character device driver may contain up to eight ASCII characters representing the name of the device driver. All operations to the character device driver are performed by referencing this name.

The device drivers need to request some system services. The system services for device drivers offered by the kernel under OS/2 are called Device Helper (DevHelp) functions. These DevHelp functions are designed to let the device driver perform some low level functions in a consistent manner between various device drivers. The DevHelp functions are linked statically to the driver. The DevHelp functions also help the driver to process the request packet. The DevHelp interface is a register-based interface and uses a common entry point for all the functions. The device driver places the number of the DevHelp service in one of the register parameters of the DevHelp function in other registers, and then indirectly calls the DevHelp service address. The DevHelp functions are device driver mode sensitive, that is, which DevHelp functions can be called by the device driver depend upon the mode in which the device driver is programmed (Kernel, Interrupt, or Init). The DevHelp functions can be broadly grouped into the following categories.

Process Management:	This group of functions includes services for multitasking.
Hardware Management:	This group of functions provides services for managing hardware functions like issuing EOI (End Of Interrupt) to the PIC (Programmable Interrupt Controller), Setting IRQ vector, and Releasing IRQ vector.
Memory Management:	This group of functions offers memory management services. Some of the examples of the functions included in this group are Physical to Virtual and Virtual to Physical address conversion, locking a memory segment, mapping a physical address and length to a Global Descriptor Table selector, and memory allocation and de-allocation.
Semaphore Management:	The semaphore management functions provide access to 16-bit semaphores. These functions include setting a semaphore, and clearing a semaphore.
Request Packet Management:	These DevHelp functions provide request packet management. This includes functions that allocate request packets, free request packets, and sort request packets. This group also includes functions to manage the request packet queues.

Timer Management:	Timer management functions provide services such as setting a timer, resetting a timer, and counting timer ticks.
Character Queue Management:	The character queue management DevHelp functions allow character queues for supporting asynchronous and keyboard devices to be managed.
Miscellaneous Functions:	This group of DevHelp functions provides miscellaneous services such as switching processors from real to protected mode and vice versa, and obtaining inter driver communication entry points.

The DevHelp functions provide very low level functions for OS/2 device drivers. These functions offer a lot of power and flexibility to the device driver programmer under OS/2 operating system.

The OS/2 device driver request packet flow is illustrated in Figure 3-44.

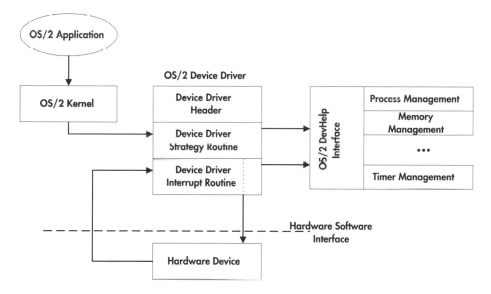

Figure 3-44. I/O Request Flow in OS/2

NOVELL NETWARE OPERATING SYSTEM

The Novell NetWare operating system is the operating system designed to provide client/server computing across an enterprise. In the PC environment, Novell NetWare operating system is used in more than 70% of the networked

PCs. By far, Novell NetWare is considered to be the defacto network operating system, providing capabilities such as file sharing, printer sharing, security, etc. The Novell operating system has gone through major enhancements in the past few years. Listed below are the main versions of the Novell NetWare operating system.

NetWare 2.x: The NetWare 2.x operating system was introduced for 286 and higher processors. This version of the operating system is also known as NetWare 286. In this version, user programs can be loaded as value added processes (VAPs). The VAPs are programs such as database management programs or any other user programs that needs to run on the network server and provide additional services to various clients. In NetWare 2.x, when a user tries to load a VAP, the VAP logs into the operating system as a user and is then loaded in the NetWare server's memory for execution. The overall architecture of the Novell NetWare 2.x operating system is very monolithic. The last version of NetWare 2.x was 2.11 and Novell is not planning to revise this operating system.

NetWare 3.x: The NetWare 3.x operating system was introduced by Novell for 386 and higher processors. The NetWare 3.x operating system is also known as NetWare 386. The NetWare 3.x operating system introduced the concept of NLM (Network Loadable Module). NLMs replaced the VAP programs for 3.x operating system. The NLMs are programs written for NetWare 3.x and higher versions of the operating system. These programs become part of the NetWare operating system when loaded under the operating system. This makes the NLMs very powerful, programs which are very tightly integrated with the operating system. The NetWare 3.x operating system is very modular in design. The easy installation of NetWare 3.x operating system is another major advantage of 3.x over the 2.x version. The latest version of NetWare 3.x operating system at the time of this publication was 3.12.

NetWare 4.x: The NetWare 4.x operating system was introduced in 1993 and is targeted for 386 and higher processors. The concepts behind user processes running as NLMs did not change for this version of the operating system. The main enhancements for the NetWare 4.x operating system were in the area of network management, easier maintenance, and better and more security options. The single biggest enhancement for NetWare 4.x is the NDS (NetWare Directory Services). NDS maintains a global, distributed, replicated database of information about network resources such as users, groups, servers, disk volumes, printers, computers, and modems. NDS allows the integration of various different network resources into a single easy to use environment. The latest version of 4.x operating system at the time of this publication is 4.02.

The NetWare operating system discussion included in the following sections is based on NetWare 3.x and NetWare 4.x operating system. The NetWare 2.x operating system is not included in the discussion because the NetWare 2.x operating system is nearly obsolete and most users have upgraded to NetWare 3.x or NetWare 4.x. Also, almost all the new installations of NetWare are either 3.x- or 4.x-based.

NetWare Operating System Basics

The NetWare based network consists of two major components: a server machine running the NetWare operating system and a client (also known as workstation) machine running the standard client operating systems like DOS, OS/2, or Windows 3.x. A server machine has the resources that are shared by the various client machines. The files that are shared among various client machines reside on the server machine. Similarly, other resources such as printers, and various application programs such as database applications. reside on the server. The client machine's operating system has to run few pieces of software (i.e., protocol stack, network shell/redirector) to gain access to the server. The client machine's software also makes the remote resources appear local. This means that the user thinks that he or she is printing on a local printer port. In reality, the network shell program provided by Novell intercepts the access to the LPT port and sends it over the network to the server where the printer is present and the document gets printed. Once a link is established between the client machine and the server machine, the user logs on the server machine and starts to use these common resources. The Novell NetWare environment consists mainly of PCs. Figure 3-45 illustrates a Novell client server environment. The client machine in this figure is running DOS operating system.

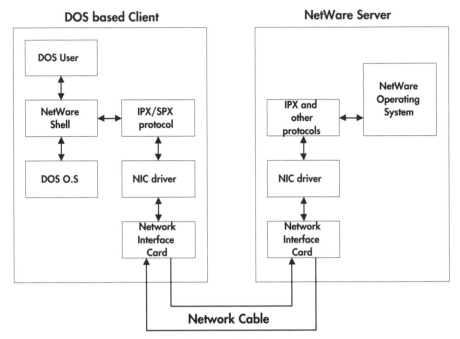

Figure 3-45. NetWare Client / Server Environment

The NetWare server is typically a 386 or higher processor based computer with variety of peripheral devices connected to it. Some of the peripheral devices are disk drives, modems, printers and other boards. The server has the basic NetWare operating system along with a core set of protocols called NetWare Core Protocols (NCPs) running under the server. The client side (workstation) has the NetWare software running in conjunction with the work-station operating system (DOS or OS/2). Novell has released two different client software packages: NetWare Shell and NetWare Redirector. NetWare shell and NetWare redirector will be discussed in the next section. The main purpose of the NetWare client software is to provide access to the remote resources located on the NetWare server. The client NetWare software extends the services of the operating system to the network. The NetWare shell inter-cepts the file access calls to the DOS operating system and decides if the file access is for the local file system or for the file system located on the server. If the file access is for the local files, the NetWare shell gives the file access call to the local operating system (DOS). However, if the file access is for the file located on the server, the NetWare shell constructs a packet and gives the packet to the protocol stack to transmit it over the network to the server. The server receives the file access request, prepares a response to it and sends it back to the client. The client shell then displays the information to the user and hence completes the file access call.

The core of the NetWare operating system based server is the kernel which performs the basic services such as adding users, security for various server resources, etc. Additional programs can be added to the server to get additional functionality. The NetWare 3.x and 4.x operating systems allows to add this extra software as NLMs (Network Loadable Modules). Also protocol stacks used for sending and receiving packets can be loaded as NLMs. The NLMs are one of the key features that distinguish the NetWare 3.x and 4.x environments from the other operating systems. The NLMs can be dynamically loaded or unloaded under the NetWare operating system. The loading and unloading of the NLMs does not disturb the rest of the operating system functions. A NLM, once loaded becomes part of the NetWare operating system . The NLMs have full access to the NetWare system resources. Most of the NetWare operating system components are built as NLMs. The list is very long and includes components such as device drivers, protocol stacks, installation programs etc. Most of the third party programs such as database servers, etc. are loaded as NLMs under NetWare. The NLMs must be well written and tested because they have access to all the system resources and can corrupt other NLMs resources. Novell offers a certification program for testing and certifying NLMs written by third party vendors. The NetWare environment is multitasking. Several different NLMs run at the same time in the NetWare server environment.

The protocol stacks and the network interface cards and the device drivers for the network interface cards constitute the networking component of the NetWare servers. The protocol stacks are responsible for implementing protocols for transmitting, receiving, sequencing, and error checking packets between the server and the client machines. The protocol stacks use the services provided by the network interface card and their drivers to send, and receive packets to and from the network. The Novell core protocol stacks are IPX and SPX. The IPX stands for Internetwork packet exchange. The IPX protocol is used to provide connectionless data exchange between the client and the server. The SPX stands for Sequenced packet exchange protocol. The SPX services are used for providing connection oriented data exchange between the client and the server.

The Novell networking protocols are derived from the Xerox Network System (XNS). The Novell protocol stack is based on the XNS layer 3 and 4 protocols. The XNS includes a protocol at layer 3 called IDP (Internetwork Datagram Protocol) which is the basis of Novell's IPX protocol. The XNS also include two transport layer protocols: PEP (Packet Exchange Protocol) and SPP (Sequenced Packet Protocol). The XNS's PEP and SPP form the basis for the Novell's Sequenced Packet Exchange (SPX) protocol.

Novell's IPX is a connectionless protocol. Connectionless protocols are low overhead protocols. There is no guarantee that a packet which is transmitted using a connectionless protocol would ever reach its destination. In a connectionless service, a packet is given to the protocol stack and it is assumed that it would be delivered to its destination. The IPX protocol stack performs the functions of a network layer of the 7 layer OSI model. The basic service provided by this protocol is forwarding the packet, segmenting, reassembling, and routing the packet. The IPX packet format is shown in Figure 3-46.

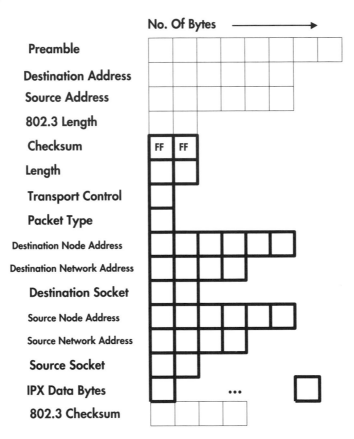

Figure 3-46. IPX Fields Embedded in 802.3 Frame Format

The IPX header (highlighted blocks) is embedded in the 802.3 raw packet format in the Figure 3-46.

The IPX header is 30 bytes in length. The first field is the checksum field. The checksum field is not used in IPX and has a value of 0xFFFF. The length field contains the length of the IPX packet. This length field includes the IPX header and the IPX data. It does not include the ethernet fields. The transport control field is used by IPX routers. This field is incremented every time the IPX frame passes a router. This field indicates the number of routers hopped by this IPX frame. This field is set to 0 at the starting station. The frame is discarded at the 16th router. The packet type field indicates the type of service that a packet will use. This field is 0, 4, 5 or 7 for IPX based communications (0 or 4 for IPX, 5 for SPX, and 7 for NCP). The destination node address is a 6 byte field which contains the destination station's node address. The value 0xFF FF FF FF FF FF is used as the broadcast address. Packets addressed to NetWare server have this address set to 0x00 00 00 00 00 01. The destination network address is a 4 byte field which contains the address of the destination node. If this field contains 0x00 00 00 00, the packet is destined for the same network as the source station and will not be routed to any other network. The destination socket is a 2 byte socket number. Socket number is the number of the process within a computer which gets the packet. The source node address is a 6 byte field which contains the source address of the node (A value of 0x00 00 00 00 00 01 for packets starting from a NetWare server). The source network field is the network address to which the source node belongs. The source socket field contains the socket number of the process that is transmitting the packet.

The SPX is a connection-oriented protocol. The SPX protocol first establishes a connection with another SPX protocol on a remote computer. The SPX protocol then starts sending sequenced packets to the destination node. The SPX packets arrive in proper order. This overhead communication in the SPX environment makes SPX based communications a little slower. The SPX protocol is used by the Novell NetWare server for its print server services, remote console services etc. The SPX packet header contains all the IPX header fields as described in Figure 3-46 plus 12 additional bytes. This makes the SPX header 42 bytes long. The SPX header begins with the same first 30 bytes as the IPX header fields. The next 12 bytes of the SPX header are shown in Figure 3-47.

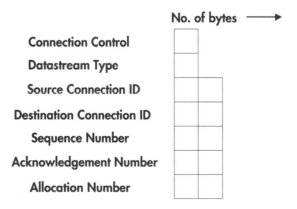

No. of bytes ⟶

Connection Control

Datastream Type

Source Connection ID

Destination Connection ID

Sequence Number

Acknowledgement Number

Allocation Number

Figure 3-47. SPX Header Fields

The first 30 bytes of the SPX header are the same as IPX. The packet type field for IPX is 0 or 4. The packet type field for the SPX packet is 5. The rest of the fields have values based on their field description. The connection control field controls the bi-directional flow of data. The datastream type field contains the type of data included in the packet. It has values such as End-Of-Connection or End-Of-Connection Acknowledgment. The source connection ID is a 2-byte field which contains the ID for the source SPX station. The destination SPX implementation puts this field in the destination connection ID. The destination connection ID is another 2 byte field that contains the connection ID number of the destination station. The sequence number is a 2 byte field that contains the count of data packets transmitted from the station. This number is incremented after the source station receives an acknowledgment for the data packet sent by the source station. The acknowledgment number field is a 2 byte field. This field indicates the value of the sequence number expected in the next SPX packet from the SPX receiving station. This field is used by the transmitting and receiving station to watch for any lost SPX packets. The allocation number field indicates the number of receive buffers available in the station. This field is used by the two SPX stations to watch out for each other's resources. If an application on the receiving side is not releasing buffers, the sending station would see this by monitoring the allocation field.

The IPX and SPX protocol stacks are used in the Novell environment to transmit and receive packets. However, a standardized language is used to define networking services (request and replies). The standardized language in Novell NetWare environment is called NCP (NetWare Core Protocols). The Novell NetWare environment defines a set of NCP standards which define the format and conventions for various messages. The NCP language is spoken by all the NetWare clients and servers. The NetWare client requests file reads, writes, print services, and drive letter mapping. These client requests are NCP requests which are interpreted by the server and acted upon by the server. Once the request is completed by the server, the server uses the NCP replies to reply to the client.

The IPX, SPX, and the NCP services of the NetWare client and server environments use the network interface card and driver to transmit and receive packets. The protocol stack is connected to the network interface card via the network device drivers. The network interface card device drivers follow an architecture called ODI (Open Data-Link Interface), described in Chapter 7.

Networking Under NetWare Operating System

The Novell NetWare operating system is written with networking in mind. In fact, the sole reason for its creation is to provide networking services to the various clients (workstations) attached to it. The *NetWare Operating System*

Basics section introduced various networking components of the NetWare operating system. This section is focused on providing some more details on the networking capabilities of NetWare operating system. The discussion in this section is broken down into two sections: NetWare as a server and NetWare client support.

NetWare as a Server

The NetWare operating system software is a multitasking environment. The server operating system services are offered by the core operating system. The basic concepts of the services offered by the NetWare operating system include a base kernel which offers the basic kernel services to various processes running under it. These services include starting a program, memory management, scheduling processes, and inter-process communication. The NetWare environment consists of a server machine, which is typically a 386 or higher processor, along with all the peripherals such as disk drives, modems, and printers. The server contains a network interface card (like ethernet) to attach itself to the network where the rest of the clients are connected. The server also contains protocol stacks for communicating to various clients. The IPX and SPX protocols are the most used protocol stacks. TCP-IP is another protocol stack that is used a lot in the NetWare server environment. The various user programs are loaded as network loadable modules under the NetWare server operating system. The NCPs (network core protocols) are request/reply messages defined for the NetWare operating system environment. The clients use the NCP services to request various actions from the server. The NCP services being requested by the client are embedded within the IPX/SPX packet. The server receives the NCP service request from the client and acts on it.

The services provided by the core set of NCP services offered by the NetWare server fall into the following categories:

- Accounting Services
- Bindery Services
- Connection Services
- Directory Services
- File Services
- File Server Environment
- Message Services
- Print Services
- Queue Services
- Transaction Tracking Services

The accounting services category of the NCP services contains services to track the service usage by the user. The supervisor on a Novell NetWare server can assign resources to users and then can monitor the usage of the user accounts.

The Novell NetWare server has a special file called bindery. The bindery is a network database that contains definitions for entities such as users, groups, and workgroups. The bindery is used for security, accounting, and name management. The bindery exists for NetWare 3.x and below. In NetWare 4.x, the bindery has been replaced by the NetWare Directory database, under NetWare Directory Services. The bindery services of the NCP services provide functions for adding, deleting and modifying bindery objects such as users, passwords for users, and security options.

The connection services are another category of the NCP services. A connection is a number assigned to any workstation that attaches to a NetWare server. Connection numbers are also assigned to processes, print servers, and applications that use NetWare server connections. Connection services provide functions to manage the connections to the server. These include functions to get the internet address, open and close connections, get station number, login and logout functions.

The directory services provide a number of functions to manage the directory structure of the NetWare file system. The functions included in this category contain functions for adding or deleting directories, managing the disk space for users, obtaining information about the NetWare volumes, mapping directories to a path, moving directories, scanning directory databases for certain information, and renaming directories.

The file services part of the NCP services contain functions to open, close, create, and delete files. There are functions defined for copying files, searching for files, scanning files for pieces of information, and setting file attributes.

The file server environment services are another subset of the NCP services. The file server environment provides services for managing the NetWare file server environment. This includes allocating resources, deallocating resources, enabling transaction tracking, getting disk utilization, and getting file server date and time information.

The message services provide mechanisms to send messages to various users. The services provide means to send broadcast messages, to get broadcast messages, and disable broadcast messages.

The print services contain functions to manage the print process under NetWare. The functions included are for print management. For example to create a spool file, to close a spool file, and to spool a disk file.

The queue services provide services for managing queues under NetWare. These include functions such as create queue, destroy queue, and add/remove jobs from queue. The synchronization services provide functions for locking and unlocking files for serializing access to the files, opening, closing, and waiting on semaphores.

The Transaction Tracking Services provide functions to track various transactions. The NetWare Transaction Tracking System (TTS) protects database applications from corruption by backing out incomplete transactions that result from failure in a network component. When a transaction is backed out, data and index information in the database are returned to the state that they were in, before the transaction began. The NCP's transaction tracking services provide functions for aborting transactions, beginning transactions, and getting status of transactions.

The protocol stacks (IPX, SPX, TCP-IP, etc.) are used by the NCP services to transmit and receive packets. The protocol stacks use the network interface card and the device driver to send and receive packets from the network. The network device driver in a Novell environment is a <driver_name>.lan file. The *.lan extension is the notation used in the NetWare server environment for the LAN device drivers. The main function of the LAN device driver is to initialize and service the LAN hardware. The LAN device driver for NetWare provides a uniform interface for the various types of network protocol stacks running above it. This interface is called ODI (Open Data-Link Interface). The ODI interface is described in detail in Chapter 7.

NetWare and Client Operating System

The Novell NetWare environment includes the software that runs in conjunction with the client operating system to provide the client access to the NetWare server environment. The client environments supported by the NetWare client software are:

- DOS and Windows 3.x
- Apple Macintosh
- OS/2 1.x and 2.x
- Windows NT 3.1

The support for the client environments is provided by the network requestor or the network shell. Novell provides ODI based network card drivers and protocol stacks for the above client environments. Novell also provides a network shell or requestor for the above environments. A network shell is a piece of software that traps all the file and print service requests made from the user applications to the client operating services. It then makes a decision as to whether the request is for the network resource or local resource. For example, if a user is on a DOS-based system and enters "dir c:" as a command on a DOS-based machine running the NetWare DOS client environment including network shell (netx.exe), the network shell from Novell traps this command and examines it. It decides that the command is for local resource (c:) and gives the command to the local operating system, DOS. If the user enters "dir f:" (assume f: is a network drive), the network shell traps this command and examines it. Since this command is for a network resource, the network shell creates a NCP request and passes it to the protocol stack and the LAN driver for transmission on the network. Various different Novell NetWare client environments work in a similar way.

The glue between the protocol stack and the network interface card, in the client environments, is the network device driver. The network device drivers for various Novell NetWare client environments also follow ODI (Open Data-Link interface) specifications. The ODI network device driver environment allows various different protocol stacks to run on the network device driver. The network device drivers for the client environments are responsible for initializing and servicing the network interface cards. The ODI environment is discussed, in detail, in Chapter 7.

The DOS client network device drivers are DOS TSRs (Terminate and Stay Resident) programs interfacing with the network interface cards and the protocol stacks. The network device drivers for the DOS operating system are DOS COM files (<driver_name>.com) that reside under the DOS operating system as TSRs. The OS/2 network device drivers follow the OS/2 device driver format and are <driver_name>.sys files that are loaded from the config.sys files.

NetWare Device Driver Architecture

The NetWare file server device drivers are NetWare Loadable Modules (NLMs). The generic applications and device drivers follow the NLM file format under the NetWare Operating system. The network supervisor can load and unload various NLMs without affecting the rest of the functionalities of the NetWare server. This means that the supervisor can add or delete a functionality by loading or unloading NLMs providing the functionality. Also, the supervisor can add or delete device drivers from a NetWare server while the system is running. The network device drivers, protocol stacks, disk drivers, and the various utilities, all follow the NLM format under NetWare server. Before we look into the device driver format and routines and its interface with the NetWare server, we examine the compilation process for a NLM under NetWare.

The NetWare NLMs are mostly written in 386 assembly language. The NetWare server runs in the 386 or higher processor in protected mode. The memory architecture is 32-bit flat mode. Once the source file is completed, it is assembled into an object code file. For example, the source file name for the device driver that we are writing is landrvr.386. The corresponding object file is called landrvr.obj. The assembler which is used to assemble the source file into the object file should support the 32-bit flat memory model. The most common assembler used for NetWare environment is Phar Lap 386asm assembler. The object file has to be converted from object file format to the special NetWare Loadable Module format. The Novell NetWare environment has a linker which is supplied by Novell. The linker provided by Novell is called nlmlink. The nlmlink is a 386 linker for NetWare environment. The landrvr.obj file is linked into a landrvr.lan file by the nlmlink. The nlmlink reads a module definition file (landrvr.def) which is a ASCII text file providing various parameters to the nlmlink. Each NetWare Loadable Module must have a corresponding definition file with .DEF extension. The definition file contains the name of the input object file, name of output executable file, copyright statement, NetWare services that this loadable module would need to import, and services this module will export. The NetWare linker can produce NLM executable files with three types of extensions. They are:

- **.LAN**: The NetWare linker attaches this extension to the executable file when the definition file tells the linker that the type = 1. The .lan type is used for the LAN device drivers.

- **.DSK**: The NetWare linker attaches this extension to the executable file when the definition file tells the linker that the type = 2. The .dsk type is used for the disk device drivers.

- **.NLM**: This is the default extension for the executable files produced by the NetWare linker. This extension is used by protocol stacks, applications etc. under NetWare.

The device drivers for the NetWare operating system have three major interfaces. These interfaces are:

- The Loadable Module Interface
- IOCTL (I/O Control) Operations Interface
- I/O Interface

The NetWare Loadable Module (NLM) interface requires that all the NLMs support three routine entry points: initialize driver, check driver, and remove driver.

The **InitializeDriver** routine is called when the driver is first loaded under NetWare. The InitializeDriver routine is typically called for each adapter card when the device driver for that adapter card is loaded. The InitializeDriver routine initializes the hardware by checking for its presence, making sure that the hardware is fully operational, setting the I/O ports and interrupts, for the hardware. The InitializeDriver routine also initializes various internal and external data structures for the device driver. On completion, the InitializeDriver routine returns either a success or a failure signal to the

NetWare operating system. If it signals failure for any reason, the load process for the device driver is aborted. The CheckDriver routine is called by the NetWare when the user enters the unload command for that loadable module. The **CheckDriver** routine is used for .DSK drivers. This routine checks all the storage devices and makes sure that they are not being used by any other applications. If the storage device is being used, the NetWare displays an error message and allows the user to abort the DSK driver unload process. The **RemoveDriver** routine is called by the NetWare operating system to unload the driver. This routine removes the entire code and data image from the memory. The RemoveDriver routine returns all the allocated memory, and frees all the resources like I/O and interrupts, that are used by the hardware device.

The **IOCTL interface** is a special interface that exists for the Loadable Modules under NetWare. The IOCTL interface is used to implement functions specific to the Loadable Modules. For example, the IOCTL interface in the case of the ODI-based network device drivers implements functions to read statistics from the network device drivers. Any applications can call the network device driver IOCTL interface via the NetWare operating system and can request the statistics from the network device driver. The NetWare operating system and the loadable modules can access the device driver's IOCTL routines by passing an IOCTL request structure to the IOCTL Operations Interface that contains a function and a subfunction number. The device driver parses the function number and the subfunction number and performs the appropriate task.

The I/O Interface includes **Timeout** and **Interrupt Service Routines**. The device driver **Timeout routine** is used by the driver to schedule periodic tasks. At the initialization time, the driver determines the timeout value and sets the Timeout routine. The NetWare operating system calls the Timeout routine of the driver asynchronously, each time the specified timeout value expires. This means the driver can do all the tasks it needs to do every so often (timeout value). The **Interrupt Service Routine (ISR)** is the routine that services all the hardware interrupts generated by the hardware device. The NetWare server environment has a system Interrupt Service Routine. The system ISR receives the interrupt when the hardware interrupts. The system ISR calls the driver's ISR routine. The driver ISR routine determines the reason for the hardware interrupts and takes appropriate action for the hardware interrupt. In case of LAN hardware, an interrupt is generated by the hardware to tell the driver that a new packet was received properly, or that a transmission of a packet was completed successfully. The driver ISR routine is also responsible for clearing the interrupt condition for the hardware device.

The device driver interface for the Novell NetWare environment follows the Loadable Module Interface for NLMs. The Novell NetWare environment provides a set of NetWare services, such as memory management, or asynchronous event scheduling, for the device drivers. The device drivers can use these services when needed. The overall architecture of Novell NetWare provides a very flexible yet powerful environment for device driver operation.

UNIX OPERATING SYSTEM

The UNIX operating system has been under development since 1970s. This operating system includes the base operating systems and the commands associated with it. The very early UNIX systems provided only character based user interface. The user entered commands for processing by the operating system and the operating system would execute the commands and the programs. Today, most of the UNIX systems provide a very easy to use graphical interface. For example, Open Desk Top (ODT) from SCO UNIX, and X-Windows under UNIX from a number of vendors. The base UNIX operating system, underneath the text based user interface, and the graphical interface, is the same. The UNIX operating system manages the resources of the computer by providing commands for file management, process management and other general housekeeping functions. The UNIX system also provides various tools for program development. These include editors, compilers, assemblers, and text formatters.

The UNIX system contains basic architecture concepts from a number of operating systems being used in 1960s and 1970s. The basic research which provided the foundation of the UNIX operating system was done at AT&T Bell Laboratories by Dennis Ritchie and Ken Thompson. A number of other people also provided input to the base development. The first UNIX implementation was completed on a PDP 11 machine in 1970. In 1971, the first manual documenting the UNIX operating system was written by Ritchie and Thompson. This implementation contained the file system description, process management, system interface, and all major commands. The second edition of UNIX came in 1972. This implementation had the inclusion of pipes in it. In parallel Thompson was working on a language that he called B. The B language came from BCPL (Basic Command Programming Language). The B programming language produced interpretive code in one pass and was typeless. B. Kernighan and Ritchie carried on more work on the language B and introduced a new language, C, in 1978. The C language provided the foundation of all the program development under UNIX. In fact, the C language has become the defacto programming environment under a number of UNIX and non-UNIX environments. The UNIX system was rewritten in 1977 to allow porting of the operating system from one computer to another. This work resulted in a general release of the UNIX operating system version 7 in 1979. At this point the UNIX system development was split between AT&T and University of California at Berkeley. This resulted in two major releases in 1980s of the

UNIX: AT&T UNIX System V and Berkeley BSD (Berkley Software Distribution) 4.3. Since the releases of the UNIX operating systems, many commercial companies have obtained the license of the base operating system from AT&T and have released commercial versions of UNIX implementations. Some of these companies are SUN Microsystems, Hewlett Packard, Santa Cruz Operations, and Novell (UNIX Systems Labs). The UNIX operating system is a very widely used operating system. This is one operating system which has now been ported to micro, mini-, and mainframe computers. The UNIX operating system is available from various manufacturers. The list below is a non-exhaustive list of the UNIX manufacturers.

- Santa Cruz Operation—UNIX 3.2.4 and Open Desk Top
- Interactive UNIX (Now part of SUN Microsystems)
- Novell—UNIXWARE 1.1 and 2.0
- Sun Microsystems—SUN OS and Solaris 2.4
- Hewlett Packard—HP UX
- International Business Machines—IBM AIX
- Digital—Digital Ultrix

The next few sections discuss the basic features of the UNIX operating system which are common to the various flavors of UNIX.

UNIX Operating System Basics

The UNIX operating system is responsible for managing various hardware resources that exist in a computer like processor, memory, and hard disk video. It also provides an environment for a user to build a program and execute it. The main components of the UNIX operating system that make this happen are:

- Kernel
- User Processes
- Shell
- File System

The kernel is the main component of the UNIX operating system. The kernel is the main program which has complete control of the system hardware including processor, main memory, and I/O devices. The kernel provides a set of system calls for various user level programs. The user programs use these system calls to interface with the hardware. This ensures that all the system resource management is performed in a unified manner by the kernel. This also means that the system resources are shared evenly and properly between various user programs. The kernel acts as an arbitrator between various different user processes competing for the resources. The kernel of the UNIX operating system is a single binary file containing modules mainly written in C with some assembly language usage for critical components. The UNIX kernel is called during the boot process of a computer (different for different computer hardware architectures). However, during the power on boot process, the kernel is the first piece of software that is initialized and loaded in the computer memory. The kernel then is responsible for creating and scheduling user processes. It provides resources to the user processes for them to be able to execute.

The user processes under UNIX are responsible for doing all the user related work. This may include text processing, and number crunching. The user processes under UNIX are written in a programming language like C and are compiled and linked to produce a binary file known as an executable image. The kernel loads the executable image in the memory (code and data). The UNIX allows for multiple user processes to be executed at the same time. This is achieved by the kernel keeping the current user process code and data in the memory and its registers and program counter values in the processor registers. The kernel lets the processor execute this process for some time. If the user has to wait for some external event to happen, the kernel swaps this process with another process. The kernel may also swap the process with another process just because it has to run multiple processes at the same time, effectively providing a multiprocess environment to the users. The kernel manages the processor and the main memory to perform the process execution function.

The shell is a command language that provides a user interface to the UNIX operating system. The shell has the capability to execute from a user terminal or from a file. Users can write batch files consisting of UNIX commands and pass the patch file to the shell for execution. This provides the flexibility for users to create their own commands which are built around general UNIX commands.

The UNIX file system allows the users to store information (files) by name. This file system also provides features like security of files from unauthorized access, and backup for protection from hardware failures. The UNIX file system contains ordinary files that contain characters forming the basis of documents, and programs. The executable programs are also stored in ordinary file formats. The UNIX file system contains a feature called a directory. A directory is like a folder which contains files or directories. This directory provides the concept of file system hierarchy under UNIX.

Networking Under UNIX Operating System

The UNIX operating system is one of the first operating systems to provide networking in its base operating system. The UNIX networking follows the client/server model. In a client/server model, the server is started and initialized. The server waits for commands from the client. The client is a user process which may be running on the same machine or a different machine. If the client is running on a different machine than a server, then the client and server machines are connected via a computer network like Ethernet. The client passes commands to the server like read a file from the server's file area, write to a file, and print a document. The server receives this command and executes it and provides the status back to the client process.

The client/server networking is implemented in UNIX with the help of protocol stacks and inter-process communications between the protocols and applications that implement the networking infrastructure under UNIX. The next few paragraphs will discuss the protocol stack and the inter process communication under UNIX.

The UNIX operating system has the following protocol suites available. The list provided below is not an exhaustive list. There are a number of protocol suite implementations which are beyond the scope of the discussion in this book. The following list contains the most popular set of protocol suites under UNIX.

- TCP-IP Protocol Suite

- Xerox Networking System (XNS)

- System Network Architecture (SNA)

- NetBIOS

The TCP-IP suite of protocols is the most popular protocol implementation under UNIX. The TCP-IP protocol suite was developed under the Defense Advanced Research Projects Agency (DARPA) sponsored development of a networking project called ARPANET. The TCP-IP protocol suite has been implemented on almost all types of UNIX operating systems running on personal computers to main frames. The TCP-IP protocol stack implementation and its relationship with various OSI layers is shown in Figure 3-48.

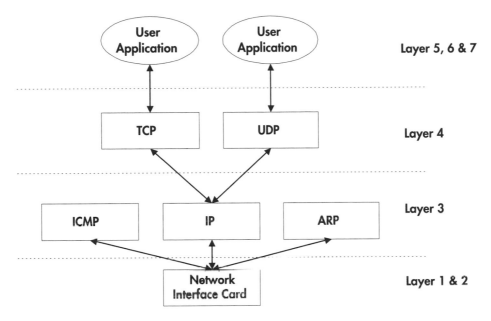

Figure 3-48. TCP-IP Protocol Stack and OSI Layers

The TCP-IP protocol suite and the description of the various components of TCP-IP are explained in Chapter 8. The key concept presented here is that the TCP-IP protocol suite is the most used protocol suite under UNIX and is made up of various protocols.

The XNS is the networking architecture developed by Xerox Corporation in the late 1970s. The XNS protocol suite is similar in implementation to the TCP-IP. The XNS protocol suite resides on layers 3 and 4 of the OSI reference model. The application processes communicate to the XNS protocol suite which consists of PEX (Packet Exchange Protocol), SPP (Sequenced Packet Protocol), ECHO (Echo Protocol), and RIP (Routing Information Protocol). All the XNS protocols listed here use an underlying IDP (Internet Datagram Protocol) to provide layer 3 type of services.

The SNA architecture is a networking architecture developed by IBM. Most UNIX vendors provide add on support for IBM's SNA architecture. The NetBIOS interface is the implementation of network and transport layer interface in personal computers. The name NetBIOS is derived from Net-Basic Input Output System. The first implementation of the NetBIOS stack was in a ROM on the network adapter card. However, the subsequent implementations have been implemented as software drivers under various operating systems. The NetBIOS interface provides a defacto standard interface to provide networking under the various operating systems. The NetBIOS interface may use different protocol stacks to provide this functionality. The most common protocol stack for NetBIOS interface is called NetBEUI. The TCP-IP protocol stack can also be used for the NetBIOS interface implementation.

The networking implementation under UNIX involves some complex protocols that are implemented as separate processes under UNIX. The interprocess communication (IPC) is the key to such a networking implementation as the networking components have to exchange data and commands via the IPC mechanisms discussed here to run properly. The UNIX operating system provides IPC mechanisms and various processes involved in the networking use these IPC methods. For two processes to communicate properly, they both have to follow the same IPC mechanism. The most common IPC mechanisms implemented and used under UNIX are:

- Pipes

- FIFOs

- Message Queues

- Semaphores

- Shared Memory

The concepts behind these IPCs were discussed in the *IBM OS/2 2.x Operating System* section of this chapter. The exact same concepts apply here.

There are three application programming interfaces for UNIX operating system specific to networking. These API mechanisms apply to the networking component of UNIX. They are:

- Sockets

- Transport Layer Interface (TLI)

- Streams

The Sockets are APIs (Application Programming Interfaces) providing application level interfaces for the communication protocols. The socket interface was first developed for BSD (Berkeley Software Distribution) UNIX 4.1 system. The socket interface supports the TCP-IP and XNS protocol implementations. The socket interface provides a set of socket based system calls which the networking applications can use to perform networking I/O. This interface mimics the file I/O calls like read(), write() etc. for the network files. The implementation of the sockets will use a protocol stack like TCP-IP to send and receive packets and hence complete the network I/O requested by the application via the socket interface. Some of the socket system calls are: socket(), bind(), listen(), accept(), connect(), read(), write(), recv(), send(), recvfrom(), sendto(), close(), and shutdown().

Another application programming interface which is used a lot under UNIX is TLI (Transport Layer Interface). The TLI interface was introduced in AT&T UNIX System V Release 3.0 in 1986. The TLI interface provides interface to the transport protocol layer. The TLI interface is implemented as a static library of function calls which are linked during the application link processes. The TLI interface uses a transport protocol stack like TCP-IP as the communication protocol. The TLI function calls consist of various different function calls such as t_open(), t_bind(), t_alloc(), t_connect(), t_accept(), t_snd(), and t_rcv(). These function calls provide the applications an API for communicating with the transport provider in the UNIX system.

The Streams I/O mechanism was first introduced by Dennis Ritchie of AT&T Bell Laboratories in 1984. The main reason for introducing the streams I/O mechanism was to provide networking protocol programmers with a UNIX kernel mechanism for implementing the various layers of OSI model as separate processes and linking them together with a very efficient full duplex I/O pipe with minimum latency in the communication path. Since the streams first appeared in the AT&T system V release 3.0 they are very widely used in various UNIX implementations to implement protocol modules. The streams mechanism is a character based full duplex communications path that links a user process and a streams device driver. This is illustrated in Figure 3-49.

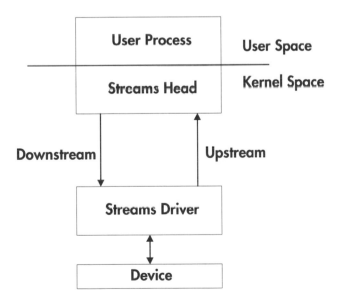

Figure 3-49. A Basic Streams Configuration

The streams device driver is responsible for communicating with the device. In the networking implementation of streams-based systems, the streams device driver is responsible for communicating with the network interface card. The streams driver implements various routines to transmit and receive packets on the network via the network interface card. It also implements the interrupt processing routine for the network interface card. In a streams based system, streams head is next to the user process. The link between the streams head and the streams driver is established when the user process opens the device and the user process can make system calls such as open(), close(), read(), and write(). Data is passed in a structure called a message. One or more modules can be inserted in a stream between the stream head and stream driver. Examples of modules which would need to present in a networking implementation using streams mechanism are TCP and IP. Figure 3-50 illustrates a basic Streams configuration.

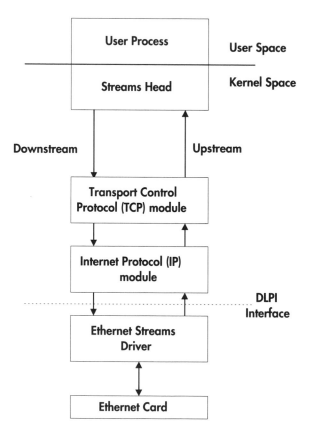

Figure 3-50. A Basic Streams Configuration

Figure 3-50 shows the TCP-IP implementation under a streams configuration. The data exchange between streams modules take place via passing a basic data type used by stream. The stream interface and messaging is discussed in detail in Chapter 8. Another major point to note here is the DLPI (Data Link Provider Interface) interface. The DLPI interface is a specification for protocol stacks implemented using the streams mechanism to communicate with the Streams based networking drivers. The DLPI interface and specification are also discussed, in detail, in Chapter 8.

UNIX Device Driver Architecture

A UNIX device driver is a set of routines that are linked into the UNIX kernel. This set of routines is responsible for translating the general I/O calls like open(), close(), read() & write() into commands that will operate the specific hardware device being accessed. The specific hardware device commands differ from one hardware to another, and hence the device driver is very dependent on the hardware that it is responsible for managing. The device driver is a glue between the operating system and the hardware. This layered architecture ensures that operating system is hardware-independent. When a hardware component of the operating system changes, the only component of the operating system that has to change is the device driver for that hardware device. The rest of the operating system remains untouched. The device drivers provide software interfaces to hardware devices. These interfaces are used by the UNIX kernel and the applications which need to access the hardware devices.

The device drivers are an integral part of the UNIX operating system. They are linked statically to the operating system. In older versions of UNIX, the device drivers could not be dynamically loaded and unloaded. The device drivers were written in C and were compiled into object modules that were linked into the UNIX kernel image using the loader (ld). The UNIX system administrator had to rebuild the UNIX kernel to add, modify or delete a UNIX device driver and reboot the system. This whole process could be very painful under UNIX. However, some of the newer UNIX implementations (1993 onwards) are supporting an interface under UNIX that allows the dynamic loading and unloading of the device drivers. The newer UNIX implementations that allow dynamic loading and unloading of the drivers are Novell's UNIXWARE and Sun Microsystem's Solaris UNIX operating systems. In general, the UNIX device drivers are linked into the kernel, and hence become integral parts of the kernel. The UNIX kernel interfaces with the device driver by using the file system commands like open(), close(), read(), and write. This makes the device driver look like an extension to the UNIX file system. The peripheral devices and their corresponding device drivers appear as extensions to the UNIX file system, and hence the interfacing to these peripherals is very simple from an application standpoint. An application would perform read() and write() operation on a peripheral in the same way as it would perform read and write on a UNIX file.

UNIX device drivers can be of two types: block or character. A block driver is usually written for devices which hold the UNIX file system such as disks etc. These devices read and write fixed sized blocks of data at any time. All transactions with such devices are block-based. The character device drivers are written for all other devices which are non block based. The peripherals which have character device drivers written for them usually interact with the UNIX operating system without any restriction on the size of data block. The user can check if a device driver is character or block by executing "ls -l /dev" command. The files under /dev directory are the device drivers. The field on the left of the device files has either a "b" which stands for block or a "c" which stands for character. A UNIX device driver has a defined set of entry points from UNIX kernel perspective. These entry points follow certain well defined rules. The different classes of UNIX drivers support different subsets of entry points. For example, a CD-ROM device does not need a write() function as the device is read only. The set of entry points also depends on whether the device driver is character or block-based. The entry points that a UNIX device driver has to support are:

- An initialization routine (called during boot process)

- Open and close routines

- Read and write routines

- I/O control interface

The above entry points are the ones that the device driver has to provide to the kernel. Besides these routines, the device driver has to provide entry points for the hardware device. One such entry point is the device driver interrupt service routine which is called when the device needs any service.

As mentioned above, the entry points of the device driver have to follow certain rules. The generic rule is that the entry point of a device driver constitutes a specific prefix followed by the generic name of that entry point. The following list shows the typical entry points for a device driver:

xx_init: This is the driver initialization routine which is called during the kernel bootup process. This routine initializes the hardware and the software components of the device driver. This routine also detects whether or not the device is present in the system. If the device is not present in the system, the initialization routine informs the kernel, and hence no resources (Interrupt, I/O address, etc.) are assigned to the device.

xx_open: The driver open routine is called by the kernel whenever any user process issues an open system call to the device. The device driver opens the device in this routine. For example, in a networking driver, the open routine might implement starting the network controller for transmit and receive operation.

xx_close: The driver close routine is called when the last process which has opened the device closes it. The device driver performs general housekeeping in the close routine and shuts the device down. In case of a networking adapter, a close routine should stop the networking controller from sending and receiving any further frames.

xx_read: The device driver read routine is called by the kernel when the user issues a read system call to a specific file which is a character device driver. The device driver read routine performs the read only if the device is not busy. If the device is busy, the read routine queues the read operation and completes it later.

xx_write: The device driver write routine is called by the kernel when the user issues a write system call to a specific file which is a character device driver. The device driver write routine performs the write if the device is not busy. If the device is busy, the write routine queues the write operation and completes it later.

xx_strategy: The strategy routine is used by block device drivers only. The kernel calls the clock device driver strategy routine to perform block read and write functions. The kernel passes a pointer to a data structure that contains a buffer to be written and a block to be read. This data structure is called buf structure. The strategy routine maintains internal queues for queuing requests among other functions.

xx_intr: The device driver interrupt service routine is called when the device generates a hardware interrupt. The interrupt service routine is very device specific and is responsible for implementing the device specific interrupt handling. Generally speaking, an interrupt service routine for a networking device driver handles interrupts such as a receive packet interrupt, a transmit complete packet interrupt, and error interrupt.

xx_ioctl: The I/O control interface routine is a special interface for functions other than general purpose read and write functions. This routine is called when the user process issues a ioctl system call. The ioctl interface is also device driver specific. In case of networking device drivers, the ioctl interface is used for obtaining statistics, and changing the multicast address list.

Please note that the xx_prefix would be replaced by the actual device driver prefix.

The UNIX device drivers are implemented following the guidelines described in the section above. The function naming convention must be followed for the device driver to operate correctly. The UNIX device drivers are part of the system kernel, and hence any operational errata can have severe consequences. Caution should be exercised when writing UNIX device drivers.

SUMMARY

This chapter provides the background information needed for the next few chapters. The development of device drivers is a very complicated process and requires a thorough understanding of the operating system internals and the hardware device. This chapter provides the basic architecture and the networking components of various operating systems. The generic device driver interface for all these operating systems is also discussed in this chapter. The operating systems covered by this chapter include DOS, Windows 3.x, Windows NT 3.x, OS/2 2.x, NetWare, and UNIX.

REFERENCES

Adams, Phillip M. and Tondo, Clovis L. 1990. *Writing DOS Device Drivers in C*. Prentice-Hall, Englewood Cliffs, NJ.

Bourne, Stephen R. 1987. *The UNIX System V Environment*. Addison-Wesley Publishing Company, Inc., MA.

Brown, Ralf and Kyle, Jim 1994. *Network Interrupts—A Programmer's Reference to Network APIs*. Addison-Wesley Publishing Company, Inc., MA.

Custer, Helen 1992. *Inside Windows NT*. Microsoft Press.

Day, Michael 1991. *Troubleshooting LAN Manager 2*. M&T Publishing, Inc.

Deitel, H.M. and Kogan, M.S. 1992. *The Design of OS/2*. Addison-Wesley Publishing Company, Inc., MA.

Duncan, Ray 1989. *Advanced OS/2 Programming*. Microsoft Press.

Egan, Janet I. and Teixeira, Thomas J. 1988. *Writing a UNIX Device Driver*. John Wiley & Sons, Inc., New York, NY.

Kettle, Peter and Statler, Steve 1992. *Writing Device Drivers for SCO UNIX— A Practical Approach*. Addison-Wesley Publishing Company, Inc., MA.

Lai, Robert S. 1992. *Writing MS-DOS Device Drivers*. Addison-Wesley Publishing Company, Inc., MA.

Norton, Daniel A. 1992. *Writing Windows Device Drivers*. Addison-Wesley Publishing Company, Inc., MA.

Pajari, George 1992. *Writing UNIX Device Drivers*. Addison-Wesley Publishing Company, Inc., MA.

Petzold, Charles 1992. *Programming Windows 3.1, Third Edition*. Microsoft Press.

Schulman, Andrew et al. 1994. *Undocumented DOS*. Addison-Wesley Publishing Company, Inc., MA.

Stevens W. Richard 1990. *UNIX Network Programming*. Prentice-Hall, Inc. Englewood Cliffs, NJ.

Thielen, David and Woodruff, Bryan 1993. *Writing Windows Virtual Device Drivers*. Addison-Wesley Publishing Company, Inc., MA.

_____. 1993. *Microsoft Windows NT Device Driver Kit—Kernel-mode Driver Reference*. Microsoft Corporation.

_____. 1993. *Microsoft Windows NT Device Driver Kit—Win32 Subsystem Driver Reference*. Microsoft Corporation.

4

NDIS 2.0.1 Drivers

INTRODUCTION AND BACKGROUND

Until the late 1980s many networking protocol stack implementations were using a completely monolithic approach to provide multiple protocol stack functionality. They had multiple protocols, and the software that drives the network card all built into the same monolithic piece of software. That meant that even if users did not need some of the functionality built into these monolithic drivers, they still had to load the complete driver.

The network software vendors for MS-DOS and OS/2, traditionally have used the monolithic/ad hoc methods to implement the protocols and the drivers that link applications to their resident network hardware. Figure 4-1 shows the monolithic architecture which was used before NDIS (Network Driver Interface Specification). In a typical implementation, the complete software is implemented as a single executable software with all layers of functionality built into it. It is also possible to implement the Datalink, Network, and Transport layers as three separate system drivers. In this case, the interfacing between the layers would be accomplished through a proprietary interface developed by the vendor, and the application would communicate via some inter-layer communication mechanism (e.g., TCP-IP sockets).

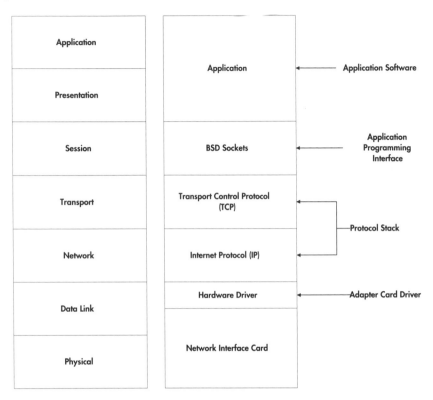

Figure 4-1. Typical networking system implementation without NDIS

   The proprietary interfaces made compatibility between applications, protocol implementation, and network cards nonexistent. This meant that a single
vendor had to supply all the possible components of the networking solution.
The vendor had to provide the hardware drivers for all popular networking
hardware, various protocol stack implementations, and applications that followed its proprietary interfaces.
   In May of 1988, 3COM and Microsoft released NDIS (Network Driver
Interface Standard). The NDIS specification defines a standard interface for
communication between MAC layer and the protocol drivers that reside on layers 3 and 4 of the OSI model. The NDIS interface is a software interface which
allows a flexible data exchange environment which is used by the protocols to
communicate with the network adapter card. The current version of the NDIS
specification is 2.0.1 dated June 1991. The NDIS specification is mainly used
in DOS and OS/2 operating systems. Figure 4-2 illustrates the NDIS specification in relation to the 7 layer OSI model.

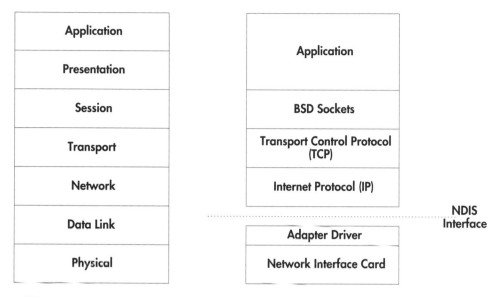

Figure 4-2. NDIS in a TCP-IP environment

The flexibility of NDIS comes from the standardized implementation used by the network industry. Any NDIS compatible protocol can pass data to any NDIS compatible MAC driver, and vice versa.

NDIS OVERVIEW

The device driver interface is described in the NDIS specification functions within the data link layer of the OSI reference model. Figure 4-3 shows the NDIS protocol driver and the NDIS MAC driver in relation to the OSI layer.

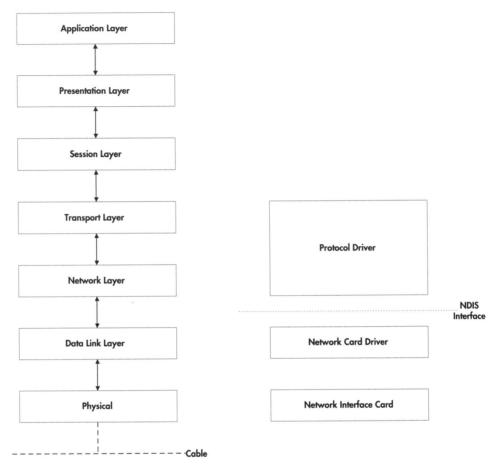

Figure 4-3. NDIS and the OSI reference model

All network software components that comply with the NDIS definitions are drivers. These drivers can be classified into two types: Protocol Drivers and Media Access Control (MAC) drivers.

The MAC driver is at the bottom of the stack and is the driver that directly controls the hardware. The remaining higher layers of the protocol stack are implemented in one or more protocol drivers. Any NDIS-compatible MAC driver can communicate with any NDIS-compatible protocol driver.

Protocol drivers provide higher-level communication services by handling the various network data formats. A protocol driver may be a device driver, a terminate and stay resident (TSR), or a transient application program.

MAC drivers provide low level access to the network adapters. MAC drivers are loaded at system initialization time and they stay in the system memory.

The primary function of the MAC driver is to transmit and receive packets. MAC driver also provides some basic network card management functions like initializing the card, and maintaining statistics.

The three most important software pieces in a NDIS environment are protocol driver, MAC driver, and the protocol manager. Figure 4-4 explains the role of these three software pieces.

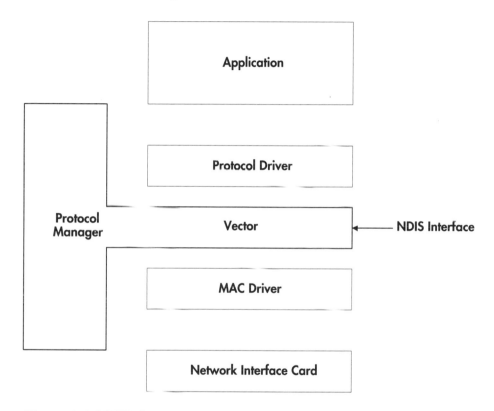

Figure 4-4. NDIS Overview

All NDIS drivers, both MAC and protocol, share a basic common structure. Each driver has an upper and lower boundary. The drivers are linked to form a stack by connecting, or binding, the upper boundary of one driver to the lower boundary of another driver during initialization. This binding process can be repeated several times, linking several drivers to form a protocol stack. The Protocol Manager is used to coordinate binding between drivers. Vector is an extension to the Protocol Manager which is introduced only when multiple protocol drivers want to bind to a single MAC driver. The Protocol Manager and the binding process is explained in more detail in the next section.

The simplest configuration of the drivers is one MAC driver bound to a single protocol driver. NDIS allows two completely parallel stacks in one machine, each with its own network card, MAC driver, and protocol driver. NDIS also allows one network card and a single MAC driver bound to two separate protocol drivers (see Figure 4-5).

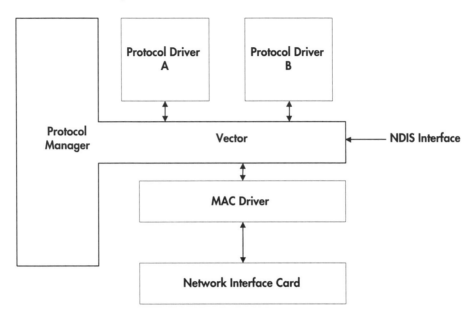

Figure 4-5. Multiple protocol NDIS setup

The above configuration allows multiple protocol stacks like TCP-IP, and XNS etc. to share the same MAC driver, and hence the same network card. NDIS environment allows a single protocol driver bound to multiple MAC drivers (see Figure 4-6). This configuration can be used to create network bridging configuration where a single protocol is connected to two networks.

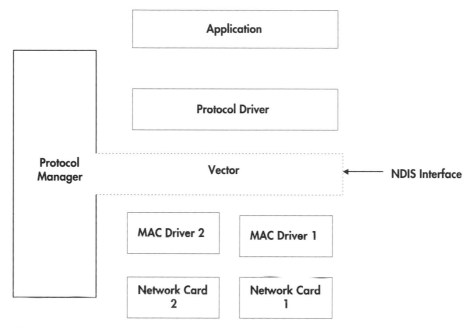

Figure 4-6. Multiple MACs with single protocol

NDIS DRIVER INITIALIZATION AND BINDING

The MAC driver has to be connected to the right protocol driver to form a NDIS protocol stack. This is accomplished in the initialization and binding process. Three components are used to manage and control the binding process. They are:

    (i) Protocol.ini (an ASCII configuration parameter file)

   (ii) Protman.dos or Protman.os2 (the protocol manager)

  (iii) Netbind.exe (a program that initiates the final binding process)

The initialization and binding process is the same for DOS and the OS/2 operating system.

The Protocol Manager (Protman.dos or Protman.os2) must be loaded prior to any MAC driver or Protocol driver being loaded. The Protocol Manager is loaded by placing an entry in the config.sys file. The Protocol Manager reads network configuration information from a file named protocol.ini. The ASCII file protocol.ini contains the instructions for assembling the protocol stack from the NDIS MAC and protocol drivers. It also contains parameters that are needed to configure the individual drivers. This file is created by the automatic installation programs or manually by the administrator.

The protocol.ini information is grouped into a number of logical sections of the form:

```
[module_name]
        parameter = value
```

The module_name is the name of the NDIS driver. There is one module section for each NDIS driver (MAC or protocol) that describes the drivers configuration. Each section can have multiple parameters. The DRIVERNAME parameter is mandatory for each module_name. Figure 4-7 shows the contents of a simple protocol.ini file that has entries for three drivers. The first is Protocol Manager. The second module section is for AMD's AM2100 adapter MAC driver. The last section is for NETBEUI protocol driver.

```
;****************************
; Example Protcol.ini file
;****************************

[PROTMGR]
        DriverNAME=PROTMAN$

[AM2100_NIF]
        DRIVERNAME=AM2100$
        INTERRUPT=3
        DMA=5
        IOADDRESS=300

[NETBEUI_XIF]
        DRIVERNAME=NETBEUI$
        BUFFSIZE=2048
        BINDINGS=AM2100_NIF
```

Figure 4-7. Sample PROTOCOL.INI File

The first parameter in all module sections is DRIVERNAME which is the same as the driver name that the driver registers with the operating system during initialization. The driver uses the DRIVERNAME entry as a key when searching Protocol.ini data for its relevant module section. Any number of additional, optional parameters entries can be included in a module section. These parameters provide the driver with the necessary configuration information.

The BINDINGS= parameter is a special parameter that is valid only for protocol drivers. The BINDINGS= parameter specifies the module name of the driver with which the protocol should attempt to bind on its lower boundary. In Figure 4-7 the NETBEUI protocol driver is instructed to bind to the AM2100 MAC driver.

The Protocol Manager (Protman.dos or Protman.os2) and the Netbind.exe program are available from 3COM or Microsoft. Vendors can obtain these executables and ship them with their products.

The Protocol Manager reads the Protocol.ini file and parses the information into a set of structures, called the Configuration Memory Image. As the config.sys processing continues, the other MAC drivers or protocol drivers are directed to initialize by the Operating System. During initialization the MAC or protocol driver must open the Protocol Manager device (PROTMAN$) and then issue a GetProtocolManagerInfo primitive to obtain from the Protocol Manager a pointer to the Configuration Memory Image. The driver then finds the section of the protocol.ini data that belongs to it and uses any parameters found there to adjust its initialization process. Finally, the driver issues a RegisterModule primitive to the Protocol Manager to register itself. The MAC driver passes some addresses to the Protocol Manager during registration. Similarly, the protocol driver passes to the Protocol Manager, the MAC driver that it needs to bind to (obtained from BINDINGS = statement). After config.sys processing completes, the Protocol Manager has a list of active NDIS drivers, their entry points and the desired bindings (specified in Protocol.ini).

The actual binding of the NDIS drivers starts when some program issues the BindAndStart primitive call to the Protocol Manager. For Microsoft operating systems this call comes from the execution of NETBIND.EXE file.

After receiving the BindAndStart primitive call, the Protocol Manager builds a binding hierarchy tree. This binding information is obtained by the Protocol Manager during the module registration earlier. Starting at the bottom of this tree (the MAC end) the Protocol Manager works up the tree and issues an InitiateBind primitive to each protocol module that needs a driver bound to its lower boundary. As part of the InitiateBind call, the driver is given a pointer to the information (common characteristic table) of the module to be bound. The protocol driver that was instructed to initiate the bind will issue a Bind primitive directly to the MAC driver to which it wishes to bind. When binding is completed, the two drivers (MAC and Protocol) will have a pointer to each other's common characteristics table (described in the next section) and therefore have access to each other's entry points. The drivers can call each other by calling each other's entry points.

MAC drivers can have only one binding at their upper boundary. To link one MAC driver to multiple protocols, the Protocol Manager inserts a component called Vector (see Figure 4-5). The Vector is responsible for the multiplexing of incoming packets. The MAC driver is bound to the Vector. The Multiple Protocol Drivers are also bound to the Vector. The net effect is that the Protocol Drivers are bound to the MAC drivers via the Vector.

Figure 4-8 summarizes the binding process in a DOS platform running the NDIS drivers.

```
Step 1:  Config.sys initialization begins
         1. Protocol Manager driver is loaded
                * Protocol Manager reads the PROTOCOL.INI file and builds
                  the Configuration Memory image
         2. MAC Driver loads
                * Opens the PROTMAN$ device
                * Calls GetProtocolManagerInfo to gain access to Protocol
                  Manager Configuration Image
                * Reads its configuration parameters from the image and uses
                  them to complete its initialization
                * Calls RegisterModele to register with Protocol Manager
                  passing its name and pointers to Protocol Manager
         3. Protocol Driver Loads
                * Opens the PROTMAN$ device
                * Calls GetProtocolManagerInfo to gain access to Protocol
                  Manager Configuration Image
                * Reads its configuration parameters from the image and uses
                  them to complete its initialization
                * Calls RegisterModule to register with Protocol Manager
                  passing its name and pointers to Protocol Manager
                * Protocol Driver also indicates the name of the MAC driver
                  that the Protocol wants to bind to
Step 2:  Binding Process Starts
         1. Netbind.exe program is executed. It opens PROTMAN$ and issues a
            BindAndStart to Protocol Manager
                * Protocol Manager builds the binding tree from
                  RegisterModule information
                * Protocol Manager starts at the bottom of the tree and
                  calls drivers with InitiateBind
                * Protocol issues a Bind to MAC
                * Protocol and MAC exchange entry points
                * Protocol and MAC call each other to transmit and receive
                  packets
```

Figure 4-8. Initialization and Binding

NDIS DRIVER DATA STRUCTURES

All protocol and MAC modules are described by an internal data structure called a Characteristics Table. The Characteristics Table consists of a master section called the Common Characteristic Table and four sub-tables. The Common Characteristic Table contains module independent information, including a dispatch address for issuing system commands (e.g., InitiateBind) to the module.

The four module specific sub-tables are chained off the Common Characteristics Table. These sub-tables define module specific parameters and the entry points used for inter-module communication. When two modules bind they exchange pointers to the Common Characteristics Table so that each module gets access to the other module's information and entry points.

Figure 4-9 lists the various fields of Common Characteristics Table.

Width	Name
WORD	Size of Common Characteristics table (in bytes) BYTE Major NDIS Version
BYTE	Minor NDIS Version
WORD	Reserved
BYTE	Major Module Version
BYTE	Minor Module Version
WORD	Module function flags bit mask 0: Binding at upper boundary supported 1: Binding at lower boundary supported 2: Dynamically bound 3-31: Reserved, must be 0
Byte[16]	Module Name (ASCII format)
BYTE	Protocol level at upper boundary
BYTE	Type of interface at upper boundary
BYTE	Protocol level at lower boundary
BYTE	Type of interface at lower boundary
WORD	Module ID filled by Protocol Manager on return from RegisterModule
WORD	Module DS (Data Segment)
Pointer	System request dispatch entry point
Pointer	Pointer to service specific characteristics table
Pointer	Pointer to service specific status table
Pointer	Pointer to upper dispatch table
Pointer	Pointer to lower dispatch table
Pointer	Reserved
Pointer	Reserved

Figure 4-9. NDIS Common Characteristics Table

The common characteristics table contains four pointers that are used to chain sub-tables off the characteristics table. These are:

- Service Specific characteristics table
- Service Specific status table
- Upper dispatch table
- Lower dispatch table

NDIS MAC and Protocol drivers have Common Characteristics Tables. They may or may not have the other 4 sub-tables. If a particular sub-table does not exist for the driver then the corresponding pointer in the Common Characteristics Table must point to NULL.

MAC Module-Specific Sub-table

The MAC module-specific sub-tables are chained off the Common Characteristics Table.

MAC Service-Specific Characteristics Table

This table contains descriptive information and parameters. All MACs use the following format for the Service-Specific Characteristics Table (see Figure 4-10).

Width	Name
WORD	Length of MAC Service-Specific Characteristics Table
BYTE[16]	Type name of MAC (ASCII): 802.3, 802.4 etc.
WORD	Length of Station Address (in bytes)
BYTE[16]	Permanent Station Address
BYTE[16]	Current Station Address
DWORD	Current functional address of adapter
Pointer	Multicast address list
DWORD	Link speed (bits per second)
DWORD	Service flags (a bit mask)
WORD	Maximum frame size
DWORD	Total transmission buffer capacity in the driver (bytes)
WORD	Transmission buffer allocation block size (bytes)
DWORD	Total reception buffer capacity in the driver (bytes)
WORD	Reception buffer allocation block size (bytes)
CHAR[3]	IEEE vendor code
CHAR	Vendor adapter code
Pointer	Vendor adapter description
WORD	RQ Interrupt level used by adapter
WORD	Transmit Queue Depth
WORD	Maximum number of data blocks in buffer descriptors supported
..	Remaining bytes are vendor specific

Figure 4-10. MAC Service-Specific Characteristic Table

MAC Service-Specific Status Table

This table contains the run time operating status and statistics of the MAC.

Width	Name
WORD	Length of status table
DWORD	Date/Time when diagnostics last run
DWORD	MAC status, a 32 bit mask
WORD	Current packet filter, a bit mask
Pointer	Pointer to media specific statistics table
DWORD	Date/Time when last ClearStatistics issued
DWORD	Total frames received
DWORD	Frames with CRC error
DWORD	Total bytes received
DWORD	Frames discarded, no buffer space
DWORD	Multicast frames received
DWORD	Broadcast frames received
DWORD	Frames received with errors (obsolete)
DWORD	Frames exceeding maximum size (obsolete)
DWORD	Frame smaller than minimum size (obsolete)
DWORD	Multicast bytes received (obsolete)
DWORD	Broadcast bytes received (obsolete)
DWORD	Frames discarded, hardware error
DWORD	Total frames transmitted OK
DWORD	Total bytes transmitted
DWORD	Multicast frames transmitted
DWORD	Broadcast frames transmitted
DWORD	Broadcast bytes transmitted (obsolete)
DWORD	Multicast bytes transmitted (obsolete)
DWORD	Frames not transmitted, timeout
DWORD	Frames not transmitted, hardware error

Figure 4-11. MAC Service-Specific Status Table

The remainder of Figure 4-11 is used for MAC statistics. Counters that are not supported must be set to 0xFFFFFFFF.

MAC Upper Dispatch Table

The MAC upper dispatch table provides dispatch addresses for the upper boundary of the MAC. The various fields of the MAC Upper Dispatch Table are listed in Figure 4-12. The various pointer fields and their functions are explained in later sections.

Width	Name
Pointer	Back pointer to Common Characteristic Table
Pointer	Generic request address
Pointer	TransmitChain address
Pointer	TransferData address
Pointer	ReceiveRelease address
Pointer	InidicationOn address
Pointer	IndicationOff address

Figure 4-12. MAC Upper Dispatch Table

MAC Lower Dispatch Table

The lower dispatch table provides addresses for the lower boundary of MAC. As MAC is the lowest software module, it does not have a Lower Dispatch Table.

Protocol Module-Specific Sub-tables

The protocol specific sub-tables are chained off the Common Characteristic Table.

Protocol Service-Specific Characteristic Table

All protocols must provide Protocol Service-Specific Characteristics Table. The table format is shown in Figure 4-13.

Width	Name
WORD	Length of table
BYTE[16]	Type name of protocol ASCII format
WORD	Protocol type code
..	Protocol specific information

Figure 4-13. Protocol service-specific characteristic table

Protocol Service-Specific Status Table

The NDIS 2.0.1 specification does not specify a format for this table.

Protocol Upper Dispatch Table

The NDIS 2.0.1 specification does not standardize the protocol upper interface.

Protocol Lower Dispatch Table

This table is chained off the protocol common characteristics table. The format of this table is defined in Figure 4-14.

Width	Name
Pointer	Back pointer to common characteristic table
DWORD	Interface flags (used by VECTOR)
Pointer	RequestConfirm Address
Pointer	TransmitConfirm Address
Pointer	ReceiveLookahead Indication Address
Pointer	IndicationComplete Address
Pointer	ReceiveChain Indication Address
Pointer	Status Indication Address

Figure 4-14. Protocol Lower Dispatch Table

FRAME DATA DESCRIPTORS

The MAC describes the frame data with a data structure called a Buffer Descriptor. The descriptor is composed of pointers and lengths that describe a logical frame. A Buffer Descriptor can contain one or more data blocks of length zero. In this case, the other fields (pointers) in the data block may not be valid and must be ignored.

NDIS 2.0.1 specification defines three types of buffer descriptors. They are:

- Transmit Buffer Descriptor
- Transmit Data Buffer Descriptor
- Receive Chain Buffer Descriptor

Transmit Buffer Descriptor

All transmit data is passed using a pointer to a Transmit Buffer Descriptor. The format of Transmit Buffer Descriptor is shown in Figure 4-15.

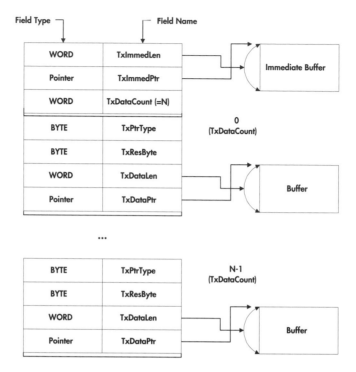

Figure 4-15. Transmit Buffer Descriptor

In this data structure the first two fields describe the immediate data, followed by TxDataCount numbers of buffer blocks. The immediate data referenced by the first two fields of the Transmit Buffer Descriptor may only be referenced during the scope of the call that references it. The maximum length of the immediate data is 64 bytes. The first three fields are followed by TxDataCount number of buffer blocks. Each buffer block describes the length of the buffer and a pointer to the buffer. The TxPtrType field of the buffer block indicates the type of pointer which is included in the TxDataPtr field. The allowed values for TxPtrType are 0=physical or 2=GDT. The TxResByte is a reserved byte and must be 0.

Transfer Data Buffer Descriptor

The transfer data buffer descriptor is used during the reception of a packet. If Receive Lookahead mechanism (described later) is being used, the protocol makes a transfer data call to get the remaining bytes. This call has a pointer to a Transfer Data Buffer descriptor attached to it. Figure 4-16 describes a Transfer Data Buffer Descriptor.

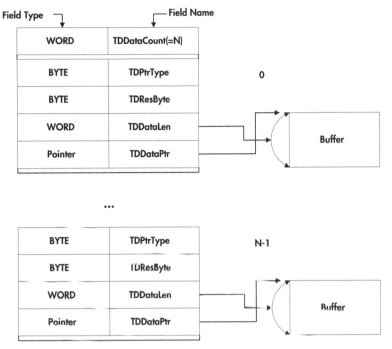

Figure 4-16. Transfer Data Buffer Descriptor

The TDDataCount field counts the number of transfer data blocks which follow in the data structure. Each transfer data block points to a buffer. The transfer data block consists of 4 fields. The first field is a TDPtrType which indicates the type of pointer (0=physical or 2=GDT). The TDResByte is a reserved byte and must be zero. The TDDataLen contains the length of the buffer pointer by the TDDataPtr field.

Receive Chain Buffer Descriptor

The Receive Chain Buffer Descriptor is used to describe the received frame (see Figure 4-17). The RxDataCount field defines the number of receive data blocks. This is followed by RxDataCount number of Receive Data Block fields. Each Receive Data Block contains a length field (RxDataLen) and a pointer to a buffer (RxDataPtr).

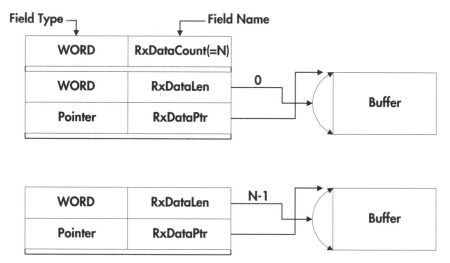

Figure 4-17. Receive Chain Buffer Descriptor

NDIS PRIMITIVES

The main purpose of the NDIS interface is to let the bound drivers communicate with each other. To that end, the NDIS is largely concerned with defining a set of functions that dictate how the MAC driver will communicate with the protocol bound on its upper layer. This section describes the various primitives that are defined for MAC-to-Protocol communication. All of the NDIS primitives are grouped in 5 categories. They are:

- Direct Primitives
- General Requests
- Status Indications
- System Requests
- Protocol Manager Primitives

Direct Primitives

The direct primitives are those that are called directly by MAC or Protocol. The calling address of these primitives is passed directly to MAC or to Protocol to accomplish direct calls. The MAC Upper Dispatch Table and the Protocol Lower Dispatch Tables are used to pass the calling address of these primitives (see sections *MAC Module-Specific Sub-table* and *Protocol Module-Specific Sub-table*). The direct primitives contain all the main functions needed to transmit and receive frames via the NDIS 2.0.1 interface.

Figure 4-18 lists all the direct primitives and the function they perform.

Name	Direction	Function
TransmitChain	P→M	Initiates transmission of a frame
TransmitConfirm	M→P	Indicates completion of frame transmit
ReceiveLookahead	M→P	Indicates arrival of received frame from MAC to Protocol
TransferData	P→M	Requests transfer of received frame (issued in response to ReceiveLookahead)
IndicationComplete	M→P	Allows Protocol to do post processing on indication
ReceiveChain	M→P	Indicates reception of a frame (attaches MAC managed buffer list)
ReceiveRelease	P→M	Returns frame buffer to the MAC that owns it
IndicationON	P→M	Enables indications from the MAC
IndicationOff	P→M	Disables indications from the MAC

P→M: Protocol to MAC; M→P: MAC to Protocol

Figure 4-18. Direct Primitives

Most of the direct primitives are used for the transmission and reception of frames. Frames move between the MAC and Protocol interfaces using these primitives. The passing of frames across the interface between Protocol and MAC is accomplished by exchanging the pointers to buffers or to a descriptor that, in turn, points to several data buffers (see the *Frame Data Descriptors* section). The objective is to avoid unnecessary, time consuming copying of data between buffers.

In the transmit process, the frame data buffers are owned by the host system and managed by the Protocol Driver. The Transmit Data Buffer Descriptor (see Figure 4-5) is used for transmit. To initiate a transmit, the Protocol assembles the frame data into buffers, puts the buffer addresses in the Buffer Descriptor structure, and calls the MAC with the TransmitChain primitive. The primitive contains a pointer to the buffer descriptor. The Protocol must build the entire packet including the MAC fields like source and destination addresses in the buffer(s).

The MAC has two options for processing the transmit. The MAC may choose one or the other at its own discretion; the Protocol must be capable of handling either. The first option is called Synchronous Transmission. In the Synchronous Transmission Option, the MAC copies all the packet data and returns to the Protocol with a code signifying that the data buffers are free and the transmit is complete. The second option is called Asynchronous Transmission. In the Asynchronous Transmission Option, the MAC can return a code signifying that the transmit is queued. This implies that the buffers are not free and the transmit has not yet completed. Later, after the MAC has copied all the transmit data, it will call the Protocol with a TransmitConfirm primitive (asynchronous response) to inform the Protocol that the transmit is complete and the buffers are now free.

An additional feature available in transmit is immediate data. The protocol has the option of beginning the Transmit Buffer Descriptor with up to 64 bytes of immediate data. This immediate data, if present, is always the first data to be transmitted. The MAC must fully process or copy this data before returning from TransmitChain call even if it will asynchronously process any remaining data buffers for the call. This feature allows the protocol to have a small, locally managed buffer that only needs to be valid during TransmitChain primitive call. A protocol may use this feature for building packet header information, or for entire small protocol generated packets, such as acknowledgments.

Packet Reception is defined in two ways. The first option for the MAC is to use ReceiveChain primitive. The MAC builds a buffer descriptor for the incoming packet and it calls the protocol with ReceiveChain. When the protocol gets the ReceiveChain indication, it has two options. The protocol can copy all of the packet data and return to the MAC specifying that the receive is complete and buffers are free. The other option is that the protocol can defer copying the buffers and return to the MAC specifying that the buffers are still in use. The protocol will later complete the processing of buffer and then call MAC with a ReceiveRelease primitive to indicate that the receive is complete and the buffers are free.

The second receive option that MAC has, is to use ReceiveLookahead and TransferData primitives. When the MAC receives a packet that it wants to present to the protocol, it indicates this by calling the ReceiveLookahead primitive of the protocol. The ReceiveLookahead call contains a pointer to a short portion of the data at the beginning of the packet. At this point, the protocol driver examines the Lookahead data to determine whether it wants the packet. If the packet is not needed, the protocol returns to the MAC indicating a reject and the receive is complete. If the packet is needed, the protocol calls the TransferData primitive of the MAC which results in the MAC transferring the remainder of the data to a protocol buffer.

Reception Indications can be controlled by the protocol by two primitives: IndicationOn and IndicationOff. A protocol may call a MAC with IndicationOff to prevent the MAC from generating any further indications and forcing the MAC to queue any indications that would be generated during the time that the indications are turned off. After calling IndicationOff, a protocol cannot block and must re-enable indications as soon as possible.

The IndicationOn function is called by the protocol to re-enable indications.

The IndicationComplete is a call from the MAC to allow the protocol to complete its indications processing. All MAC indications must be followed by an IndicationComplete call to the protocol.

General Requests

General requests are commands from a protocol to a MAC directing it to do adapter management operations like setting the station address, running diagnostics, and changing operating parameters or modes. A MAC may choose to implement any of the request functions synchronously, or asyncronously. If the MAC completes the request synchronously then it returns the status of the request on completion of the request. If the MAC chooses to complete the request asynchronously, then it returns REQUEST_QUEUED return code to inform the protocol that a given request will be processed later. In this case, the MAC will call back to the protocol's RequestConfirm entry point to indicate when the processing of the request is complete.

The NDIS driver (MAC or Protocol) contains a field by the name of "System Request Dispatch Entry" in its Common Characteristics Table. The protocol calls this entry point of the MAC when it wants to pass a general request to the MAC. The protocol passes a number of parameters including the Opcode of the request. The MAC looks at the Opcode and performs the appropriate function. If the MAC decides to complete the request asynchronously, it returns REQUEST_QUEUED. The MAC later calls the protocol's RequestConfirm entry point to indicate completion of request. The MAC obtains the RequestConfirm entry point from the Protocol's lower dispatch table.

Figure 4-19 lists all the general request primitives.

Name	Direction	Opcode	Function
InitiateDiagnostics	P→M	1	Starts MAC runtime diagnostics
ReadErrorLog	P→M	2	Gets error log from MAC
SetStationAddress	P→M	3	Sets network address of the MAC
OpenAdapter	P→M	4	Issues open request to adapter
CloseAdapter	P→M	5	Issues close request to adapter
ResetAdapter	P→M	6	Resets MAC driver and adapter
SetPacketFilter	P→M	7	Specifies filtering parameters for received packets
AddMulticastAddress	P→M	8	Specifies multicast address for the adapter
DeleteMulticastAddress	P→M	9	Removes previously added multi-cast address
UpdateStatistics	P→M	10	Forces Mac to update statistics counters
ClearStatistics	P→M	11	Forces MAC to clear statistics counters
InterruptRequest	P→M	12	Protocol Requests asyn-chrounous indication from MAC
SetFunctionAddress	P→M	13	Forces adapter to change its function address
SetLookahead	P→M	14	Sets the length of lookahead data for ReceiveLookahead
GeneralRequestConfirm	M→P	N/A	Confirms the completion of a pre-vious general request

Figure 4-19. General Request Primitives

All General Request Primitives are passed from protocol to MAC. The GeneralRequestConfirm is the only primitive which is issued by the MAC to the protocol. This primitive is issued by the MAC only when the MAC queues a previous general request and wants to indicate its completion. The MAC calls the protocol's RequestConfirm entry point to pass this primitive.

Status Indication Primitives

Status Indication Primitives are spontaneous calls from a MAC to a protocol. These inform the protocol of changes in the MAC status.

The Protocol Lower Dispatch Table contains a pointer to the status indication address. The MAC calls this address to report a status change. Before calling the protocol's status indication address, the MAC has to push MAC ID, Opcode of status indication, and some other parameters on the stack so that the protocol can identify the MAC and also the Status Indication Primitives.

Figure 4-20 lists all the status indication primitives and their functions.

Name	Direction	Opcode	Function
RingStatus	M→P	1	Indicates a change in Ring Status
AdapterCheck	M→P	2	Indicates an error from adapter
StartReset	M→P	3	Indicates adapter has started a reset
Interrupt	M→P	4	MAC response to InterruptRequest general request primitive from Protocol (see Figure 4-19)
EndReset	M→P	5	Indicates adapter has completed reset

Figure 4-20. Status Indication Primitives

System Request Primitives

All MAC and protocol modules implement a set of system request functions that support module-independent functions, such as binding. The caller of these functions is usually the Protocol Manager. The entry point for system requests is defined in the Common Characteristics Table for the module. The caller (usually Protocol Manager) obtains the system request entry point and calls it. The caller of the system requests also has to pass the system request Opcode and any parameters on the stack so that the module knows what to do. Figure 4-21 lists all the system requests, their Opcodes and functions.

Name	Direction	Opcode	Function
InitiateBind	PM→MO	1	Instructs a module to bind to another module
Bind	MO→MO	2	Exchanges Characteristics Table information with another module
InitiatePrebind (OS/2)	PM→MO	3	In OS/2 only, instructs a module to restart its prebind initialization
InitiateUnbind	PM→MO	4	Instructs a module to unbind from another module
Unbind	MO→MO	5	Deletes linkage information with another module

Figure 4-21. System Request Primitives

Note*: MO: MAC/Protocol Module, PM: Protocol Manager.*

Protocol Manager Primitives

These are the set of primitives which are used by the MAC driver or the protocol driver to access various services provided by the Protocol Manager. In DOS, the Protocol Manager primitives are called via the DOS IOCTL (I/O Control) function. The Protocol Manager provides various services. These services are demultiplexed via an Opcode specified in a structure called ReqBlock.

The ReqBlock structure is defined as follows:

```
structReqBlock{
        unsigned     Opcode;    /* Opcode for Protocol Manager Request */
        unsigned     Status;    /* Status at Completion of request */
        char far     *Pointer1; /* Pointer to Parameter 1 */
        char far     *Pointer2; /* Pointer to Parameter 2 */
        unsigned     Word1;     /* Parameter Word */
};
```

All Protocol Manager requests are supported by a single DOS IOCTL function. The MSDOS input/output control (IOCTL) functions provide a consistent and expandable interface between programs and device drivers. The MAC or protocol module obtain a handle for protocol manager device from DOS. This is accomplished by issuing a DOS open call for PROTMAN$. The IOCTL is then requested via interrupt 21 general registers loaded with the following contents.

```
AH=44h for IOCTL request
AL=02h for device input
DS:DX=Pointer for ReqBlock structure
CX=14 for the size of ReqBlock structure
BX=Handle from DOS open of PROTMAN$
```

When the IOCTL is issued, the Protocol Manager looks at the ReqBlock and performs the appropriate function. Usually, this method of communication is used for the first command between MAC/Protocol and the Protocol Manager. The first command is GetProtocolManagerLinkage. The protocol manager returns its entry point in the ReqBlock. The MAC or protocol can now make direct calls to Protocol Manager.

The ReqBlock defined above has an Opcode field. This field is used to distinguish various Protocol Manager primitives. Figure 4-22 lists all the primitives provided by the Protocol Manager.

Name	Direction	Opcode	Function
GetProtocolManagerInfo	MO→PM	1	Retrieves pointer to Configuration Image
RegisterModule	MO→PM	2	Registers a module with Protocol Manager
BindandStart	EXE→PM	3	Initiates the binding process
GetProtocolManagerLinkage	MO→PM	4	Retrieves Protocol manager entry point
GetProtocolIniPath	DP→PM	5	Gets file path for the protocol.ini file
RegisterProtocolManagerInfo	DP→PM	6	Dynamic mode, registers new configuration image
InitAndRegister	DP→PM	7	Dynamic mode OS/2, restarts prebind initialization
UnbindAndStop	DP→PM	8	Dynamic mode, Unbinds and terminates a module
BindStatus	EXE→PM	9	Retrieves information on current bindings
RegisterStatus	EXE→PM	10	Queries if a specific module is registered

Figure 4-22. Protocol Manager Primitives

Note: *MO: MAC/Protocol Module, PM: Protocol Manager, DP: Dynamic Protocol, EXE: Any Executable Program.*

The dynamic mode of the NDIS driver is explained in the *NDIS VECTOR Function* section.

NDIS VECTOR FUNCTION AND DYNAMIC BINDING

The vector allows multiple protocols to bind to a single MAC. The vector module is present in two cases. First, if multiple protocols want to communicate to a single MAC, the vector (static binding) is used. Second, the vector is always present in dynamic mode. The dynamic mode is defined as the mode that allows a protocol to be added to, or removed from an existing network configuration after the initialization process has been completed. The vector shields static MAC from dynamic binding/unbinding of protocol modules.

Static VECTOR Binding

In static mode, the VECTOR is a function that is implemented within the Protocol Manager that allows more than one protocol stack to drive a single MAC. If more than one MAC is attached to multiple protocol stacks, then a VECTOR is created for each MAC.

Multiple protocols request the use of the same MAC via the binding hierarchy contained in the protocol.ini. At the initialization time, various MACs and protocols call RegisterModule function of Protocol Manager. This tells the Protocol Manager that more than one protocol wants to bind to a single MAC. The Protocol Manager responds by inserting the VECTOR. The Protocol Manager binds to the MAC and passes the Characteristics Table that contains entry point into the VECTOR module. The MAC passes to the Protocol Manager a pointer to MAC's Characteristics Table. The Protocol Manager binds to the protocol by issuing InitiateBind and passing entry point into the VECTOR. The protocol module passes its Characteristics Table to the VECTOR. The Protocol Manager gives a Characteristics Table containing MAC's entry point to the protocol. The VECTOR filters calls going across MAC/Protocol interface.

Dynamic VECTOR Binding

Dynamic protocols can be loaded and bound after system initialization. In dynamic mode, the VECTOR function is always present for protocol/MAC intermodule communications. There can be zero, one, or more protocol stacks that bind to MAC, but the VECTOR function is still present. The presence of a dynamic environment is indicated to the protocol manager by a statement

"DYNAMIC=YES" in the Protocol Manager section of the protocol.ini file. The VECTOR shields all static binding MACs from the interactions of dynamic binding and unbinding protocol modules.

In the dynamic mode the protocol re-reads the protocol.ini. The protocol module uses the GetProtocolIni primitive to obtain the location of the protocol.ini file. A pointer to this new memory image is passed to the Protocol Manager via the RegisterProtocolManagerInfo primitive. This is required since the configuration memory image created by the Protocol Manager at INIT time is not valid at post-INIT time. After the protocol module loads, it initializes and registers with the Protocol Manager via RegisterModule. The bind sequence is initiated by an application (Netbind.exe). The bind sequence in dynamic binding is the same as in static vector binding. The protocol binds to the VECTOR, and the VECTOR binds to the MAC. After the bind, the dynamic protocol is ready for use. The main advantage of the dynamic binding is freeing system memory until it is actually needed. Hence, the protocols are only loaded when they are required, and they can be unloaded when not required.

SUMMARY

The main goal of the NDIS specification is to make the protocol stacks independent of the networking hardware. A protocol stack which is written to the NDIS specification should be able to work with networking hardware that has NDIS MAC drivers available. The networking hardware vendors do not have to be concerned with the compatibility of the their hardware with protocol stacks. If hardware vendors provide NDIS-compatible MAC drivers, then the NDIS compatible protocol stacks will work with these drivers.

The NDIS specification also allows sharing of the same networking hardware for multiple protocols in a machine. This leads to very efficient use of all the resources in a machine. The NDIS specification is well accepted and adopted in the industry. Microsoft follows it in its LAN Manager and Windows for Workgroups 3.1 products. IBM follows it in its LAN Server 2.0 and 3.0 products, and Sun Microsystems implements it in PC-NFS product line. Almost all the networking card manufacturers also support this specification.

REFERENCES

Alters, Alex 1991. "NDIS Concepts," *3TEC Journal*, Winter 1991, 3COM.

1991. "Network Driver Interface Specifications," *3COM / Microsoft Version 2.0.1*, Final Draft, June, 1991.

5

NDIS 3.0 Drivers

INTRODUCTION

The NDIS (Network Driver Interface Specification) 3.0 was introduced by Microsoft for Windows NT 3.1 Operating System. The NDIS 3.0 architecture is very different in implementation as compared to the NDIS 2.0.1 architecture (see Chapter 4). The underlying protocols and basic data transfer concepts are the same, however the architecture and implementation of NDIS 3.0 is different enough from the NDIS 2.0.1 that it is fair to consider NDIS 3.0 as a new device driver architecture for networking.

The main architecture change for NDIS 3.0 as compared to the NDIS 2.0.1 is its portability. The NDIS 3.0 driver is written in C, and as we will see later on in this chapter, it is designed to be portable across various Microsoft Operating Systems. The NDIS 3.0 data structure is designed to be 32-bits, and the NDIS 3.0 architecture is multiprocessor safe. The device architecture can handle multiple adapter cards running multiple transport protocols above it. As in other networking device driver architectures, the NDIS 3.0 architecture hides the implementation details of transport layers from the implementation details of the networking adapter hardware-related (send, receive, etc.) functions. The manufacturers of network card provide the networking hardware along with NDIS 3.0-compatible device driver. The manufacturers of protocol stacks provide the NDIS 3.0 compatible protocol stacks. These two components work together seamlessly if both follow certain guidelines documented by Microsoft regarding the implementation of NDIS 3.0-compatible MAC and protocol drivers.

Windows NT Networking Model

The Windows NT networking architecture is built of various layers of software. The breaking of a software architecture into layers allows for future expandability by allowing other functions and services to be added. Figure 5-1 shows various components of the Windows NT networking model.

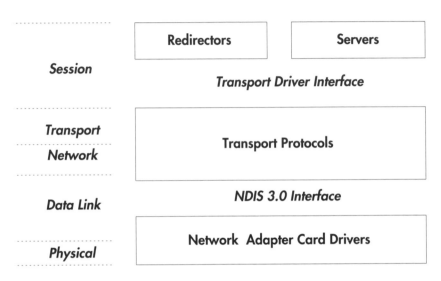

Figure 5-1. Windows NT Networking Model

Microsoft Windows NT includes integrated networking capabilities and support for distributed applications. Windows NT provides a platform on which vendors can develop distributed applications. The NDIS interface provides a unified interface at a significant break point in the architecture. Another significant break point is provided at the session layer. The TDI (Transport Driver Interface) provides a common interface for networking components that communicate at the Session Layer. These boundaries allow software components above and below a given level to be mixed and matched without reprogramming. Figure 5-2 illustrates the NDIS and TDI interface related software components.

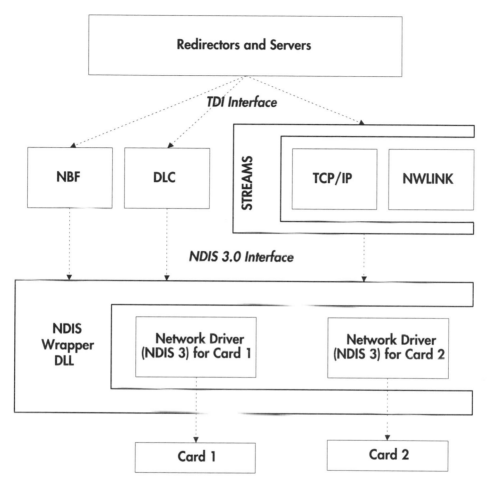

Figure 5-2. Windows NT and NDIS 3.0

In Windows NT architecture, two software components, the server and the redirector, provide server and workstation functionality. Both of these components reside above the TDI and are implemented as file systems drivers. The redirector is a component through which one computer gains access to another computer. The Windows NT redirector allows connection to other Windows NT computers as well as LAN Manager, LAN Server, and MS-Net Server. The redirector communicates with the protocol stacks to which it is bound, via the TDI. The server component entertains the connections requested by client-side redirectors and provides them with access to resources requested.

The transport protocols communicate with a network adapter card via a NDIS 3.0 compliant device driver. The Windows NT includes the following protocol stacks:

(i) **NBF**: is the Net BIOS Extended User Interface (Net-BEUI) protocol driver used in Windows NT.

(ii) **TCP/IP**: is the NDIS compliant implementation of the standard TCP-IP Protocol suite.

(iii) **NWLink**: is an NDIS-compliant implementation of Novell's IPX/SPX protocol.

(iv) **DLC**: Microsoft's Data Link Control provides an interface for access to mainframes and network-attached printers.

At the bottom of the networking architecture is the Network Card Device Driver. Windows NT supports Network Device Drivers written to the NDIS 3.0 specification. NDIS 3.0 allows a single computer to have several network adapter cards installed in it. In turn, each network adapter card can support multiple transport protocols. Each NDIS driver is responsible for sending and receiving packets over its network connection and for managing the physical card on behalf of the operating system. At its lowest boundary, the NDIS driver communicates directly with the card or cards it services, using NDIS routines to access it. The NDIS driver starts I/O on the cards and receives interrupts from them. In addition, it calls protocol drivers to indicate that it has received data and notifies its completion of an outbound transfer.

The NDIS architecture allows network drivers to be portable without containing embedded knowledge of the processor or operating system upon which it is running. The network drivers can call NDIS routines to shield themselves from platform-specific information so that they can move easily from Windows NT to future MSDOS/Windows systems. This is achieved by implementing all NDIS routines which are processor and operating system dependent in a piece of software called NDIS 3.0 wrapper. The NDIS 3.0 wrapper links together the network driver, transport protocol, and operating system routines.

Windows for Workgroup 3.11 Networking Model

Microsoft introduced Windows for Workgroups 3.1 and then 3.11 as extensions to the Windows 3.1 architecture. The Windows for Workgroups architecture builds on the architecture implemented in Windows 3.1 by providing integrated network functionality in the base operating system. The incorporation of networking components in Windows for Workgroups helps to define a standard platform for Workgroup members to communicate and exchange information with each other.

The Windows for Workgroups 3.1 uses NDIS 2.0.1 compatible adapter card drivers for running various protocol stacks. The main components of the Windows for Workgroups 3.1 network functionality consist of the following components:

- Protocol Manager (PROTMAN.DOS)

- NDIS2 Compatible Network Adapter Card Driver (*.DOS)

- Workgroup Driver (workgrp.sys)

- NetBEUI Transport Protocol

- NetBIOS Interface

- Network Redirector

- Windows for Workgroups WinNet Driver

- Windows for Workgroups Server Virtual Device Driver

Figure 5-3 describes the Windows for Workgroups 3.1 386 enhanced mode configuration.

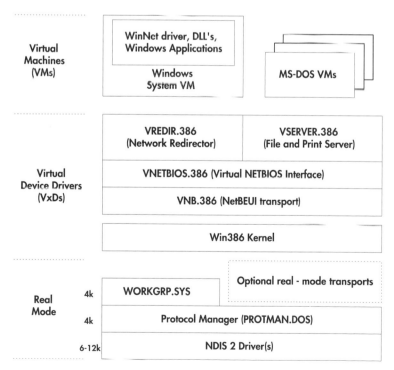

Figure 5-3. Windows for Workgroups 3.1 386 Enhanced Mode Configuration

Windows for Workgroups 3.11 extends the 32-bit architecture first delivered in Windows for Workgroup 3.1 to support 32-bit network adapter card drivers and 32-bit File Access. The 32-bit network adapter card support is obtained under Windows for Workgroup 3.11 by following the NDIS 3.0 specification. The 32-bit File Access is also implemented under Windows for Workgroups 3.11. This provides a full 32-bit code path from the network adapter card, through the network protocol and network client and server software, to the hard disk in the local computer. This provides improved performance for network I/O and disk and file I/O access.

The networking components found in Windows for Workgroups 3.11 are tightly integrated with the Windows 3.1 environment. Each network component is implemented as a Windows virtual device driver (VxD) and provides better integration than MS-DOS based solutions. The Windows for Workgroups 3.11 provides the best level of client support for Windows NT and Windows NT Advanced Server. It also has the ability to run on top of Open Datalink Interface (ODI) based network adapter card drivers and can act as a client to Novell servers.

As with the Windows for Workgroups 3.1, Windows for Workgroups 3.11 provides support for 16-bit NDIS 2.0 network adapter card. The NDIS 2 drivers are real mode drivers, and reside in the MS-DOS conventional memory. Figure 5-4 describes the configuration of Windows for Workgroups 3.11 network components when NDIS 2.0 network adapter card drivers are used.

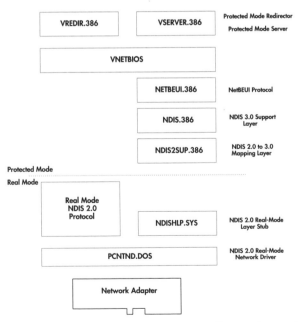

Figure 5-4. Windows for Workgroup 3.11 configuration using NDIS 2.0.1 drivers

If the network adapter card driver is NDIS 2.0 compliant, an NDIS 3.0 protocol (e.g., NetBEUI.386) requires the NDIS 2.0 mapping layer (NDIS2SUP.386) and the real-mode stub (NDISHLP.SYS) to bind to the NDIS 2.0 network adapter card driver. Also, the NDIS 3.0 protocols require the NDIS 3.0 support layer (NDIS.386) also known as NDIS 3.0 wrapper. There is a slight performance penalty in this configuration as memory is buffered into the first megabyte of physical memory in order to allow transmission and reception by the real mode NDIS 2.0 network adapter card driver.

The NDIS2SUP.386 is the NDIS2.0.1/3.0 support layer. It is also referred to as a mapper because it translates real mode addressing into protected-mode addressing and vice versa. It also translates NDIS 2.0 instructions to NDIS 3.0 instructions. NDIS2SUP appears as an NDIS 3.0 network adapter card driver to the NDIS 3.0 protocol driver and an NDIS 2.0 protocol driver to an NDIS 2.0 network adapter card driver.

The NDISHLP.SYS driver is the real-mode stub for the NDIS2SUP.386 VxD and assists in the binding process between real-mode NDIS 2.0 network adapter card drivers and NDIS 2.0 protocols.

As stated earlier, the NDIS 3.0 drivers are used in Windows for Workgroups 3.11 and Windows NT. The NDIS 3.0 differs from NDIS 2.0 in several ways:

- NDIS 3.0 uses 32-bit C language APIs to access the network adapter card driver whereas NDIS 2.0 uses 16-bit assembly language APIs.

- NDIS 3.0 provides code portability allowing OEMs to take NDIS 3.0 drivers written for Windows NT, modify them slightly, and recompile and use them for Windows for Workgroups 3.11.

- NDIS 3.0 drivers on Windows for Workgroups 3.11 run in protected mode and reside in extended memory, whereas NDIS 2.0 drivers run in real mode and reside in conventional memory.

- NDIS 3.0 network adapter card drivers cannot be used with NDIS 2.0 protocols. NDIS 2.0 protocols require the use of NDIS 2.0 network adapter card drivers.

The Windows for Workgroups 3.11 uses NDIS 3.0 native architecture also. In a pure NDIS 3.0 system, only three layers are necessary to compose the protocol stack:

- The NDIS 3.0 compliant network adapter card driver

- The NDIS 3.0 support layer (NDIS.386)

- The NDIS 3.0 protocol

Figure 5-5 depicts the configuration of Windows for Workgroups network components when NDIS 3.0 network adapter card drivers are used.

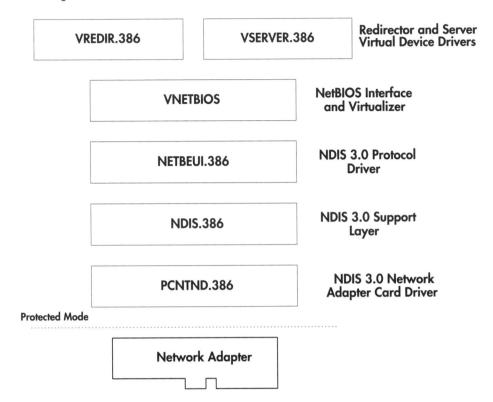

Figure 5-5. WFW 3.11 using NDIS 3.0 drivers

In addition to supporting NDIS 2.0 and NDIS 3.0 network adapter card drivers, Windows for Workgroups 3.11 also features the ability to run on top of Open Datalink Interface (ODI) drivers. Figure 5-6 explains the architecture of Windows for Workgroups 3.11 when running above ODI drivers.

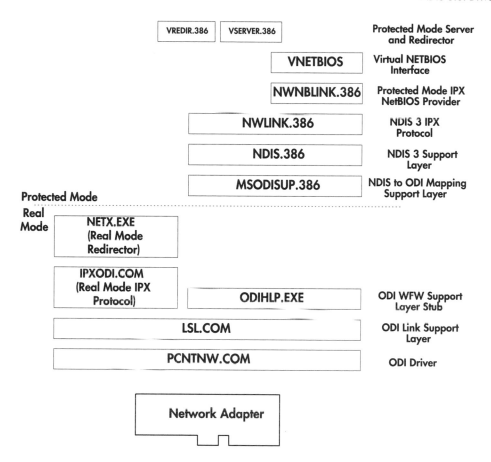

Figure 5-6. WFW 3.11 using ODI drivers

The ODI and the NDIS 2.0 device driver architectures are covered in Chapter 7 and Chapter 4, respectively. This chapter focuses on NDIS 3.0 architecture.

NDIS 3.0 ARCHITECTURE

NDIS 3.0 is a specification introduced by Microsoft for implementing networking device drivers and transport layer drivers. This specification outlines the initialization, registration, transmit, and receive paths between a Netcard Driver (device driver handling a LAN hardware) and a Transport Driver (like a TCP/IP stack).

Figure 5-7 describes the NDIS 3.0 architecture.

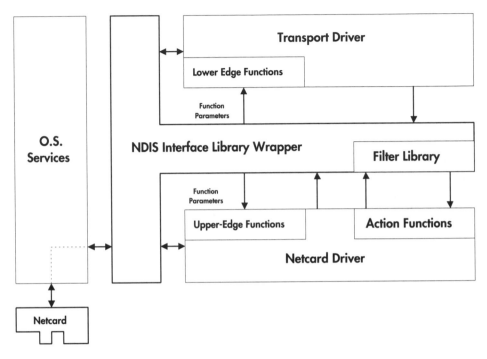

Figure 5-7. NDIS 3.0 Driver Architecture

The NDIS 3.0-based netcard and Transport Drivers use the NDIS interface library wrapper to access each other and the operating system functions. At the beginning of network communication, the Netcard Driver must register itself with the network. Each Transport Driver opens the corresponding netcard and creates a binding. After this, the bound Transport Driver can submit requests to the netcard by calling Netcard Driver functions through related wrapper functions/macros, specifying the netcard handle.

The NDIS 3.0 supports the following netcard types:

- Ethernet (802.3)
- Token Ring (802.5)
- FDDI
- WAN (point-to-point and WAN netcards)
- Local Talk
- Ethernet DIX (Digital Intel Xerox)

The NDIS 3.0 Transport drivers generate and respond to/from higher-level transports. All interactions between Transport Drivers and Netcard Drivers use the NDIS interface library wrapper. In a Windows NT implementation, the entire interface library is packaged in a DLL (Dynamic Link Library) as a set of abstract functions, with emphasis on macros for maximum performance. Both NDIS 3.0 transport and Netcard Driver link against this DLL. The main role of a wrapper function/macro is to exchange calls with network driver upper-edge functions and Transport Driver lower-edge functions, usually forwarding information from one driver to the other.

Figure 5-7 illustrates a block called Filter Library which resides within the NDIS Interface Library Wrapper. The filter libraries are special sets of NDIS interface library wrapper functions that route a received packet to a specific bound Transport Driver, based upon packet target address. The NDIS 3.0 currently supports filter libraries for Ethernet, Token Ring, and FDDI. Each filter library maintains a database for a netcard. The database associates each netcard binding with a list of addresses. The filter library processes a packet and passes it to each Transport Driver that has an address entry matching the destination address of the packet.

Netcard Driver Function Description

The Netcard Driver must provide the minimum upper-edge functions defined in Figure 5-8. A bound Transport Driver makes all calls to these functions indirectly, through the NDIS interface library. The *NDIS 3.0 Operation* section lists the exact steps which are taken to pass the entry points (addresses) of all upper-edge functions. The entry points are used to call these upper-edge functions.

The Netcard Driver can optionally make use of the NDIS interface filter libraries (Ethernet, Token Ring, and FDDI). These libraries are used to manage multiple Transport Driver bindings to a netcard. If a netcard uses a filter library, it must supply the action functions listed in Figure 5-9.

Function	Description
DriverEntry	Called by the operating system to activate and initialize the Netcard Driver.
MacAddAdapter	Called by the NDIS interface library to add support for a netcard.
MacCloseAdapter	Called by a Transport Driver to close an open binding.
MacDeferredProcessingRoutine	Called by the operating system to complete interrupt processing that MacInterrupt-ServiceRoutine does not perform.
MacInterruptServiceRoutine	Called by the O.S. as an ISR that invokes processing associated with a netcard interrupt.
MacOpenAdapter	Called by a Transport Driver to open a binding between itself and a netcard.
MacQueryGlobalStatistics	Called by the O.S. to get Netcard Driver statistics about a logical driver.
MacRemoveAdapter	Called by O.S. to remove a registered netcard.
MacRequest	Called by a Transport Driver to query or set Netcard Driver information.
MacReset	Called by a Transport Driver to issue a hardware reset to a netcard.
MacSend	Called by a Transport Driver to instruct the Netcard Driver to transmit a packet through a netcard onto the network.
MacSynchronizeFunction	Called by a Netcard Driver function to synchronize access to shared data by the ISR and non-ISR netcard functions.
MacTimerFunction	Called by the O.S. for time delayed processing after the timer expires.
MacTransferData	Called by a Transport Driver to copy the data from a received packet.
MacUnload	Called by the O.S. to instruct the Netcard Driver to unload itself.

Figure 5-8. Netcard Driver Upper-Edge Functions

Function	Description
MacChangeEthAddresses	Called by the Ethernet filter library to initiate processing if there is a change in the multicast address list for a netcard.
MacChangeFddiAddresses	Called by the FDDI filter library to initiate processing if there is a change in the multicast address list for a netcard.
MacChangeFilter	Called by Ethernet, Token Ring, or FDDI filter libraries to initiate processing when a binding sets or clears a filter class.
MacChangeGroup	Called by the Token Ring filter library to initiate processing if there is a change in the group address for all bindings.
MacChangeTrAddress	Called by the Token Ring filter library to initiate processing if the functional address for a netcard changes.
MacCloseAction	Called by one of the library to complete processing when a binding closes while the Netcard Driver is indicating a received packet to a bound Transport Driver.

Figure 5-9. Netcard Driver Action Functions for Filter Libraries

Transport Driver Functions

An NDIS 3.0-compatible Transport Driver includes the lower-edge functions as described in Figure 5-7. The minimum set of these lower-edge functions is defined in Figure 5-10. All calls to and from these functions go through the NDIS interface library.

Function	Description
DriverEntry	Called by the O.S to activate and initialize the Transport Driver.
ProtocolCloseAdapterComplete	Called by a Netcard Driver to indicate asynchronous completion of MacCloseAdapter operation.
ProtocolOpenAdapterComplete	Called by a Netcard Driver to indicate asynchronous completion of MacOpenAdapter operation.
ProtocolReceive	Called by a Netcard Driver to indicate that all or part of a packet is available for the Transport Driver to inspect.
ProtocolReceiveComplete	Called by a Netcard Driver to indicate that a receive operation has completed and to request post processing.
ProtocolRequestComplete	Called by a Netcard Driver to indicate asynchronous completion of a MacRequest operation.
ProtocolResetComplete	Called by a Netcard Driver to indicate asynchronous completion of a MacReset operation.
ProtocolSendComplete	Called by a Netcard Driver to indicate asynchronous completion of a MacSend operation.
ProtocolStatus	Called by a Netcard Driver to notify a Transport Driver of changes in netcard status.
ProtocolStatusComplete	Called by a Netcard Driver to indicate completion of status reporting for a logical adapter.
ProtocolTransferDataComplete	Called by a Netcard Driver to indicate asynchronous completion of a MacTransferData operation.

Figure 5-10. Transport Driver Lower-Edge Functions

NDIS Interface Library

The interaction between the Transport Driver and the netcard takes place with the help of NDIS interface library. The NDIS library functions accept Transport Driver requests and Netcard Driver event indications. These call the Netcard Driver upper-edge functions, Transport Driver lower-edge functions, or operating system functions to satisfy the driver requests.

In Windows NT, the NDIS interface library is implemented as a DLL (Dynamic Link Library) which the Transport Driver and the Netcard Driver link. This allows the Transport Driver and the Netcard Driver access to the functions provided by this library. The NDIS interface library functions are:

(i)   Functions called by the Netcard Driver

(ii)   Functions called by a Transport Driver

(iii)   Buffer, packet, and pool functions

(iv)   Memory functions

(v)   File Management functions

(vi)   Timer functions

(vii)   Interrupt Handling functions

(viii) Configuration functions

(ix)   Send Flag functions

(x)   Spin Lock functions

(xi)   Interlocked functions

(xii)   Non-interlocked list manipulation functions

(xiii) DMA related functions

The following sections detail the NDIS interface library functions called by the Netcard and Transport Driver. The other library functions are explained in the following sections in summary format. For detailed description of all the functions, please refer to Microsoft Windows NT Device Driver Kit.

Figure 5-11 lists all the NDIS interface library functions called by the Netcard Driver.

Function	Description
NdisCompleteCloseAdapter	Forwards netcard close data to ProtocolCloseAdapterComplete (see Figure 5-10).
NdisCompleteOpenAdapter	Forwards netcard open data to ProtocolOpenAdapterComplete.
NdisCompleteQueryStatistics	Performs post processing for asynchronous completion of a MacQueryGlobalStatistics operation.
NdisCompleteRequest	Forwards request information to ProtocolRequestComplete.
NdisCompleteReset	Forwards reset information to ProtocolResetComplete.
NdisCompleteSend	Forwards send data to ProtocolSendComplete.
NdisCompleteTransferData	Forwards information about a data transfer to ProtocolTransferDataComplete.
NdisDeregisterAdapter	Terminates the registration of a netcard with the NDIS interface library wrapper.
NdisDeregisterAdapter-ShutdownHandler	Removes a registered adapter MacShutdown function.
NdisDeregisterMac	Removes the Netcard Driver.
NdisIndicateReceive	Forwards a receive indication to ProtocolReceive.
NdisIndicateReceiveComplete	Forwards a receive complete indication to ProtocolReceiveComplete.
NdisIndicateStatus	Forwards an indication of changes in netcard status to ProtocolStatus.
NdisIndicateStatusComplete	Forwards a status complete indication to ProtocolStatusComplete.
NdisInitializeWrapper	Initializes the data structures that the wrapper associates with the Netcard Driver.
NdisMapFile	Associates a virtual address with an opened file so the Netcard Driver can access the file contents.
NdisOpenFile	Opens a disk file, typically one the Netcard Driver will download to an intelligent network card.

Figure 5-11. NDIS Interface Library Netcard Driver Functions

Function	Description
NdisRegisterAdapter	Registers with the wrapper each netcard that the Netcard Driver supports.
NdisRegisterAdapter-ShutdownHandler	Registers MacShutdown with the O.S. so the system can call the function later when it shuts down.
NdisRegisterMac	Provides the wrapper with the Netcard Driver information.
NdisTerminateWrapper	Completes Netcard Driver removal from the wrapper connection.
NdisUnmapFile	Disassociates a virtual address from a file previously mapped by NdisMapFile.
NdisWriteErrorLogEntry	Writes an I/O error log.

Figure 5-11. NDIS Interface Library Netcard Driver Functions (Continued)

Figure 5-12 lists all the NDIS interface library functions called by a Transport Driver. These functions are called by the Transport Driver to communicate with the Netcard Driver.

Function	Description
NdisCloseAdapter	Forwards a netcard close request to MacCloseAdapter.
NdisDeregisterProtocol	Deregisters the Transport Driver from the wrapper connection after the Netcard Driver has unloaded itself.
NdisOpenAdapeter	Forwards a netcard open request to MacOpenAdapter.
NdisRegisterProtocol	At initialization, provides the wrapper with information about the Transport Driver.
NdisRequest	Forwards to MacRequest a request to query or set Netcard Driver information.
NdisReset	Forwards a reset request to MacReset.
NdisSend	Forwards a packet send request to MacSend.
NdisTransferData	Forwards a transfer data request to MacTransferData.

Figure 5-12. NDIS Interface Library Transport Driver Functions

The following discussion provides the overview of various other functions provided by NDIS interface library.

The Netcard and Transport Driver allocate and manage virtual memory buffers in the host. The NDIS interface library provides functions that allow the drivers to allocate, construct, and inspect such buffers. The NDIS 3.0 defines a packet as a chain of one or more buffers that compose a network message.

A NDIS buffer is described by a structure NDIS_BUFFER. A packet is described by a structure of type NDIS_PACKET. The NDIS interface library includes functions that NDIS 3.0 drivers can call to allocate, construct, and inspect packets. The packet descriptor is used by the Netcard Driver and the Transport Driver to send and/or receive packets from the network.

The NDIS interface library provides a set of memory functions that translate general operating system requests into operating system-specific calls. This allows a standard portable interface that supports the various operating environments for NDIS 3.0 drivers. The memory functions allow:

- Allocate/DeAllocate memory
- Map/UnMap I/O space
- Read/Write I/O space
- Read/Write Memory Space
- Copy From/To memory

The NDIS interface library provides file management functions that allow the Netcard Driver or the Transport Driver to access and manipulate system files. The timer functions allow the Netcard Driver or the Transport Driver to suspend execution for a specified period of time.

The NDIS interface library provides several interrupt handling functions for use in a multiprocessor environment. These functions provides the initialization, removal, and synchronization of interrupts. The NDIS interface library provides configuration functions. These functions allow the drivers to read configuration information from the configuration registry.

The NDIS interface library spin lock functions deal with initialization, acquisition, release and freeing of spin locks. A spin lock is a low-level, synchronization mechanism defined by Windows NT kernel. A driver or any other component can use the spin lock to synchronize access to a shared resource, particularly in a multiprocessor machine.

The NDIS interface library also provides certain DMA-related functions. These DMA functions allow the Netcard Driver to allocate/free DMA channels. It also allows the Netcard Driver to set up DMA transfers.

Filter Libraries

Filter libraries are special sets of NDIS interface library wrapper functions that route a packet from the Netcard Driver to specific bound Transport Drivers. Microsoft provides filter libraries for Ethernet, FDDI, and Token Ring Networks. The Netcard Driver passes a received packet to the filter library appropriate to the network. The filter looks at the destination address of the received packet and passes the packet onto each Transport Driver that has its source address match the destination address of received packet.

This section discusses the Ethernet Filter library. The FDDI and Token Ring libraries are similar and are covered in Windows NT Device Driver Kit (DDK).

Function	Description
EthChangeFilterAddress	Changes the multicast address list.
EthCreateFilter	Creates and initializes the Ethernet filter library database associated with one netcard.
EthDeleteFilter	Deletes memory associated with the Ethernet filter library database.
EthDeleteFilterOpenAdapter	Deletes netcard binding filter information from the Ethernet filter library database.
EthFilterAdjust	Adjusts the Ethernet filter library database.
EthFilterIndicateReceive	Indicates a receive packet.
EthFilterIndicateReceiveComplete	Indicates to all bound Transport Drivers that EthFilterIndicateReceive has returned.
EthNoteFilterOpenAdapter	Adds a binding filter to the Ethernet filter library database.
EthNumberOfOpen-FilterAddresses	Counts the number of Ethernet filter library database multicast addresses in a binding filter.
EthQueryGlobalFilterAddresses	Queries the Ethernet filter library database for a list of multicast addresses associated with a particular netcard.
EthQueryOpenFilterAddresses	Queries the Ethernet filter library database for a list of multicast addresses associated with a binding.
EthShouldAddressLoopBack	Determines if the Netcard Driver should place a packet on the netcard logical adapter loop-back queue to avoid transmitting the packet on the network.

Figure 5-13. Ethernet Filter Library Functions

Statistics

The Netcard Driver has to maintain certain mandatory statistics. The Netcard Driver may also maintain certain optional counters. The NDIS 3.0 classifies each statistical or operational counter by an Object Identifier (OID). The Netcard Driver and the Protocol Driver can access these OIDs by NdisRequestQueryInformation, NdisRequestSetInformation, and MacQueryGlobalStatistics. The NDIS 3.0 OIDs are four-byte values, encoded as follows:

Most significant byte:

> 0x00   General Information
>
> 0x01 — 0xfe Media-specific information
>
> > 0x01 802.3
> >
> > 0x02 802.5
> >
> > 0x03 FDDI
> >
> > 0x04 Async
> >
> > 0x05 LocalTalk
>
> 0xff Implementation-specific information

Second most significant byte:

> 0x01 Operational characteristics
>
> 0x02 Statistics

Third most significant byte:

> 0x01 Mandatory
>
> 0x02 Operational

The fourth most significant byte is a unique value differentiating the OID from the others with the same three high bytes.

Figure 5-14 Lists the general operational characteristics and general mandatory statistics.

OID (hex)	Length	Name
General Operational Characteristics		
00 01 01 01	n * 4	List of supported OIDs
00 01 01 02	4	Hardware Status
00 01 01 03	n * 4	Media types supported
00 01 01 03	n * 4	Media types in use
00 01 01 05	4	Max. Receive lookahead size
00 01 01 06	4	Max frame size
00 01 01 07	4	Link Speed
00 01 01 08	4	Transmit buffer space
00 01 01 09	4	Receive buffer space
00 01 01 0A	4	Transmit block size
00 01 01 0B	4	Receive block size
00 01 01 0C	4	Vendor adapter code
00 01 01 0D	Variable	Vendor adapter descriptor
00 01 01 0E	4	Current packet filter
00 01 01 0F	4	Current lookahead size
00 01 01 10	2	Driver version number
General Statistics (Mandatory)		
00 02 01 01	4	Frames transmitted OK
00 02 01 02	4	Frames received OK
00 02 01 03	4	Frames not transmitted or transmitted with error
00 02 01 04	4	Frames received with error
00 02 01 05	4	Frames missed, no buffers

Figure 5-15. General Operational Characteristics and Statistics

Figure 5-15 list the Ethernet (802.3) specific operational characteristics and mandatory statistics.

OID (hex)	Length	Name
802.3 Operational Characteristics		
01 01 01 01	6	Permanent Station Address
01 01 01 02	6	Current Station Address
01 01 01 03	n * 6	Current multicast address list
01 01 01 04	4	Max. size of multicast address list
802.3 Mandatory Statistics		
01 02 01 01	4	Frames received with alignment error
01 02 01 02	4	Frames transmitted with 1 collision
01 02 01 03	4	Frames transmitted with > 1 collision

Figure 5-15. 802.3 Specific Operational Characteristic and Statistics (mandatory)

NDIS 3.0 OPERATION

These are three main modules which constitute the NDIS 3.0 sub-system:

- Netcard Driver
- NDIS interface library
- Transport driver

These three modules interact with each other while performing functions like sending a packet, receiving a packet, and so on. This section defines the main operations involved under NDIS 3.0.

Initializing Wrapper and Registering Drivers

The NDIS 3.0 initialization and registering of drivers process is described in Figure 5-16.

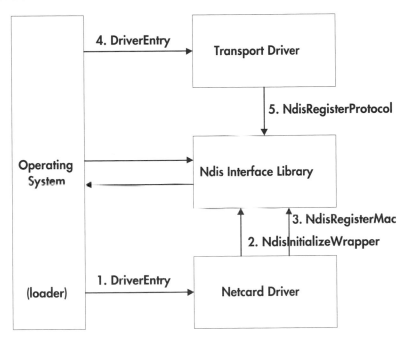

Figure 5-16 Initializing Wrapper and Registering Drivers

The operating system creates a Netcard Driver object and calls the Netcard Driver at its DriverEntry function. The Netcard Driver object is a software object managed by the operating system. The software object contains information about the netcard, such as name, network address, and the current state of driver in relation to the hardware, such as number of bindings, or binding handler. The driver object also keeps track of buffer resources used for sending and receiving data.

The Netcard Driver's DriverEntry function is passed the driver object pointer. The DriverEntry in turn calls NdisInitializeWrapper and passes the address of the driver object.

After NdisInitializeWrapper returns, the Netcard Driver calls NdisRegisterMac to register itself as a driver on the network. The Netcard Driver constructs a data structure that contains the addresses of all functions that it needs to provide to NDIS Interface Library (Netcard Driver upper-edge functions) and passes that data structure via NdisRegisterMac.

When all Netcard Drivers for the network have registered, the O.S. loader calls the DriverEntry function of a Transport Driver. The Transport Driver makes a NdisRegisterProtocol to register itself with NDIS Interface Library. The NDIS interface library allocates a block of memory for driver information, including addresses of event handlers and capability data, and provides the Transport Driver with a handle to this information. When the Transport Driver is registered, it is ready to send/receive packets to/from the network. The NDIS interface library has to register all netcards before the tx/rx process starts.

Registering Netcards

Figure 5-17 explains the NDIS interface library registering the netcards to each Netcard Driver on network.

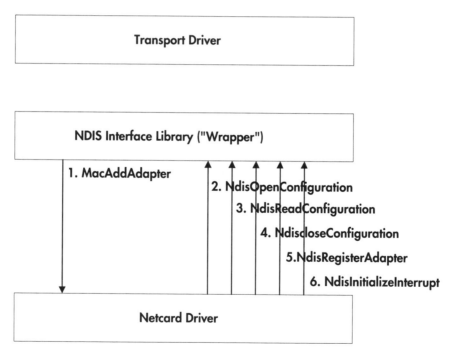

Figure 5-17. Registering a Netcard

The registration process starts by the NDIS Interface Library calling MacAddAdapter. The Netcard Driver calls NdisOpenConfiguration, NdisReadConfiguration, and NdisCloseConfiguration to read the configuration registry database to determine parameters for the netcard. The Netcard Driver obtains the necessary configuration data and then calls NdisRegisterAdapter. This allows the NDIS interface library wrapper to recognize the netcard name when the Transport Driver opens the card later.

The Netcard Driver can further initialize the netcard by calling the NDIS interface library functions such as NdisAllocateMemory, NdisMapIoSpace, and NdisAllocateDmaChannel. When it has completely initialized the netcard, the Netcard Driver must initialize the interrupts by calling NdisInitializeInterrupt. After the registration of one netcard is complete, the NDIS interface library completes the above procedure for the remainder of the netcards.

Opening a Netcard

The Transport Driver has to open a netcard before it can send or receive from the netcard. A Transport Driver opens any netcard to which it is bound by calling MacOpenAdapter through NdisOpenAdapter. The NdisOpenAdapter writes an NDIS binding handle to the Transport Driver. The Transport Driver must keep track of this handle, which is its only link to the Netcard Driver and which the Transport Driver must use in all future calls to the NDIS interface library.

The NdisOpenAdapter calls MacOpenAdapter to inform the Netcard Driver that Transport Driver has been bound to the associated netcard. The Netcard Driver starts the netcard hardware.

The MacOpenAdapter can complete synchronously or asynchronously. If the MacOpenAdapter operation is completed synchronously, it returns a status code other than NDIS_STATUS_PENDING. If the MacOpenAdapter returns a status code NDIS_STATUS_PENDING, this indicates that MacOpenAdapter is not complete. When the MacOpenAdapter completes (asynchronously) then the Netcard Driver calls NdisCompleteOpenAdapter which in turn calls ProtocolOpenAdapterComplete.

After the MacOpenAdapter is complete, a number of network activities such as sending data, and receiving data, can be accomplished. The MacOpenAdapter function call flow sequence is listed in Figure 5-18.

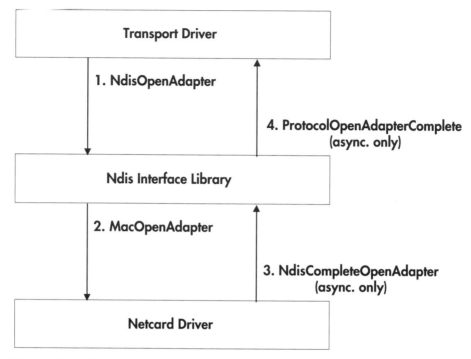

Figure 5-18. Opening a Netcard

Sending Data

The Transport Driver creates a packet consisting of data and header information. The Transport Driver can send additional send information to the Netcard Driver by optionally calling NdisSetSendFlags. This additional information is returned by the Netcard Driver by calling NdisQuerySendFlags (see Figure 5-19).

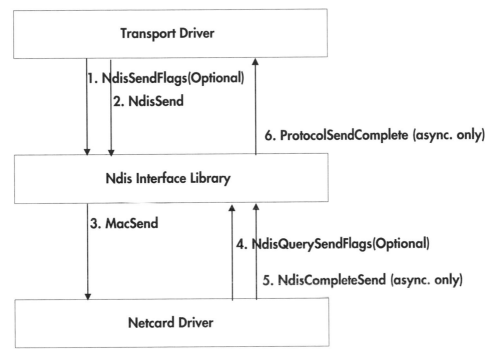

Figure 5-19. Sending Data

The Transport Driver initiates a send by calling NdisSend. The NDIS Interface Library forwards this call and the associated packet data to Netcard Driver by calling MacSend. The MacSend translates the packet into network data frame and carries the send operation.

The Netcard Driver can complete send synchronously or asynchronously. If the Netcard Driver completes the send operation asynchronously, it sends a status code NDIS_STATUS_PENDING for MacSend and then calls NdisCompleteSend asynchronously. The NDIS interface library calls ProtocolSendComplete asynchronously to indicate to the Transport driver that a send is completed and to pass the ownership of packet to the Transport Driver.

Receiving Data

The Figure 5-20 indicates the complete receive path under NDIS 3.0.

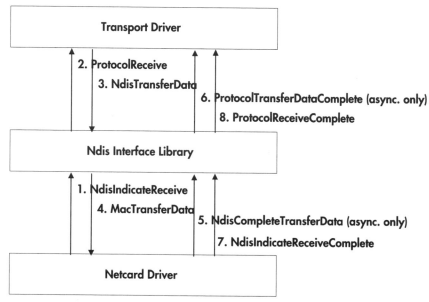

Figure 5-20. Receiving Data

When a Netcard Driver receives a data packet over the network, it issues a call to NdisIndicateReceive. The NDIS interface library calls ProtocolReceive with all the binding context it received from NdisIndicateReceive.

The Transport Driver initiates the transfer of data packet by calling MacTransferData through NdisTransferData. The Netcard Driver copies the received data frames into the packet structure that the Transport Driver provides in its call.

The MacTransferData can complete synchronous or asynchronous. If the function is not able to complete the transfer data operation before returning, it returns status code NDIS_STATUS_PENDING. The Netcard Driver later calls NdisCompleteTransferData which is followed by NDIS interface library calling ProtocolTransferDataComplete for completing the reception of copied data frame.

Any post receive processing is indicated by the Netcard Driver by calling NdisIndicateReceiveComplete which calls ProtocolReceiveComplete.

Indicating Status

The Netcard Driver calls NdisIndicateStatus to communicate a status change to the bound Transport Driver along with the binding context, its only link to the Transport Driver. The NDIS interface library forwards the call to the Transport Driver via ProtocolStatus call. The Netcard Driver calls NdisIndicateStatusComplete which in turn calls ProtocolStatusComplete to stop indicating the status changes (see Figure 5-21).

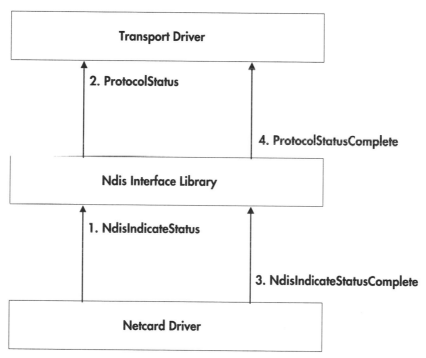

Figure 5-21. Indicating Status

Querying and Setting Netcard Driver Capabilities

The NdisRequest and MacRequest calls are used to query and set netcard information. The Transport Driver calls NdisRequest along with a data structure called NDIS_REQUEST and passes it to NDIS interface library. The NDIS interface library calls MacRequest (see Figure 5-22). The NDIS_REQUEST structure contains the OID (see the *Statistics* section) for an object that it wants to query or set. MacRequest either queries or sets the object that corresponds to the Transport Driver provided OID. The MacRequest fills in the NDIS_REQUEST data structure and passes it back to the Transport Driver.

The MacRequest can complete synchronously or asynchronously. If MacRequest completes asynchronously, the function returns NDIS_STATUS_PENDING, and the Netcard Driver later completes the request operation by a call to NdisCompleteRequest. The NdisCompleteRequest function forwards the call to ProtocolRequestComplete for post processing.

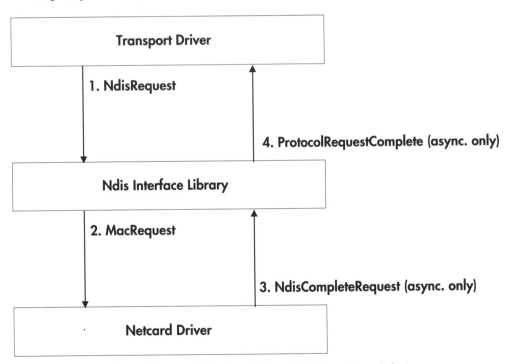

Figure 5-22. Querying and Setting Netcard Driver Capabilities

Querying Global Statistics

The NDIS interface library acts as a network management entity and calls MacQueryGlobalStatistics to make a statistics request. This function is similar to MacRequest. The MacQueryGlobalStatistics returns all the global statistics counters.

Figure 5-23 illustrates the functional flow of calls.

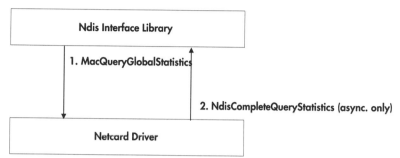

Figure 5-23. Querying Global Statistics

Closing Netcards

Figure 5-24 shows the function call flow for closing netcards.

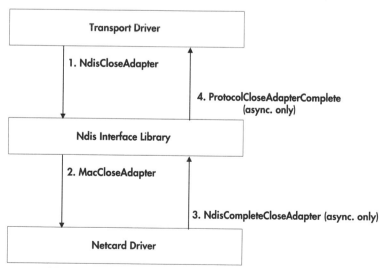

Figure 5-24. Closing Adapters

As shown in Figure 5-24, a Transport Driver unbinds itself from a netcard by calling MacCloseAdapter via NdisCloseAdapter along with the NDIS binding handle. The Netcard Driver uses MacCloseAdapter to close the netcard binding, cancel the ISR, and prevent further requests to the netcard. After the Netcard Driver has closed the netcard binding, the Transport Driver cannot submit further requests on this binding.

The MacCloseAdapter can also be asynchronous, returning NDIS_STATUS_PENDING.

Resetting a Netcard

Figure 5-25 shows the resetting sequence of the netcard. The Transport Driver initiates a reset of a netcard by calling MacReset through NdisReset along with NDIS binding handle. MacReset tells the Netcard Driver to issue a hardware reset to the netcard and also set its own reset software state.

The Netcard Driver calls the ProtocolStatus via NdisIndicateStatus twice during reset. This is to deliver two status codes: NDIS_STATUS_ RESET_START and NDIS_RESET_STATUS_END. When the Netcard Driver no longer needs to indicate status changes, it calls ProtocolStatusComplete through NdisIndicateStatusComplete.

MacReset can complete synchronously with a success or error status code, or asynchronously with NDIS_STATUS_PENDING. If MacReset completes asynchronously, the Netcard Driver calls ProtocolResetComplete through NdisCompleteReset to request post processing.

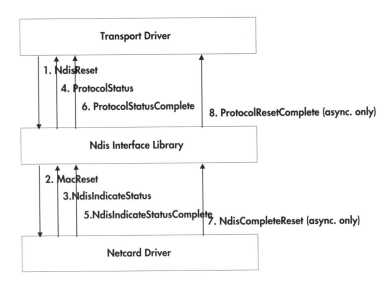

Figure 5-25. Resetting a Netcard

Removing a Netcard

When all netcard bindings have been closed, the NDIS interface library initiates removal of the associated netcard (see Figure 5-26). The library calls MacRemoveAdapter. The Netcard Driver removes associated resources by calling NdisRemoveInterrupt. After all resource removal, the driver calls NdisDeregisterAdapter. At this point, the NDIS interface library informs the operating system that the netcard has been removed.

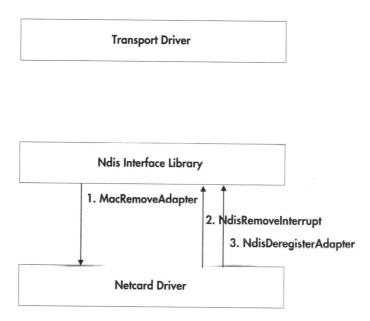

Figure 5-26. Removing a Netcard

Unloading and Deregistering Drivers

The sequence of events described here takes place when the network is shutting down. The NDIS interface library calls MacUnload (see Figure 5-27). The MacUnload function frees allocated resources. The Netcard Driver calls NdisDeregisterMac to remove the Netcard Driver from the NDIS interface library connections.

If the Netcard Driver is the last driver being unloaded, MacUnload makes a call to NdisTerminateWrapper to close the NDIS interface library wrapper.

The Transport Driver calls NdisDeregisterProtocol when it wishes to unload.

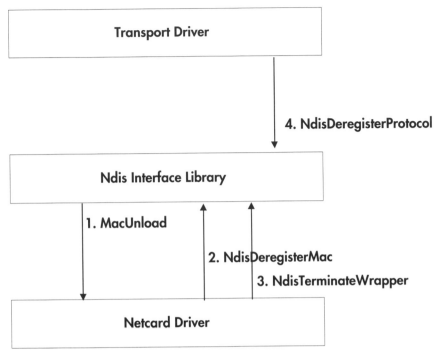

Figure 5-27. Unloading Drivers

SUMMARY

This chapter discussed the NDIS 3.0 networking device driver interface from an architectural and operational standpoint. The chapter discussed how the NDIS 3.0 interface works, how the services are implemented, and how they are used by MAC and Protocol drivers.

The NDIS 3.0 interface can be modeled as a set of abstract services, that when requested, cause a request to be submitted to another NDIS module, or cause a local action to be performed. The main purpose of the NDIS interface is to allow protocols to send and receive packets on a network.

NDIS 3.0 is implemented as a distributed interface, so that the NDIS interface requests in a caller's code are implemented as macros or function calls. This reduces the extra overhead of routing and clearing formalized requests.

The NDIS 3.0 architecture is implemented in Microsoft's Windows NT and Windows for Workgroup 3.11 products. It is also the networking interface for the new version of Windows 3.1x code-named "Chicago" product from Microsoft. Although Microsoft supports ODI architecture from Novell, NDIS 3.0 is the strategic networking interface for Microsoft.

REFERENCES

Custer, Helen 1992. *Inside Windows NT*. Microsoft Press.

_____. *Microsoft Windows NT Device Driver Kit, Network Drivers*, Microsoft Corporation, 1 Microsoft Way, Redmond, WA.

_____. *Microsoft NT Resource Guide, Volume 1*, Microsoft Corporation, 1 Microsoft Way, Redmond, WA.

_____. *Microsoft LAN Manager*, Network Driver Interface Specification (NDIS), Version 3.0, Microsoft Corporation, 1 Microsoft Way, Redmond, WA.

6

Packet Driver

INTRODUCTION

This chapter describes the development and internals of Packet Driver Architecture. The packet driver architecture is commonly used in the TCP-IP world. This chapter introduces the TCP-IP protocol suite evolution. It explains the TCP-IP protocol and its application under IEEE 802 LANs. It introduces various protocols which belong to the suite of the TCP-IP protocol.

This chapter covers, in complete detail, the packet driver architecture. It explains the DOS environment which is the most commonly used environment for packet driver operation. It explains the packet driver internals with respect to the packet driver specification. The packet driver specification is compared to the NDIS and ODI driver models. The interoperability between NDIS, ODI, and packet driver specification is also covered under this chapter. Various packet driver internal classes and functions are described, in detail, in this chapter.

TCP-IP (TRANSMISSION CONTROL PROTOCOL–INTERNET PROTOCOL)

This section describes the TCP-IP protocol evolution. It describes the TCP-IP protocol suite, its members, and the functionality provided by various members of the TCP-IP family of the protocols. The operation of the TCP-IP protocols over IEEE 802 LANs is covered here.

Evolution of TCP-IP

The TCP-IP Internet Protocol Suite commonly referred to as TCP-IP (after the name of its two main standards TCP and IP), evolved from the research funded by the Defense Advanced Research Projects Agency (DARPA). (See Figure 6-1.) The DARPA technology includes a set of network standards that specify the details of how computers communicate, as well as a set of conventions for interconnecting networks and routing traffic.

The DARPA belongs to the U.S. Department of Defense. The military need- ed a non-proprietary way of connecting widely different computers that could perform peer-to-peer communications at high data rates. DARPA funded researchers at Bolt Beranek & Newman (BBN) to provide the hardware and routers, and to manage the network infrastructure. DARPA also contracted with a number of educational and defense-related research institutions to implement the new protocols on various host systems, as well as the applica- tions that would allow end users to access the network.

The TCP-IP protocol suite is designed to be media-independent so that it could be routed across an internet made up of many different types of media connected together. This is achieved by layering an "internet protocol (TCP- IP)" above the low-level, media specific framing and addressing schemes.

To encourage University researchers to adopt and use the new protocol suites, DARPA contracted the University of California at Berkeley to integrate the protocols with its software distribution. At that time, most university com- puter science departments were running a version of UNIX operating system available in the University of California's Berkeley Software Distribution, com- monly called Berkeley UNIX or BSD UNIX. By integrating TCP-IP with BSD, DARPA was able to reach the computer science departments of over 90% of the Universities in the U.S. The TCP-IP protocol suite became a defacto standard to connect computers over a local area network.

Today, all major corporations and universities are connected together using the TCP-IP family of protocol suite. In addition, many companies use the TCP- IP protocols on their internal corporate networks.

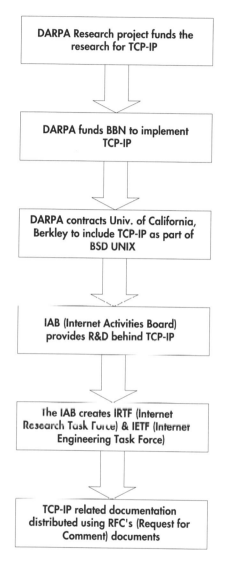

Figure 6-1. Evolution of TCP-IP

Introduction to TCP-IP Protocol Suite

A networking protocol is a set of rules that governs communications between connected computers. The communication protocols that run over IP, alongside TCP protocol, are grouped together and are often referred to as TCP-IP protocol suite.

The generic term "TCP-IP" usually means anything and everything related to the specific protocols of TCP (Transmission Control Protocol) and IP (internet Protocol). It also is used to refer to some other protocols, for example, UDP, ARP, and ICMP. Some applications that are also part of TCP-IP suite are TELNET, FTP and RCP.

The architecture of the TCP-IP protocol suite is shown in Figure 6-2. Figure 6-2 shows the TCP-IP architecture, including applications, transport protocols and the Internet protocol. The TCP-IP applications use the TCP protocol or UDP protocol to transport data across a network. The applications include file transfer, terminal emulation, mail, network management, and printing.

The Transport Control Protocol (TCP) offers a connection oriented byte stream. The TCP service is reliable, and it transfers data sequentially between local or remote hosts. TCP guarantees that data reaches its destination and retransmits any data that did not get through.

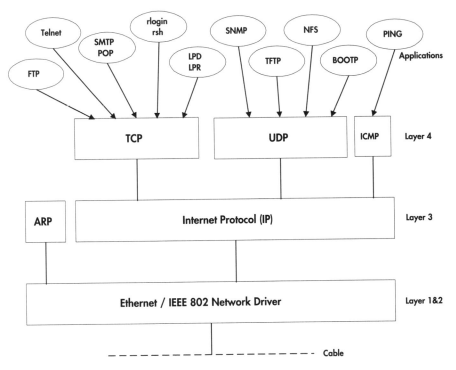

Figure 6-2. TCP-IP Family Protocols

User Datagram Protocol (UDP) is a connectionless datagram delivery service that does not guarantee delivery. UDP does not maintain an end-to-end connection with the remote UDP modules. UDP pushes the datagram out on the network and accepts incoming datagrams off the network.

Internet Control Message Protocol (ICMP) sends error and control messages from routers or hosts to the message originator. ICMP is considered as a network management protocol which uses the services provided by the IP layer.

Internet Protocol (IP) receives data bytes from data link layer, assembles them into an IP datagram, and routes it to the appropriate protocol address on a subnet. If the IP datagram is for this host, then IP will pass it to TCP or UDP protocol. If the IP datagram is for a host residing on another subnetwork, then IP will send the datagram to a router to be forwarded to that subnetwork.

Address Resolution Protocol (ARP) is used to translate IP addresses to Ethernet addresses. The translation is done for outgoing IP packets, because this is when the IP header and the Ethernet header are created. Each TCP-IP protocol suite implementation maintains an ARP table. If the ARP table cannot be used to translate an address, an ARP request packet is transmitted with a broadcast ethernet address. All ethernet nodes receive this packet. If the receiving ethernet node's IP address matches the IP address of the ARP request, the receiving node has to respond with an ARP response which contains its IP address. This is how the ARP table is built in the host machine.

The TCP-IP datagram format is shown in Figure 6-3.

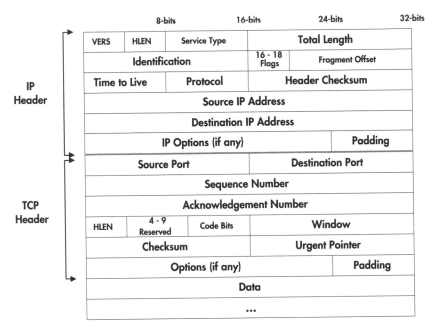

Figure 6-3. TCP-IP Datagram Format

The UDP-IP datagram format is shown in Figure 6-4.

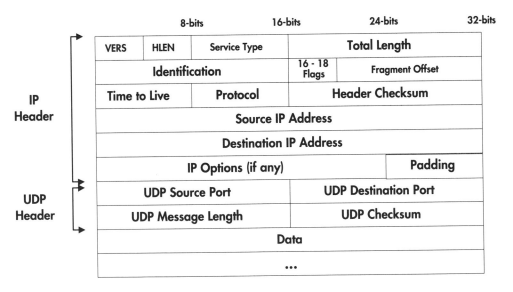

Figure 6-4. UDP Datagram Format

TCP-IP and the Packet Driver

The packet driver is the generic interface between the TCP-IP protocol stack and the software drivers responsible for driving the communication hardware (ethernet hardware). Figure 6-5 shows the relationship between the 7 layer OSI model and the TCP-IP protocol stack implementation.

The packet driver interface hides the hardware dependent functions from the protocol stack. It also hides the protocol dependent issues from the networking hardware. The packet driver interface is typically implemented in the TCP-IP solutions running on an IBM PC-AT under DOS operating system.

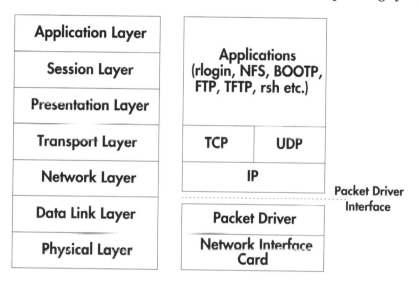

Figure 6-5. TCP-IP and Packet Driver Relationship

PACKET DRIVER ARCHITECTURE

Figure 6.5 illustrates the typical implementation of a networking protocol software and hardware. A very specific piece of software which drives and manages the networking hardware is called the networking device (hardware) driver. The networking driver operates at Media Access Control (MAC) layer, and hence it is often referred to as MAC layer driver. In a typical networking stack implementation, the MAC driver hides the details of a specific network card from the communication protocol using the card. This is illustrated in Figure 6-6.

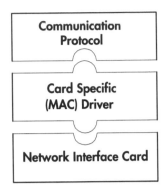

Figure 6-6. The MAC Layer Driver

It is possible to have the MAC driver functions built into the Protocol Stack. This type of implementation, however, makes the protocol implementation dependent upon the network card. As there are a wide variety of network cards available, the protocol stack implementation must have a version available for each network card. Also, only one piece of software can reliably control the Network Card. This means that in a monolithic architecture one cannot run two protocol stacks on the same network card. These two restrictions make the architecture in which MAC driver is part of the Protocol Stack impossible to use.

To solve the above problem, various driver specifications evolved to provide a common interface between the network card and the protocol stacks. A MAC driver, which is written to a standard specification, can have different protocol stacks run on top of it. A MAC driver implementor can implement the driver to a common specification. This will ensure that all the protocol stacks written to the common specification can work above this particular network card. Similarly, a protocol stack developer can develop a protocol stack that is compatible to a common specification and can run this protocol stack on top of all network cards which have MAC drivers implemented to the common specification (see Figure 6-7).

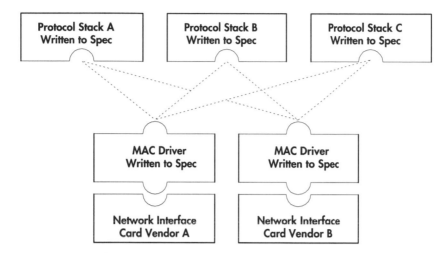

Figure 6-7. Compatibility provided by Common Specifications

One such common specification is Packet Driver. The packet driver specification was developed by FTP Software, Inc. in 1987. The packet driver specification defines how the MAC driver loads and operates under DOS. It defines a common software interface for various protocol stacks. Using the common software interface, which is defined by the packet driver, one or more protocol stacks can run above an Ethernet Card, or a Token Ring Card, for example. The packet driver protocol stack implementation is independent of the actual brand of the network card. A network card, which has a MAC driver compatible with packet driver specification, is independent of the protocol stacks. Using the packet driver specification, multiple protocol stacks can use the same network card simultaneously (see Figure 6-8).

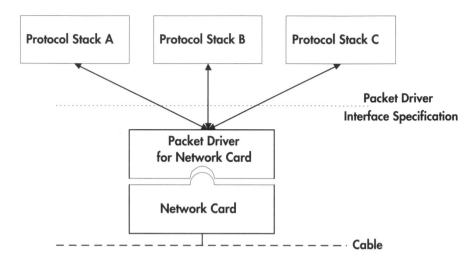

Figure 6-8. Packet Driver Architecture

A packet driver examines the packet type of every packet (frame) received from the network. It then passes the packet to the appropriate protocol stack.

Packet drivers are widely accepted among DOS TCP-IP users. Several commercial packages support packet drivers including the FTP Software PC/TCP, Beame & Whiteside BW-NFS, Wollongong Pathway Access, and SUN PC-NFS. A number of freeware TCP-IP packages support packet driver. They are PC/IP developed by MIT, CMU, and Harvard; NCSA Telnet, Phil Karn's KA9Q TCP/IP package; and Clarkson University's CUTCP.

The packet driver loads in a PC as a TSR (Terminate and Stay Resident) or a DOS device driver. The packet driver provides calls to service various needs of the protocol stacks. It provides calls to initiate access to a specific packet type, to end access to it, to send a packet, to receive a certain packet type, and to get statistics. Packet driver loads and stays in the PC memory. Any protocol stack that wants to use the services provided by the packet driver can call it by using a software interrupt. The packet driver upper interface uses a software interrupt between 60h–80h to provide the services to the protocol stacks.

Almost all available packet drivers provide a way to the user to select one of the software interrupt between 60h–80h. The user has to make sure that the interrupt it chooses does not conflict with other pieces of software interrupts that also use software interrupts. Once the packet driver is loaded into DOS using a certain software interrupt, the protocol stacks use the software interrupt for any communication with the packet driver.

The packet driver specification has no provision for the support of multiple network cards via a single packet driver and associated software interrupt. This issue of the architecture can be addressed by loading multiple packet driver (one for each network card) with different interrupts.

PACKET DRIVER INTERNALS

Packet driver has three levels of functionality that it can provide:

- Basic (mandatory)
- Extended (Optional)
- High Performance (Optional)

A basic packet driver provides functionality to send and receive packets. The extended packet driver is a superset of the basic packet driver. It provides functions to handle multicast address, and statistics gathering among other things. The high performance functionality packet drivers support performance improvement and tuning which is not available with either basic or extended packet drivers. In a packet driver environment, a network interface is identified by a combination of three fields: <class, type, number>. The class of a network interface is a 8-bit integer field that identifies the kind of media interface. Some of the class values used under packet driver are listed in the Figure 6-9.

Class	Network Type
1	DEC/Intel/Xerox Ethernet
2	ProNet-10 Token Ring
3	IEEE 802.5 Token Ring
4	Omninet
5	Appletalk
6	Serial Line IP (SLIP)
7	StarLAN
8	ArcNet
9	AX.25
10	KISS
11	IEEE 802.3 with 802.2 headers
12	FDDI with 802.2 headers
13	Internet X.25
14	N.T. LANSTAR

Figure 6-9. Packet Driver—Class Field Members

Each class of a network interface may have one or multiple "type" of interface. A "type" of interface specifies a product from a specific manufacturer that belongs to that particular class. Interface types for Ethernet class are 3COM 3C503, and 3C505 Interface types for IEEE 802.5 class are IBM Token Ring adapter, and Proteon p1340. The "number" field specifies the interface number. If a machine is equipped with more than one interface of a class and type: the interface must be numbered using the "number" field to distinguish between them.

The "class" and "type" field values are managed by FTP Software. The type 0xFFFF is a wildcard type that matches any interface in the specified class. An interface number should start with a 0 to correspond with the first interface of the specified class and type.

Initiating Packet Driver Operations

A typical packet driver implementation is a DOS TSR which is loaded from CONFIG.SYS or AUTOEXEC.BAT in a DOS system. When a packet driver is invoked, the user also specifies the software interrupt to be used (60h–80h) to communicate with the protocol stack. Various other initialization parameters may be passed to the packet driver. For example, the hardware I/O address, or the IRQ number. A packet driver, at initialization time, initializes the network interface card (hardware). This process includes the initialization of the hardware IRQ vector and the appropriate software interrupt vector to point to the internal functions of the packet driver. This ensures that if a protocol stack issues a software interrupt, the packet driver functions will be called for processing. Similarly, the network interface card may generate a hardware interrupt and the packet driver function will be called to handle it.

The packet driver specification also specifies a mechanism that enables a protocol stack to scan and see if a packet driver is loaded and resident in a machine. The protocol stack scans the software interrupts from 60h–80h for the presence of the packet driver. Each software interrupt has an entry in the interrupt vector table which provides the address of the handler for that interrupt. The protocol stack looks for a null terminated string "PKT DRVR" presence starting at byte 4 of the interrupt handler. The first three bytes provide a jump instruction to the interrupt handler code.

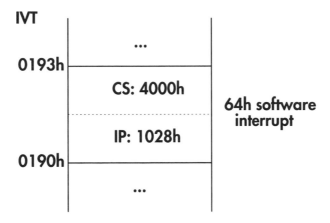

Figure 6-10. IVT entry for 64h software interrupt

Figure 6-10 shows the interrupt vector table entry for the software interrupt 64h. The lower 2 address bytes 190h–191h indicate the instruction pointer value, say 1028h. The upper 2 address bytes indicate the value that goes into the code segmented register of the 80x886 processors. The CS:IP represents the address of the packet driver routine that should be called by the 80x86 microprocessor when any application in the PC-AT invokes interrupt 64h. In this example the CS:IP is 4000:1028h which corresponds to 41028h physical address (CS shift left 4-bits and add IP). The memory location starting at 4000:1028 should look like Figure 6-11.

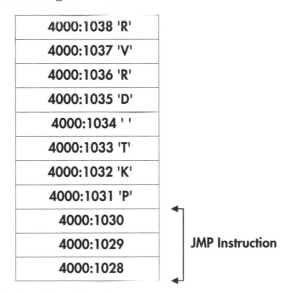

Figure 6-11. Packet Driver Identification

The protocol stack scans the interrupt handlers for interrupts between 60h–80h and looks for "PKT DRVR" string starting at byte 4. If a "PKT DRVR" string is identified, the protocol stack assumes that a packet driver is present at that software interrupt. All the packet driver functions are accessed by the protocol stack using the software interrupt determined via the mechanism described above. The protocol stack sets the function code (standard) in register AH and then calls the software interrupt. The packet driver interrupt handler looks at register AH for the function code and performs the appropriate service.

Running Multiple Protocols Above Packet Driver

Various MAC layer headers have embedded in their frames, a field defining the type of protocol. In Ethernet II (DIX), the 16-bit "ethertype" field immediately following the 6 byte destination and 6 byte source address defines the type of protocol. In IEEE 802.3 frame which uses 802.2 headers, the type of protocol is in the 802.2 header. The packet driver examines the incoming packet type and decides which protocol (TCP-IP, XNS, and OSI) for which the packet is intended. Each protocol stack registers with the packet driver and registers the type of packet it wants to receive. This is done by the protocol stack by calling access_type() function provided by the packet driver. Each access_type() call establishes a destination for a particular type of packet, which remains in effect until release_type() is called with the handle returned by the particular access_type().

All functions provided by the packet driver are accessed via the software interrupt (60h–80h). The register AH of 80x86 processor contains the function code of the desired service.

Service Provided by the Packet Driver

The packet driver has to provide certain services to the protocols running above it. These services include receiving packets, transmitting packets, and statistics gathering. These services are provided by the packet driver as various functions which are called by the protocol stack via software interrupts. As described earlier, the packet driver provides three type of functions.

- Basic Functions
- Extended Functions
- High Performance Functions

Figure 6-12 lists all the functions provided by a packet driver and the category of packet driver functionality to which they belong.

Function Name	AH	Level of Function
driver_info	1	Basic
access_type	2	Basic
release_type	3	Basic
send_pkt	4	Basic
terminate	5	Basic
get_address	6	Basic
reset_interface	7	Basic
get_parameters	10	High Performance
as_send_pkt	11	High Performance
set_rcv_mode	20	Extended
get_rcv_mode	21	Extended
set_multicast_list	22	Extended
get_multicst_list	23	Extended
get_statisstics	24	Extended
set_address	25	Extended

Figure 6-12. Packet Driver Functions

The functions which are labeled extended and high performance are considered optional. The protocol stacks which wish to use these functions should use the driver_info() function to determine if they are available in a given packet driver.

driver_info() function

The packet driver function provides information about the packet driver and the network interface that it is managing. This function provides the class, type and number information. It provides name of the driver and the functionality it supports: basic, extended, and/or high-performance.

access_type() function

A protocol stack calls this function to register the type of packets it wants to receive from the packet driver. The protocol stack also registers a pointer to its own receiving function which a packet driver calls when a packet of registered type arrives from the network.

When a packet is received, and the packet type matches the type of packet registered by access_type function called by a protocol stack, the packet driver will call the corresponding receiver function provided by the protocol stack. The packet driver calls the receiver function of the protocol stack twice. The first time it requests a buffer from the protocol stack into which to copy the packet and the second time it copies the packet to the final destination. After the copy is completed, the packet driver calls the receiver function of the protocol stack to indicate that the copy is completed and the protocol stack can use the buffer.

Release_type() function

A call to this function de-registers the packet type and receiver function address which was registered earlier by the protocol stack by calling the access_type function.

send_pkt() function

This function is called by the protocol stack to request a transmission of a packet on the wire. The protocol stack provides a buffer which has the complete packet including all MAC layer headers. The packet driver takes the buffer and transmits the packet on the wire.

terminate() function

This function call terminates the packet driver.

get_address() function

This function returns the current local network address of the interface card to the protocol stack. The network address, typically, is the 6 byte MAC address.

reset_interface() function

This function call is given by the protocol stack to request a hardware and software reset of the packet driver and the associated network hardware.

get_parameters() function

This function is provided by the packet drivers which are supporting high performance extensions. When a protocol stack executes a get_parameters() function call to the driver, the packet driver returns a data structure which contains a number of performance-related functions. For example, the packet driver returns the number of receive buffers and the number of transmit buffers when get_parameters() function is invoked. The number of transmit and receive buffers that the packet driver maintains can be used by the protocol stack to streamline its successive transmit and receive algorithms.

as_send_pkt() function

This function belongs to the high performance category of packet driver functions. It is used by the protocol stack for high performance functionality. This function is responsible for sending packets on the network. However, this function is different from send_pkt() function. In the send_pkt() function when the packet driver returns, the protocol stack can assume that the packet driver has sent the frame (or an error has occurred), and the protocol stack can use the buffer for next packet. In as_send_pkt(), the protocol stack uses this function to queue the send buffer in the packet driver. When the packet driver transmits the buffer, it makes a call to the protocol stack to indicate that an earlier packet which was queued has been transmitted and the protocol stack is free to reuse the transmit buffer.

set_rcv_mode() function

This is an extended driver function. This function is used by the protocol stack to instruct the packet driver to set the receive mode on the network card. The packet driver executes the network card specific commands to achieve the desired receive modes. Some of the receive modes that this function has to support are:

- turn receiver off
- receive packets sent to this network card only
- receive packets sent to this network card and all broadcast packets
- receive all packets

get_rcv_mode() function

This is an extended driver function. This function returns the current receive mode of the network card.

set_multicast_list() function

This is an extended driver function. This function is used by the protocol stack to pass a list of multicast addresses to the packet driver. The packet driver sends a command to the hardware (if hardware supports multicast filtering) to update the multicast list. Otherwise, the packet driver maintains a software filter to filter the multicast addresses given by this command.

get_multicast_list() function

This function is an extended driver function. This function is used by the protocol stack to get the list of multicast addresses from the packet driver. Typically, if a protocol stack wants to add a multicast address in the filter list, it gets the multicast list, adds the address to the list, and then performs a sct_multicast_list function call.

get_statistics() function

This is an extended driver function. The packet driver returns the statistics table on execution of this function call. The statistics table contain the packets transmitted, packets received, total bytes transmitted, and total bytes received.

set_address() function

This is an extended driver function. This function call is used by the protocol stack to change the MAC address of the network card.

SUMMARY

This chapter provides complete details of the packet driver architecture, its evolution in the TCP-IP world, and its packet driver internals. The packet driver specification is very much a defacto standard in the TCP-IP based DOS software. One can obtain a number of public domain TCP-IP stacks and utilities based on the packet driver. Some of the TCP-IP stacks and utilities are NCSA Telnet, Phil Karn's KA9Q TCP-IP package, and Clarkson University's CUTCP. Providing a packet driver for a network card makes the network hardware run under all these environments.

REFERENCES

Postel, J. and Reynolds, J. 1988. RFC-1042, *A standard for the Transmission of IP Datagrams over IEEE 802 Networks*.

_____. *PC/TCP Interoperability*. FTP Software, Inc. 2 High Street, North Andover, MA.

_____. *PC/TCP Packet driver Specification*, Revision 1.09, September 14, 1989. FTP Software, Inc. 26 Princess Street, Wakefield, MA.

7

Novell NetWare Open Data-Link Interface Drivers

INTRODUCTION/OVERVIEW

The Open Data-Link Interface (ODI) specification was developed by Novell and was published in 1989. The goal of ODI is to provide seamless network integration at the transport, network and data-link levels. ODI allows multiple network protocols and LAN adapters to be used concurrently on the same workstation or file server. ODI provides a flexible, high-performance Data Link Layer interface to the Network layer protocol stacks. The ODI specification describes the set of interface and software modules used to decouple device drivers (MAC level) from protocol stacks and to enable multiple protocol stacks to share the network hardware and media in a transparent fashion. The ODI consists of three major components:

- Multiple Link Interface Drivers (MLIDs)
- Link Support Layer (LSL)
- Protocol Stacks

Figure 7-1 illustrates the relationship between the three ODI components:

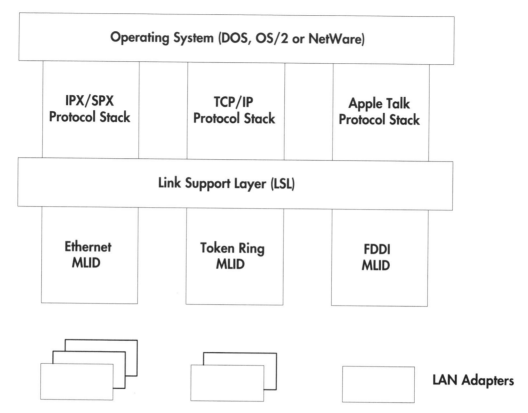

Figure 7-1. ODI Model

Multiple Link Interface Drivers (MLIDs)

Multiple Link Interface Drivers are LAN drivers written to the ODI specification. Each MLID driver is unique to the adapter hardware and the LAN media (Ethernet, Token Ring, FDDI, etc.). The ODI specification eliminates the need for separate drivers to be written for each specific protocol stack.

MLIDs are device drivers that handle the sending and receiving of packets to and from a physical or logical LAN medium. MLIDs control communication between the LAN adapter and the Link Support Layer. MLIDs interface with the LAN adapter and handle frame header appending and stripping. They also help demultiplex the incoming packets by determining their frame format.

The ODI specification expects that the smallest packet size which all MLIDs send and receive is 586 bytes. This value does not include any low-level header information maintained by the MLID. If the underlying LAN medium does not support this minimum value, the MLID fragments the packets to be sent, and reassembles the packets when they are received, in order to meet the minimum packet size requirement.

When the MLID receives a packet, it removes the media access information (MAC) header and passes the packet to the Link Support Layer. Since the media details are invisible to the LSL, this modular design provides true media independence, which means that any MLID can communicate with any ODI protocol stack through the LSL.

The MLID is partitioned into three modules: MSM (Medial Specific Module), TSM (Topology Specific Module), and HSM (Hardware Specific Module). Figure 7-2 shows the three modules and their respective functions.

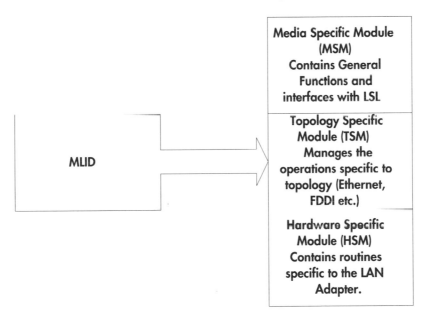

Figure 7-2. Multiple Link Interface Driver

Link Support Layer (LSL)

The Link Support Layer (LSL) is the core of the Open Data-Link Interface. The LSL allows a single MLID driver to support multiple protocols and allows a single protocol to use multiple MLID drivers (see Figure 7-3).

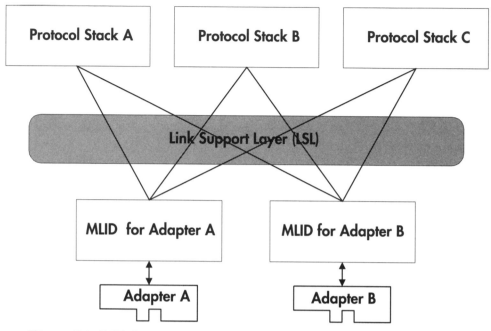

Figure 7-3. LSL Acting as a Multiplexer

The LSL handles the communication between protocol stacks and MLIDs. It acts like a multiplexer, directing packets between the appropriate MLIDs and protocol stacks. The MLID receives the packets destined for different protocol stacks that might be present in the system. The LSL then determines the protocol stack to which the packet is to be delivered. Next, the protocol stack determines what should be done with the packet or where it should be sent. When the protocol stack has to transmit a packet, it hands the packet to the LSL which then routes the packet to the appropriate MLID.

The LSL provides procedures for the following services:

(i.)   Allows a protocol stack to bind with MLIDs.

(ii.)   Allows a protocol stack to transmit and receive packets through an MLID.

(iii.)   Registers and deregister MLIDs and protocol stacks.

(iv.)   Allows a protocol stack to obtain and return Event Control Blocks (ECBs). ECBs are control structures that are used to send or receive packets or to schedule timers.

(v.)   Queues and recovers ECBs for later use.

(vi.)   Allows a protocol stack to obtain MLID statistics.

Protocol Stacks

Protocol stacks receive packets from the LSL and are unaware of the media or the LAN adapter type through which the packet was received. They transmit and receive data over a logical or physical network. The protocol stacks provide an interface to allow higher level protocols or applications to access their services which include routing, segmentation and reassembly of packets, error handling, and other similar functions. The popular ODI protocol stacks are IPX/SPX, TCP/IP, AppleTalk, and OSI.

The relationship between the ODI architecture and the 7 layer OSI model is shown in Figure 7-4.

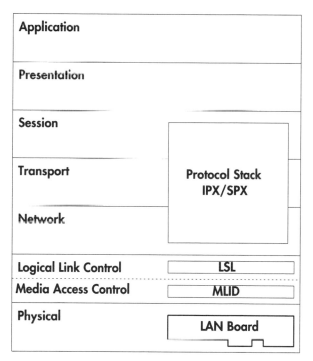

Figure 7-4. ODI and OSI

ENVIRONMENT

The ODI architecture applies to the device drivers written for DOS and NetWare Server (3.x and above) environments. The ODI architecture also applies to OS/2 operating system. The OS/2 ODI architecture is beyond the scope of this book. However, the DOS and NetWare ODI concepts apply to OS/2 also.

In the DOS environment, the following files are needed for setting the ODI environment:

- LSL.COM   ; Link Support Layer

- NE2100.COM   ; MLID Hardware Dependent Driver

- IPXODI.COM   ; IPX Protocol Stack

- NETX.COM   ; DOS NetWare Shell

- NET.CFG   ; ODI Configuration File

The DOS ODI drivers run under DOS real mode environment. They may also operate under Microsoft Windows environment.

The operating system environment of the NetWare 3.1x and 4.x server is significantly different from DOS. Protocol stacks and MLIDs for NetWare server operate in a NetWare environment. A key NetWare feature is NetWare Loadable Module (NLM). The NLMs are software modules that are dynamically linked to the NetWare Operating system at run time. Once an NLM is loaded, its functions become an integral component of the NetWare Operating system.

Different types of loadable modules have unique filename extensions that signify their respective functions. LAN drivers are the ".LAN" file name extension, disk drivers are ".DSK," and general utility or support modules are ".NLM."

NetWare supervisors can load or unload additional functionalities to the NetWare 3.1x, 4.x server operating system without disturbing the functionality of other modules by using NetWare Loadable Modules.

The NetWare Operating System is a multitasking operating system and is non-preemptive. This means that the Protocol Stacks, MLIDs, and other applications can be called reentrantly. The programs run in a 32-bit protected mode with a flat memory model. As the NetWare Operating system is non-preemptive, the operating system requires every module executing in this environment periodically to release control to the operating system.

INITIALIZATION OF PROTOCOLS, MLIDs, AND LSL

The Protocols, MLIDs and LSL have to follow a loading sequence for proper initialization. In DOS environment, the sequence is as follows:

(i.) LSL is loaded first.

(ii.) All the MLIDs are loaded after LSL.

(iii.) Protocol stacks are loaded last.

The loading sequence ensures that all the necessary components required for initialization are in place before a module loads.

The loading and initialization sequence is slightly different for DOS and NetWare environments. This section will first discuss the DOS environment followed by NetWare environment.

Initialization Under DOS Environment

The initialization of LSL, MLIDs, and Protocol stacks under DOS environment involves the following steps:

(i.) Load LSL

(ii.) Load and register MLID

(iii.) Load and register Protocol stacks

(iv.) Determine the logical board and obtain Protocol ID value

(v.) Bind the Protocol stack to the logical board

The LSL is a TSR (Terminate and Stay Resident) program under DOS. When LSL loads, it installs an interrupt handler for DOS Multiplex Interrupt (INT 2FH). Multiplex interrupt is a common entry point for DOS resident programs and device drivers that carry out requests for other programs. To provide services to other programs, a service program (like LSL) must add its multiplex handler to the interrupt chain and choose a multiplex identifier. This identifier is an integer that distinguishes the program's multiplex handler from all others in the interrupt chain. When a program requests service, it places the service program's multiplex identifier in the AH register. When multiplex interrupt is issued, each multiplex handler in the interrupt chain checks the AH register—if the register contains its identifier, the handler processes the service request. The DOS uses multiplex identifiers from 00H to 0BFH. The LSL can use identifiers in the range of 0C0H-0FFH.

Once the LSL is installed with an identifier (multiplex), any program can reach the LSL via the DOS multiplex interrupt (2FH).

Every MLID scans for the presence of LSL in the system. The MLID calls DOS multiplex interrupt 2FH with identifier 0C0H-0FFH in the AH register. The multiplex interrupt is called with every identifier and it checks the presence of LSL signature "LINKUPS$" at the location pointed by the ES:SI registers. If the LSL signature is present, the register DX:BX points to the LSL initialization entry point. When the LSL initialization entry point is called, the resident LSL returns in the registers ES:SI or DS:DI the following parameters as shown in Figure 7-5.

If BX equals	Action	Return Parameters
01h	MLID requests registration	DS:DI has a pointer to the LSL information block
02H	Request Protocol stack and general service API entry points	ES:SI has a pointer to the LSL information block
03H	Request MLID API entry points (without having to register the MLID)	ES:SI has a pointer to the MLID entry point

Figure 7-5. LSL initialization entry points

The LSL information block contains pointers to the various API services provided by LSL. The three API services which are used by protocol stacks and MLIDs are:

- LSL Protocol Support API
- LSL General Services API
- LSL MLID Services API

Once protocol stacks and MLID have obtained their API entry points, they can call various services by calling their entry points. Each LSL API has several functions. These functions are distinguished by a function ID which is assigned by Novell and is placed in the BX register before calling the API entry point of LSL. The LSL looks at register BX and decides which function of the API is being called by the protocol stack or MLID. Figures 7-6 to 7-8 list the functions contained in various LSL APIs.

LSL Protocol Stack Services API	Description	Function Code
GetECB	This function is called by the protocol to obtain an Event Control Block (ECB).	0
ReturnECB	This function is called to return the ECB to LSL pool.	2
ScheduleAES event event	This function is called to schedule an asynchronous event. The LSL makes sure that the specified protocol event is invoked when the specified time has expired.	3
CancelAES event	This function is called to cancel the event scheduled by Schedule AES Event.	4
GetIntervalMarker	This function returns a timing marker in milliseconds. It is used to measure delta times.	5
RegisterStack	This function registers a bound protocol stack with LSL and assigns an LSL handle (the stack ID).	6
DeregisterStack	This function removes a stack from the LSL's list of bound protocol stacks.	7
RegisterDefaultStack	This function registers a default protocol stack with LSL. Default stack receives all leftover frames not claimed by bound or prescan stacks.	8
DeregisterDefaultStack	This function removes a default protocol stack.	9
Register prescan stack	This function registers a prescan protocol stack with LSL for a specified board. This allows prescan stack to view all incoming packets on a particular board.	10

Figure 7-6. LSL Protocol Stack Services

LSL Protocol Stack Services API	Description	Function Code
DeregisterPrescanStack	This function removes a prescan protocol stack.	11
SendPacket	This function sends a packet as described by an ECB.	12
GetStackIDFromName	This function allows a protocol stack to obtain its own or any other stack ID.	16
GetStackIDFrom-StackID Board	This function returns a protocol ID that corresponds to a protocol and frame type.	17
GetMLIDControlEntry	This function returns the specified MLID's control handler routine entry point.	18
GetProtocolControlEntry	This function returns the specified protocol stack's control handler routine.	19
GetLSLStatistics	This function returns a pointer to the LSL's statistics table.	20
BindStack	This function binds a protocol stack to an adapter/frame type combination (logical board) that allows and enables packet reception.	21
UnbindStack	This function unbinds a protocol stack from a logical board.	22
AddProtocolID	This function allows a protocol stack to register a Protocol ID for a given frame type/protocol stack combination.	23
RelinquishControl	This function allows a protocol stack to yield control to LSL, allowing the LSL to perform the necessary background processing.	24

Figure 7-6. LSL Protocol Stack Services (Continued)

LSL Protocol Stack Services API	Description	Function Code
GetLSLConfiguration	This function returns a pointer to the LSL's configuration table.	25
GetTickMarker	This function returns the number of ticks that have occurred since LSL was loaded. (1 tick= 55 milliseconds)	26

Figure 7-6. LSL Protocol Stack Services (Continued)

The LSL provides a number of services to all modules in a system. The LSL's general services can be invoked by calling the general service entry point that the protocol stack obtains when it locates the LSL. Figure 7-7 lists the general services defined and implemented in LSL.

LSL General Service API	Description	Function Code
AllocateMemory	Allows an application to allocate to allocate memory.	0
FreeMemory	Allows an application to free memory which is allocated by Allocate Memory	1
ReallocateMemory	Allows an application to reallocate memory.	2
MemoryStatistics	Provides the complete statistics of LSL's memory usage.	3
AddMemoryToPool	Adds a block of memory to LSL's memory pool.	4
AddGeneralServices	Allows protocol stacks, MLIDs and applications to add new commands to the LSL's General Service entry point.	5
RemoveGeneralService	Removes a general service that was previously added.	6
GetNETcfgPath	Returns a fully formed path specification to the NET.CFG file as found by the LSL when the LSL was initialized.	7

Figure 7-7. LSL General Services API

The LSL also provides services for MLIDs. The LSL MLID services can be called by calling the required LSL MLID service API entry points that the MLID obtains when it registers with LSL. Figure 7-8 lists the LSL MLID service functions as defined and implemented under LSL.

LSL MLID Service API	Description	Function Code
GetECB	Allocates an ECB to the MLID.	0
ReturnECB	Returns an ECB which was previously allocated to Get ECB.	1
DefragECB	Assembles a defragmented ECB.	2
ScheduleAESEvent	Schedules an asynchronous event. The LSL makes sure that the specified MLID event is invoked when the specified time has expired.	3
CancelAESEvent	Cancels the event scheduled by Schedule AES Event.	4
GetIntervalMarker	Returns a timing marker in milliseconds. It is used to measure delta times.	5
DeregisterMLID	Removes a MLID from the LSL's list of bound MLIDs.	6
HoldReceiveEvent	Holds a receive event for processing.	7
StartCriticalSection	This function is called by the MLID before starting a critical section of the code.	8
EndCriticalSection	This function is called by the MLID to end the critical section of its code.	9
CriticalSectionStatus	Returns the status of critical section processing.	10
ServiceEvents	The MLID invokes Service Events to complete the processing of sent and received events.	11

Figure 7-8. LSL MLID Service API

LSL MLID Service API	Description	Function Code
SendComplete	The MLID uses SendComplete to indicate completion of a transmit request.	14
AddProtocolID	This function is used by MLID to add a Protocol ID to the LSL tables.	15
GetStackECB	Returns a ECB on the stack.	16

Figure 7-8. LSL MLID Service API (Continued)

When a protocol stack registers with LSL, one of the parameters it passes is a pointer to the protocol stack's entry point. Applications and other stacks can obtain this entry point from the LSL (see Figure 7-6) and then invoke protocol supplied control commands. The protocol supplied control procedures are described in Figure 7-9.

Protocol Control Procedure	Description	Function Code
GetProtocolStack Configuration	This function call returns a pointer to the protocol stack's configuration table.	0
GetProtocolStack Statistics	This function call returns a pointer to the protocol stack's internal statistics table.	1
BindToMLID	This function call informs the protocol stack that it should bind to a specific board.	2
UnbindFromMLID	This function call informs the protocol stack that it should unbind from a specific board.	3
MLIDDegistered	The LSL invokes MLID Deregistered whenever the logical board that a protocol is using is deregistered.	4

Figure 7-9. Protocol Stack Control Procedures

The ODI requires an MLID to provide a number of control procedures to protocol stacks and LSL. The protocol stack can obtain the MLID control entry point by calling GetMLIDControlEntry (see Figure 7-4) and then invoking the returned entry point with the proper register set. The MLID provides the control procedures as listed in Figure 7-10.

MLID Control Procedure	Description	Function Code
GetMLIDConfiguration	This function returns a pointer to the MLID's configuration table for the specified logical board.	0
GetMLIDStatistics	This function returns a pointer to the MLID's statistics table for the specified board.	1
AddMulticastAddress	This function adds a multicast address to the MLID's multicast table.	2
DeleteMulticastAddress	This function removes a multicast address from the specified board's multicast table.	3
MLIDShutdown	This function allows an application to shut down physical adapter.	5
MLIDReset	This function causes the MLID to totally re-initialize the physical adapter.	6
CreateConnection	This function is used by MLID users to create connections.	7
RemoveConnection	This function is used by MLID users to delete connections.	8
SetLookAheadSize	This function tells the MLID the amount of Look Ahead data that is needed by the caller to properly process the received packets.	9

Figure 7-10. MLID Control Procedures

MLID Control Procedure	Description	Function Code
PromiscousChange	This function is called by the protocol stack to enable or disable the promiscuous mode on the MLID's adapter.	10
RegisterReceiveMonitor	This function is invoked by Protocol stacks when they want to monitor the packets that the adapter is receiving and transmitting.	11
DriverPoll	This function is called by the LSL after a set amount of time. The MLID sets the time. This function contains tasks that MLID wants to repeat every time the timer expires.	12

Figure 7-10. MLID Control Procedures (Continued)

Initialization Under NetWare Environment

The initialization of LSL, MLIDs, and Protocol stacks under NetWare environment is very similar to the DOS initialization process. The user does not have to load the LSL in NetWare environment. The LSL is an integral component of NetWare environment. The user has to load the MLID and also load the protocol stack. The protocol stack is not fully functional until the user binds the protocol to a board.

The NetWare environment is very different from the DOS environment. As explained in the previous section, the DOS modules exchange entry points by means of software interrupts (DOS multiplex interrupts). The NetWare environment provides a very simple means of exchanging entry points between various modules. A module exports a set of functions when it loads. A module can also import a set of functions at the time when it loads. The functions that a module is importing must have been exported earlier by some other module. This type of importing and exporting is also called dynamic linking. This means that the module dynamically links the function it wants to import at load time.

As in DOS environment, the NetWare environment provides various support functions for protocols, MLIDs, and LSL among others. Figure 7-11 lists all the functions that the NetWare Operating System provides.

O.S. Function Name	Description
AddPollingProcedureRTag	This function is used by the driver to register its polling procedure.
Alloc	This function is used to get memory.
AllocateMappedPages	This function is used to allocate memory on 4K boundaries.
AllocateResourceTag	This function is called by the driver to obtain a resource tag to get resources from the O.S.
AllocateBufferBelow16Meg	This function is used to allocate memory below 16 Meg for the 16-bit host adapters that cannot address above 16 Meg.
CancelInterruptTimeCallback	This function is called by the driver to cancel an event previously scheduled using ScheduleInterruptTime Callback.
CancelNoSleepAESProcessEvent	This function removes the specified AES event from the operating system's list of events to be called by the AES No-Sleep process.
CancelSleepAESProcessEvent	Same as above, but the events are called by the AES process instead of AES No-Sleep process.
ClearHardwareInterrupt	This function releases a processor hardware interrupt previously allocated by SetHardwareInterrupt for a physical board.
CPSemaphore	This function is used to lock the real mode workspace when making an EISA BIOS call.
CRescheduleLast	This function places the task in the last place on the list of active tasks to be executed.
CVSemaphore	This function clears a semaphore that was set with CPSemaphore.
DeallocateMappedPages	This function is used to return previously allocated 4K page boundary buffer allocated using AllocateMappedPages Procedure.
DeRegisterHardwareOptions	This function releases previously registered hardware options.

Figure 7-11. NetWare O.S. Support Procedures

O.S. Function Name	Description
DisableHardwareInterrupt	This routine marks off the specified interrupt on the programmable interrupt controller, preventing the adapter from interrupting the driver.
DoEndOfInterrupt	This routine sends an EOI to one or both PICs.
DoRealModeInterrupt	This routine is used to perform real mode interrupts, such as BIOS or DOS interrupts
EnableHardwareInterrupt	This routine enables the adapter's interrupt line on the programmable interrupt controller if DisableHardwareInterrupt was previously used.
Free	This routine returns the memory previously allocated by the driver.
FreeBufferBelow16Meg	This routine returns the memory previously allocated by AllocBufferBelow16Meg.
GetCurrentTime	This routine determines the current relative time.
GetHardwareBusType	This routine returns a value indicating the processor bus type.
GetProcessorSpeedRating	This routine is used to determine the relative processor speed.
GetRealModeWorkSpace	This routine is used in conjunction with DoRealModeInterrupt to allow the driver access to memory in real mode.
GetServerPhysicalOffset	This routine returns the physical address of the operating system's logical address 0. This routine is used to convert physical to logical address 0 and vice-versa.
OutputToscreen	This routine is used to display a driver error message in the screen console.
ParseDriverParameters	This routine is used to instruct the server to parse various driver parameters obtained from command line and various data structures.

Figure 7-11. NetWare O.S. Support Procedures (Continued)

O.S. Function Name	Description
QueueSystemAlert	This routine allows a system notification of driver hardware or software problems during regular operation of the board.
ReadEISAConfig	This procedure reads the EISA configuration block for the specified slot into a 320 byte buffer.
ReadRoutine	This routine allows drivers to read custom data into system memory during initialization.
RegisterForEventNotification	This routine is called at initialization to register an event call back routine.
RegisterHardwareOptions	This routine reserves hardware options for a particular board.
RemovePollingProcedure	This routine is used to remove a driver's poll routine from the server's list of polling procedures.
ScheduleInterruptTime Callback	This routine is used to add an event to the list of events that will be called by the timer interrupt handler.
ScheduleNoSleepAESProcess Event	This routine sets a process that will be executed at a desired interval.
ScheduleSleepAESProcess Event	This routine sets a process that will be executed at desired intervals but can be blocked.
SetHardwareInterrupt	This routine allocates the specified interrupt and provides an ISR entry point.
UnregisterEventNotification	This routine is used to unhook the driver from event notification.

Figure 7-11. NetWare O.S. Support Procedures (Continued)

Figure 7-11 lists all the support procedures provided by the NetWare Operating system to MLIDs and Protocol Stacks. The LSL, which is an integral part of the O.S., provides support procedures/routines to MLID and Protocol Stacks. The MLID and Protocol Stacks use these procedures to perform the binding, transmitting and receiving as described in the next few sections.

Figure 7-12 lists the LSL support commands that can be called by the protocol stacks and MLIDs. Although MLIDs may also use some of these calls, protocol stacks might use these calls differently.

LSL Commands for Protocols and MLIDs	Description
LSLAddProtocolID	Allows a protocol Stack to register a Protocol ID for a given frame type/protocol stack combination.
LSLBindStack	Binds a protocol stack to an MLID.
LSLCancelAESEventRTag	Cancels an AES event.
LSLDeFragmentECB	Consolidates packet fragments before processing the ECB.
LSLDeRegisterDefaultStack	Removes the specified protocol stack associated with the specified MLID from the LSL's internal default stack tables.
LSLDeRegisterPreScanStack	Removes the specified protocol stack associated with the specified MLID from the LSL's internal prescan stack table.
LSLDeRegisterStack	Removes the specified protocol stack from the LSL's internal protocol stack tables.
LSLGetHeldPocketRTag	Allows a protocol to remove an ECB placed in the hold queue.
LSLGetIntervalMarker	Measures the delta time.
LSLGetLinkSupportStatistics	Obtains a pointer to the LSL's statistics table.
LSLGetMaximumPacketSize	Returns the largest physical packet size for which the LSL has been configured.
LSLGetMLIDControlEntry	Returns the MLID Control Entry Point.
LSLGetPIDFromStaackIDBoard	Returns a protocol ID that corresponds to a combination of the protocol stack ID and a board number.
LSLGetProtocolControlEntry	Returns the pointer to the control entry point for the specified protocol stack.
LSLGetRcvECBRTag	Allocates a receive buffer. The protocol stack should return the buffer using LSL ReturnRcvECB.

Figure 7-12. LSL Commands for Protocols

LSL Commands for Protocols and MLIDs	Description
LSLGetStackIDFromName	Allows a protocol stack or application to obtain its own or any other stack ID.
LSLHoldPacket	Allows a protocol stack to queue an incoming packet in the LSL for later processing.
LSLRegisterDefaultStackRTag	Binds the protocol stack to the MLID as a default stack. The default stack accepts packets not destined for other stacks.
LSLRegisterPreScanStackRTag	Binds the protocol stack to the MLID as a prescan stack. A prescan stack receives all the incoming packets.
LSLRegisterStackRTag	Registers a stack with the MLID. This call is required when a stack wants to receive packets.
LSLReturnRcvECB	Returns a previously allocated receive ECB buffer to the LSL.
LSLScanPacket	Scans the hold queue in search of ECBs that correspond to the stack ID.
LSLScheduleAESEventRTag	Schedules an AES (Asynchronous Event Schedule) Event.
LSLSendPacket	Sends a packet to one of the registered MLIDs.
LSLUnbindStack	Unbinds a protocol stack from an MLID.

Figure 7-12. LSL Commands for Protocols (Continued)

As stated earlier, the MLIDs and Protocol Stacks have to provide control procedures for each other and for LSL.

Implementors of the protocol stacks have to provide the control procedures. When a protocol stack control command is called, the caller has to place a function code into the EBX register and then call the protocol stack's control entry point. The address of this entry point is obtained by calling LSL Get Protocol Control Entry function (see Figure 7-12). As the Protocol stack is loaded last, the functions it exports cannot be imported by LSL or MLID. Figure 7-13 lists the mandatory and optional calls which the protocol has to support.

Protocol Control Commands	Function Code	Status	Description
Bind	2	Mandatory	This function provides a consistent method of binding a protocol stack with an MLID.
GetProtocolStack Configuration	0h	Mandatory	This function returns a pointer to the protocol stack configuration table.
GetProtocolStack Statistics	1h	Mandatory	This function returns a pointer to the protocol stack statistics table.
GetProtocolString ForBoard	100h	Optional	This function obtains a unique ID string for a protocol.
MLID DeRegistered	4h	Optional	This function is used by the LSL to inform all protocol stacks bound to a specific MLID that the MLID has deregistered.
Unbind	3h	Required	Unbind provides a consistent method of unbinding a protocol stack from an MLID.

Figure 7-13. Protocol Stack Control Commands

The ODI architecture requires an MLID to provide a number of control procedures to protocol stacks and other NetWare Loadable Modules (NLMs). The protocol stack can obtain the MLID control entry point by calling LSLGetProtocolControlEntry (see Figure 7-12). Once the protocol stack has obtained the control entry point, the protocol stack places the function code in EBX register and then calls the MLID control entry point. Figure 7-14 lists the MLID Control Procedures.

MLID Control Procedures	Function Code	Status	Description
Get MLID Configuration	0	Mandatory	This procedure returns a pointer to the logical board's configuration table.
GetMLIDStatistics	1	Mandatory	This procedure returns a pointer to the statistics table of the MLID.
AddMulticast Address	2	Optional	This procedure adds the specified node address to a physical card's multicast address table.
DeleteMulticast Address	3	Optional	This procedure deletes a specified node address from a physical card's multicast table.
MLIDShutdown	5	Mandatory	This procedure shuts down a card partially or completely.
MLIDReset	6	Mandatory	This procedure either resets a card or reactivates a card that has been partially shut down.

Figure 7-14. MLID Control Procedures

Here are some items which must be kept in mind when initializing a protocol stack. The protocol stack is not fully operational until the user binds the protocol to a board. Therefore, it should not send or receive frames until after the protocol stack has been issued a bind command. The protocol stack does a limited initialization when it is loaded and then returns control to the operating system. The protocol stack must get a stack ID from the LSL by using LSLRegisterStackRtag function. This registration informs the LSL about the protocol stack. The operating system invokes the protocol stack BIND to start servicing the board specified by the user.

After binding, the protocol stack determines the maximum physical packet size it can send and receive on the board by examining the MLID configuration table fields. The protocol first obtains the MLID control handler by calling LSLGetMLIDControlEntry (see Figure 7-12). The protocol then invokes the proper function code to obtain the pointer to the MLID Configuration Table (Figure 7-14). The DriverRecvSize field of MLID configuration table represents the largest amount of data that the protocol stack can send or receive using that board.

All bound protocol stacks call the LSL, using LSLGetPIDFromStack ID board, and ask for a defined Protocol ID (PID) before they can transmit and receive on a board. If a PID is returned, the protocol stack can add a PID by calling LSLAddProtocolID (see Figure 7-12). The protocol stack blindly uses this value when it transmits a packet.

ODI DATA STRUCTURES

There are several data structures that are defined and used under the ODI environment. This section defines several of these data structures as defined for the DOS ODI environment. The NetWare Server Operating system uses very similar data structures and hence are not repeated in this section.

The various data structures which are described here are LSL, MLID, and protocol stack statistics and Configuration Tables. The Event Control Block (ECB) is also discussed in this section.

Event Control Block (ECB)

The ECB data structure is the main structure which is used define the protocol data during packet transmission and packet reception. The various fields on an ECB are described in Figure 7-15.

Offset	Name	Size (in bytes)	Description
00h	NextLink	4	This field is used as a forward link to manage a list of ECBs.
04h	PreviousLink	4	This field is used as a back link to manage a list of ECBs.
08h	Status	2	This field indicates the completion status of an ECB.
0Ah	EventService Routine	4	The protocol stack sets this field to point to an appropriate routine that is to be called when the send or receive event is complete.

Figure 7-15. Event Control Block

Offset	Name	Size (in bytes)	Description
0Eh	StackID	2	This field represents the stack ID. On the transmit ECB, this field is filled by the protocol. On the receive path, the LSL fills this field.
10h	ProtocolID	6	This field contains the Protocol ID for sends and receives.
16h	BoardNumber	2	When an MLID registers with the LSL, the MLID is given a logical board number. The protocol obtains the board number from the configuration table of the MLID and fills it in on send.
18h	Immediate Address	6	In a send ECB, this field contains the destination node address. In a receive ECB, this field contains the packet source node address.
1Eh	Driver Workspace	4	This field is reserved for MLID use. The MLID uses this field to indicate to the Protocol if the packet received was a direct, multicast or broadcast.
22h	Protocol Workspace	8	This field is used by the Protocol stack.
2Ah	Datalength	2	This field indicates the total length of the send or receive packet.
2ch	Fragment Count	2	This field contains the number of fragment buffer descriptors immediately following this field. This value cannot be zero or larger than 16.
2Eh	Fragment N Address	4	This field specifies a far pointer to a data buffer of FragmentNlength.
32h	Fragment N Length	2	This field specifies this length of the buffer pointed to by Fragment-Naddress. This field can be 0, in which case the MLID will skip over it when transmitting or receiving data.

Figure 7-15. Event Control Block (Continued)

Protocol Stack Statistics Table Format

All ODI protocol stacks keep Statistics tables for the purpose of Network management. Figure 7-16 lists the various fields of a statistics table.

Offset	Name	Size (in bytes)	Description
00h	StatMajorVersion	01	This field has the major version number of the statistics table.
01h	StatMinorVersion	01	This field has the minor version number of the statistics table.
02h	GenericCounters	02	This field has the number of counters in the statistics table.
04h	ValidCountersMask	04	This field contains a bit mask indicating which generic counters are used. The value 0 indicates Yes, the value 1 indicates No.
08h	TotalTxPackets	04	This field contains the total number of transmit packets.
0ch	TotalRxPackets	04	This field contains the total number of packets received by the Protocol Stack.
10h	IgnoredRxPackets	04	This field contains the number of packets which were ignored by the Protocol Stack for any reason.
14h	NumberCustom	02	This field contains the total number of custom counters that follow this field.
16h	CustomCounter0	04	This is the Custom counter 0 field.
1Ah	CustomCounter1	04	This is the Custom counter 1 field.
1Eh	CustomCounter0 Name	04	This is the pointer to length preceded ASCII string that describes the name of custom counter 0.
22h	CustomCounter 1 Name	4	Same as above but for custom counter 1.
	..... so on		

Figure 7-16. Protocol Stack Statistics Table

Note: *Figure 7-16 used two custom counters as an example. In reality, custom counters can be as many as can be supported by the NumberCustom field.*

Protocol Stack Configuration Table Format

The protocol stack configuration table contains the configuration information of the protocol. Figure 7-17 describes various fields of the protocol stack configuration table.

Offset	Name	Size (in bytes)	Description
00h	ConfigMajorVersion	01	This is the Major version of the table.
01h	ConfigMinorVersion	01	This is the Minor Version of the table.
02h	ProtocolLongName	04	This field contains a far pointer to a length preceded ASCII Protocol stack description string.
06h	ProtocolShortName	04	This field contains a pointer (far) to a length preceded ASCII string used to register the Protocol stack. The short name should be 15 or less characters.
0Ah	StackMajorVersion	01	This field contains the major version of the Protocol stack.
0Bh	StackMinorVersion	01	This field has the minor version of the Protocol stack.
0Ch	Reserved	16	This field is reserved for future use.

Figure 7-17. Protocol Stack Configuration Table Format

LSL Statistics Table Format

The LSL keeps a statistics table for the purpose of network management. The format of the statistics table is described in Figure 7-18.

Offset	Name	Size (in bytes)	Description
00h	StatMajorVersion	01	The LSL statistics table major version field.
01h	StatMinorVersion	01	The LSL statistics minor version field.
02h	GenericCounters	02	This field contains the number of 4 byte static counters of this table.
04h	ValidCountersMark	04	This field contains the bit mark which indicates which generic counters are used.
08h	TotalTxPackets	04	This field contains the total number of transmit packets.
0ch	Reserved	04	Reserved.
10h	Reserved	04	Reserved.
14h	AESEventCount	04	This field contains the number of completed AES events.
18h	PostponedEvents	04	This field contains the number of AES Send and Receive events that were postponed.
1ch	CancelAESFailures	04	This field contains the number of times CancelAESEvent was called and failed to find and cancel the specified AES ECB.
20h	Reserved	04	Reserved.
24h	Reserved	04	Reserved.
28h	TotalRxPackets	04	This field contains the total number of receive packets.
2ch	UnclaimedPackets	04	This field contains the total number of times a packet was received and was not consumed by a Protocol stack.
30h	NumberCustom	02	This field contains the total number of custom variables that follow this field.

Figure 7-18. LSL Statistics Table Format

Note: *The Custom Counters (1 byte each) start at offset 32 h. Following these 4 byte Custom Counters, Custom pointers (4 byte each) point to the length-preceded ASCII strings that describe each custom counter.*

LSL Configuration Table Format

Figure 7-19 describes the LSL Configuration Table fields.

Offset	Name	Size (in bytes)	Description
00h	ConfigMajorVersion	01	The major version of LSL Configuration table.
01h	ConfigMinorVersion	01	The minor version of LSL configuration table.
02h	Reserved	08	Reserved.
0Ah	LSLMajorVersion	01	The major version of the LSL.
0Bh	LSLMinorVersion	01	The minor version of the LSL.
0Ch	MaxBoardsNum	02	This field contains the maximum number of boards for which the LSL is configured.
0Eh	MaxStacksNum	02	This field contains the maximum number of Protocol stacks for which the LSL is configured.
10h	Reserved	12	Reserved.

Figure 7-19. LSL Configuration Table Format

MLID Statistics Table Format

This section describes the MLID Statistics table for MLIDs that interface directly with the LSL. Figure 7-20 describes the various fields of the MLID Statistics Table.

Offset	Name	Size (in bytes)	Description
00h	DriverStatMajorVer	01	The major version of statistics table.
01h	DriverStatMinorVer	01	The minor version of statistics table.
02h	NumberGenericCounters	02	This field contains the number of 4 byte generic counters defined in the statistics table.
04h	ValidCountersMark	04	This bit field is used to signal which generic counters the MLID is actually using.
08h	TotalTxCount	4	This field contains the total number of transmit packets
0Ch	TotalRxCount	4	This field contains the total number of receive packets.
10h	NoECBAvailableCount	4	This field is used to count the total number of incoming packets that were lost because of unavailable ECBs.
14h	TxTooBigCount	4	This field has the number of requested packets for transmission that were too big to send.
18h	TxTooSmallCount	4	This field contains the number of requested packets for transmission that were too small to be transmitted.
1Ch	RxOverflowCount	4	This field indicates the total count of the physical card running out of internal receive buffers.
20h	RxTooBigCount	4	This field contains the number of incoming packets that were bigger than the maximum allowed receive size.
24h	RxTooSmallCount	4	This field contains the number of incoming packets that were smaller than the minimum legal size for the media.

Figure 7-20. MLID Statistics Table Format

Offset	Name	Size (in bytes)	Description
28h	TxMiscCount	4	This field contains the number of Tx packets not sent due to errors.
2Ch	RxMiscCount	4	This field contains the number of Rx packets not received due to errors.
30h	TxRetryCount	4	This counter counts the number of transmit retries.
34h	RxCheckSumErrorCount	4	This counter counts the total number of receive packets with bad CRC.
38h	RxMismatchCount	4	This field counts the total number of incoming packets lost due to conflicting information given to hardware.
3Ch	NumberCustomCounters	2	This field has the total number of Custom counters (4 byte) following this field.

Figure 7-20. MLID Statistics Table Format

Note: *The Custom Counters (4 bytes each) start at offset 3Eh. Following these 4 byte Custom Counters, Custom pointers (4 bytes each) point to the length-preceded ASCII strings that describe each custom counter.*

MLID Configuration Table Format

This section defines the MLID configuration table for MLIDs that interface directly with the LSL. Figure 7-21 describes all the fields of the configuration table.

Offset	Name	Size (in bytes)	Description
0h	Signature	26	This field contains the string "Hardware Driver MLID" with eight spaces appended.
1Ah	ConfigTableMajorVer	1	This field contains Major Version of Configuration Table.
1Bh	ConfigTableMinorVer	1	This field contains Minor Version of Configuration Table.
1Ch	NodeAddress	6	This field contains the card's node address.
22h	ModeFlags	2	ODI defines certain Mode flags. This field combines the state of various mode flags of MLID.
24h	BoardNumber	2	This field contains the board number returned by LSL during initialization.
26h	BoardInstance	2	The MLID should set this field to the physical board instance.
28h	MaxPacketSize	2	This field contains the maximum packet size that the driver/card combination can transmit and/or receive.
2Ah	BestDataSize	2	The total data size = MaxPacketSize - the MAC header (smallest).
2Ch	WorstDataSize	2	The total data size = MaxPacketSize - all the headers (max).
2Eh	NICLongName	4	Pointer to the NIC (card) long name.
32h	NICShortName	4	Pointer to the NIC (card) short name.
36h	FrameTypeString	4	Pointer to the string describing the frame and media type being used by MLID.
3Ah	Reserved	2	Reserved should be 0.

Figure 7-21. MLID Configuration Table

Offset	Name	Size (in bytes)	Description
3Ch	FrameTypeID	2	This field describes the frame and media type being used by this MLID.
3Eh	TransportTime	2	This contains the number of milliseconds it takes MLID and card to transmit a 512 byte packet.
40h	SourceRouteHandler	4	Used for source routing in token ring drivers.
44h	LookAheadSize	4	This field holds the configured look ahead size as set by the Protocol stacks.
46h	LineSpeed	2	This field holds the data route used by physical card's media.
48h	QueueDepth	2	This field contains the current number of transmit ECBs queued by the MLID.
4Ch	Reserved	6	Reserved.
54h	DriverMajorVer	1	This field defines the current revision level of MLID.
55h	DriverMinorVer	1	This field defines the current minor version of the MLID.
56h	Flags	2	This field reflects the bustype (ISA, EISA, etc.) of the physical card.
58h	SendRetries	2	This field represents the number of times an MLID will retry errored transmission.
5Ah	ConfigTableLink	4	This field should be set to 0.
5Eh	SharingFlags	2	This field indicates which hardware resources (IO, Memory, Interrupt, and DMA) an MLID/card can share with another MLID/card.
60h	Slot	2	This field is for PS/2 or EISA cards. This indicates the slot MLID is driving.

Figure 7-21. MLID Configuration Table (Continued)

Offset	Name	Size (in bytes)	Description
62h	IOAddress 1	2	Default I/O port base address.
64h	IORange 1	2	This defines the number of I/O ports used by the card at I/O Address 1.
66h	IOAddress 2	2	This field allows the MLID to have a second I/O port base address.
68h	IORange 2	2	I/O address range for IOAddress 2.
6Ah	MemoryAddress 1	4	Card's default memory base address.
6Eh	MemorySize 1	2	Size of Memory Address 1.
70h	MemoryAddress 2	4	MLID's second memory base address.
74h	MemorySize 2	2	Size of MemoryAddress 2.
76h	IntLine 1	1	Cards default IRQ.
77h	IntLine 2	1	MLID's second IRQ (if needed).
78h	DMALine 1	1	Card's default DMA channel number.
79h	DMALine 2	2	Card's second DMA channel number (if needed).

Figure 7-21. MLID Configuration Table (Continued)

Frame Types and Protocol IDs

The ODI specification defines various frame types and their corresponding Protocol ID numbers for IPX and other protocols. For proper communication under Novell ODI, the user must set the same frame type protocol ID combination at both the transmitting and the receiving ends (client and server). Some most commonly-used frame type and Protocol IDs are described in Figure 7-22.

Frame ID	Frame Type String	Protocol	Protocol ID	Description
2	Ethernet_II	IPX / SPX	8137h	Ethernet using a DEC Ethernet II envelope
3	Ethernet_802.2	IPX / SPX	E0h	Ethernet (802.3) using an 802.2 envelope
10	Ethernet_SNAP	Appletalk ...... so on	809Bh	Ethernet (802.3) using an 802.2 envelope with SNAP

Figure 7-22. Frame Types and Protocol IDs

PACKET TRANSMISSION AND RECEPTION

Packet transmission and reception are a complicated sequences of events. The main data structure that supports packet transmission and reception from protocol stack, LSL and MLID, is an Event Control Block (ECB). Packet transmission and reception are independent processes and are defined in the following sections.

Packet Transmission

In ODI architecture, packet transmission is an asynchronous operation. Packets sent through LSL are connectionless and are neither guaranteed to reach their destination, nor guaranteed to be placed onto the LAN medium. The protocol stacks may use checksum to increase the data integrity and may also provide guaranteed packet delivery to upper layers. In this case, the protocol stacks have to provide the necessary time-outs, retries, and packet acknowledgments to realize a guaranteed delivery system.

The packet transmission process begins when the Protocol stacks gets a request to send a packet or decides that it needs to send a packet. The protocol stack builds an ECB and fills all the necessary fields (see the *Event Control Block (ECB)* section). The ECB is then passed from protocol stack to the LSL by calling SendPacket LSLProtocolStackServicesAPI (see Figure 7-6).

The LSL calls the underlying MLID transmit handler with a pointer to the ECB. The LSL passes the ownership of the ECB and its associated packet data buffers to the MLID. The MLID transmits the packet on the wire. The MLID passes back the ownership of the ECB and its associated packet data buffers to the LSL, regardless of whether the packet transmission was completed successfully or with an error.

The LSL calls the Protocol stack's Event Service Routine specified in the ECB. The Event Service Routine field contains a pointer to a protocol routine (transmit complete) which does the housekeeping operations on the ECB as the transmit is completed.

Packet Reception

The packet reception in ODI architecture is a more complicated process than packet transmission.

The ODI defines three methods of packet reception for protocol stacks:

- Bound protocol stack

- Prescanned protocol stack

- Default protocol stack

The bound protocol stack receives packets with the appropriate protocol ID (PID) in the ECB's Protocol ID field. A bound protocol stack can choose to consume or reject a packet.

Prescan protocol stacks use the Receive Look Ahead method (see the *Receive Look Ahead* section below) to look at all packets received by a particular logical board. The Prescan protocol stack decides to either consume or reject the packet based on the lookahead data.

The default protocol stack receives packets not consumed by the prescan and bound protocol stacks. A default stack can choose to consume or reject a packet. If a packet is rejected by the default protocol stack, it is discarded from the system.

Normal Packet Reception

The following events occur in an ODI system during a packet reception:

The packet comes from the wire into a temporary storage space/memory. Typically, the memory is on the LAN adapter card or in the system. Once the complete packet is received, the LAN controller invokes the MLID (by generating an interrupt), requesting MLID to initiate a packet reception.

The MLID fills out a LookAhead structure and calls the MLID LSL support routine GetStack ECB to obtain a receive buffer from a protocol stack for the packet data (see Figure 7-6). The LookAhead structure is passed to the GetStack ECB call so that the protocol can look at the receive data and decide if it needs the received packet or not.

The LSL decides whether bound, Prescan, or default protocol stacks will be receiving the packet. It calls the protocol that is to receive the data and passes to the protocol stack a pointer to the LookAhead structure describing the received packet.

The protocol stack decides whether it wants to receive the packet or not. It builds an ECB describing a set of receive buffers into which the packet should be placed. It signals to the protocol stack that this protocol stack will consume the packet. The MLID copies the packet data into the provided data buffers, puts the ECB into the LSL hold queue, and calls the Service events (see Figure 7-6), indicating LSL to service the hold queue. The LSL calls the Event Service Routine (ESR field of ECB) signaling to protocol that the packet reception is complete.

Receive Look Ahead Packet Reception

The receive look ahead method passes the beginning portion of the packet to the protocol stack. The protocol stack uses the look ahead data to make decisions like the name of the application that needs the data, size of buffers, and other similar determinations. The protocol stack then obtains the buffers directly from the application and the rest of the packet is dispersed directly into the application buffers. This is the optimal situation because the receive data only crosses the host's bus once. The Receive Look Ahead structure has the following fields:

- MediaHeaderPtr → This is a pointer to a buffer containing the complete low level media header.

- DataLookAheadPtr → This is a pointer to a buffer containing the start of the protocol's header (IPX header).

- DataLookAheadLen → This contains the length of the Data Look Ahead Ptr buffer. This value is normally the MLID's currently configured look ahead size.

- ProtocolID → This contains the protocol ID value.

- BoardNumber → This contains the logical board number that received this packet.

- DataLookAheadDataSize → This contains the total number of data bytes in the received packet.

The size of the receive look ahead data needed by a protocol's receive handler is usually different for each type of protocol stack. The protocol stack can configure the amount of receive look ahead data that the MLID provides by invoking the SetLookAheadSize MLID control functions.

EXAMPLE OF ODI-BASED COMMUNICATION

In this example, let us assume that a user wants to send a mail message to another user. Let us also assume that the mail utility knows the destination address and network address of the mail recipient user. Let us further assume that the complete message fits into a single packet. The complete flow of messages is listed below.

- The mail utility passes the message to the IPX Protocol stack.

- The IPX encapsulates the packet with an IPX header and inserts destination and source addresses into the packet.

- IPX passes the packet to the LSL.

- The LSL checks the board number to which the Protocol stack is bound and passes the packet to the appropriate LAN driver.

- The LAN driver encapsulates the packet in the appropriate frame type (Ethernet_802.3, in this case).

- The LAN driver passes the packet to the LAN board, which adds an 8 byte preamble to the packet. The LAN board also calculates and puts the 4 byte CRC at the end of the packet. The LAN boards transmits the packet on the ethernet wire.

- The destination LAN board receives the packet. The destination LAN board uses the first 8 bytes of preamble to adjust the timing to receive correctly. The receiving LAN board checks the CRC to make sure that the contents of packet is intact.

- The LAN board strips the preamble and CRC and passes the packet to the receiving LAN driver.

- The LAN driver strips the Ethernet_802.3 header from the packet.

- The LAN board gives the Protocol Identification Number (PID) to the LSL. This enables the LSL to determine to which LAN board the Protocol stack is bound.

- The LSL checks the PID and passes the packet to the appropriate Protocol stack (IPX in this case).

- IPX strips off the IPX header and passes the mail message to the receiving portion of the mail utility.

The flow of information involves various different pieces of software under the ODI model. The above steps lists some of the handshake which a packet goes through. It is important to note that the complete process is very compli- cated and hence care should be taken when designing various different pieces for system performance.

SUMMARY

This chapter covers the complete ODI architecture for Novell environment. The ODI architecture is one of the most popular network device driver environ- ments. It also provides the most flexible operation.

The ODI environment initialization is different for DOS and NetWare Operating systems. The data structures used under ODI, although complicat- ed, are very complete for an efficient networking operation.

The packet transmission and reception in ODI is defined in a streamlined manner. This is very important because after initialization (which is not time critical), the packet transmission and reception should be very streamlined.

The ODI architecture presents the most common and flexible architecture to run multiple protocol stacks on top of multiple boards with LSL acting as mul- tiplexer between protocol stacks and LAN boards. The ODI's modular design provides better and improved memory management. Smaller modules require smaller portions of contiguous memory, which makes it easier to load these modules. The ODI architecture allows for very flexible configuration via the NET.CFG file. The LSL passes the incoming packets to the specific Protocol stack. This increases the performance of ODI architecture over the other architectures.

REFERENCES

Malamud, Carl 1990. *Analyzing Novell Networks*. Van Nostrand Reinhold, New York, NY.

____. 1992, *Open Data-Link Interface, Developer Guide for NetWare Server Driver*, Revision E.2, Novell, Inc.

____. 1992, *ODI Developer's LAN Driver Toolkit Guide for DOS Workstation*, Version B, Novell, Inc.

____. 1992, *ODI Developer's Guide for NetWare 3.1x Server Driver Protocol Stacks*, Version 1.00, Novell, Inc.

____. 1992, *ODI Developer's Guide for DOS Workstation Protocol Stacks*, Version 1.10, Novell, Inc.

8

UNIX DLPI Drivers

The UNIX device drivers are very different from some of the other operating systems that we have discussed in this book. In UNIX a device driver becomes part of the UNIX operating system. Hence, in UNIX, a device driver is a collection of routines that make up part of the operating system. The device driver in UNIX hides the hardware specific details from the operating system and the user. It provides a uniform interface between the kernel and the device which allows the device to be accessed using the same system calls as those associated with accessing a regular file. Figure 8-1 illustrates a UNIX device driver along with other parts of UNIX operating system.

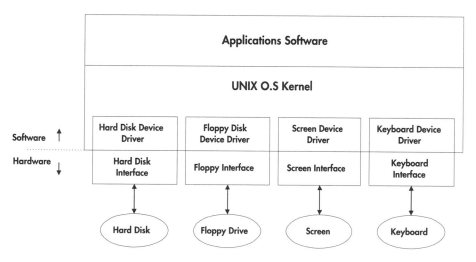

Figure 8-1. UNIX Device Drivers

INTRODUCTION TO DLPI AND LLI SPECIFICATIONS

The Data Link Provider Interface (DLPI) is an interface specification which enables a data link service user to access and use any of a variety of conforming data link service providers without special knowledge of the provider's protocol. The term data link is used in accordance with the definition contained in the standard ISO Data Link Service Definition (DIS 8886—Draft International Standard 8886). The standard defines a standard way for any protocol to access media without the detailed knowledge and implementation of the media (e.g., Ethernet, Token Ring, FDDI, etc.). The service layer definition contained in DIS 8886 standard assumes that a Logical Link Control (LLC) layer is present which conforms to the ISO DIS 8802/2 LLC standard. The relationship between the ISO 7 layer OSI model and the DLPI interface is shown in Figure 8-2.

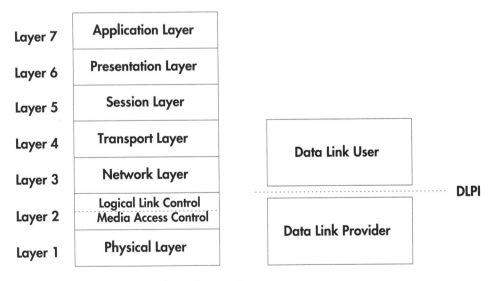

Figure 8-2. DLPI Interface Comparison

The DLPI based interface specifies access to data link service providers (e.g., Ethernet, FDDI, etc.), and does not define a specific protocol implementation. The implementation of the DLPI specification is done by using the STREAMS-based communication mechanism which is explained in the next section. Hence, it is accurate to refer to DLPI based implementation as a STREAMS-based data link provider interface. Almost all commercial implementations of UNIX available today, use the STREAMS-based DLPI implementation for its networking subsystem. The specific implementation that is discussed in this chapter is Santa Cruz Operation's (SCO's) Logical Link Interface (LLI).

The SCO's LLI interface describes the interface to a LAN/WAN card driver as it is used by all SCO transport stacks. The goal of defining this interface is to make sure that any driver conforming to this specification can interoperate with any transport stack (like TCP/IP, NETBEUI, etc.) conforming to the LLI specification. The drivers based on the LLI specification perform some Logical Link Control (LLC) processing to route packets to and from the transport stacks. This processing will be discussed in the later sections of this chapter. The SCO's LLI specification defines the LLI interface which is identical to the AT&T's Data Link Provider Interface (DLPI). The INCLUDE file which is used to build a DLPI or LLI driver is the same INCLUDE file, <sys/dlpi.h>. The data structures and the primitives used are the same between DLPI and LLI specification. The LLI specification defines some semantics of various fields more strictly than DLPI specification. The LLI specification focuses on three main media access control layers: IEEE 802.3 (Ethernet), IEEE 802.4 (Token Bus) and IEEE 802.5 (Token Ring) networks.

There is no restriction on the type of LAN/WAN access method which the LLI driver may use. Also, there is no restriction on the number of interface boards (NIC) a driver may handle nor is there any restriction on the number of transport protocol stacks which may bind to the driver. The specification provides flexibility and extensivibility.

The DLPI and the LLI architecture are based on UNIX System V Stream design. It is very important to understand streams messaging concepts before getting into the technical details of DLPI and LLI specifications. The next section is devoted to basics of streams.

STREAMS OVERVIEW

The STREAMS input-output system was added to UNIX System V implementation. The STREAMS mechanism was first described by Dennis Ritchie in the *AT&T Bell Laboratories Technical Journal Volume 63*, Number 8, October 1984. The STREAMS mechanism was introduced in the UNIX kernel to facilitate the separation of network protocols into functionally distinct layers implemented as separate STREAMS modules. Also the traditional live discipline solution to character based I/O was becoming too slow for certain applications. These drivers were difficult to write, debug and maintain. In addition, only a single live discipline can be active at any given time. STREAMS is designed to overcome all these shortcomings. It is designed to create modular building blocks to connect a wide variety of hardware and software configurations.

STREAMS first appeared in AT&T's System V Release 3.0 in 1986. SCO UNIX has made STREAMS available since 1988 and has used it to implement various SCO's networking products, including TCP-IP.

A STREAM is a flexible character-based full duplex communication link that connects a user process to a device driver. In a simple minimum configuration STREAMS has a STREAMS head that is connected to the user process, and a STREAMS driver that controls the hardware (see Figure 8-3).

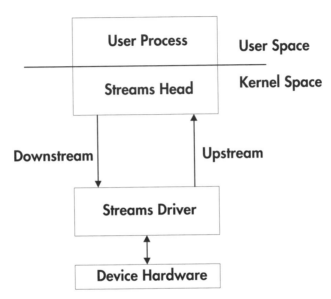

Figure 8-3. A Basic STREAMS Configuration

STREAMS offers a system of linked lists of kernel data structure that combined with special routines to access the structures, provides a full duplex data path between a user process and a device. Each linked list of structures is referred to as a STREAMS message. The message is the basic data type used by the streams. The message contains a description of the message type and the data associated with the message. A message is constructed from one or more message blocks, and is passed downstream from the streams head towards the streams driver, or upstream from the streams driver towards the streams head. The upstream and downstream flow of messages is completely independent of each other and hence, STREAMS messaging becomes full duplex. A streams may also include one or more pushable modules that a user adds or removes from within streams head and streams driver. A typical example of STREAMS configuration would be the implementation of TCP-IP protocol stack over a Ethernet Streams driver. In this configuration two modules are inserted: a TCP streams module and an IP streams module. These two modules are responsible for performing intermediate processing of messages. The Ethernet driver implements the LLC protocol and the manipulating of the underlying Ethernet hardware (see Figure 8-4).

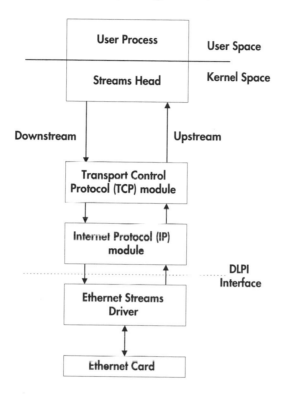

Figure 8-4. A Basic STREAMS Configuration

The connection between the streams head and the streams driver is established automatically when the device is first opened, and a user process can make open(s), close(s), read(s), write(s), and ioctl(s) system calls in exactly the same way as for ordinary character device drivers. A user process may also build the streams to meet its needs by pushing and/or removing modules from a streams using the ioctl(s) system call.

A streams module in its simplest form is two queues. A queue is an instance of queue_t data structure as shown in Figure 8-5. A streams head is an interface provided by the STREAMS system and is standardized. Each streams module is responsible for processing the upstream and downstream messages as it passes through the module.

```
/*
 * queue_t structure
 */
  struct queue {
     struct qinit  *q_qinfo;   /* procs and limits for queue *
     struct msgb   *q-first;   /* first data block */
     struct msgb   *q_last;    /* last data block */
     struct queue  *q_next;    /*queue of next stream */
     struct queue  *q_link;    /*to next queue for scheduling */
     caddr_t       *q_ptr;     /*to private data structure */
     ushort        *q_count;   /*number of block on queue */
     ushort        *q_flag;    /*queue state */
     short         *q_minpsz;  /*minimum packet size accepted by this module */
     short         *q_maxpsz;  /*max packet size accepted by this module */
     ushort        *q_hiwat;   /*queue high water mark */
                   *q_lowat;   /*queue low water mark */
           }
     typedef struct queue queue_t;
```

Figure 8-5. queue_t data structure

A streams driver is the last element in the streams queue. The streams driver provides a uniform interface between the kernel and the hardware.

As shown in Figure 8-5, the data blocks in the queue are of type *msgb*. This data type is the head of a triplet of data structures defining a complete message. A message block is a linked, three-way unit consisting of the *msgb* and *datab* structures and a variable length block.

The message block points to the structure *datab*, called a data block. The data block describes the message type and contains a pointer to a buffer containing the actual data. Figure 8-6 describes the *msgb* structure and Figure 8-7 describes the *datab* data structure.

```
/*
 * Message block descriptor
 */
struct msgb{
      struct msgb     *b_next;    /* next message on queue */
      struct msgb     *b_prev;    /* previous message on queue */
      struct msgb     *b_cont;    /* next message block on queue */
      unsigned char   *b_rptr;    /* first unread byte in buffer */
      unsigned char   *b_wptr;    /* first unwritten byte in buffer */
      struct datab    *b_datap;   /* data block */
      };

typedef struct msgb mblk_t;
```

Figure 8-6. Message Block Descriptor

```
/*
 * Data Block Descriptor
 */
struct datab {
      struct datab    *db_freep; /* Internal Use           */
      unsigned char   *db_base;  /* first byte of buffer   */
      unsigned char   *db_lim;   /* last byte +1 of buffer */
      unsigned char   db_ref;    /* # of messages pointing to this block */
      unsigned char   db_type;   /* message type */
      unsigned char   db_class;  /* Internal Use */
      };

typedef struct datab dblk_t;
```

Figure 8-7. Data Block Descriptor

The three data structures described above form the basis of all STREAMS-based communication. Let us take a typical flow of data in a networking module. If the data or a packet is flowing from a higher layer to a lower layer (layer 4 to layer 3), each layer typically adds few bytes of its own data to the incoming packet. Let us assume that the transport layer receives a message of the type M_DATA (message types are explained in later sections) containing 64 bytes of data and it needs to add another 32 bytes of data to it.

Figure 8-8 shows the message of type M_DATA, containing 64 bytes of data.

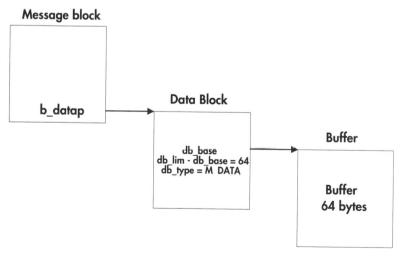

Figure 8-8. An M_DATA Message of 64 bytes

The transport layer streams module, as discussed earlier, would like to extend this message by adding another buffer of length 32 bytes. The transport streams module has two options:

(i)   To allocate a new buffer of size 96 bytes and copy the old buffer and new data in this new buffer and replace the *dl_base* and *dl_lim* pointers to point to this new buffer.

(ii) To allocate a new message block describing the additional buffer space and attach it to the original message block (see Figure 8-9).

The transport layer streams module can choose either of the above two options. The final messages generated, are identical in semantics, irrespective of the option used.

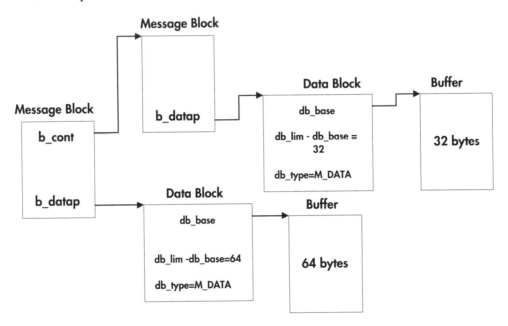

Figure 8-9. A Total Message of 96 bytes

The streams messages have 24 different types (dl_type). The messages are grouped in two different classes called ordinary messages and priority messages. The message types differ in their intended purposes, their treatment at the streams head, and their message queue priorities. Ordinary messages are subject to the regular flow control mechanisms of the streams. These are placed on STREAMS queue on a FIFO basis and are processed on a FIFO basis. Priority messages are not subject to flow control. The priority messages are always placed at the front of the message queue with other priority messages.

STREAMS does not prevent a module or a driver from generating any message type and sending it in any direction on the streams. Each streams module has to follow the established processing and direction rules for each message posted. Figure 8-10 lists the various message types and the classes to which they belong.

Ordinary Message	Priority Message
M_DATA, M_PROTO, M_BREAK, M_PASSFP, M_SIG, M_DELAY, M_CTL, M_IOCTL, M_SETOPTS, M_RSE	M_IOCACK, M_IOCNAK, M_PCPROTO, M_PCSIG, M_READ, M_FLUSH, M_STOP, M_START, M_HANGUP, M_ERROR, M_COPYIN, M_COPYOUT, M_IOCDATA, M_PCRSE

Figure 8-10. Ordinary and Priority Messages

In certain cases, two messages may perform similar functions, but they differ in the classes they belong to and hence, the priority levels.

The DLPI and LLI specifications support the message types which are defined in the <sys/stream.h> file. Currently, only M_PROTO, M_DATA, M_PCPROTO, M_FLUSH, and M_IOCTL messages are used. The discussion below explains the currently used five message types. The remaining message types are described in *Appendix B* of the *AT&T STREAMS Programmer's Guide*. The five different message types which are used to communicate the LLI/DLPI service primitive are discussed below.

M_PROTO: This message type contains internal control information and associated data. The message format is one M_PROTO message block followed by zero or more M_DATA message blocks. M_PROTO messages are generally sent bi-directional on a streams. The semantics of the M_PROTO and M_DATA message blocks are determined by the STREAMS module that receives the message.

For DLPI/LLI modules, a M_PROTO type message block contains the type of primitive (described later) and all the arguments associated with that primitive. The M_DATA type block contains the data associated with the primitive. Figure 8-11 shows an example of M_PROTO type message.

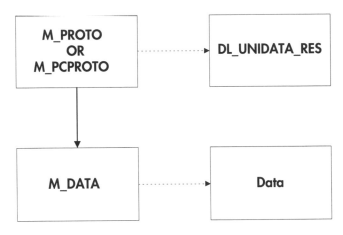

Figure 8-11. M_PROTO type message

M_DATA: This message type is intended to contain ordinary data. M_DATA messages are generally send bi-directional on a streams.

M_PCPROTO: This message has the same format and characteristics as the M_PROTO message type, except for priority. Only one M_PCPROTO message is allowed by the streams head to be placed in its read queue at a time. This message type is intended to allow data and control information to be sent with the constraints of the normal flow control.

M_FLUSH: The M_FLUSH message type requests all the modules and drivers that receive this message to flush their message queues. The first byte of the M_FLUSH message contain flags that specify the module to flush its read queue, write queue, or read and write queue (FLUSHR, FLUSHW, FLUSHRW).

M_IOCTD: The M_IOCTL messages are intended to perform the general ioctl functions of character device drivers. The streams head creates a M_IOCTL message in response to ioctls received from a user process. The format of a M_IOCTL message consists of one M_IOCTL message block linked to zero or more M_DATA message blocks. Streams head constructs an M_IOCTL message block by placing an ioctl structure in its data buffer. The ioctl data structure is explained in Figure 8-12.

```
Struct iocblk
{
      int ioc_cmd;        /* ioctl command type */
      ushort ioc_uid;     /* effective user ID number */
      ushort ioc_gid;     /* effective group ID number */
      uint ioc_id;        /* ioctl identifier */
      uint ioc_count;     /* byte count for ioctl data */
      int ioc_error;      /* error code */
      int ioc_rval;       /* return value */
};
```

Figure 8-12. iocblk structure placed in M_IOCTL data buffer

The response to the M_IOCTL message is contained in an M_IOCACK (positive acknowledgment) or an M_IOCNACK (negative acknowledgment) message. The *ioc_id* field of *iocblk* structure (see Figure 8-12) is used to match response sent to the original message.

The message blocks are allocated by a kernel routine called allocb();

```
mblk_t *
allocb(size, pri)
int size, pri;
```

The *allocb* routine returns a pointer to a message block of type M_DATA with a single data block describing a buffer of at least size bytes attached, or NULL if no message blocks are available. The *pri* parameter indicates the priority of the *allocb* request.

The kernel interface to a streams module and a streams driver is via routines like XXput, XXservice, XXopen, XXclose, and XXadmin. The discussion on the Streams kernel interface, flow control and STREAMS scheduling is beyond the scope of this chapter. Please consult the references list for more details on the kernel interface.

LLI DRIVER SPECIFICATION

This section describes the interface used between SCO transport protocol stacks and the Link Level Interface (LLI) drivers. The LLI specification from SCO is based on AT&T's Data Link Provider Interface (DLPI). The LLI and DLPI drivers use the same data structures, and hence use the same include file <sys/dlpi.h>. The main advantage of following a common specification like LLI is that a driver based on LLI specification will be able to communicate with any SCO transport stack or any other SCO OEM stack conforming to the LLI specification. The LLI driver performs the network hardware manipulation and a small amount of Logical Link Control (LLC) processing. The protocol stack does all the protocol specific processing. This ensures that the protocol stack implementation is hardware-independent and the LLI driver implementation is independent of any protocol specifications. This enables mixing of protocol stacks and hardware very easy. The LLI driver can provide access to any type of LAN/WAN interfaces. However, the SCO's LLI specification focuses on IEEE 802 LANS (802.3/802.4/802.5).

The LLI architecture from SCO has two main versions: LLI 3.1 and LLI 3.2. The LLI 3.1 implementation was used in SCO UNIX 3.2.4 and open Desktop version (ODT) 2.0 and 3.0. The LLI 3.1 based driver implemented the complete LLI interface along with the hardware manipulation. Figure 8-13 illustrates the LLI 3.1 architecture.

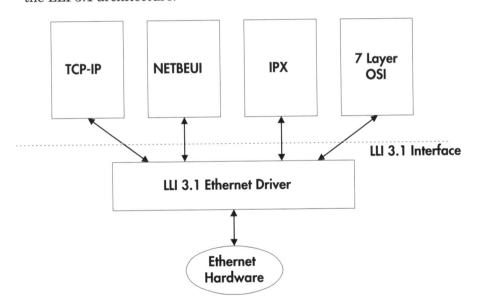

Figure 8-13. LLI 3.1 Architecture

As shown above, LLI 3.1 is an interface definition which defines interfaces between protocol stacks and device drivers. Protocol stacks and drivers are written to LLI 3.1 interfaces. SCO introduced LLI 3.2 specification for its new operating systems. The main objective behind LLI 3.2 specification is to make driver development simpler. The LLI interface is considered to be very complex. Also, the LLI 3.1 specification had a number of problems when it came to Service Access Point (SAP) handling. For example, for a protocol stack to receive 802.3 native frames, it had to bind with address 0xFFFFFFFE. Also, two protocols could not bind to the same address. This meant that only one stack could send and receive 802.3 frames under LLI 3.1. This SAP limitation was overcome in LLI 3.2 specification.

The LLI 3.2 architecture is modular in nature. SCO broke the traditional LLI 3.1 driver into two modules: a module responsible for handling LLI interface and common driver processing, and another module responsible for implementing the hardware specific send and receive functions. This new LLI 3.2 architecture defines an interface between the LLI module and the hardware specific driver. This interface is labeled as Mac Driver Interface (MDI). The protocol stacks still use the LLI interface. The new LLI interface between protocol stacks and the driver has been improved. From a driver developer standpoint, the LLI 3.2 based driver is very easy to develop because it has to implement the hardware dependent module only. Two generic LLI modules are provided by SCO.

Figure 8-14 illustrates the LLI 3.2 architecture.

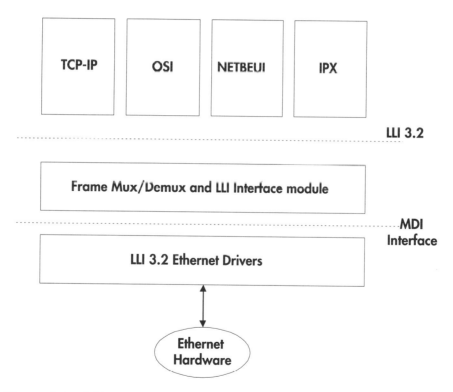

Figure 8-14. LLI 3.2 Interface

The discussion in the various subparts of this section is for LLI 3.1 specification. LLI 3.2 specification has not been completed or implemented at the time of the publication of this chapter.

STREAMS Messages and Primitives

The following section describes various LLI 3.1 primitives. The LLI primitives are based on the IEEE 802.2 Logical Link Control (LLC) Service layer definition. In the LLC service layer model, request/response primitives are passed from a higher layer (3 or above) down to second layer (Data Link Layer). Similarly, indication/confirmation primitives are passed from second layer to its users like layer 3.

Figure 8-15 illustrates the flow of primitives.

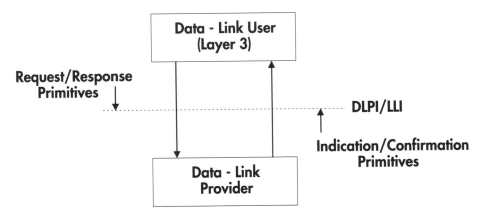

Figure 8-15. Flow of Primitives

The message/primitive flow discussed in this section uses the direction convention as seen for the LLI driver. Hence, a data link command primitive going upward means that it was initiated by the LLI and is destined for the LLI user. A primitive going down means that it was initiated by the LLI user (e.g., transport layer) and is directed to the LLI layer.

The primitives which move up and down carry very specific messages/data. The exact function or message that each primitive is responsible for is discussed in the next few sections.

Figure 8-16 contains the summary definitions of all the primitives supported by LLI 3.1 specification. The dl_primitive column lists the values for the fields in the data structure which define these primitives.

Mnemonic	dl_primitive	Description	Direction
DL_INFO_REQ	0	Request for Protocol parameter information.	DOWN
DL_BIND_REQ	1	Request for Protocol address binding.	DOWN
DL_UNBIND_REQ	2	Request for unbinding with Protocol address.	DOWN
DL_UNIDATA_REQ	7	Request for sending/ transmitting data.	DOWN
DL_INFO_ACK	3	Providing Protocol parameter information.	UP
DL_BIND_ACK	4	Acknowledging Protocol address binding.	UP
DL_ERROR_ACK	5	Error Indicator.	UP
DL_OK_ACK	6	Acknowledging successful completion.	UP
DL_UNITDATA_IND	8	Indicates data reception.	UP
DL_UDERROR_IND	9	Indicates Unit data error.	UP

Figure 8-16. LLI Primitives

The discussion which follows, explains the flow of primitives between the local and remote LLI Streams environment. Some of these primitives are used within a local LLI Streams environment to obtain local information. Other primitives are used to send and receive information from remote LLI Streams driving different LAN hardware.

A DL_INFO_REQ primitive is used by the LLI user to obtain information about the LLI Streams. The LLI driver returns the information in a DL_INFO_ACK message (see Figure 8-17).

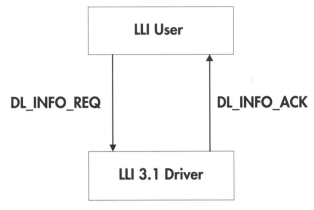

Figure 8-17. Information Reporting

Another service used in the LLI 3.1 specification is bind service. A data link user's identity (or LLI user) is established by associating it with a data link service access point (DLSAP) which is the point through which the user will communicate with the data link provider. A DLSAP is identified by a DLSAP address. This address is very important because multiple data link users might be using the same data link and hence, some level of addressing is needed to identify the recipient of the message. A DLSAP address is associated with a particular streams. The bind service associates a data link service access point (DLSAP) address with a stream.

The DL_BIND_REQ message requests the LLI driver to bind a DLSAP with a stream. The LLI driver indicates a success by sending DL_BIND_ACK, or a failure by sending a DL_ERROR_ACK (see Figure 8-18).

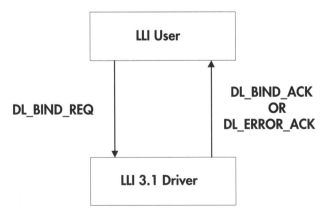

Figure 8-18. Bind Service

The bind request, if successful, will make the streams active for processing data transfers.

The DL_UNBIND_REQ message is sent by the LLI user to the LLI Streams driver requesting to unbind all DLSAPs from a stream. The LLI driver responds by sending DL_OK_ACK, or failure with a DL_ERROR_ACK message.

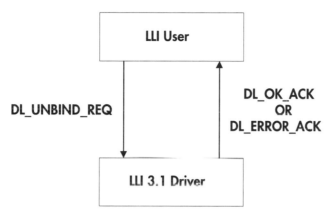

Figure 8-19. Unbind Service

The LLI architecture supports connectionless mode of data transfer service. This means that there is no guarantee of data delivery between peer LLI users. The advantage of connectionless service is that the LLI user does not have to carry the overhead of establishing and releasing a connection.

A LLI user uses DL_UNITDATA_REQ message to request LLI driver to transmit data on the LAN. The peer LLI driver receives the data and uses DL_UNITDATA_IND message to pass the received data to the peer LLI user (see Figure 8-20).

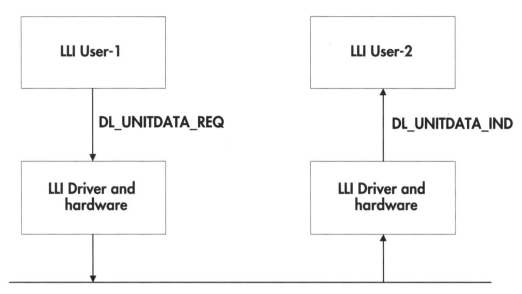

Figure 8-20. Data Transfer Service

If the data reaches the peer LLI user correctly, no action is taken by the peer LLI user. However, if the LLI driver detects an error in the data unit received, the LLI driver sends a DL_UDERROR_IND message to the LLI user.

The following sub-sections discuss each of these LLI primitives, their format and structures. This sub-section should provide more insight into these streams LLI primitives/messages.

Figure 8-16 listed all the LLI primitives. The following sections list the detail format of these primitives.

DL_INFO_REQ Message (Down)

The LLI user uses this message to request information about the LLI streams from the LLI driver. The format of this message is one M_PCPROTO message block, which contains the following structure:

```
typedef struct {
        ulong dl_primitive;  /* DL_INFO_REQ */
} dl_info_req_t;
```

The LLI driver has to perform one of the following tasks on receipt of this message:

(i)   Generate a DL_INFO_ACK response message containing all information

(ii)   If an error occurred and DL_INFO_ACK message cannot be sent by the LLI driver, it should send a DL_ERROR_ACK response message.

The LLI user has to wait for one of the above acknowledgments before it can issue any other primitives.

DL_INFO_ACK message (Up)

The message is generated by the LLI driver in response to DL_INFO_REQ. This message contains the result of DL_INFO_REQ message and hence, indicates successful completion of the DL_INFO_REQ message. The message consists of one M_PCPROTO message containing the following structure:

```
typedef struct {
    ulong    dl_primitive;     /* DL_INFO_ACK   */
    ulong    dl_max_sdu;       /* Maximum packet size   */
    ulong    dl_min_sdu;       /* Minimum packet size     */
    ulong    dl_addr_length;   /* Mac address length 2 or 6 bytes   */
    ulong    dl_mac_type;      /* Type of Mac/Media     */
    ulong    dl_reserved;      /* Reserved    */
    ulong    dl_current_state; /* Current state of LLI layer    */
    ulong    dl_reserved[9];   /* Reserved     */
    } dl_info_ack_t;
```

The dl_info_ack_t data structures fields/parameters are defined below:

dl_primitive: Is always set to DL_INFO_ACK for this message type.

dl_max_sdu: This parameter defines the maximum data packet size. For Ethernet networks, this is 1500. This parameter has positive integer values which are greater than or equal to dl_min_sdu.

dl_min_sdu: This parameter defines the minimum data packet size. The Ethernet networks define a value of 1 for this field. The LLI driver is responsible for padding the packet with extra bytes to make the packet data size = 46 bytes for Ethernet networks (total packet size = 64 bytes), if the data bytes passed by LLI user is less than 46.

dl_addr_length: This is the Mac address length field. IEEE 802.3 standard defines Mac address of length 2 or 6 bytes. Typically, all 802.3 networks use 6 byte addresses.

dl_mac_type:	This field defines the media supported by the LLI driver. The possible values are defined in <sys/dlpi.h>. This field indicates to LLI user if the underlying media is 802.3, 802.4, 802.5, and FDDI, HDLC.
dl_reserved:	Reserved field.
dl_current_state:	Indicates the current state for the link level streams to the LLI user. The list of values are defined in <sys/dlpi.h> see *Appendix C*.
dl_reserved2:	Reserved

DL_BIND_REQ message (Down)

This message is generated by the LLI user for the LLI driver requesting the LLI driver to bind an address to the user streams. This message consists of one M_PROTO message block containing the following structure:

```
typedef struct {
      ulong   dl_primitive;    /* DL_BIND_REQ    */
      ulong   dl_sap;          /* Local SAP address to bind    */
      ulong   dl_max_coniud;   /* Ignored by LLI    */
      ushort  dl_service_mode; /* Always DL_CLDLS    */
      ushort  dl_conn_mgmt;    /* Ignored    */
} dl_bind_req_t;
```

The detailed description of various fields/parameters is as follows:

dl_primitive:	This field describes the primitive being represented by this data structure. This field is DL_BIND_REQ for this message.
dl_sap:	This field indicates to the LLI driver the SAP address which should be bound to this user streams. LLI uses 0xFFFFFFFE as the default address and 0xFFFFFFFF as the broadcast address.
dl_max_conind:	The LLI driver only supports connectionless mode of service. However, this field has no meaning for connectionless mode of service. Hence, this field is ignored for LLI drivers.
dl_service_mode:	The field indicates the type of service for this streams. LLI drivers/users only support connectionless mode and hence this field contains DL_CLDLS value for LLI streams.

dl_conn_mgmt: This field is meaningful for connection oriented mode of service only. This field is ignored for connectionless service and hence, for LLI environment.

The LLI driver has to provide one of the following responses after receiving a DL_BIND_REQ primitive:

(i) Sends a DL_BIND_ACK to LLI user indicating successful processing of DL_FIND_REQ

(ii) Sends a DL_ERROR ACK message indicating an error condition

DL_BIND_ACK message (Up)

This message reports a successful binding of an address (SAP) to a stream. This primitive is generated in response to a DL_BIND_REQ primitive. The message consists of one M_PROTO message block containing the following structure:

```
typedef struct {
      ulong     dl_primitive;   /* DL_BIND_ACK    */
      ulong     dl_sap;         /* SAP which as bound   */
      ulong     dl_addr_length; /* Mac address length   */
      ulong     dl_addr_offset; /* Mac address offset   */
      ulong     dl_reserved[2]; /* Reserved      */
} dl_bind_ack_t;
```

The detailed description of all the fields is as follows:

dl_primitive: This field describes the primitive being represented by this data structure. This field value is DL_BIND_ACK for this message.

dl_sap: This field indicates the SAP which was bound to by DL_BIND_REQ message.

dl_addr_length: This field indicates the length of the Mac address in bytes. Typically this field has a volume of 6.

dl_addr_offset: This field indicates the offset from the beginning of the M_PROTO message block where the local Mac address starts. Typically, the Mac address starts after the dl_bind_act_t structure fields.

dl_reserved[2]: Reserved field.

DL_UNBIND_REQ Message (Down)

This message requests the LLI driver to unbind a SAP from a stream. The SAP was previously bound to the streams by using DL_BIND_REQ message. This message consists of one M_PROTO message block. The structure of this message block contains:

```
typedef struct {
     ulong dl_primitive;   /* DL_UNBIND_REQ   */
} dl_unbind_req_t;
```

The dl_primitive field contains the value of DL_UNBIND_REQ for this message. The LLI driver has to respond with one of the following responses after receiving a DL_BIND_REQ message.

(i)   The successful processing of DL_UNBIND_REQ is indicated by sending a DL_OK_ACK message with dl_correct primitive field set to DL_UNBIND_REQ.

(ii) Any error in processing of DL_UNBIND_REQ is indicated by a DL_OK_ACK message being sent upward.

DL_OK_ACK message (Up)

This message is initiated by the LLI driver. It indicates to the LLI user that a previously issued request was received correctly. This message is only initiated for request primitives that require positive acknowledgment (e.g., DL_UNBIND_REQ message). This message consists of a M_PCPROTO message block. The structure of this message block contains:

```
typedef struct {
     ulong   dl_primitive;         /*  DL_OK_ACK   */
     ulong   dl_correct_primitive; /*  Previous successful primitive   */
} dl_ok_ack_t;
```

The dl_primitive field contains the type of this primitive and should be set to DL_OK_ACK. The dl_correct_primitive contains the type of the successfully received primitive that is being acknowledged.

DL_ERROR_ACK Message (Up)

This message is initiated by the LLI driver. It indicates to the LLI user that an error occurred in the previously-issued message. The error code included in this message explains the nature of the error. This message consists of one M_PCPROTO message block. The structure of this message block contains:

```
typedef struct {
      ulong   dl_primitive;            /* DL_ERROR_ACK    */
      ulong   dl_error_primitive;      /* Error primitive    */
      ulong   dl_errno;                /* DLPI/LLI error code     */
      ulong   dl_unix_errno;           /* UNIX error code    */
} dl_error_ack_t;
```

The detailed description of all the primitives are as follows:

dl_primitive: Indicates the type of primitive. This field is always DL_ERROR_ACK for this message.

dl_error_primitive: This field contains the type of primitive which caused this DL_ERROR_ACK primitive to be generated.

dl_errno: This field contains the DLPI/LLI error code associated with the error which occurred. The error codes are one of the following:

DL_BADSAP: Illegal dl_sap value in DL_BIND_REQ message.

DL_ACCESS: Indicates access privileges problems

DL_OUTSTATE: Indicates that LLI driver is in a state where it cannot act on the previously received primitive.

DL_SYSERR: Indicates that a UNIX system error has occurred.

DL_UNITDATA_REQ Message (Down)

The LLI driver supports only the connectionless mode of data transfer. This means that a data packet is transmitted on the network without establishing any connection. This message primitive is used to request data transmission on the network. The message is generated by the LLI user and passed to LLI driver. The connectionless mode of data transfer does not guarantee the transfer to reach the other end. It also has less overhead associated with it.

The DL_UNITDATA_REQ message consists of one M_PROTO message block containing the structure below, followed by one or more M_DATA blocks containing data bytes which need to be transmitted. The total amount of data included in the DL_UNITDATA_REQ is limited by the parameter dl_man_sdu in the DL_INFO_ACK primitive. The M_PROTO message block contains:

```
typedef struct {
      ulong   dl_primitive;            /* DL_UNITDATA_REQ     */
      ulong   dl_dest_addr_length;     /* Mac address length     */
      ulong   dl_dest_addr_offset;     /* Mac address offset     */
      ulong   dl_reserved[2];          /* Reserved    */
} dl_unitdata_req_t;
```

The detailed description of all the primitives are as follows:

dl_primitve: Indicates the type of primitive. This field is always DL_UNITDATA_REQ for this message.

dl_dest_addr_length: This field represents the length of the Mac address in bytes. This length should match the address length returned in DL_INFO_ACK primitive.

dl_dest_addr_offset: This field indicates the offset from the beginning of the M_PROTO message block where the destination Mac address begins.

dl_reserved[2]: Reserved field.

This primitive is not acknowledged in LLI architecture. The LLI driver accepts this primitive from LLI user and queues the packet for transmission. There is no guarantee that the packet will reach its destination in the connectionless mode of service. If the LLI driver discovers an error in the request, it generates a message DL_UDERROR_IND to report the problem to the LLI user.

DL_UNITDATA_IND Message (Up)

This primitive is used to indicate to the LLI user that a data packet which is addressed to it has arrived. The message consists of one M_PROTO message block followed by one or more M_DATA blocks containing the user data of the LLI frame. The format of the M_PROTO message block is as follows:

```
typedef struct {
    ulong   dl_primitive;        /* DL_UNITDATA_IND     */
    ulong   dl_src_addr_length;  /* Source Mac length      */
    ulong   dl_src_addr_offset;  /* Source Mac address offset   */
    ulong   dl_dest_addr_length; /* Destination Mac address length   */
    ulong   dl_dest_addr_offset; /* Destination Mac address offset   */
    ulong   dl_reserved;         /* Reserved    */
} dl_unitdata_ind_t;
```

The description of all the fields of the above structure is as follows:

dl_primitve: This is the type of the primitive. It should always be DL_UNITDATA_IND.

dl_dest_addr_length: This is the length of Mac address (destination) in bytes. Typically, for 802 networks this field is 6.

dl_dest_addr_offset: This is the offset from the beginning of the M_PROTO message block where the destination Mac address begins.

dl_src_addr_length: The is the length of Mac address (source) in bytes. Typically, for 802 networks this field is 6.

dl_src_addr_offset: This is the offset from the beginning of the M_PROTO message block where the source Mac address begins.

dl_reserved: Reserved field.

DL_UDERROR_IND Message (Up)

This primitive indicates to the LLI user that a previously sent DL_UNITDATA_REQ had an error. The primitive is sent by the LLI driver to the LLI user. The message consists of either one M_PROTO message block or one M_PCPROTO message block. The structure shown below is contained in the message block.

```
typedef struct {
      ulong   dl_primitive;         /* DL_UDERROR_IND    */
      ulong   dl_dest_addr_length;  /* Destination Mac address length   */
      ulong   dl_dest_addr_offset;  /* Destination Mac address offset   */
      ulong   dl_reserved;          /* Reserved   */
      ulong   dl_errno;             /* DLPI error code    */
} dl_uderror_ind_t;
```

The description of all the fields of the above structure is as follows:

dl_primitive: This is a type of primitive. It should always be DL_UDERROR_IND.

dl_dest_addr_length: This is the length of Mac address (destination) in bytes. Typically, for 802 networks this field is 6.

dl_dest_addr_offset: This is the offset from the beginning of the M_PROTO message block where the destination Mac address begins.

dl_reserved: Reserved.

dl_errno: This field indicates the nature of the error that occurred. The value of this field is one of the error codes defined in <sys/dlpi.h> file (see *Appendix C*).

I/O Controls

Streams messages are also used to communicate I/O control messages to and from streams drivers. In LLI architecture, the LLI driver specification has its custom I/O controls which it supports, and hence the LLI user can make I/O requests via streams messages. The structure of such a request is on M_IOCTL type message block optionally followed by one or more M_DATA blocks pointed to by *b_cont* field of the *msgb* structure (see Figure 8-9). The M_IOCTL message block reception may generate two types of response from the LLI driver: M_IOCACK (positive acknowledgment) or M_IOCNACK (negative acknowledgment). Figure 8-12 illustrates the *iocblk* structure which is used to define M_IOCTL, M_IOCACK & M_IOCNACK messages.

Figure 8-21 lists all the I/O control messages supported by the LLI driver.

Name	DESCRIPTION
MACIOC_DIAG	Set Mac Diagnostics
MACIOC_UNITSEL	Mac Unit Select
MACIOC_SETMCA	Set Multicast Address
MACIOC_DELMCA	Delete Multicast Address
MACIOC_CLRMCA	Clear Multicast Table
MACIOC_GETMCA	Get Multicast Table
MACIOC_GETIFSTAT	Get BSD Style Interface Statistics
MACIOC_GETADDR	Get Mac Address
MACIOD_GETSTAT	Get Mac Statistics
MACIOC_PROMISC	Set Promiscuous Reception
MACIOC_GETRADDR	Get Factory Mac Address
MACIOC_CLRSTAT	Clear Mac Statistics
MACIOC_GETMCCSIZ	Get Multicast Table Size
MACIOC_HWDEPEND	Hardware Dependent

Figure 8-21. LLI I/O Control Interface

The detailed description of various ioctls is given in the next section.

MACIOC_DIAG—SET MAC DIAGNOSTICS

This request is issued by the LLI user to the LLI driver, requesting the LLI driver to print debugging information on the console. The amount of debugging information is controlled by the value of first two bytes contained in an M_DATA type message block pointed to by the *b_cont* field of the M_IOCTL type message block. The exact relationship between the debugging level and the amount of information printed on the console is dependent upon the implementor. The only rule that should be followed is that a higher debugging level should force more information on the console.

A successful acknowledgment is given by sending a M_IOCACK type message block to the LLI user containing the original iocblk structure with *ioc_rval* set to zero. An unsuccessful acknowledgment is sent by sending an M_IOC-NACK type message with *ioc_error* set to EINVAL and *ioc_rval* set to -1.

MACIOC_UNITSEL—MAC UNIT SELECT

This request is used by LLI user to tell the LLI driver (supporting multiple controllers) to associate itself with a certain controller. This request only applies to drivers which support multiple controllers. The M_IOCTL message block has an associated M_DATA message block which contains a *ushort* which is the controller number to be selected. Positive and negative acknowledgment is given by LLI driver via M_IOCACK and M_IOCNACK messages, respectively.

MACIOC_SETMCA—SET MULTICAST ADDRESS

The IOCTL request is used by the LLI user to add another multicast address in the list of multicast addresses being supported by the LLI driver. The LLI driver should start receiving all packets coming to this multicast address. The LLI driver receives a MAIOC_SETMCA request with one M_DATA block associated with it. The M_DATA block contains one MAC address.

MACIOC_CLRMCA—CLEAR MULTICAST TABLE

The request is issued to the LLI driver, instructing it to clear its entire multicast address table. This request has a M_IOCTL message block of type MACIOC_CLRMCA with no M_DATA message block associated with it. After this request, the LLI driver should only receive packets coming to the broadcast address and its individual address. No further multicast address packets should be received. Successful completion of this is indicated to LLI by sending an M_IOCACK type message block. Any errors are reported via M_IOCNACK type message block.

MACIOC_GETMCA—Get Multicast Address Table

This is a request for the LLI driver to return the contents of the multicast address table. The LLI driver receives a M_IOCTL message of type MACIOC_GETMCA with the *b_cont* field pointing to an M_DATA block. The buffer contained/pointed to by the M_DATA block contains the space for the multicast address table.

The successful completion of this request is an M_IOCACK message from LLI driver with *ioc_count* set to the size, in bytes, of the multicast address table, *ioc_rval* set to 0, and an associated M_DATA block containing a copy of the multicast address table. Errors are signaled by returning an M_IOCNACK message block.

MACIOC_GETIFSTAT—Get BSD Style Interface Statistics

This request is used to get the interface statistics. The LLI driver receives an M_IOCTL message block of type MACIOC_GETIFSTAT with the *b_cont* field pointing to M_DATA block which contains a buffer space for a data structure of the following format.

```
typedef struct{
     struct mac_ifstats *ifs_next;  /* next interface on chain */
     char *ifs_name;          /* interface name */
     short ifs_unit;          /* unit number */
     short ifs_active;        /* non-zero if this interface is running */
     caddr_t *ifs_addr;       /* list of addresses */
     short ifs_mtu;           /* max. transmission unit */
     int ifs_ipackets;        /* packets received on interface */
     int ifs_errors;          /* input errors on interface */
     int ifs_opackets;        /* packets sent on interface */
     int ifs_oerrors;         /* output errors on interface */
     int ifs_collisions;      /* collision on 802.3 interface */
} mac_ifstats_t;
```

The successful completion of this request is indicated by the LLI driver sending an M_IOCACK message with the associated M_DATA block containing the statistics. Errors are reported via M_IOCNACK message block.

MACIOC_GETADDR—Get MAC Address

This ioctl request is used by the LLI user to request the LLI driver to return the current MAC address being used by the controller. The LLI driver receives an M_IOCTL message block of type MACIOC_GETADDR with an associated M_DATA message block. The driver copies the MAC address into the M_DATA block and sets the *ioc_count* to the size of that address. It then constructs an M_IOCACK message with the associated M_DATA block containing the MAC address.

MACIOC_SETADDR—Set MAC Address

This ioctl is used to set the MAC address in use by the network controller. The LLI driver receives an M_IOCTL message block of type MACIOC_SETADDR with an M_DATA block containing the new Source MAC address. The LLI driver should configure all the outgoing packets so that the new MAC Source address is used. The driver indicates successful completion by sending an M_IOCACK message. Errors are indicated by the LLI driver by sending M_IOCNACK message block.

MACIOC_GETRADDR—Get Factory MAC Address

The request is used to get the factory MAC address of the controller. The MACIOC_GETADDR returns the current MAC address (may have been changed by MACIOC_SETADDR) whereas MACIOC_GETRADDR returns the original MAC address set at the factory. The LLI driver receives an M_IOCTL message block of type MACIOC_GETRADDR with an associated M_DATA block. The LLI driver retrieves the original MAC address (usually stored in a EEPROM on the network card) and puts it into the M_DATA block and attaches this block to M_IOCACK message block. This message block is sent to the LLI user. Any errors are returned via M_IOCNACK.

MACIOC_PROMISC—Set Promiscuous Reception Mode

The support for this ioctl is optional. The LLI driver receives an M_IOCTL message block of type MACIOC_PROMISC with no M_DATA blocks associated with it. The LLI driver, if possible, configures the controller so that all valid MAC frames are received from the network by the LLI driver and networking hardware. The frames are passed to the LLI user without any pre-processing along with headers and checksums.

The successful completion of this message is indicated to the LLI user by sending an M_IOCACK message. Any errors are acknowledged by sending M_IOCNACK message.

MACIOC_GETSTAT—Get MAC Statistics

This ioctl is used by the LLI user to request media interface statistics from the LLI driver. The LLI driver is responsible for maintaining all the media statistics. It also keeps all the statistics related to the interface. The LLI driver receives a M_IOCTL message block of type MACIOC_GETSTAT with the *b_cont* field pointing to an M_DATA block. The LLI driver, on reception, creates a M_IOCACK message with the following structure in the M_DATA block and sends it to LLI user.

```
typedef struct {
      ulong   mac_frame_xmit;  /* Frames Transmitted */
      ulong   mac_bcast_xmit;  /* Broadcast Frames Transmitted */
      ulong   mac_mcast_xmit;  /* Multicast Frames Transmitted */
      ulong   mac_lbolt_xmit;  /* Frames Transmitted per Second */
      ulong   mac_frame_recv;  /* Frames Received */
      ulong   mac_bcast_recv;  /* Broadcast Frames Received */
      ulong   mac_mcast_recv;  /* Multicast Frames Received */
      ulong   mac_lbolt_recv;  /* Frames Received per Second */
      ulong   mac_frame_def;   /* Frames Deferred */
      ulong   mac_collisions;  /* Total Collisions */
      ulong   mac_frame_coll;  /* Frames involved in a collision */
      ulong   mac_oframe_coll; /* Out of Frame Collision */
      ulong   mac_xs_coll;     /* Frames dropped due to excessive collision */
      ulong   mac_frame_nosr;  /* Frames dropped due to no streams */
      ulong   mac_no-resource; /* Frames dropped due to no resources */
      ulong   mac_badsum;      /* Bad Checksums Received */
      ulong   mac_align;       /* Bad Alignment Received */
      ulong   mac_badlen;      /* Bad length Received */
      ulong   mac_badsap;      /* Bad SAP Received */
      ulong   mac_mcast_rjct;  /* Multicast Frames Rejected */
      ulong   mac_carrier;     /* Errors due to lost carrier */
      ulong   mac_badcts;      /* Error due to lost CTS */
      ulong   mac_baddma;      /* DMA Over/Under runs */
      ulong   mac_timeouts;    /* Device Timeouts */
      ulong   mac_intr;        /* Device Interrupts */
      ulong   mac_spur_intr;   /* Spurious Interrupts */
      unsigned long  mac_ioctets;     /* received octets */
      unsigned long  mac_ooctects;    /* transmitted octets */
      unsigned long  mac_ifspeed;     /* net interface speed (bits/sec) */
      unsigned long  mac_reserved [1]; /* Reserved */
} mac_stats_t;
```

Any errors in completion of MACIOC_GETSTAT request are communicated by LLI driver by sending a M_IOCNACK message block to the LLI user.

MACIOC_CLRSTAT—Clear MAC Statistics

This ioctl is a request by the LLI user to the LLI driver to clear the Statistics counters kept by the LLI driver. The LLI driver receives an M_IOCTL message block of type MACIOC_CLRSTAT with no M_DATA block. The LLI driver clears all its statistics counters on reception of MACIOC_CLRSTAT. The LLI driver informs of successful completion via M_IOCACK message. Any errors are reported by the LLI driver via an M_IOCNACK message.

MACIOC_GETMCSIZ—Get Multicast Table Size

This ioctl is used by the LLI user to get the size of the current Multicast Table. This information is used by the LLI user to determine the size of the buffer for M_DATA associated with MACIOC_GETMCA ioctl. The LLI driver receives an M_IOCTL message block of type MACIOC_GETMCSIZ with no M_DATA associated with it. On successful completion, the LLI driver constructs an acknowledgment via an M_IOCACK message with ioc_rval set to the size of the multicast address table in bytes. Any errors are reported via M_IOCNACK.

MACIOC_HWDEPEND—Hardware Dependent

This ioctl is used for the implementator's own use.

SUMMARY

The focus of this chapter is UNIX networking devices drivers. The UNIX networking device drivers are based upon STREAMS messaging concepts. This chapter, discusses the STREAMS messaging concepts and the implementation of the 7 layer OSI networking model using STREAMS. In addition, the chapter discusses the DLPI/LLI device driver interface for networking cards running under UNIX. The LLI specification/architecture is unique to SCO, the most popular UNIX implementation on IBM PCs. The various primitives implemented under LLI and the flow of primitives from LLI user to and from LLI driver are also discussed in this chapter. The LLI architecture has a very flexible I/O control interface. This interface can be used by LLI users to obtain various kinds of information like detailed statistics, multicast address tables, and factory MAC addresses. This I/O control interface is also discussed in this chapter. The LLI specification is a subset of the AT&T's DLPI specification. This chapter focuses only on the LLI specification. Readers interested in the DLPI specification should read the DLPI specification as referenced in the *References* section.

REFERENCES

Egan, Janet I. and Teixeira, Thomas J. 1988. *Writing UNIX Device Drivers*, John Wiley and Sons, Inc., New York, NY.

Kettle, Peter and Steve Statler 1993. *Writing Device Drivers for SCO UNIX, A Practical Approach*, Addison-Wesley Publishing Company, MA.

Pajari, George 1992. *Writing UNIX Device Drivers*, Addison-Wesley Publishing Company, MA.

____. 1992, *LLI Driver Interface Specification*, Version 3.1 Rev 3a, The Santa Cruz Operation, Inc. 400 Encinal Street, P.O. Box 1900, Santa Cruz, CA.

____. 1992. *SCO UNIX Operating System,* Version 4.0, Device Driver Writer's Guide Supplement, The Santa Cruz Operation, Inc. 400 Encinal Street, P.O. Box 1900, Santa Cruz, CA.

____. 1989. *SCO UNIX System V/386 Development System, Device Driver Writer's Guide,* The Santa Cruz Operations, Inc. 400 Encinal Street, P.O. Box 1900, Santa Cruz, CA.

____. 1991. *A Streams-based Data Link Provider Interface—Version 2*, UNIX International, 20 Waterview Boulevard, Parsippany, NJ.

APPENDIX A

Chip Architecture

INTRODUCTION

The networking card marketplace has various networking cards following various data movement architectures. Typically, a network interface card (NIC) is responsible for implementing the media access control protocol like ethernet, token ring, and FDDI. The NIC is also responsible for moving the data to and from the network cable. The data movement is the most important function which a NIC has to perform. Typically, the data that comes to and from the cable has to be moved to and from the system memory. The protocols that operate above the NIC use the system memory to store the packet data. The packet that comes from the network cable has to be placed in the system memory before the protocol can use it. This is done by using one of the following three different architectures:

- Direct Memory Access (DMA)
- Shared Memory Access
- Programmed I/O

The DMA mode of operation is again split into two separate architectures: bus master DMA or slave DMA. In the bus master DMA architecture, the NIC is responsible for accessing the system memory directly and reading or writing data from/to the system memory. In the slave DMA architecture, a system DMA controller (like 8237 chip in an IBM PC-AT) is used to move data to and from the system memory and the NIC.

The shared memory mode architecture based NIC contains static RAM on the NIC which is dual port RAM. This means that the RAM on the NIC is visible as a memory resource to the system and also to the NIC (dual ported). The NIC can write data into the RAM and this data can be read by the system. Similarly, the system can write the data into this RAM and the NIC can read it out. The main point in the shared memory mode architecture is that the Niche's shared RAM appears as system memory on the system processor side and can be accessed (read/write) by using standard memory "move" instructions.

The third architecture is based on the programmed I/O(PIO) mode of data transfer. In a PIO based NIC some RAM is configured as two separate FIFOs— one for transmit and the other for receive path. Data is written or read from the FIFO via two I/O ports. The 80x86 processor instructions which are used in this case are IN and OUT instructions. The data is written or read a byte or a word at a time from the receive and transmit FIFOs.

A NIC may be based on one of the above three architectures. The fastest method of moving data is bus master DMA. Each architecture has advantages and disadvantages associated with it. The example NIC discussed in this section is a single chip ethernet controller from Advanced Micro Devices called PCnet-ISATM (Am79C960). This single chip ethernet controller is a bus master DMA controller on the ISA bus. The next few sections discuss the architecture and transmit/receive data flow for this NIC. These sections are intended to provide the reader with a typical NIC architecture and the software interface for a typical NIC. This background information should help the reader with understanding networking device drivers.

PCnet-ISA CHIP ARCHITECTURE

The PCnet-ISA chip is a single chip ethernet controller for the industry standard ISA bus. The PCnet-ISA chip interfaces directly to the ISA bus. The chip supports the IEEE 802.3/ANSI 8802-3 and Ethernet standards.

PCnet-ISA is a bus master DMA-based device. The bus master DMA interface of the chip performs all the DMA transfers on the ISA bus. This configuration enhances system performance because the PCnet-ISA chip DMA controller will be performing the DMA cycles while the CPU and the system DMA controller (8237) perform other functions. The PCnet-ISA has the capability of addressing 16 Meg of system memory directly (24 address bits). The chip also has individual transmit and receive FIFOs which are 136 bytes and 128 bytes respectively. These FIFOs provide packet buffering for increased system latency. This means that an incoming packet comes in the receive FIFO before the PCnet-ISA DMA unit transfers it into the system memory. Similarly, the transmit packet will be transferred using the PCnet-ISA bus master DMA unit from the system memory to the transmit FIFO.

The PCnet-ISA chip provides integrated Attachment Unit Interface (AUI) and 10Base-T transceiver. The chip can be placed in an auto mode where it monitors the AUI and 10Base-T interfaces and automatically switches from one to the other depending on which interface is active. Only one interface is active at any given time. Figure A-1 shows the block diagram of the PCnet-ISA chip.

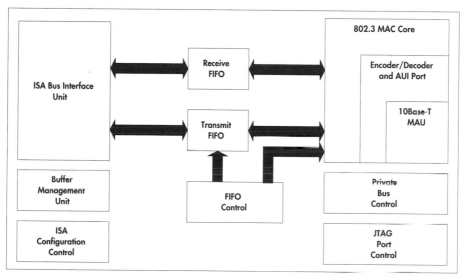

Figure A-1. PCnet-ISA Block Diagram

Bus Interface Unit

The PCnet-ISA is a bus master controller on the ISA bus. The Bus Interface Unit (BIU) block of the PCnet-ISA chip interfaces with the ISA bus and performs all the cycles on the bus. The chip performs all the data transfer in the bus master mode. The PCnet-ISA device also has a number of registers which are used for internal user control and status reporting. These registers are used to keep the internal status of the chip and also report the status to the driver. The access to the registers is via programmed I/O (PIO) mode. The programmed I/O mode is a transfer mode defined in the 80x86 microprocessors where the device registers are mapped in the processors I/O space and the software can use the IN and OUT assembly language instructions to access these registers.

The BIU of the PCnet-ISA is designed to interface directly with the ISA bus signals. It is possible to connect the ISA bus pins of the PCnet-ISA chip directly to the edge connector pads on the adapter card without using external buffers, drivers, or decoders. All system bus buffering and address decoding can be done inside the PCnet-ISA chip. The basic operation of the PCnet-ISA in the bus master mode consists of PIO cycles for register addressing and the bus master DMA(direct memory access) operations (16-bit) for the movement of transmit and receive data. These bus master DMA operations take place over the ISA bus and the host CPU stays away from the bus during the periods when the bus is granted to the PCnet-ISA for data transfer. Typically, if the host CPU has internal cache, it can perform several functions while waiting for PCnet-ISA to complete the DMA transfer. The PCnet-ISA requires a 16-bit host platform such as PC-AT. The PCnet-ISA will not function as a bus master in a 8-bit environment like PC-XT. The PIO accesses to the PCnet-ISA can be 8- or 16-bit.

Buffer Management Unit (BMU)

The PCnet-ISA implements a very simple but very powerful and flexible buffer management. The complete management of the transmit and receive buffers is done by the buffer management unit block of the PCnet-ISA (see Figure A-1).

The PCnet-ISA buffer management consists of user register (Control & Status Registers) CSR1 and CSR2. The CSR1 and CSR2 contain a 24-bit physical address pointer to the system memory where the initialization block is kept. The initialization block of PCnet-ISA is 24 bytes and contains the following:

- Mode Information (2 bytes)
- Physical MAC Address (6 bytes)
- Logical Address Filter (8 bytes)
- Receive Descriptor Address and Length (4 bytes)
- Transmit Descriptor Address and Length (4 bytes)

Figure A-2 illustrates the complete buffer management architecture of the PCnet-ISA chip.

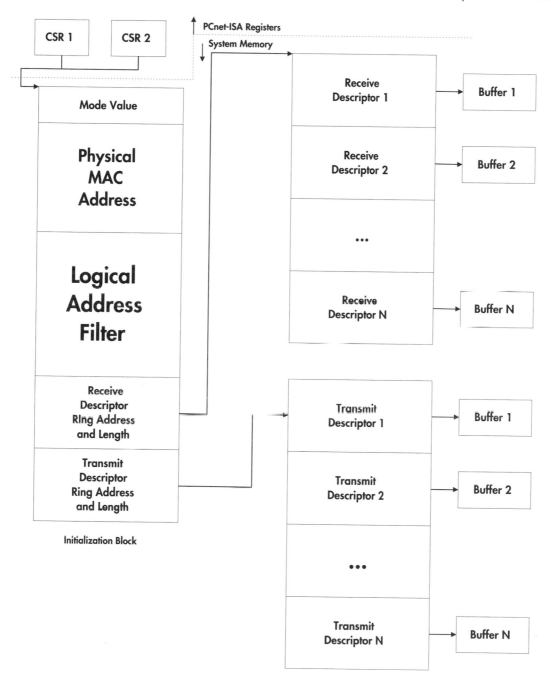

Figure A-2. PCnet-ISA Buffer Architecture

The CSR 1 and CSR 2 registers contain a 24-bit physical address to the initialization block. As shown in figure A-2, the initialization block contains fields like Mode, Physical MAC Address, Logical Address Filter, and Receive and Transmit Descriptor Address and lengths. The initialization block's mode field contains various bits to control various features like putting the chip in promiscuous mode (receive all frames from the network). The physical MAC address field of initialization block contains the MAC address of the station which is being controlled by the PCnet-ISA device. The logical address filter field defines a filter which controls the reception of multicast addresses. Multicast addresses are defined as special addresses which are used to address a group of stations. This logical address filter field provides a mechanism to selectively filter some or all of the packets addressed to a multicast address. The next field in the initialization block is Receive Descriptor Ring Address and Length. This field contains a 24-bit pointer to the receive descriptor ring. It also contains the number of receive descriptor ring entries (specified in power of 2). The next field in the initialization block is Transmit Descriptor Ring Address and Length. This field contains a 24-bit pointer to the transmit descriptor ring. It also contains the number of transmit descriptor ring entries (specified in power of 2).

The receive descriptor ring is a data structure in the system memory which is pointed to by the initialization block. The receive descriptor ring contains descriptors which occupy 8 bytes each. The number of descriptor entries in the receive descriptor ring is controlled by the initialization block. The receive descriptors in PCnet-ISA can have 1 to 128 number on entries (2^0 to 2^7). The receive descriptor ring contains a bit called OWN (ownership) bit. This bit is used to indicate the ownership of the receive descriptor. The descriptor can be owned by the host or by the PCnet-ISA chip. When a packet is received by the chip, the chip puts the packet and the status information of that packet in one of the descriptors that it owns. It then gives the ownership of that packet to the host by toggling the OWN bit. The host owns the receive descriptor at this point. The host device driver performs the necessary processing of the packet and then it gives the ownership back to the PCnet-ISA chip by toggling the OWN bit.

The receive descriptor also contains a 24-bit pointer to a buffer. The length of the buffer is also contained in the receive descriptor. The status of the incoming frame is defined by some status bits in the receive descriptor. The PCnet-ISA chip puts the incoming frame in the buffer pointed to by the receive descriptor which is owned by the PCnet-ISA chip. If the receive packet is smaller than the buffer, PCnet-ISA writes the actual size of the incoming packet in the length field of the receive descriptor. If the incoming packet is larger than the buffer pointed to by the current receive descriptor, the PCnet-ISA chip checks the ownership of the next receive descriptor in the chain. If the next descriptor is owned by the chip then the PCnet-ISA will start putting the rest of the incoming packet in the next buffer. The start and end of the incoming packet is indicated by the PCnet-ISA chip by writing into the STP (Start of Packet) and ENP (End of Packet) bits of the receive descriptor.

The transmit descriptor ring data structure is very similar to the receive descriptor ring data structure. Each entry in the transmit ring data structure is 8 bytes. The transmit ring data structure is constructed by the device driver in the host system memory. The initialization block contains a 24-bit pointer to the transmit descriptor ring data structure. The transmit descriptor ring can have 1 to 128 entries (2^0 to 2^7) in the increments of power of 2s. The transmit descriptor entry contains the 24-bit physical address of the data buffer and the length of the data buffer. It also contains some status bits which are updated by the PCnet-ISA chip to communicate the status of the transmit to the host device driver.

The transmit descriptor entry contains a bit called OWN bit which has the same function as the receive descriptor OWN bit. This OWN bit is used as an ownership indicator between the host and the PCnet-ISA chip. When the host driver wants to transmit a packet on the network, it constructs that packet and points to that packet via the transmit descriptor buffer pointer. It also updates the number of bytes to be transmitted in the buffer length field of the transmit descriptor. The host device driver then instructs the PCnet-ISA to send this packet. This instruction is given to the PCnet-ISA by performing a PIO operation and setting a bit in the control and status register 0 called TDMD (transmit demand). As soon as the host driver sets this bit, the PCnet-ISA goes to the current transmit descriptor entry and checks the ownership bit. If the descriptor is owned by the chip, the PCnet-ISA chip starts the transmission of the packet.

At the end of the packet transmission, the PCnet-ISA chip updates the status bits indicating a successful or erroneous transmission (as the case might be). The host driver is interrupted at the end of transmission (if the interrupts are enabled) or the host driver can poll the ownership bit to check when the packet transmission is complete.

Register Access

The PCnet-ISA has internal user control and status registers (CSRs) that facilitate configuration and status transfer between the PCnet-ISA and the host device drivers. The CSRs are addressed using an indirect addressing scheme in PCnet-ISA. The PCnet-ISA has in excess of 100+ 16-bit CSR registers. If these registers were directly I/O mapped in the processor space, the device registers will occupy a lot of processor I/O space—which is undesirable. Hence, the indirect indexing scheme is implemented to access these registers.

The PCnet-ISA has a single register address port (RAP) into which the device driver writes the CSR number. Another port which is labeled as register data port (RDP) contains the data. If the device driver wants to read the contents of CSR 0, it will write 0 into the RAP and then read the RDP. If the device driver wants to write a value of 0x10 into the CSR 0 register, it will write a 0 into the RAP followed by a write of 0x10 into the RDP. PCnet-ISA also contains another set of internal registers called the ISA bus configuration registers (ISACSRs). These registers are accessed in the same way as CSRs. They use the same RAP to indicate the register being accessed. However, the data port for these registers is different than the RDP. The data port for these registers is called ISA bus data port (IDP).

The PCnet-ISA also has a EEPROM interface. An adapter card vendor uses the serial EEPROM to store information like the permanent MAC address of this station. This EEPROM is electrically connected to the PCnet-ISA device and can be read by the host device driver via the PCnet-ISA device. The EEPROM stores 16 bytes of data and is mapped in the same I/O space as the rest of PCnet-ISA register ports. The I/O address map for the PCnet-ISA device is shown in the table below.

Offset	# of Bytes	Register
0h	16	MAC Address EEPROM
10h	2	Register Data Port (RDP)
12h	2	Register Address Port (RAP)
14h	2	Reset Port
16h	2	ISA bus configuration data port (IDP)

The reset port (offset 14h) is used by the device drivers to perform a complete reset of the device. The 24-bit of I/O space can be located at I/O base address of 300h, 320h, 340h, or 360h. The PCnet-ISA supports the four base addresses and the user can configure the adapter for one of these four base addresses.

Media Access Control (MAC) Unit

The PCnet-ISA Media Access Control (MAC) unit implements the IEEE 802.3 compatible MAC protocol. It provides the interface between the bus interface unit and the core MAC engine. The MAC unit interfaces with the transmit and receive FIFOs. This unit is responsible for transmitting/receiving data bytes to and from the 802.3 media into the FIFOs. The MAC engine for the PCnet-ISA device has a number of programmable features. Two of these features are the dynamic frame check sequence (FCS) generation on a packet-by-packet basis, and automatic PAD field insertion to ensure that the packet transmitted on the 802.3 network meets the minimum allowed packet size of 64 bytes.

The two primary attributes of the MAC engine are:

- Transmit and receive message data encapsulation

- Media access management

The MAC engine is responsible for performing the data encapsulation for transmit and receive packets. On the transmit side, the MAC engine of the PCnet-ISA device performs the auto PAD function as described earlier. The receive part of the MAC engine monitors the size of the incoming frame and if the size is <64 bytes it considers this frame as a runt packet and discards it. This feature of discarding runt packets can be disabled by the device driver. The MAC engine prepares the packet for transmission by sending 7 bytes of preamble followed by 1 byte of start of frame delimiter (SFD). This initial preamble of the packet provides receive clock synchronization at the receiving station. This initial preamble is followed by actual bytes of the packet including destination address, source address, length of the packet, and data bytes. The MAC transmit engine also monitors the ethernet media for any errors. It monitors the collision state of the media and if it encounters a collision state, it aborts the transmission, performs the random backoff, and then attempts a re-transmission. If the attempts for re-transmission fail, it aborts the transmission and marks the transmit descriptor with the collision error.

The MAC engine monitors the first six bytes of the incoming packet (destination address) and attempts to match it with its own MAC address. If the address matches, the MAC engine starts receiving the packet and putting the incoming bytes in the receive FIFO. The bus interface unit of the PCnet-ISA device takes the bytes from the receive FIFO and starts to DMA them into a receive descriptor buffer owned by the PCnet-ISA device. The MAC receive engine also monitors the media for any errors during the receive process. It calculates the checksum of the receive packet and compares it with the checksum received. It also monitors the media for any collision. If it encounters any collision activity on the media, the PCnet-ISA device aborts the reception and marks the receive descriptor with an error status.

The basic requirement for all stations on the ethernet network is to provide fairness of channel allocation. The IEEE 802.3/Ethernet protocol defines a media access mechanism which permits all stations to access the channel with equality. The ethernet channel is a multidrop communications medium which allows a single station to transmit and all other stations to receive. If two stations simultaneously contend for the medium, their signals will interact causing loss of data. This is referred to as collision. The MAC unit of the PCnet-ISA implements the complete protocol as discussed above. It performs functions such as medium allocation along with collision avoidance. It also implements collision resolution and handling. This is the backoff and retry algorithm as defined in the IEEE 802.3 standard. The data bytes which are transmitted on the ethernet medium are encoded using a scheme called manchester encoding. This encoder is also built in the PCnet-ISA chip. The receive data bytes have to be decoded using a manchester decoder, also in the PCnet-ISA chip.

INTERFACING SOFTWARE DRIVERS TO PCnet-ISA

A networking device driver interfaces the operating system and applications to the networking adapter card device. As explained in the previous chapters, the implementation of the networking device driver is dependent on the environment for which the device driver is written. The only common portions that these networking device drivers have are the modules that interface with the device. The implementation of the code which handles the networking devices such as PCnet-ISA may also be different (C vs. Assembly), however the code flow and sequence of events stay approximately the same. This section describes the various steps a device driver has to implement to handle a PCnet-ISA device. The four main modules which each device driver has to implement are as follows:

- Initialization module
- Transmit module
- Receive and ISR module
- I/O control module

The following sections describe, in general, the steps which a device driver implements for these modules.

Initialization Module

The initialization steps discussed here are the general steps necessary for initializing the PCnet-ISA device. A networking device driver may have to implement additional steps to perform operating system specific initialization. The main steps that the driver has to take to initialize PCnet-ISA are to set up the initialization block, the transmit and receive descriptor rings, the transmit and receive descriptors. The driver is also responsible for initializing the PCnet-ISA device and then starting it.

The PCnet-ISA drivers first allocate system memory space for the initialization block. They also allocate memory for the receive and transmit descriptors and the associated buffers. The initialization block is fixed in size (24 bytes). The memory required for the transmit and receive descriptor blocks depends upon the number of entries in the transmit and receive descriptor rings (between 1 to 128). After the memory allocation the device driver starts initializing various individual fields of the initialization block data structure, transmit descriptor ring data structure and receive descriptor ring data structure.

The device driver takes the physical address of the initialization block data structure and programs it into the CSR 1 and CSR 2 registers by using the RAP and RDP ports. It sets the mode of the chip in the first 2 bytes of the initialization block data structure. It also sets the physical MAC address in the physical MAC address field. In the PCnet-ISA architecture the device driver obtains the physical MAC address from the MAC address EEPROM located on the adapter card. The device driver also fills the starting address of the transmit and receive descriptor rings and their corresponding lengths (power of 2 format) in the initialization block.

The device drivers then initializes the receive descriptor ring. It puts the buffers addresses in the corresponding receive descriptors and the buffer size in the corresponding size field of each descriptor. It also clears all the error bits in all the descriptors and then assigns the ownership of all the descriptors to the PCnet-ISA device.

The initialization of the transmit descriptor ring is very similar to that of the receive descriptor ring. The networking device driver assigns the buffer addresses of the transmit buffers to the transmit descriptors and the length of the buffer to the transmit descriptor length field. The driver clears all the error counters, and assigns the ownership of all the transmit descriptors to the host.

The PCnet-ISA device driver is also responsible for initializing the DMA channel and the programmable interrupt controller (PIC). The device driver finds out the DMA channel which the PCnet-ISA is using from the user and then puts the DMA channel into cascade mode. In the cascade mode the PC-AT DMA controller (8237) performs the bus arbitration, but lets the bus master DMA controller (PCnet-ISA) provide read/write control signals. The device driver also unmasks the DMA channel which the device is planning to use. The device driver also sets the PIC to generate the interrupt request (IRQ) which the PCnet-ISA device is using. The device driver programs the interrupt vector table with its interrupt handler routine address and unmasks the IRQ channel which the PCnet-ISA device is using.

When the device driver is ready to instruct the PCnet-ISA device to initialize, it passes a command to the PCnet-ISA device by setting a bit called Initialize in the CSR 0 register. The PCnet-ISA device gets the initialization block from the system memory and starts the initialization process. When the device initialization is complete, the PCnet-ISA device sets a bit called initialization done (IDON) bit in the CSR 0. The device driver can poll this bit to check if the device initialization was successful. After successful initialization the device driver starts the chip by setting the START bit the CSR 0 register of the PCnet-ISA device. Figure A-3 contains the flow chart of the PCnet-ISA initialization sequence.

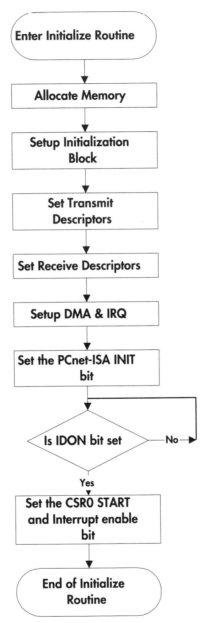

Figure A-3. Initialization of PCnet-ISA

Transmit Module

The transmit routine for the PCnet-ISA is very simple. When the protocol layer running above the networking device driver has a packet to send, it passes the buffer containing the packet to the device driver. The PCnet-ISA device driver will check to see if the buffer has a transmit descriptor which the driver owns. If the driver owns a descriptor, it will either copy the transmit data into the buffer associated with the transmit descriptor, or it will put the pointer of the buffer it received from the protocol into the transmit descriptor. In either case, the device driver is responsible for making sure that the transmit descriptor buffer pointer points to the buffer that contains the data to be transmitted.

The device driver starts the transmission process by toggling the OWN bit of the transmit descriptor and hence assigning the ownership of the transmit descriptor to the PCnet-ISA device and then setting the transmit demand (TDMD) bit in the CSR0. The PCnet-ISA device starts the DMA engine to move the data into its transmit FIFO and then starts the transmission on the ethernet media (see Figure A-4).

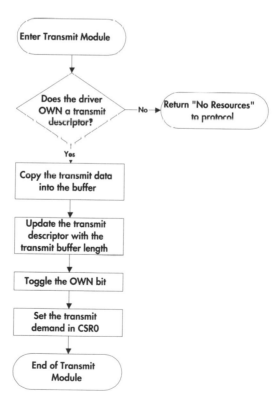

Figure A-4. Transmit Packet Flow

Interrupt Service Module Including Receive Frame Processing

The interrupt service routine (ISR) is the most critical piece of code within any device driver. In case of a typical PCnet-ISA's ISR, the functions such as receive packet handling, end of transmit interrupt, error condition handling, are all handled within the interrupt service routine. The statistics counter maintenance is also handled within the ISR.

The device driver ISR routine is called when the PCnet-ISA generates an interrupt. The device driver reads the CSR0 register which contains the cause of the interrupt. The CSR0 of the PCnet-ISA chip is designed so that when the device driver writes the same value back to the register, it will clear the interrupt condition. Typically, the device driver reads the CSR0, stores it into a local variable and then writes the same value back to CSR0 thus clearing the reason for the interrupt. Also, to avoid re-entry into the ISR routine, the device driver ISR code clears the interrupt enable bit in the CSR0 and then enables the system interrupts. This means that the rest of the PC-AT system has all the interrupts enabled and hence can function normally while the PCnet-ISA ISR code processes the stored value of the CSR0 to process the interrupt. At the end of the ISR, the device driver will disable the system interrupts and then enable the PCnet-ISA interrupts by setting the interrupt enable bit of the CSR0 register and then executing the IRET (return from interrupt) instruction which also enables the system interrupt. The system along with the PCnet-ISA device is now fully functional once again.

The PCnet-ISA device driver checks for various reasons for the interrupt by examining the stored value of the CSR0, one bit at a time. It first checks the error bit of the CSR0 to check if the interrupt was caused due to one of the following errors: Babbling transmitter—transmitter staying on the ethernet channel for longer than maximum allowed time, Collision error—transceiver test feature which indicates a bad 10Base link or no transceiver present on the AUI port; Missed Frame—when the PCnet-ISA cannot receive a frame because of lack of resources, or Memory error—PCnet-ISA cannot get the system bus within a set period. If the error bit of the CSR0 is set, the device driver ISR handles the appropriate error condition and updates the statistics counter associated with that error condition.

The ISR then checks to see if the reason for the interrupt was the completion of a previously started transmission. If the cause of the interrupt is the completion of the transmit packet, the device driver ISR checks the status of the transmit packet, the device driver ISR checks the status of the transmission by examining the error bits of the transmit descriptor. The device driver ISR updates the statistics and performs some other housekeeping functions such as informing the protocol of the status of packet transmission. If the interrupt is caused due to a reception of a packet, the device driver ISR routine examines the receive descriptor error bits to make sure that the packet is received without any error. If the status of the received packet is good, the device driver ISR informs the protocol that it has received a packet and lets the protocol take over the packet for further processing. The ISR also updates the statistics counters associated with the reception of the packet. If the packet received had errors, the ISR will inform the protocol that an error packet was received. The ISR will also update the necessary counters. In the case of transmit and receive paths, once the device driver ISR has finished handling the packet, it toggles the ownership bit to reassign the ownership to the correct entity—host vs. PCnet-ISA. Figure A-5 describes the PCnet-ISA ISR in a flow chart format.

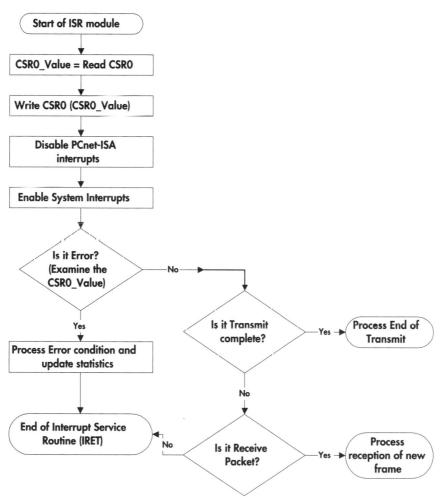

Figure A-5. PCnet-ISA Interrupt Service Routine Flow

I/O Control Interface

The networking device drivers offer various I/O control routines to the protocol layer. This I/O control interface is implemented according to the operating system environment. However, almost all the standard device drivers implement certain I/O control commands via the I/O control interface. The specific I/O control interface is discussed in the corresponding device driver chapter. This section describes the most common I/O control commands and how they are implemented with the PCnet-ISA device.

The first most common I/O control command is used to get the statistics. Each device driver maintains various kinds of statistics. For example, the device driver will maintain the number of frames transmitted, number of frames received, number of collisions on the network and so on. These statistics are passed back when a protocol or an application uses the I/O control command to get the statistics. In case of PCnet-ISA device, the driver uses its own software logic and the on chip statistics registers (CSR 112: Missed Frame Count, CSR 114: Receive Collision Count) to maintain all the statistics counters and then report them to the user of the I/O control interface.

The I/O control interface also requires most of the device drivers to implement the functions like adding and removing multicast addresses. The PCnet-ISA implements a hashing algorithm (Am79C960 1992) to calculate which multicast address it has to receive. The PCnet-ISA recalculates the 8 byte, logical address filter after receiving the add/remove multicast address command and then reprograms the initialization block to reflect the correct logical address filter based on the correct set of multicast addresses. The PCnet-ISA device driver has to re-initialize the device after changing the initialization block.

SUMMARY

This appendix focuses on AMD's PCnet-ISA bus mastering single chip ethernet controller chip and its interaction with the device drivers. The reader should have been able to gain some understanding of a real networking controller and how various pieces of the device driver interact with the networking controller. The transmit, receive and the interrupt service routines of a device driver managing the PCnet-ISA chip have also been discussed in this appendix. This appendix however covers only the general flow of the device drivers and not the detailed chip and device driver interaction. The detailed interactions are very specific to operating systems, and hence are not discussed in this appendix.

APPENDIX B

Remote Program Load (RPL) Operation

INTRODUCTION

This appendix outlines the Remote Program Load (RPL) process and the RPL protocol. The RPL process is used to allow workstations connected to a network to boot from a server. This boot process from the server is used in place of the boot from a floppy or a hard disk. This boot process is typically used in workstations that do not have a hard disk support (diskless workstations).

The RPL protocol which is discussed in this chapter is the IBM Find/Found RPL protocol. The IBM RPL protocol allows a hardware-independent boot strap program to boot a diskless workstation. The IBM RPL protocol is generic, and it allows the board manufacturer to provide a single Boot ROM that will boot from any network server supporting the RPL protocol. Currently, this includes Novell NetWare, Microsoft LAN Manager and IBM LAN Server.

OVERVIEW OF THE RPL PROCESS

The RPL functionality can be separated into two categories:

(a)   Remote Workstation

(b)   RPL Server

The remote workstation is responsible for taking control of the remote machines after the initial boot process and then initiating RPL requests to any potential RPL servers. The RPL servers process the requests from the remote workstations.

The RPL process begins when the remote workstation is either warm booted or powered up. The system BIOS performs the POST (Power On Self Test) operation. The system BIOS scans memory locations between C0000h and EE000h in 2k (2048) byte increments, looking for a 55AAh signature that denotes the presence of a valid option ROM. Typically, the RPL code is resident in an option ROM on the Network Interface card (NIC). If the signature is found, the BIOS uses the third byte of the option ROM (containing the number of 512 byte pages) to perform a checksum on the ROM. If the checksum result is 0, the system BIOS calls the option ROM's initialization code by issuing a far call to the offset 03 (the fourth byte) of the option ROM.

The option ROM's initialization code initializes its resources and optionally replaces any of the various BIOS INT vectors such as the boot fail vector (INT 18h), the diskette driver vector (INT 13h), or the boot strap vector (INT 19h). The option ROM then returns control to the system BIOS to allow it to complete its system initialization. Various RPL implementations differ as to the method by which the option ROM takes control of the workstation to begin the RPL boot process. The two main methods are by trapping INT 18h or INT 19h.

To start the boot process, the system BIOS calls INT 19h (boot strap). If the option ROM replaced the INT 19h vector such that it calls the option ROM, the option ROM then takes control of the system and attempts to find a RPL server on the network. If the option ROM replaced the INT 18h vector such that it calls the option ROM, the systems INT 19h call will fail because there is no local media (or the local media is unable to boot), and the system BIOS will call the boot fail vector INT 18h. The option ROM then takes control of the system and attempts to find a RPL server on the network to boot from.

The Novell remote workstation implementation uses the INT 18h mechanism while the Microsoft LAN Manager uses the INT 19h vector to take control from the system BIOS.

The next step in the RPL process requires the RPL option ROM to use some type of protocol to communicate with potential RPL servers. The remote workstation and the RPL servers must implement the same protocol. The IBM Find/Found protocol is used in most popular server environments like Novell, Microsoft, and IBM.

The IBM Find/Found RPL protocol is used by the remote workstation to locate a RPL server. The workstation sends a find frame to a multicast address (03 00 02 00 00 00h). The RPL servers typically monitor a network constantly for new RPL requests. The server responds to the find frame by transmitting a found frame to the workstation address. Once a workstation receives the found frame, the workstation transmits the Send File Request frame to download the Boot Strap Program. The RPL server responds with a File Data Response frame. This frame contains a copy of the Boot Strap Program to be sent to the loader application. Once the transfer is complete, the option ROM in the workstation passes control to the loader or equivalent program in the data just transferred into memory. The loader application continues the boot process and loads the necessary operating system from across the network. Figure B-1 illustrates the flow of operations after the BIOS calls the loader application.

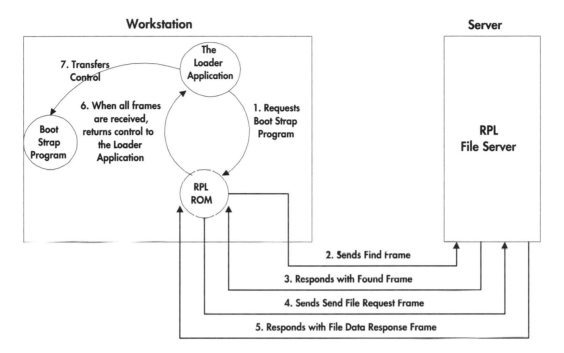

Figure B-1. RPL Flow of Operations

IBM FIND/FOUND PROTOCOL

Figure B-2 provides the flow diagram for the IBM Find/Found frame RPL protocol.

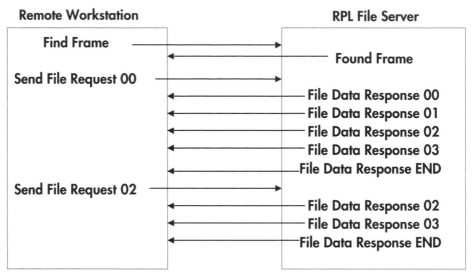

Figure B-2. IBM Find/Found RPL Protocol

The remote workstation option ROM attempts to locate an RPL server by transmitting a find frame using the multicast address 03 00 02 00 00 00h. The find frame format is given in Figure B-3.

Offset Decimal	Length	Value	Description
00	02	0053h	Frame Length
02	02	0001h	FIND Command
04	04	0008 4003h	Correlator Vector
08	04	0000 0000h	Correlator Value
12	04	0010 0008h	Connect Info Vector
16	04	0006 4009h	Frame size sub-vector
20	02	Max Frame	Max Frame from Driver Config Table
22	04	0006 400Ah	Connect Class Sub-Vector
26	02	0001h	Class I only

Figure B-3. Format of the Find Frame (Novell)

Offset Decimal	Length	Value	Description
28	04	000A 4006h	Address Vector
32	06	Address	6 Byte MAC Address
38	04	0005 4007h	Logical SAP Vector
42	01	FCh	Remote SAP Vector
43	04	0028 0004h	Search Vector
47	04	0024 C005h	Leader info Sub-Vector
51	08	Config	Configuration obtained by issuing INT 15h
59	02	Equipment	Register AX from INT 11h
61	02	Memory Size	Register AX from INT 12h minus 32k minus the Boot ROM size
63	02	Version	Major, Minor Version
65	06	00 00 00 00 00 00h	Rest of RPL EC
71	02	5342h	Adapter ID
73	10	Short Name	The short name from the Driver Config Table

Figure B-3. Format of the Find Frame (Novell) (Continued)

The connection class field at offset 26h is set to accept class I frames. This means that the Boot ROM is not capable of accepting File Data Response Frames that are broadcast to a group or functional address. The memory size field at offset 61 (decimal) is set to <RAM_Memory_size> – 32K Bytes – <Boot ROM Size> in Novell environment. This is because the Boot ROM is relocated from ROM to RAM. 32K bytes are subtracted from the memory size to allow room for the transient portion of DOS.

The RPL file server responds to the find frame with a found frame. The format of the found frame is shown in Figure B-4.

Offset Decimal	Length	Value	Description
00	02	003Ah	Frame Length
02	02	0002h	Found Frame
04	04	0008 4003h	Correlator value
08	04	0000 0000h	Correlator value
12	04	0005 400B	Response Correlator
16	01	00	Response code
17	04	000A 400Ch	Set address vector
21	06	00 00 00 00 00 00h	Group address not supported
27	04	000A 4006h	Loader address vector
31	06	Node Addr	RPL server node address
37	04	0010 0008h	Connect info vector
41	04	0006 4009h	Frame size sub-vector
45	02	Max Frame	Maximum frame size
47	04	0006 400Ah	Connect class sub-vector
51	02	0001	Connection class
53	04	0005 4007h	Loader SAP Vector
57	01	RSAP	SAP value of the RPL server

Figure B-4. Found Frame Format

After receiving the Found Frame, the Boot ROM transmits the Send File Request Frame to download the Boot Strap program. Figure B-5 lists the format of the Send File Request frame.

Offset Decimal	Length	Value	Description
00	02	0053h	Frame Length
02	02	0010h	Send File Request Command
04	04	0008 4003h	Correlator value
08	04	0000 0000h	Correlator value
12	04	0010 0008h	Connect Info Vector
16	04	0006 4009	Frame size sub-vector
20	02	Max Frame	Max Frame from Driver Config Table
22	04	0006 400A	Connect Class Sub-Vector
26	02	0001h	Class I only
28	04	000A 4006h	Address Vector
32	06	Address	MAC Address of this adapter
38	04	0005 4007h	Logical SAP Vector
42	01	FCh	Remote SAP Value
43	04	0028 0004h	Search Vector
47	04	0024 C005h	Loader info sub-vector
51	08	Config	Configuration obtained by issuing INT 15h
59	02	Equipment	Register AX from INT 11h
61	02	Memory Size	Register AX from INT 12h minus 32K minus the Boot ROM size
63	02	Version	Major, Minor Version
65	06	00 00 00 00 00 00h	Rest of the RPL EC
71	02	5342h	Adapter ID
73	10	Short Name	The short name from the Driver Config Table

Figure B-5. Send File Request Frame Format

The RPL file server responds to the Send File Request Frame with a File Data Response Frame. This frame contains a copy of the boot strap program to be sent to the loader application. Figure B-6 describes the format of the file data response frame.

Offset Decimal	Length	Value	Description
00	02	0019h + nn	Frame Length nn= File Data Length
02	02	0020h	File Data Response Frame
04	04	0008 4011h	Sequence Header
08	04	0000 nnnnh	Sequence Number
12	04	000D C014h	Loader Header
16	04	Locate Addr	Address of Data
20	04	XFER Addr	Transfer Control Address
24	01	Flags	Bit Significant Option Flag
25	02	0004h + nn	File Data Vector Length
27	02	4018h	File Data Vector
29	nn	File Data	Binary File Data

Figure B-6. File Data Response Format

The copy of the Boot Strap Program is loaded into the RAM by the Loader Application and the Loader Application transfers the control to the Boot Strap Program. The Boot Strap program is responsible for getting the Boot Disk Image residing on the RPL file server. In the Novell NetWare environment, a DOS boot disk image is created by utilities provided by Novell. This DOS boot disk image is downloaded by the Boot Strap Program from the RPL file server. The Boot Strap Program also initializes the network card device driver and any other components of software involved in transmitting/receiving frames. The Boot Strap Program downloads the complete boot disk image from the RPL server, loads it into the RAM, and starts executing it. The boot disk contains the operating system files, startup files, and various device drivers to complete the boot process and start various programs needed by the user. The remote boot process appears to the user very similar to the normal boot process. At the end of the remote boot, the user has the operating system loaded, and the workstation is ready for use by the user.

APPENDIX C

DLPI.H File for UNIX DLPI Drivers

DLPI.H INCLUDE FILE

This appendix is provided as a reference appendix. It contains the SCO LLI 3.1 DLPI.H header file. This header file contains all the key definitions and the data structures for the LLI device driver. This file is also the key between the architecture compatibility of SCO's LLI and the AT&T's DLPI architectures. The LLI and the DLPI drivers use the same header file for various data structures and hence follow the same basic STREAMS device driver architecture.

```
#ifndef _SYS_DLPI_H
#define _SYS_DLPI_H

#ident "@(#)head.sys:dlpi.h    1.1.1.1"

/*
 * dlpi.h header for Data Link Provider Interface
 */

/*
 * This header file has encoded the values so an existing driver
 * or user which was written with the Logical Link Interface(LLI)
 * can migrate to the DLPI interface in a binary compatible manner.
 * Any fields which require a specific format or value are flagged
 * with a comment containing the message LLI compatibility.
 */

/*
 * Primitives for Local Management Services
 */
#define DL_INFO_REQ             0x00    /* Information Req, LLI compatibility */
```

```
#define DL_INFO_ACK          0x03    /* Information Ack, LLI compatibility */
#define DL_ATTACH_REQ        0x0b    /* Attach a PPA */
#define DL_DETACH_REQ        0x0c    /* Detach a PPA */
#define DL_BIND_REQ          0x01    /* Bind dlsap address, LLI compatibility
*/
#define DL_BIND_ACK          0x04    /* Dlsap address bound, LLI compatibility
*/
#define DL_UNBIND_REQ        0x02    /* Unbind dlsap address, LLI compatibili-
ty */
#define DL_OK_ACK            0x06    /* Success acknowledgment, LLI compati-
bility */
#define DL_ERROR_ACK         0x05    /* Error acknowledgment, LLI compatibili-
ty */
#define DL_SUBS_BIND_REQ     0x1b    /* Bind Subsequent DLSAP address */
#define DL_SUBS_BIND_ACK     0x1c    /* Subsequent DLSAP address bound */

/*
 * Primitives used for Connectionless Service
 */
#define DL_UNITDATA_REQ      0x07    /* datagram send request, LLI compatibil-
ity */
#define DL_UNITDATA_IND      0x08    /* datagram receive indication, LLI com-
patibility */
#define DL_UDERROR_IND       0x09    /* datagram error indication, LLI compat-
ibility */
#define DL_UDQOS_REQ         0x0a    /* set QOS for subsequent datagram trans-
missions */

/*
 * Primitives used for Connection-Oriented Service
 */
#define DL_CONNECT_REQ       0x0d    /* Connect request */
#define DL_CONNECT_IND       0x0e    /* Incoming connect indication */
#define DL_CONNECT_RES       0x0f    /* Accept previous connect indication */
#define DL_CONNECT_CON       0x10    /* Connection established */

#define DL_TOKEN_REQ         0x11    /* Passoff token request */
#define DL_TOKEN_ACK         0x12    /* Passoff token ack */

#define DL_DISCONNECT_REQ    0x13    /* Disconnect request */
#define DL_DISCONNECT_IND    0x14    /* Disconnect indication */

#define DL_RESET_REQ         0x17    /* Reset service request */
#define DL_RESET_IND         0x18    /* Incoming reset indication */
#define DL_RESET_RES         0x19    /* Complete reset processing */
#define DL_RESET_CON         0x1a    /* Reset processing complete */


/*
 * DLPI interface states
 */
```

```
#define DL_UNATTACHED 0x04      /* PPA not attached */
#define DL_ATTACH_PENDING       0x05    /* Waiting ack of DL_ATTACH_REQ */
#define DL_DETACH_PENDING       0x06    /* Waiting ack of DL_DETACH_REQ */
#define DL_UNBOUND    0x00      /* PPA attached, LLI compatibility */
#define DL_BIND_PENDING         0x01    /* Waiting ack of DL_BIND_REQ, LLI com-
patibility */
#define DL_UNBIND_PENDING 0x02          /* Waiting ack of DL_UNBIND_REQ, LLI com-
patibility */
#define DL_IDLE       0x03 /* dlsap bound, awaiting use, LLI compatibility */
#define DL_UDQOS_PENDING        0x07    /* Waiting ack of DL_UDQOS_REQ */
#define DL_OUTCON_PENDING       0x08    /* outgoing connection, awaiting
DL_CONN_CON */
#define DL_INCON_PENDING 0x09 /* incoming connection, awaiting DL_CONN_RES */
#define DL_CONN_RES_PENDING  0x0a       /* Waiting ack of DL_CONNECT_RES */
#define DL_DATAXFER             0x0b    /* connection-oriented data transfer */
#define DL_USER_RESET_PENDING 0x0c      /* user initiated reset, awaiting
DL_RESET_CON */
#define DL_PROV_RESET_PENDING 0x0d      /* provider initiated reset, awaiting
DL_RESET_RES */
#define DL_RESET_RES_PENDING  0x0e      /* Waiting ack of DL_RESET_RES */
#define DL_DISCON8_PENDING      0x0f    /* Waiting ack of DL_DISC_REQ when in
DL_OUTCON_PENDING */
#define DL_DISCON9_PENDING      0x10    /* Waiting ack of DL_DISC_REQ when in
DL_INCON_PENDING */
#define DL_DISCON11_PENDING  0x11       /* Waiting ack of DL_DISC_REQ when in
DL_DATAXFER */
#define DL_DISCON12_PENDING  0x12       /* Waiting ack of DL_DISC_REQ when in
DL_USER_RESET_PENDING */
#define DL_DISCON13_PENDING  0x13       /* Waiting ack of DL_DISC_REQ when in
DL_DL_PROV_RESET_PENDING */
#define DL_SUBS_BIND_PND        0x14    /* Waiting ack of DL_SUBS_BIND_REQ */


/*
 * DL_ERROR_ACK error return values
 */
#define DL_ACCESS       0x02 /* Improper permissions for request, LLI compati-
bility */
#define DL_BADADDR      0x01 /* DLSAP address in improper format or invalid */
#define DL_BADCORR      0x05 /* Sequence number not from outstanding
DL_CONN_IND */
#define DL_BADDATA      0x06 /* User data exceeded provider limit */
#define DL_BADPPA       0x08 /* Specified PPA was invalid */
#define DL_BADPRIM      0x09 /* Primitive received is not known by DLS provider
*/
#define DL_BADQOSPARAM 0x0a /* QOS parameters contained invalid values */
#define DL_BADQOSTYPE 0x0b /* QOS structure type is unknown or unsupported */
#define DL_BADSAP       0x00 /* Bad LSAP selector, LLI compatibility */
#define DL_BADTOKEN     0x0c /* Token used not associated with an active stream
*/
#define DL_BOUND        0x0d /* Attempted second bind with dl_max_conind or  */
```

```
                                      /*        dl_conn_mgmt > 0 on same DLSAP or PPA */
#define DL_INITFAILED 0x0e   /* Physical Link initialization failed */
#define DL_NOADDR      0x0f   /* Provider couldn't allocate alternate address
*/
#define DL_NOTINIT     0x10   /* Physical Link not initialized */
#define DL_OUTSTATE    0x03   /* Primitive issued in improper state, LLI com-
patibility */
#define DL_SYSERR      0x04   /* UNIX system error occurred, LLI compatibility
*/
#define DL_UNSUPPORTED 0x07   /* Requested service not supplied by provider */
#define DL_UNDELIVERABLE 0x11 /* Previous data unit could not be delivered */
#define DL_NOTSUPPORTED  0x12 /* Primitive is known but not supported by DLS
provider */


/*
 * DLPI media types supported
 */
#define DL_CSMACD      0x0    /* IEEE 802.3 CSMA/CD network, LLI Compatibility
*/
#define DL_TPB         0x1    /* IEEE 802.4 Token Passing Bus, LLI
Compatibility */
#define DL_TPR         0x2    /* IEEE 802.5 Token Passing Ring, LLI
Compatibility */
#define DL_METRO       0x3    /* IEEE 802.6 Metro Net, LLI Compatibility */
#define DL_ETHER       0x4    /* Ethernet Bus, LLI Compatibility */
#define DL_HDLC        0x05   /* ISO HDLC protocol support, bit synchronous */
#define DL_CHAR        0x06   /* Character Synchronous protocol support, eg
BISYNC */
#define DL_CTCA        0x07   /* IBM Channel-to-Channel Adapter */
#define DL_SLIP        0x08   /* Serial-Line IP (RFC 1055) */
#define DL_PPP         0x09   /* Point-to-point Protocol (RFC 117[12]) */
#define DL_LOOP        0x0a   /* Loopback */


/*
 * DLPI provider service supported.
 * These must be allowed to be bitwise-OR for dl_service_mode in
 * DL_INFO_ACK.
 */
#define DL_CODLS       0x01   /* support connection-oriented service */
#define DL_CLDLS       0x02   /* support connectionless data link service */


/*
 * DLPI provider style.
 * The DLPI provider style which determines whether a provider
 * requires a DL_ATTACH_REQ to inform the provider which PPA
 * user messages should be sent/received on.
 */
#define DL_STYLE1      0x0500 /* PPA is implicitly bound by open(2) */
```

```
#define DL_STYLE2      0x0501  /* PPA must be explicitly bound via
DL_ATTACH_REQ */

/*
 * DLPI flag for MORE IDU's for a single SDU
 */
#define DL_MORE        0x08

/*
 * DLPI Originator for Disconnect and Resets
 */
#define DL_PROVIDER    0x0700
#define DL_USER        0x0701

/*
 * DLPI Disconnect Reasons
 */
#define DL_CONREJ_DEST_UNKNOWN                  0x0800
#define DL_CONREJ_DEST_UNREACH_PERMANENT        0x0801
#define DL_CONREJ_DEST_UNREACH_TRANSIENT        0x0802
#define DL_CONREJ_QOS_UNAVAIL_PERMANENT         0x0803
#define DL_CONREJ_QOS_UNAVAIL_TRANSIENT         0x0804
#define DL_CONREJ_PERMANENT_COND                0x0805
#define DL_CONREJ_TRANSIENT_COND                0x0806
#define DL_DISC_ABNORMAL_CONDITION              0x0807
#define DL_DISC_NORMAL_CONDITION                0x0808
#define DL_DISC_PERMANENT_CONDITION             0x0809
#define DL_DISC_TRANSIENT_CONDITION             0x080a
#define DL_DISC_UNSPECIFIED                     0x080b

/*
 * DLPI Reset Reasons
 */
#define DL_RESET_FLOW_CONTROL 0x0900
#define DL_RESET_LINK_ERROR   0x0901
#define DL_RESET_RESYNCH      0x0902

/*
 * DLPI Quality Of Service definition for use in QOS structure definitions.
 * The QOS structures are used in connection establishment, DL_INFO_ACK,
 * and setting connectionless QOS values.
 */

/*
 * Throughput
 *
 * This parameter is specified for both directions.
 */
typedef struct dl_through {
            long    dl_target_value;    /* desired bits/second desired */
            long    dl_accept_value;    /* min. acceptable bits/second */
```

```
            } dl_through_t:

            /*
             * transit delay specification
             *
             * This parameter is specified for both directions.
             * expressed in milliseconds assuming a DLSDU size of 128 octets.
             * The scaling of the value to the current DLSDU size is provider dependent.
             */
            typedef struct dl_transdelay {
                        long    dl_target_value;  /* desired value of service */
                        long    dl_accept_value;  /* min. acceptable value of service */
            } dl_transdelay_t;

            /*
             * priority specification
             * priority range is 0-100, with 0 being highest value.
             */
            typedef struct dl_priority {
                        long    dl_min;
                        long    dl_max;
            } dl_priority_t;


            /*
             * protection specification
             *
             */
            #define DL_NONE      0x0B01 /* no protection supplied */
            #define DL_MONITOR   0x0B02 /* protection against passive monitoring */
            #define DL_MAXIMUM   0x0B03 /* protection against modification, replay, */
                                        /* addition, or deletion */

            typedef struct dl_protect {
                        long    dl_min;
                        long    dl_max;
            } dl_protect_t;


            /*
             * Resilience specification
             * probabilities are scaled by a factor of 10,000 with a time interval
             * of 10,000 seconds.
             */
            typedef struct dl_resilience {
                        long    dl_disc_prob;  /* probability of provider init DISC */
                        long    dl_reset_prob; /* probability of provider init RESET */
            } dl_resilience_t;


            /*
```

```
 * QOS type definition to be used for negotiation with the
 * remote end of a connection, or a connectionless unitdata request.
 * There are two type definitions to handle the negotiation
 * process at connection establishment. The typedef dl_qos_neg_t
 * is used to present a range for parameters. This is used
 * in the DL_CONNECT_REQ and DL_CONNECT_IND messages. The typedef
 * dl_qos_sel_t is used to select a specific value for the QOS
 * parameters. This is used in the DL_CONNECT_RES, DL_CONNECT_CON,
 * and DL_INFO_ACK messages to define the selected QOS parameters
 * for a connection.
 *
 * NOTE
 *     A DataLink provider which has unknown values for any of the fields
 *     will use a value of DL_UNKNOWN for all values in the fields.
 *
 * NOTE
 *     A QOS parameter value of DL_QOS_DONT_CARE informs the DLS
 *     provider the user requesting this value doesn't care
 *     what the QOS parameter is set to. This value becomes the
 *     least possible value in the range of QOS parameters.
 *     The order of the QOS parameter range is then:
 *
 *             DL_QOS_DONT_CARE < 0 < MAXIMUM QOS VALUE
 */
#define DL_UNKNOWN          -1
#define DL_QOS_DONT_CARE    -2

/*
 * Every QOS structure has the first 4 bytes containing a type
 * field, denoting the definition of the rest of the structure.
 * This is used in the same manner has the dl_primitive variable
 * is in messages.
 *
 * The following list is the defined QOS structure type values and structures.
 */
#define DL_QOS_CO_RANGE1    0x0101
#define DL_QOS_CO_SEL1      0x0102
#define DL_QOS_CL_RANGE1    0x0103
#define DL_QOS_CL_SEL1      0x0104

typedef struct dl_qos_co_range1 {
            ulong          dl_qos_type;
            dl_through_t    dl_rcv_throughput;
            dl_transdelay_t dl_rcv_trans_delay;
            dl_through_t    dl_xmt_throughput;
            dl_transdelay_t dl_xmt_trans_delay;
            dl_priority_t   dl_priority;
            dl_protect_t    dl_protection;
            long            dl_residual_error;
            dl_resilience_t dl_resilience;
}     dl_qos_co_range1_t;
```

```
typedef struct dl_qos_co_sel1 {
            ulong           dl_qos_type;
            long            dl_rcv_throughput;
            long            dl_rcv_trans_delay;
            long            dl_xmt_throughput;
            long            dl_xmt_trans_delay;
            long            dl_priority;
            long            dl_protection;
            long            dl_residual_error;
            dl_resilience_t dl_resilience;
}       dl_qos_co_sel1_t;

typedef struct dl_qos_cl_range1 {
            ulong           dl_qos_type;
            dl_transdelay_t dl_trans_delay;
            dl_priority_t   dl_priority;
            dl_protect_t    dl_protection;
            long            dl_residual_error;
}       dl_qos_cl_range1_t;

typedef struct dl_qos_cl_sel1 {
            ulong           dl_qos_type;
            long            dl_trans_delay;
            long            dl_priority;
            long            dl_protection;
            long            dl_residual_error;
}       dl_qos_cl_sel1_t;

/*
 * DLPI interface primitive definitions.
 *
 * Each primitive is sent as a stream message.  It is possible that
 * the messages may be viewed as a sequence of bytes that have the
 * following form without any padding. The structure definition
 * of the following messages may have to change depending on the
 * underlying hardware architecture and crossing of a hardware
 * boundary with a different hardware architecture.
 *
 * Fields in the primitives having a name of the form
 * dl_reserved cannot be used and have the value of
 * binary zero, no bits turned on.
 *
 * Each message has the name defined followed by the
 * stream message type (M_PROTO, M_PCPROTO, M_DATA)
 */

/*
 *     LOCAL MANAGEMENT SERVICE PRIMITIVES
 */
```

```
/*
 * DL_INFO_REQ, M_PCPROTO type
 */
typedef struct dl_info_req {
      ulong   dl_primitive;
} dl_info_req_t;

/*
 * DL_INFO_ACK, M_PCPROTO type
 */
typedef struct dl_info_ack {
      ulong    dl_primitive;
      ulong    dl_max_sdu;
      ulong    dl_min_sdu;
      ulong    dl_addr_length;
      ulong    dl_mac_type;
      ulong    dl_reserved;
      ulong    dl_current_state;
      ulong    dl_max_idu;
      ulong    dl_service_mode;
      ulong    dl_qos_length;
      ulong    dl_qos_offset;
      ulong    dl_qos_range_length;
      ulong    dl_qos_range_offset;
      long     dl_provider_style;
      ulong    dl_addr_offset;
      ulong    dl_growth;
} dl_info_ack_t;

/*
 * DL_ATTACH_REQ, M_PROTO type
 */
typedef struct dl_attach_req {
      ulong    dl_primitive;
      ulong    dl_ppa;
} dl_attach_req_t;

/*
 * DL_DETACH_REQ, M_PROTO type
 */
typedef struct dl_detach_req {
      ulong   dl_primitive;
} dl_detach_req_t;

/*
 * DL_BIND_REQ, M_PROTO type
 */
typedef struct dl_bind_req {
      ulong   dl_primitive;
      ulong   dl_sap;
      ulong   dl_max_conind;
```

```
        ushort  dl_service_mode;
        ushort  dl_conn_mgmt;
} dl_bind_req_t;

/*
 * DL_BIND_ACK, M_PCPROTO type
 */
typedef struct dl_bind_ack {
        ulong   dl_primitive;
        ulong   dl_sap;
        ulong   dl_addr_length;
        ulong   dl_addr_offset;
        ulong   dl_max_conind;
        ulong   dl_growth;
} dl_bind_ack_t;

/*
 * DL_SUBS_BIND_REQ, M_PROTO type
 */
typedef struct dl_subs_bind_req {
        ulong   dl_primitive;
        ulong   dl_subs_sap_offset;
        ulong   dl_subs_sap_len;
} dl_subs_bind_req_t;

/*
 * DL_SUBS_BIND_ACK, M_PCPROTO type
 */
typedef struct dl_subs_bind_ack {
        ulong dl_primitive;
        ulong dl_subs_sap_offset;
        ulong dl_subs_sap_len;
} dl_subs_bind_ack_t;

/*
 * DL_UNBIND_REQ, M_PROTO type
 */
typedef struct dl_unbind_req {
        ulong   dl_primitive;
} dl_unbind_req_t;

/*
 * DL_OK_ACK, M_PCPROTO type
 */
typedef struct dl_ok_ack {
        ulong   dl_primitive;
        ulong   dl_correct_primitive;
} dl_ok_ack_t;

/*
 * DL_ERROR_ACK, M_PCPROTO type
```

```
 */
typedef struct dl_error_ack {
      ulong   dl_primitive;
      ulong   dl_error_primitive;
      ulong   dl_errno;
      ulong   dl_unix_errno;
} dl_error_ack_t;


/*
 *      CONNECTION-ORIENTED SERVICE PRIMITIVES
 */

/*
 * DL_CONNECT_REQ, M_PROTO type
 */
typedef struct dl_connect_req {
      ulong   dl_primitive;
      ulong   dl_dest_addr_length;
      ulong   dl_dest_addr_offset;
      ulong   dl_qos_length;
      ulong   dl_qos_offset;
      ulong   dl_growth;
} dl_connect_req_t;

/*
 * DL_CONNECT_IND, M_PROTO type
 */
typedef struct dl_connect_ind {
      ulong   dl_primitive;
      ulong   dl_correlation;
      ulong   dl_called_addr_length;
      ulong   dl_called_addr_offset;
      ulong   dl_calling_addr_length;
      ulong   dl_calling_addr_offset;
      ulong   dl_qos_length;
      ulong   dl_qos_offset;
      ulong   dl_growth;
} dl_connect_ind_t;

/*
 * DL_CONNECT_RES, M_PROTO type
 */
typedef struct dl_connect_res {
      ulong   dl_primitive;
      ulong   dl_correlation;
      ulong   dl_resp_token;
      ulong   dl_qos_length;
      ulong   dl_qos_offset;
      ulong   dl_growth;
} dl_connect_res_t;
```

```
/*
 * DL_CONNECT_CON, M_PROTO type
 */
typedef struct dl_connect_con {
      ulong   dl_primitive;
      ulong   dl_resp_addr_length;
      ulong   dl_resp_addr_offset;
      ulong   dl_qos_length;
      ulong   dl_qos_offset;
      ulong   dl_growth;

} dl_connect_con_t;

/*
 * DL_TOKEN_REQ, M_PCPROTO type
 */
typedef struct dl_token_req {
      ulong   dl_primitive;
} dl_token_req_t;

/*
 * DL_TOKEN_ACK, M_PCPROTO type
 */
typedef struct dl_token_ack {
      ulong   dl_primitive;
      ulong   dl_token;
} dl_token_ack_t;

/*
 * DL_DISCONNECT_REQ, M_PROTO type
 */
typedef struct dl_disconnect_req {
      ulong   dl_primitive;
      ulong   dl_reason;
      ulong   dl_correlation;
} dl_disconnect_req_t;

/*
 * DL_DISCONNECT_IND, M_PROTO type
 */
typedef struct dl_disconnect_ind {
      ulong   dl_primitive;
      ulong   dl_originator;
      ulong   dl_reason;
      ulong   dl_correlation;
} dl_disconnect_ind_t;

/*
 * DL_RESET_REQ, M_PROTO type
 */
```

```
typedef struct dl_reset_req {
      ulong   dl_primitive;
} dl_reset_req_t;

/*
 * DL_RESET_IND, M_PROTO type
 */
typedef struct dl_reset_ind {
      ulong   dl_primitive;
      ulong   dl_originator;
      ulong   dl_reason;
} dl_reset_ind_t;

/*
 * DL_RESET_RES, M_PROTO type
 */
typedef struct dl_reset_res {
      ulong   dl_primitive;
} dl_reset_res_t;

/*
 * DL_RESET_CON, M_PROTO type
 */
typedef struct dl_reset_con {
      ulong   dl_primitive;
} dl_reset_con_t;


/*
 *      CONNECTIONLESS SERVICE PRIMITIVES
 */

/*
 * DL_UNITDATA_REQ, M_PROTO type, with M_DATA block(s)
 */
typedef struct dl_unitdata_req {
      ulong   dl_primitive;
      ulong   dl_dest_addr_length;
      ulong   dl_dest_addr_offset;
      ulong   dl_reserved[2];
} dl_unitdata_req_t;

/*
 * DL_UNITDATA_IND, M_PROTO type, with M_DATA block(s)
 */
typedef struct dl_unitdata_ind {
      ulong   dl_primitive;
      ulong   dl_src_addr_length;
      ulong   dl_src_addr_offset;
      ulong   dl_dest_addr_length;
      ulong   dl_dest_addr_offset;
```

```
            ulong   dl_reserved;
    } dl_unitdata_ind_t;

    /*
     * DL_UDERROR_IND, M_PROTO type
     *     (or M_PCPROTO type if LLI-based provider)
     */
    typedef struct dl_uderror_ind {
            ulong   dl_primitive;
            ulong   dl_dest_addr_length;
            ulong   dl_dest_addr_offset;
            ulong   dl_reserved;
            ulong   dl_errno;
    } dl_uderror_ind_t;

    /*
     * DL_UDQOS_REQ, M_PROTO type
     */
    typedef struct dl_udqos_req {
            ulong   dl_primitive;
            ulong   dl_qos_length;
            ulong   dl_qos_offset;
    } dl_udqos_req_t;

    union DL_primitives {
            ulong                   dl_primitive;
            dl_info_req_t           info_req;
            dl_info_ack_t           info_ack;
            dl_attach_req_t         attach_req;
            dl_detach_req_t         detach_req;
            dl_bind_req_t           bind_req;
            dl_bind_ack_t           bind_ack;
            dl_unbind_req_t         unbind_req;
            dl_subs_bind_req_t      subs_bind_req;
            dl_subs_bind_ack_t      subs_bind_ack;
            dl_ok_ack_t             ok_ack;
            dl_error_ack_t          error_ack;
            dl_connect_req_t        connect_req;
            dl_connect_ind_t        connect_ind;
            dl_connect_res_t        connect_res;
            dl_connect_con_t        connect_con;
            dl_token_req_t          token_req;
            dl_token_ack_t          token_ack;
            dl_disconnect_req_t     disconnect_req;
            dl_disconnect_ind_t     disconnect_ind;
            dl_reset_req_t          reset_req;
            dl_reset_ind_t          reset_ind;
            dl_reset_res_t          reset_res;
            dl_reset_con_t          reset_con;
            dl_unitdata_req_t       unitdata_req;
            dl_unitdata_ind_t       unitdata_ind;
```

```
            dl_uderror_ind_t          uderror_ind;
            dl_udqos_req_t            udqos_req;
     };

     #define DL_INFO_REQ_SIZE          sizeof(dl_info_req_t)
     #define DL_INFO_ACK_SIZE          sizeof(dl_info_ack_t)
     #define DL_ATTACH_REQ_SIZE        sizeof(dl_attach_req_t)
     #define DL_DETACH_REQ_SIZE        sizeof(dl_detach_req_t)
     #define DL_BIND_REQ_SIZE          sizeof(dl_bind_req_t)
     #define DL_BIND_ACK_SIZE          sizeof(dl_bind_ack_t)
     #define DL_UNBIND_REQ_SIZE        sizeof(dl_unbind_req_t)
     #define DL_SUBS_BIND_REQ_SIZE sizeof(dl_subs_bind_req_t)
     #define DL_SUBS_BIND_ACK_SIZE sizeof(dl_subs_bind_ack_t)
     #define DL_OK_ACK_SIZE                sizeof(dl_ok_ack_t)
     #define DL_ERROR_ACK_SIZE         sizeof(dl_error_ack_t)
     #define DL_CONNECT_REQ_SIZE       sizeof(dl_connect_req_t)
     #define DL_CONNECT_IND_SIZE       sizeof(dl_connect_ind_t)
     #define DL_CONNECT_RES_SIZE       sizeof(dl_connect_res_t)
     #define DL_CONNECT_CON_SIZE       sizeof(dl_connect_con_t)
     #define DL_TOKEN_REQ_SIZE         sizeof(dl_token_req_t)
     #define DL_TOKEN_ACK_SIZE         sizeof(dl_token_ack_t)
     #define DL_DISCONNECT_REQ_SIZE        sizeof(dl_disconnect_req_t)
     #define DL_DISCONNECT_IND_SIZE        sizeof(dl_disconnect_ind_t)
     #define DL_RESET_REQ_SIZE         sizeof(dl_reset_req_t)
     #define DL_RESET_IND_SIZE         sizeof(dl_reset_ind_t)
     #define DL_RESET_RES_SIZE         sizeof(dl_reset_res_t)
     #define DL_RESET_CON_SIZE         sizeof(dl_reset_con_t)
     #define DL_UNITDATA_REQ_SIZE  sizeof(dl_unitdata_req_t)
     #define DL_UNITDATA_IND_SIZE  sizeof(dl_unitdata_ind_t)
     #define DL_UDERROR_IND_SIZE   sizeof(dl_uderror_ind_t)
     #define DL_UDQOS_REQ_SIZE         sizeof(dl_udqos_req_t)

     typedef struct mac_ifstats {
            struct mac_ifstats *ifs_next;    /* next if on chain */
            char            *ifs_name;       /* interface name */
            short           ifs_unit;        /* unit number */
            short           ifs_active;      /* non-zero if this if is running */
            caddr_t         *ifs_addrs;      /* list of addresses */
            short           ifs_mtu;         /* Maximum transmission unit */

            /* generic interface statistics */
            int             ifs_ipackets;    /* packets received on interface */
            int             ifs_ierrors;     /* input errors on interface */
            int             ifs_opackets;    /* packets sent on interface */
            int             ifs_oerrors;     /* output errors on interface */
            int             ifs_collisions;  /* collisions on csma interfaces */
     } mac_ifstats_t;

     #endif /* _SYS_DLPI_H */
```

Glossary

802.2

The IEEE 802 standard for Logical Link Control (LLC). The IEEE 802.2 standard is responsible for providing link layer services for various IEEE Media Access Control layers.

802.3

The IEEE 802 standard for Collision Sense Multiple Access with Collision Detect (CSMA/CD) media access. The IEEE 802.3 standard was derived from the very popular Ethernet standard from Digital/Intel/Xerox. The media cables defined in the IEEE 802.3 standard are Coaxial cable (thin and thick), Twisted Pair cable, Fiber Optics cable, etc. The media speed is 10 Mbps.

802.4

The IEEE 802 standard for Token Passing Bus Media Access Control. The IEEE 802.4 standard is used in environments which require a guaranteed response time. This standard defines a token passing scheme for media access, forcing stations to wait for the token before they start transmission. The media type or cables supported in the IEEE 802.4 standard are coaxial cable and fiber optics cable. The media speed is 10 Mbps.

802.5

The IEEE 802 standard for Token Ring Media Access Control. The IEEE 802.3 Token Ring environment was initially defined by IBM and is primarily used in the IBM networks. The media speed defined in the IEEE 802.5 standard is 4 Mbps and 16 Mbps. The media type or cables supported are Twisted Pair cable and Fiber Optics cable.

Address Resolution Protocol

See ARP.

AES

Asynchronous Event Service. This is a service provided by NetWare Operating System. The AES service allows a driver or a application to schedule a routine which will be called later on a regular time interval by the AES service.

ANSI

ANSI stands for American National Standards Institute. The ANSI is the United States national standards body. ANSI members are various corporations, universities and U.S. Government Organizations interested in standardization. ANSI standardization committee is divided into number of working sub-committees attended by individuals from its various members. ANSI represents the U.S. in the International Standards Organization (ISO).

API

Application Programming Interface. This is a general software term used for standard programming interfaces that are defined by operating systems or other application programs. An example of an API is the Win32 Application Programming Interface that is defined by Microsoft for Windows NT operating system. Win32 defines functions to aid the programmers in writing Windows applications.

ARP

Address Resolution Protocol. The ARP is a member of the TCP-IP suite of protocols responsible for resolving the IP address for a MAC address. The TCP-IP protocol family needs the IP address and the MAC address of the destination node to link it to the source node. If the source node does not know the MAC address of the destination node, it uses the ARP to send a broadcast message to all the nodes requesting the node whose IP address matches the IP address of the ARP packet, to respond with its MAC address.

ARPA

Advanced Research Projects Agency. The ARPA was a Department of Defense agency which funded the ARPANET project and the development of the TCP-IP protocol suite. The new name of the ARPA is DARPA (Defense Advanced Research Projects Agency).

ATM

Asynchronous Transfer Mode. The ATM is the upcoming standard for LAN/WAN communications based on packet switching technique. It uses packets (cells) of fixed size. The ATM also allows for dynamic bandwidth allocation based on the fixed size cells.

BIOS

Basic Input-Output System. The BIOS is the program that resides in EPROM (Erasable Programmable Read Only Memory) in an IBM PC system and is responsible for initializing the various hardware components of the PC. The BIOS is also responsible for providing the basic input/output functions for reading and writing to and from hard disks, floppy disks, keyboard, video, timer, and other similar peripherals.

Bootrom

Bootrom is a term used for the code resident on a networking interface card in a EEPROM. This piece of code is initialized during the PC boot process and once called, it takes control of the boot process and completes the boot process by getting the boot operating system from the network server. Bootrom is used in diskless workstations where the workstation is booted from the network server.

Bridge

Bridge is a device that connects networks based on different access methods all together. The example of a bridge device would be a device connecting a CSMA/CD based network to a Token Ring network. The bridge is a device that operates at the MAC level and moves traffic between the networks connected to the bridge. It performs very simple functions such as CRC checking. It does not perform functions such as segmentation and reassembly of the packets.

Broadcast

Broadcast is a term used in networking to indicate a message which is received by all receiving stations. An example of a MAC layer broadcast message would be a message with its MAC destination address equal to all 1s. The MAC address of all 1s is defined by the 802 MACs as a broadcast MAC address and all the MACs on the network are required to receive this message.

BSD

Berkeley Software Distribution. This is the UNIX operating system from University of California's Berkeley Software Distribution, commonly called Berkeley UNIX or BSD UNIX.

Client

The client is a machine which is dependent on another machine for some of the other machine's services. The term client is used in the client/server model where the server machine provides centralized services such as file sharing, printer sharing, and one or more clients access the server services via a computer network.

CLNP

Connectionless Network Protocol. CLNP is the network layer protocol which is the OSI equivalent to the IP layer of the TCP-IP protocol suite. The CLNP provides connectionless network layer services to the layer above it.

CMIP

Common Management Information Protocol. The CMIP is the management protocol defined in the OSI protocol stacks. The CMIP provides the network management functions and services in an OSI based network.

Collision

Collision is a term mainly used in CSMA/CD based networks. In a CSMA/CD based network, collision is caused when two or more nodes try to transmit on the network at the same time. Electrically, a collision is a situation when the average DC on the wire is more than the average DC when a single station is transmitting.

Connection-Less

Connection-Less is a term used in networking to indicate that the communication between two or more nodes is executed without forming a connection first. This means that there is no guarantee that the message transmitted in a connection-less mode of operation will reach its final destination. The connection-less mode of operation is used in networking environments which require less overhead and where the error rate is very low.

Connection-Oriented

Connection-oriented service is the mode of service where the message transmitting node establishes a connection with the receiving node(s) and then starts the message transmission. The overhead of a connection oriented service is higher than the connection-less service. The reliability offered by the connection-oriented mode of operation is higher than the connection-less service.

CRC

Cyclic Redundancy Check. The CRC is used at the MAC level frames to confirm the integrity of the frame. The transmitting station generates a CRC based on the packet data contents and attaches the CRC at the end of the packet. The receiving station also computes the CRC based on the packet data and compares it with the CRC transmitted with the packet. If the two CRCs match, the packet is transmitted and received without error. A polynomial is used to generate the CRC and the CRC is attached to the data. When the packet data along with the CRC is put through the same polynomial, the remainder value is zero.

CSMA/CD

Collision Sense Multiple Access with Collision Detect. The CSMA/CD is a media access method defined in the IEEE 802.3 standard. This access method is implemented by all the nodes on a CSMA/CD based network. The CSMA/CD access method defines rules which must be followed by all the nodes on the network for access to the network. The access method defines network access rules for the nodes. The protocol is based on the basic principle that if a node wants to transmit on the network, it should monitor the media and ensure that no other station is transmitting. If another station is transmitting, the node must wait until the previous transmission is complete. The node may then start its transmission. However, if two or more nodes were waiting for a previous transmission to complete, they may start transmitting simultaneously as soon as the previous transmission is complete. This will cause a collision. All nodes monitor for collisions and if a collision happens, they stop transmission, backoff and wait for a random amount of time before attempting to transmit again.

DARPA

Defense Advanced Research Project Agency. The TCP-IP protocol suite evolved from the ARPANET project funded by DARPA.

Data-Link

Data-Link is the layer number two of the 7 layer OSI networking model. The data-link layer is responsible for providing data transfer services to its upper layer. It implements the protocols and services that make data transfer possible.

Device Driver

The device driver is a piece of software responsible for controlling a hardware device. The device driver provides an application independent view of the hardware within an operating system. This means that various pieces of software (operating system, applications, etc.) can use the device driver to communicate with the hardware device. This also means that if the hardware device is changed in the system the device driver needs to be changed as well. The rest of the applications and the operating system stay the same, providing the same functionality to the user.

DIS

Draft International Standard. The DIS is a review stage that all the ISO standards must go through. The ISO standards go through the following stages: DP (Draft Proposal) followed by DIS (Draft International Standard) followed by IS (International Standard).

DIX

Digital Intel Xerox. DIX is a term used to refer to the three corporations (Digital, Intel and Xerox) that worked together to invent Ethernet which finally gave birth to CSMA/CD based networks.

DLC

Data Link Controls (DLCs) are those protocols residing at the Data-Link Layer that define the addressing (source and destination), control information, etc., for two or more links to exchange data.

DLL

Dynamic Link Library (DLL) is a function library which is linked to the program when a program is loading (dynamically). DLLs are the next step after the static linking.

DLPI

Data Link Provider Interface. DLPI is the networking device driver interface defined initially by AT&T to standardize the networking hardware interface for the networking protocol stacks. The DLPI specification is based on UNIX STREAMS messaging technique and allows multiple protocol layers to use a single networking hardware via a DLPI interface based device driver. It also allows multiple DLPI device drivers to use a single protocol.

DLS

Data Link Service. This service is provided by the Data Link Layer to the protocols above it.

DMA

Direct Memory Access. DMA is a data transfer mechanism used in computer systems where an external device accesses the memory directly and moves the data within the memory or from the memory to an external device. The system processor does not get involved in the DMA mode of data transfer.

DOS

See MS-DOS.

DSAP

Destination Service Access Point. DSAP is the address of the Data Link Layer service residing above the Data Link Layer protocol. Remote users trying to access this service would have to input the correct DSAP address to reach to and use the service.

ECB

Event Control Block. ECB is a data structure defined and used in the Novell NetWare Open Data-Link Interface (ODI) environment. The ECB data structure is used to pass the transmit and receive buffers and associated fields between various pieces of ODI NetWare architecture.

EISA

Extended Industry Standard Architecture. EISA is a bus signal and protocol definition which was defined as a follow up to the ISA bus by a consortium of companies led by Compaq Computer Corporation.

EPROM

Erasable Programmable Read Only Memory. The EPROM is a type of Read Only Memory which can be occasionally erased and reprogrammed.

Ethernet

Ethernet is the specification which defines the media access mechanism for one or more nodes residing on the same network. The Ethernet protocol is very similar to the CSMA/CD (802.3) protocols (*see CSMA/CD* for protocol details). Ethernet was initially developed by Digital/Intel/Xerox.

FDDI

Fiber Distributed Data Interface. FDDI is a standard developed by ANSI X3T9.5 committee. The FDDI standard specifies the electrical signaling for running the FDDI token passing protocol and the data transfer mechanism over 100 Mbps fiber and copper cabling.

FIFO

First In First Out. The term FIFO is used with respect to memory/stack which runs on the basis of the first in first out. This means that the data that enters memory first always gets out first.

Frame

Frame is a term used to define the collection of bits which contain the addressing, control and data information. A frame is an entity which is transmitted and received as a complete package between various nodes.

Frame Relay

Frame relay is a switching interface that operates in packet mode.

FTP

File Transfer Protocol. FTP is a protocol used in the TCP-IP suite of protocols. The FTP is responsible for transferring files between two or more stations in the Internet domain.

GOSIP

Government Open System Interconnect Profile. GOSIP is a set of recommendations from the U.S. Government specifying the OSI protocols and specifications that must be followed by the networking vendors if they wish to sell to the U.S. Government. The GOSIP is a U.S. Government procurement specification for OSI protocols.

HDLC

High Level Data Link Control. HDLC is an ISO protocol for X.25 communication.

IAB

Internet Activities Board. IAB is the technical body that is responsible for developing and maintaining the Internet suite of protocols. The Internet suite consists of the TCP-IP suite of protocols. The IAB has number of subgroups which produce RFCs (Request For Comment) documents which contain specifications and standards for different protocols.

ICMP

Internet Control Message Protocol. ICMP protocol is part of the IP layer of the TCP-IP protocol suite. ICMP protocol is responsible for providing routing control messages on the network. It is also used to handle all the error and control messages at the IP level.

IETF

Internet Engineering Task Force. IETF is one of the task forces of IAB (Internet Advisory Board). IETF is responsible for solving engineering problems. It is divided into a number of working groups that focus on various aspects of Internet.

IEEE

Institute of Electrical and Electronics Engineers. IEEE is a professional institute whose principal members are electrical and electronics engineers. The IEEE plays a very important role in producing standards for OSI and LANs.

Internet

Internet is a collection of computers connected by phone lines and various other interconnection mechanisms. The computers connected on the Internet act as a virtual network exchanging files, mail messages, and other similar data.

I/O Address

I/O address is the address of any hardware device register which is mapped in the I/O space of the x86 microprocessor. The x86 microprocessor has 64k bytes of I/O space and different devices can use the I/O space to map their registers.

IP

Internet Protocol. The IP protocol is network layer protocol (layer 3) for the TCP-IP suite of protocols. The IP protocol implements segmentation/reassembly of the network messages. The IP protocol also implements the routing functions.

IPC

Inter Process Communication. IPC is a term used to define the inter process communication which exists in systems that have more than one process running in the system. The most common ways of interprocess communication are shared memory, semaphores, and pipes.

IPX

Internet Packet Exchange. The IPX is the network layer protocol implementation used in Novell environment. The IPX protocol implements the network layer segmentation and reassembly functions and routing functions. The IPX implementation was derived from the Xerox XNS protocol suite.

IRQ

Interrupt Request. IRQ is a hardware line which is driven by one or more hardware devices indicating to the CPU that the hardware device needs attention from the software. The IBM PC has 16 IRQ lines going into a PIC (Programmable Interrupt Controller). The PIC interfaces with the CPU. The CPU is supposed to call predefined software routines when the interrupt is generated.

IRTF

Internet Research Task Force. The IRTF is a task force working for IAB. The IRTF is responsible for research and development of Internet protocol suites.

ISA

Industry Standard Architecture. The ISA is a PC bus specification describing the implementation details of a 16-bit bus architecture for plugging hardware devices in a PC.

ISDN

Integrated Services Digital Network. The ISDN is a specification which defines the mechanism to transmit voice and data together on a single medium. The ISDN standards are being developed by CCITT. The ISDN service is being offered by some telephone carriers. This makes the integration of voice and digital data possible on a single wire.

ISO

International Standards Organization. The ISO is an international organization responsible for producing worldwide standards on most technical issues.

IVT

Interrupt Vector Table. The PCs have a number of Interrupts which are used by hardware and software components of the PC. Each interrupt has a defined software entry point which must be called when the interrupt is called. The various software routine entry points are stored in the Interrupt Vector Table in the system memory.

KA9Q

A popular implementation of TCP-IP protocol suite. The KA9Q TCP-IP suite of protocols is available in the public domain format from many FTP sites. The KA9Q TCP-IP works on top of the standard packet driver interface.

Kernel

The Kernel is a term used to refer to the core software component of an operating system. In most operating systems, the kernel is responsible for coordinating the major centralized tasks like memory management, scheduling tasks, and managing hardware resources.

LAN

Local Area Networks. A term used to indicate the networks which are geographically local in nature. The maximum geographic area covered by a LAN is a few kilometers. A LAN consists of hardware and software components installed in a computer system which assist in the communication over the cabling media.

LAN Manager

LAN Manager is the Microsoft Network Operating System add-on component for various Microsoft operating systems. LAN Manager components add client and server services on various operating systems. The LAN Manager server components are available for OS/2 1.3, SCO UNIX, and Windows NT operating systems. The client components of LAN Manager are available for DOS, OS/2, Windows 3.x, and Macintosh.

LAN Server

The LAN Server is the IBM Network Operating System add-on component for IBM operating systems. The LAN Server is very similar to the core of the LAN Manager network operating system. The LAN Server's server component is available for the various versions of the OS/2 operating system. The client components of the LAN Server are available for DOS and OS/2.

Late Collision

In an Ethernet/802.3 network, a collision usually occur within 512-bit times or 51.2 micro-seconds after message transmission. If a collision occurs on the Ethernet/802.3 network after the 51.2 micro-second period, it is called late collision.

LLC

Logical Link Control. The LLC is a layer 2 standard defined in the IEEE 802.2 specification. The LLC defines the link layer data transmission and reception.

LLI

Logical Link Interface. The LLI is a specification from Santa Cruz Operation specifying the interface between the LAN device drivers and the protocol stacks running in a SCO UNIX operating system. The LLI specification is based on the DLPI (Data Link Provider Interface) specification which in turn is based on STREAMS interprocess communication from AT&T.

Local Talk

Local Talk is a baseband network using the CSMA/CD access method used mainly in the Apple Macintosh computer networking.

LSL

Link Support Layer. The LSL is the piece of software layer specified in Novell's Open Data-Link Interface (ODI) specification. The LSL separates the LAN device drivers from Novell protocol stacks and acts as a multiplexer for incoming and outgoing packets.

MAC

Media Access Control. The MAC layer is the bottom half layer of the layer 2 of the OSI 7 layer model. The MAC layer provides the media access protocols for accessing the LAN media. The MAC layer protocols are defined in the IEEE 802 standards such as IEEE 802.3—CSMA/CD, IEEE 802.4—Token Bus, and IEEE 802.5—Token Ring.

MAC Driver

The MAC driver is the software device driver responsible for driving the hardware devices implementing the MAC access protocols. The networking device drivers are MAC device drivers implementing the MAC/LLC layer functions.

MAN

Metropolitan Area Network. A MAN network is a computer network spanning geographical distances of up to 80 kilometers.

MDI

Media Dependent Interface. The MDI interface is a new LAN device driver interface specification from SCO. The MDI interface is used in the new operating systems from SCO. The difference between LLI and the MDI interface is the STREAMS interface. The LLI driver includes the hardware device interface and the STREAMS interface. The MDI architecture splits the LLI driver into two separate drivers: hardware driver and STREAMS driver. Hence, in the MDI based architecture, the hardware vendor has to provide a hardware device driver. The STREAMS interface is provided by the SCO.

MHS

Message Handling System. The MHS is a system of message user agents and message transfer agents, which are used to exchange messages such as electronic mail. The MHS protocol is specified in the CCITT X.400 specifications.

MIB

Management Information Base. MIB is a database of network management information stored as objects that can be accessed via a network management protocol such as SNMP (Simple Network Management Protocol), or CMIP (Common Management Information Protocol).

MLID

Multiple Link Interface Driver. The MLID is the LAN device driver component of the Novell ODI architecture. In a Novell environment, the MLID is responsible for driving the hardware. The MLID implements the media dependent functions in the LAN device driver. It is also responsible for communicating with the LSL. The MLID also implements the hardware device initialization and transmit and receive functions.

MS-DOS

Microsoft's Disk Operating System. The MS-DOS is one of the most popular operating systems for 80x86 based computers. The MS-DOS operating system implements basic operating system functions such as task management, and memory management. The MS-DOS is a single tasking operating system that provides character-based user interface to its users.

Multicast

Multicast is a term used to indicate the destination MAC address of a packet. The multicast destination MAC address in an outgoing packet means that the packet is destined for more that one user (multiuser).

Multiprocessor

Multiprocessor is a computer system based on more than one processor. The operating system used on a multiprocessor machine takes advantage of the multiprocessor architecture by dividing tasks between the processors.

Multitasking

Multitasking is an operating system environment in which multiple tasks run simultaneously on one or more processors without losing track of information on any of the tasks.

Named Pipes

Named Pipes is an Inter Process Communication method which allows high performance transfer of variable length messages between processes running on same or different machines.

NBF

NetBIOS Extended User Interface. The NBF is a protocol stack provided by Microsoft in its Microsoft Windows NT operating system. The NBF protocol stack provides NetBEUI type transport layer interface for applications.

NCP

NetWare Core Protocols. The NCP is the language that Novell NetWare servers and clients speak. Clients make requests to the Server by using the NetWare Core Protocol messages. The clients send NCP requests and the server replies with NCP replies. The NCPs run on top of Novell's IPX/SPX protocols. The client NCP requests may consist of file read, file write, file print, determine drive mappings, and file search.

NDIS

Network Driver Interface Specification. The NDIS specification was written by 3COM and Microsoft. The NDIS specification defines the communication between a LAN device driver and the NDIS based protocol stacks. The NDIS specification defines an interface at the Data Link Layer (layer 2) between the LAN device driver responsible for driving the hardware and the protocol stacks. The NDIS specification version 2.0.1 was written for MS-DOS and OS/2 operating systems.

NETBEUI

Network BIOS User Interface. The NetBEUI is an application programming interface which is provided by the NetBIOS protocol stack. The NetBEUI interface can be called by various applications to gain access to the capabilities of the NetBIOS protocol stack.

NETBIOS

Network Basic Input Output System. The NetBIOS is a protocol stack very widely used in the IBM networking environment. The NetBIOS provides layer 3 and layer 4 type of services.

NetWare

NetWare is the name of Novell's Network Operating System. The NetWare operating system runs on a x86 microprocessor machine and provides file sharing, printer sharing, user account management, and types of services to computers connected on the same network.

NFS

Network File System. The NFS is a distributed file system developed by SUN Microsystems. The NFS is SUN Microsystems's Network Operating System based on TCP-IP protocol stack. The Network File System allows a group of computers connected on a computer network to share files in a transparent manner.

NIC

Network Interface Card. A NIC is the adapter card implementing the interface to the network cable and the software running the network protocols. The NIC typically contains the media access control functions to transmit and receive frames from the network and also the hardware circuitry to attach to the network cable.

NLM

NetWare Loadable Module. The NLM is an application or a driver that loads under Novell NetWare operating system and provides to the user additional services. The database application running under NetWare is an example of a NLM running under NetWare operating system.

NOS

Network Operating System. A NOS is a software component that provides networking services to local and remote machines that need access to such services. A typical NOS provides services such as: files sharing, printer sharing, modem sharing, security access, and user account management. A NOS consists of a server software component and a client software component. The client component requests the server component to provide the required services and the server component provides these services.

NWLink

NetWare Link. The NWLink is the name of NetWare IPX/SPX protocol stack implementation under Microsoft Windows Operating System.

ODI

Open Data-Link Interface. The ODI is an architecture developed by Novell, Inc. which defines the communication mechanism between the LAN drivers and the LAN protocols in the Novell Client (DOS or OS/2) and the Novell Server environments. The ODI is an interface definition which allows multiple protocols to run on top of one or more network cards with corresponding LAN drivers.

OEM

Original Equipment Manufacturer. The OEM is a term used in the computer industry to indicate the original manufacturer of equipment.

OID

Object Identifier. Each statistical counter in the NDIS 3.0 environment is an Object Identifier (OID).

OS/2

Operating System 2. The OS/2 is the operating system which was initially developed by a collaboration between Microsoft and IBM. Microsoft decided not to focus on the OS/2 operating system. Since then, the OS/2 operating system is being developed and released by IBM. The OS/2 is a single user multitasking, multi-threaded operating system.

OSI

Open Systems Interconnection. The OSI specification is part of an international standardization program to facilitate the communication between computers from different manufacturers. The OSI specification defines the functions of the various layers of a 7 layer computer networking model with protocol definitions at each layer.

Packet

A packet is the unit of data that is transferred between various nodes on a network. It may also be defined as a collection of bytes defining data and control information.

Packet Driver

The packet driver is a specification written and maintained by FTP Software, Inc. This specification defines the interface between the protocol stacks and the LAN device drivers in a DOS environment.

PCI

Peripheral Component Interconnect. PCI is a processor independent local bus specification developed by Intel corporation which defines the interconnection between various computer subsystems like processor, video, network adapter, and disk subsystem.

PDU

Protocol Data Unit. The PDU is the OSI name for a packet. The PDU contains the protocol data and control information which is passed between the protocol layers.

Ping

Ping is an application program that is part of the TCP-IP protocol suite. The Ping program sends a ICMP echo request to a remote station and waits for the ICMP echo response from the remote station. This program is very quick way of checking the link integrity in the TCP-IP environment.

Pipes

See Named Pipes.

POST

Power On Self Test. POST is a term used in an IBM PC environment. It signifies the software test which is run on various hardware components of the PC such as keyboard, video, memory, during the IBM PC startup process.

Promiscuous

Promiscuous mode is a mode of the MAC (Media Access Control) function of a computer network environment which receives all the packets from the network. Typically, the MAC interface of a computer network receives only the frames targeted to its own address and the broadcast address. In promiscuous mode, the MAC interface receives all the frames from the network. The promiscuous mode is used for network management and network monitoring type of applications.

Protected Mode

Protected Mode is one of the modes of operation of 286 and higher microprocessors. This mode provides a mechanism to supply application level protection in the memory subsystem of a computer system based on the 286 or higher microprocessors.

Protocol Driver

The term protocol driver is used in the NDIS 2.0.1 environment for Protocol Stack. *See Protocol Stack.*

Protocol ID

Protocol ID is a field in Novell's Event Control Block data structure. This field is used by the various components in the Novell NetWare environment to uniquely identify the source or destination of an incoming or outgoing packet.

Protocol Manager

Protocol Manager is a software component used in the NDIS 2.0.1 environment (DOS or OS/2). The protocol manager is responsible for binding the MAC driver and the protocol driver in the NDIS 2.0.1 environment. The protocol manager assists the MAC and the protocol driver in exchanging their entry points and hence enables the communication between the MAC and Protocol Drivers.

Protocol Stack

A protocol stack is a set of formal rules and messages which when followed by two or more computers would allow them to communicate with each other.

These rules and messages form the basis of the data communication between various computer systems.

Queues

Queue is a mechanism for inter process communication (IPC). Queues are very similar to shared memory segments from an IPC standpoint. The inter process messages come into a queue and are taken from the queue by the other process. The queues can be of FIFO (First-In-First-Out) or LIFO (Last-In-First-Out) basis.

RAM

Random Access Memory. Data is stored in RAM on a temporary basis for processing.

RCP

Remote Copy. The RCP is an application part of the TCP-IP protocol suite which provides remote copy of files between different hosts.

Real Mode

The real mode is the basic mode of the x86 microprocessors in which the processor follows the segment/offset architecture for memory addressing. The real mode of the 8086 and higher microprocessor is used by the DOS operating system.

Redirector

The redirector is a piece of software which runs in a client machine on a network. The redirector intercepts the requests that are made to the local operating system and checks if the request is for the local operating system or the network operating system. The local operating system requests are passed to the local operating system and the requests to the remote network operating system are bundled as a packet and sent to the server running on another computer.

Repeater

Repeater is a device which takes electrical signals from one cable and regenerates these electrical signals on another cable without interpreting these signals. The repeater device is used in computer networking systems to enhance the quality of the electrical signal propagating within the computer network cables.

RFC

Request For Comments. The RFC is a series of documents which describe the Internet suite of protocols and the results of various research and development activities done on Internet projects. The documents in RFC series may be protocol specifications or meeting reports. The RFCs are uniquely numbered and are managed by the Internet Activities Board (IAB).

ROM

Read Only Memory. ROM is used to designate memory present in the computer system which is used for read only purposes. The BIOS of the IBM PC is usually kept in the ROM in a computer system.

Router

Router is a device that is responsible for routing traffic on a network. The router can be a dedicated hardware, dedicated software or a combination of hardware and software which performs the routing functions. It analyzes the incoming packet for address and other information and then takes a routing decision based on the addressing information. The router implements a set of routing algorithms which assist the router functions in determining the best/shortest route for a packet.

RPC

Remote Procedure Call. The RPC is a mechanism used in distributed computing where an application makes a RPC call to another application running on another computer. In such a system, the RPC call is sent to the remote computer with all the required parameters. The processing of the call takes place on the remote computer, and the results are returned to the application which made the original RPC call.

RPL

Remote Program Load. The RPL is a mechanism defined for a diskless client to allow remote boot from a boot server. The RPL specification was written by IBM. The client in a RPL process locates a boot server first and then requests for the boot file. When the boot file is completely loaded in the client, the client passes the control to the boot file to complete the boot process. In this way, a client can boot from a server over a computer network.

SAP

Service Access Point. The SAP is an OSI term. The SAP indicates a point defined by an address at which the services of the current OSI layer are made available to the layer above it.

SCO

Santa Cruz Operations. SCO is a software vendor, whose main product is UNIX operating system for IBM PCs.

Semaphores

Semaphores are simple flags which are used for IPC. Semaphores are used between processes to signal and synchronize the access to certain types of common resources. Semaphores typically have two states: set or clear.

Server

The term server is used to indicate a computer program running by itself or in conjunction with other programs on a dedicated machine, which provides network services like file sharing, print sharing, and communication channel sharing. The server receives requests from its clients and its job is to try to complete the requests and pass the results back to the clients.

Shared Memory

The shared memory is a segment of memory which can be shared by more than one entity. From a hardware standpoint, the shared memory is dual port memory which can be read/written from the processor and a I/O adapter card controller. From a software standpoint, the shared memory can be used for Inter Process Communication between two or more processes.

SMTP

Simple Mail Transfer Protocol. The SMTP protocol is a part of the TCP-IP protocol suite which is responsible for transferring electronic mail messages from one computer to another. SMTP also defines how two or more mail systems interact to exchange mail messages. The SMTP protocol is defined in RFC 821. The associated message format is defined in RFC 822.

SNA

Systems Network Architecture. SNA is IBM's networking architecture which defines the protocols and underlying physical layers required for mainframe communications. SNA architecture was first developed for mainframes and was then transferred to PCs.

SNMP

Simple Network Management Protocol. The SNMP is part of the TCP-IP protocol suite which is responsible for providing network management services on a TCP-IP based network.

Socket

The socket is a UNIX term used extensively in the BSD version of UNIX. The socket is an entry point for application programs to communicate with the TCP-IP protocol stack.

SPX

Sequenced Packet Exchange. The SPX is a connection-oriented layer 3 based protocol stack provided by Novell. The SPX protocol stack is used between clients and servers that want to communicate with each other using a connection-oriented protocol.

SSAP

Source Service Access Point. The SSAP is the Source SAP. This indicates the source address of the SAP which made a particular transmission. The receiving node uses the SSAP address to return its response to the SSAP address.

STREAMS

STREAMS is a inter process communication mechanism developed by AT&T in its UNIX operating system. The STREAMS mechanism provides an inter process communication to develop and implement the networking protocol stacks easily. STREAMS allows several modules to connect and to send and receive messages to each other.

TCP

See Transport Control Protocol.

TCP-IP

Transmission Control Protocol/Internet Protocol, The TCP-IP is a protocol suite developed by DARPA (Defense Advanced Research Projects Agency). The TCP-IP is by far the most used protocol suite.

TDI

Transport Driver Interface. The term TDI is used in the NDIS 3.0 device driver context where the TDI indicates the application programming interface provided by different transport layers such as TCP-IP, IPX/SPX, and NetBEUI.

Telnet

Telnet is an application program available under the TCP-IP protocol suite. The Telnet application allows a user to log on to a remote host and run a virtual terminal session as if the user is working on the remote host.

Token Ring

Token Ring is an IEEE 802.5 specification which defines the Media Access Control functions. In the Token Ring networks the media access is based on a token passing algorithm. The station that captures the passing token has the right to transmit on the network. The Token Ring environment uses coaxial cable, twisted pair or fiber as transmission media. The speed of Token Ring networks is 4 Mbps or 16 Mbps.

Transport Control Protocol

The Transport Control Protocol (TCP) is the layer 4 protocol used in the TCP-IP suite of protocols. The TCP protocol implements all transport layer services. The TCP protocol provides reliable connection oriented service to its user.

TSR

Terminate and Stay Resident. The TSR is a term used in the DOS world to indicate a program which stays in memory even after terminating its execution the first time. Some device drivers are TSRs in DOS. The TSRs stay resident in the memory waiting for the next event of their interest and then coming back into action to service the hardware or software event.

UDP

User Datagram Protocol. The UDP is a transport layer protocol in the TCP-IP suite of protocols. The UDP uses IP protocol for delivery. The UDP protocol is at the same level as TCP protocol. However, the UDP protocol does not provide guaranteed delivery service like TCP protocol as it is based on connectionless mode of transport.

UNIX

UNIX is the name of an operating system. The UNIX operating system was developed in AT&T Bell Laboratories.

Vector

Vector is a term used in the NDIS 2.0.1 LAN device driver environment. The vector is an extension of the Protocol Manager software module which allows multiple protocol stacks to run on top of multiple NDIS 2.0.1 LAN device drivers. The vector module makes the protocol stacks think that they are communicating to a single LAN device driver module. The vector is responsible for address multiplexing, etc., to accomplish the task of running multiple protocol stacks on multiple LAN device drivers.

VxD

Virtual Device Driver. The VxD is a term used to indicate the hardware device driver architecture for Microsoft Windows 3.x operating system.

WAN

Wide Area Network. The WAN is a network capable of transmission over a large geographic areas. The WAN uses transmission lines provided by telephone companies to cover very large geographic areas.

WFW

Windows for Workgroups. The WFW is the operating system from Microsoft which is an extension to Microsoft's most popular Windows 3.x operating system. The WFW operating system includes networking capabilities built into the operating system. Two or more WFW-based systems can exchange files, and mail very easily with each other.

Windows 3.x

The most popular operating system from Microsoft. The Windows 3.x operating system provides a graphical environment for its user to work in. The graphical environment makes it very easy for the user to accomplish various tasks.

Windows NT

Windows New Technology. A high end operating system from Microsoft, introduced in 1992. The Windows NT operating system provides processor independent architecture which can be ported to various processors. It also provides a multitasking environment with graphical user interface which is very similar to the Windows 3.x operating system.

XNS

Xerox Network System. The Xerox Network System is Xerox's data communication protocol suite containing network and transport protocols and some applications for communication over Ethernet networks. The XNS protocol suite contains modules equivalent to TCP-IP protocol suite. The network and transport layer protocols from XNS form the basis for similar layers in the Novell NetWare NOS.

Index